P9-ECP-636

MADAME PROSECUTOR

MADAME PROSECUTOR

Confrontations with Humanity's Worst Criminals
and the Culture of Impunity

A MEMOIR

CARLA DEL PONTE

with CHUCK SUDETIC

OTHER PRESS
NEW YORK

Copyright © 2008 Feltrinelli Editore
Originally published in Italian as *La Caccia*
by Feltrinelli Editore, Milan, 2008.

English-language edition copyright © 2009 Carla Del Ponte and
Chuck Sudetic

Production Editor: Yvonne E. Cárdenas

Text Designer: Simon M. Sullivan

This book was set in 10.75 Minion by Alpha Design & Composition
of Pittsfield, NH.

10 9 8 7 6 5 4 3 2 1

Library of Congress Cataloging-in-Publication Data

Del Ponte, Carla.
Madame prosecutor : confrontations with humanity's worst criminals and the culture of
impunity : a memoir / by Carla Del Ponte ; with Chuck Sudetic.
p. cm.
Includes bibliographical references and index.
ISBN 978-1-59051-302-6
1. Women attorneys general—Switzerland—Biography. 2. Public prosecutors—
Switzerland—Biography. 3. International Court of Justice. 4. International criminal
courts. 5. War crime trials. 6. War criminals. 7. Genocide. 8. United Nations. 9.
Criminal justice, Administration of. I. Title.
KKW110.D45A3 2008
345'.01—dc22
[B]   2008017279

Per mia madre, Angela

When he had bandaged me,
I fell asleep on his lap,
because I hadn't slept for a long, long time . . .

We remained there until the morning . . .
and he woke me
and asked, "Where shall we go?"

I said, "I don't know."

Testimony of WITNESS O,
The Prosecutor v. Radislav Krstić, April 13, 2000,
Wounded on a Srebrenica killing field,
Crawled from among the dead,
Escaped with another survivor.

MADAME PROSECUTOR

During my first visit to Washington, D.C., as chief prosecutor of the United Nations war crimes tribunals, I turned to one of the world's most powerful men to ask for his help. It was a Wednesday afternoon in late September 2000, near the beginning of a long series of appeals I made over the years to government officials and heads of international organizations. I needed them to twist the arms of uncooperative states such as Serbia, Croatia, and Rwanda; I needed them to help us obtain evidence; and, most of all, I needed them to help us apprehend fugitives indicted on war crimes charges. The setting for this particular appeal was adjacent to the White House, in the Old Executive Office Building. An aide led my advisers and me through the entrance. (So many decorative columns that feign to support so many decorative cornices and lintels. I had not seen such a failed struggle to exude vigor, stability, and permanence since my last stroll among the Bourbon palaces of central Paris.) We passed along a corridor that echoed our footsteps. Then, turning into some nondescript office, we came face to face with George Tenet, director of the Central Intelligence Agency. He had many pressing concerns. Ten years after Iraq's invasion of Kuwait and the imposition of economic sanctions that had destroyed hundreds of thousands of Iraqi lives, Saddam Hussein was still in power. Everyone was complaining that the price of oil had spiked to $35 a barrel and, in only a few hours, Likud party leader Ariel Sharon would climb onto the Temple Mount, the Haram al-Sharif, in Jerusalem and ignite the second *intifada*. Perhaps Tenet already knew that within a few weeks crowds would take to Belgrade's streets and topple Slobodan Milošević. In North Korea, Kim Jong-il was dabbling in nuclear weapons. CIA agents were pursuing Osama bin Laden. The September 11, 2001, terrorist attacks were eleven months away.

I needed Tenet to coordinate the CIA's activities with efforts by our office and other intelligence agencies to help capture two of the world's most wanted men, Radovan Karadžić and Ratko Mladić. The tribunal had indicted them on charges related to, among other things, the siege and shelling of Sarajevo, ethnic-cleansing operations that had displaced hundreds of thousands of people, and the killings of about 7,500 captive Muslim men and boys at Srebrenica, the largest massacre in Europe since the weeks after the end of World War II, when communist death squads executed untold thousands of prisoners whom the Allies had forcibly repatriated to Yugoslavia. My English was halting. All morning my aides had been peppering me with questions, some of them vicious, to prepare me for this interview. Tenet knew what Karadžić and Mladić had done in Bosnia, and especially at Srebrenica. We seemed to understand one another within a few moments. I felt he might share the CIA's surveillance information, intercepts of telephone conversations, advice and support for arrest operations—anything to expedite the apprehension of these and other fugitives.

Tenet remarked that Karadžić reminded him of a Sicilian thug. This I found ironic. I know something of Sicilian thugs. And Tenet, a jowly Greek by extraction, exuded a Mediterranean passion, an overbearing will, and other qualities of Sicilian toughs. I loved it, because any spymaster needs these qualities to perform effectively. He assured me that the CIA was active in the manhunt but that apprehending someone like Karadžić, who never speaks over the telephone or signs a document, is a daunting task: "I'm chasing guys all over the world. . . . It took us seven days to find [Panama's General Manual] Noriega with 20,000 GIs." He blurted out the name bin Laden. Then he said, "Karadžić is my number 1 priority."

I was thrilled. The top spy of the world's only superpower was assuring us that his agency was doing its utmost to track one of our most wanted fugitives. I strode back down that echoing corridor and burst out into an autumn afternoon full of possibilities. (Now, those columns and cornices seemed to exude vigor, stability, and permanence.) In a few weeks, I would be appearing before the United Nations Security Council to report that, by many criteria, we had enjoyed a successful first year. We were concentrating our efforts on indicting the highest-ranking officials we could pursue. The Rwanda tribunal's prosecution teams were preparing for trials of dozens of *génocidaires*. Croatia's government had begun handing over documents that linked the late Franjo Tudjman and other high-ranking Croats with crimes committed during the war in Bosnia and Herzegovina. The political winds seemed to be shifting in a Serbia that would not be Milošević's much longer. I thought I would be able to resolve the problems of the Yugoslavia tribunal's prosecution effort, obtain the crucial evidence, apprehend the accused, get them convicted, switch off the lights, and move on to new challenges.

I should have known better. I trusted Tenet to put action behind his words. I assumed he was not erecting something we Italian speakers call the *muro di gomma*, the wall of rubber, the rejection disguised so it won't appear as a rejection. So often, when you approach powerful people with an unwelcome request or demand, your words bounce back. You seem to hear what you want to hear. You might even sense that your effort has yielded something of substance.

My career had begun with a long series of collisions with the *muro di gomma*, sometimes followed by cruder forms of resistance as well as physical threats. I had encountered, and would encounter, the *muro di gomma* during meetings with many powerful people, from mafia financiers to Swiss bankers and politicians, from heads of state like George W. Bush and prime ministers like Silvio Berlusconi to bureaucrats in government offices and the various departments of the United Nations and, late in my tenure, European foreign ministers who seemed to be prepared to welcome Serbia into the European Union's embrace even as Serbia's political leaders, police, and army were harboring men responsible for killing thousands of prisoners in cold blood before the eyes of the world. The only way I know of breaching the *muro di gomma* and serving the interests of justice is by asserting my will, consistently and persistently.

I find it amusing that the philosophical high priest of human will, Arthur Schopenhauer, a stiff, nineteenth-century German pessimist, was silly enough to write that the fundamental flaw in the female character is a lack of a sense of justice:

> This arises from their deficiency in the power of reasoning . . . and reflection, but is also partly due to the fact that Nature has not destined them, as the weaker sex, to be dependent on strength but on cunning; this is why they are instinctively crafty, and have an ineradicable tendency to lie. For as lions are furnished with claws and teeth, elephants with tusks, boars with

fangs, bulls with horns, and the cuttlefish with its dark, inky fluid, so Nature has provided woman for her protection and defence with the faculty of dissimulation [cf. *muro di gomma*].[1]

Women have proven Schopenhauer wrong. Sadly, militant nationalists latched on to his glorification of will and, during the bloodiest two centuries of human history, presided over war crimes that extinguished millions of lives. I find this ironic, because it strikes me that the process I have been engaged in, the process I want to help improve through the revelations in this memoir—the international campaign to end the impunity that has been enjoyed through history by figures like Pol Pot, who bloodied the killing fields of Cambodia; the officers who ordered the deaths of those thousands of forcibly repatriated Yugoslav prisoners in 1945; and alleged, still alleged, mass murderers like Karadžić and Mladić—is in essence a fight that depends foremost upon human will and only secondarily upon subordinate clauses in statutes and conventions or subsections of rules of procedure. Putting war criminals behind bars depends on the will of women and men, and especially women and men of the bar, to challenge the assumption that might means right, to shout yes when the chorus is singing no, to demand justice again and again, even when it means suffering ridicule for seeming to be quixotic.

I began encountering the *muro di gomma* soon after my career in criminal prosecution began in 1981. I would visit Swiss banks to demand that the people there—men and women dressed in fine Italian suits and shoes, men and women ensconced in the bureaucracy of wealth—surrender balance sheets and deposit slips and transfer records from accounts controlled by the drug traffickers of the Italian Mafia. I was demanding that these Swiss bankers behave in a way that was alien to their subculture. I was demanding that they perform actions that would, in the short term, have a negative impact on the profits of their corporations and jeopardize their precious annual bonuses. Day after day, I would stride through sliding glass doors on floors of polished marble into rooms decorated with abstract art, follow a receptionist through a maze of corridors and cubicles to a conference room or a wood-paneled office, and explain that these financial institutions were required to surrender their records because sufficient evidence existed—even under Switzerland's banking laws, which, excuse the cliché, had more holes than Swiss cheese—to show that the money held in these accounts represented the profits of criminal activity. Smiles and denials and half-lies were the order of the day. Then, once we had breached the *muro de gomma*, there came the Mafia's telephone threats and the Mafia's remote-controlled bombs and the funerals of friends. These were a tougher test than the wall of rubber. But I had the advantage of the law and the confidence I was in the right.

The tests of will continued in a different way after I became Switzerland's ranking law-enforcement officer in 1994. I was not a stereotypical bureaucrat, congenitally calculating, conservative, and quiet. I channeled my Mediterranean passion and the authority of my office to help convince the country's parliament to amend Switzerland's laws in order to curtail bank secrecy and close loopholes that were facilitating money laundering by everyone from drug cartels to corrupt political leaders and natural resource companies that have made a shambles of so many states, especially in Africa and other parts of the developing world. Walking the halls of the Swiss parliament and government day after day, demanding that men and women bound by political and bureaucratic imperatives change a law that had helped to make so many people in Switzerland and beyond its borders so rich over the previous sixty years required almost daily confrontations with the *muro di gomma*. I was happy to contribute to this effort. And, once the parliament had adopted a new money-laundering law, I was happy to contribute to improving the image of both Switzerland and its financial institutions by aggressively pressing charges against depositors of dirty money who assumed they still enjoyed impunity.

I have been told that some Swiss bankers uncorked bottles of champagne in September 1999 when I departed my position in Berne and went to work for the United Nations as the chief prosecutor of both the International Criminal Tribunal for the former Yugoslavia and the International Criminal Tribunal for Rwanda. These combined positions were like no job I will ever hold again. They required me to confront the reality of genocide and crimes against humanity: the stench of mass graves, the empty eyes of rape victims, the desperation of uprooted millions, the nauseating sight of entire communities razed to the ground. Crimes of this magnitude are never local affairs. These crimes touch every one of us, wherever we live. They violate cherished principles and trample upon human rights and human dignity. Practically speaking, national leaders too often lack the willpower, and national courts the authority and courage, to prosecute the highest-ranking individuals responsible for these acts. International justice represents the only alternative to impunity.

Making the tribunals' prosecution efforts effective required me and the members of the Office of the Prosecutor to summon the will to confront a loftier and thicker *muro di gomma* than I had ever encountered, to keep demanding that reluctant states and leaders cooperate with these tribunals, to keep demanding the hand-over of documents that incriminate powerful political and military figures, to keep demanding protection for witnesses even as they received threats, to keep demanding that the accused be arrested and transferred to the tribunals' custody. These are narrow themes. Their constant repetition challenged the attention span of media organizations constantly looking for something new to report, so we could not count on them to drum up popular support. Our needs also exasperated bureaucrats and leaders who smiled and shook hands and made promises and, hunkering down behind a *muro di gomma*, did altogether too little. I repeated the words: arrest them, arrest them, arrest them . . . Milošević, Karadžić, Mladić, Gotovina, Lukić. I allowed myself to become a caricature of a woman suffering echolalia. I exposed myself to criticism that I was out of step with political realities in places as uncooperative as Serbia and, when it came to investigating the Tutsi militia, Rwanda. I exposed myself to the ridicule of ambassadors, ministers, and pundits, including some who had even profited from their relationships with such states. I sensed pressure not to issue indictments against certain accused in the former Yugoslavia or even to investigate killings of an archbishop, two bishops, and other Catholic clergymen in Rwanda. I remember receiving word from the secretary general of the United Nations to stop playing politics when I was lobbying the United States and the European Union to apply pressure on Serbia by withholding from it financial assistance. I remember receiving instructions from the United Nations Secretariat in New York and advice from Washington not to answer an invitation to visit Montenegro in 2000, because they had received high-grade intelligence that Milošević and his generals were going to arrest me as a war criminal. (After a seafood luncheon in Dubrovnik, I raced down the Adriatic Coast to Montenegro and encountered nothing more menacing than the tall Montenegrin *muro di gomma*.)

This memoir does not pretend to be a comprehensive accounting of the prosecutions the United Nations tribunals undertook from 1999 to 2007, the eight years I spent in The Hague. It is, rather, a recollection of how I, a public prosecutor from Switzerland who had acquired some international experience, came to these tribunals and how my team members and I strived to serve justice by obtaining cooperation from people who in too many instances did not want to cooperate and felt relatively little imperative to do so. The Yugoslavia tribunal and the Rwanda tribunal, the first international war crimes tribunals convened since the final judgments were handed down at Nuremberg and Tokyo after World War II, did not enjoy the authority of their predecessors. Dispensing victor's justice at Nuremberg and Tokyo was a relatively simple job compared with the work the United Nations Security Council expected the Yugoslavia tribunal and, in certain cases, the Rwanda tribunal to accomplish. Victorious armies gave the prosecutors at Nuremberg and Tokyo the authority to gain access to witnesses, to obtain documentary evidence, and to apprehend accused war criminals, though only from among their defeated German and Japanese enemies. Lacking this same authority, it was up to us to use our wits and will power to prosecute the highest-ranking individuals we could *on all sides* of the conflicts in Rwanda and the former Yugoslavia. We did receive some diplomatic support and, at times, crucial backing from some political leaders in Croatia and Serbia who understood that trying war criminals would help establish rule of law in their countries and reconcile peoples divided by horrible living memories. Sometimes political shifts brought us good fortune. Sometimes our timing was right. Sometimes political trends broke against us. Sometimes we made mistakes. And sometimes we fell out among ourselves.

The lessons to be drawn from the tribunals' successes and failures are valuable, because these efforts were unprecedented. They took place along the edge of the divide between national sovereignty and international responsibility, in the gray zone between the judicial and the political. This is a largely unexplored realm for prosecutors and judges. It is a realm whose native inhabitants—political leaders and diplomats, soldiers and spies, and arms merchants and criminals—assume too often that they enjoy impunity, that they can commit the big crime without being held accountable. It is a realm crisscrossed by the *muro di gomma* and dotted by hidden pitfalls, a realm for which women and men engaged in international justice from Lebanon to Sierra Leone, from Rwanda to Congo, from Holland to Cambodia, must now develop better maps and navigational instruments. I want this book to contribute to developing these tools.

Whenever I became frustrated or felt that I had had enough, I needed only to recall the victims of Yugoslavia and Rwanda, especially the women and children, and the courage they displayed day after day in The Hague and in Arusha, Tanzania, testifying against men, and a few women, alleged to have committed war crimes. One of these victims, Prosecution Witness O in the first Srebrenica trial, had been a seventeen-year-old boy in July 1995, when Serb military forces, allegedly overseen by Radovan Karadžič and Ratko Mladić, overran the town and began the slaughter. On April 14, 2000, not forty paces from my desk, Witness O took the stand against Radoslav Krstić, one of Mladić's top generals, who was later found guilty of aiding and abetting genocide. The witness recalled surrendering to Bosnian Serb soldiers in camouflage uniforms. He recalled being ordered to strip off his clothes, sticky with drying urine, and lined up at the edge of a killing field littered with dead bodies:

> There were several Serb soldiers there . . . standing behind our backs. . . . I thought that I would die very fast, that I would not suffer. And I just thought that my mother would never know where I had ended up. . . .
>
> [S]omebody said, "Lie down." And when we started to fall down . . . the shooting started . . . and I don't know what happened then. I wasn't thinking. . . . I just thought it was the end. I don't know whether I lost consciousness at that point, maybe I was still conscious . . . All I know is that while I was lying down, I felt pain in the right side of my chest. . . .
>
> I was thinking that maybe I wanted to call them to finish me off because I was suffering a lot. And I thought maybe if I don't die here, I will survive and then maybe I will . . . be taken away alive and that my suffering will only be prolonged. . . . [A]t one point . . . I could see a military boot stomping next to my face. And I kept watching, I didn't close my eyes. But the man stepped over me, it was a soldier, and he fired into the head of a man who was next to me. And at that moment, I closed my eyes and I was hit in my right shoulder. . . .
>
> I was sort of between life and death. I didn't know whether I wanted to live or to die anymore. I decided not to call out for them to shoot and kill me, but I was sort of praying to God that they'd come and kill me.

After the executioners had driven off, Witness O lifted his head and spotted another survivor among the dead. He called out and rolled over the corpses to reach the other man and maneuvered his bound hands to the mouth of the second survivor so he could bite through the cord binding them: "The man had a T-shirt on, a green one, and a vest. . . . He took it off and tore it up. . . . When he had bandaged me, I fell asleep on his lap because I hadn't slept for a long, long time. . . . We remained there until the morning . . . and he woke me and asked, 'Where shall we go?' I said, 'I don't know.'"[2]

I had heard many similar witness accounts by the spring of 2001, when I had my second meeting with George Tenet. On this occasion, the venue was the headquarters of the Central Intelligence Agency, a complex of glass, steel, and concrete topped by antennae that extended the will of this man and his superiors into every capital and war-ravaged corner of the world. By now, Milošević had fallen from power and was sitting in a Belgrade jail. George W. Bush had moved into the White House and had already proven himself to be no friend of the effort to establish a permanent international court to try war crimes. I went to the meeting with Tenet chaperoned by staff members of the State Department's office on war crimes who seemed to be most interested in reining in my rhetoric and requests. One of them reminded me to thank the people I was going to see, to thank them effusively for the outstanding support the United States was giving us. Bush's secretary of state, Colin Powell, was backing our efforts to obtain the transfer of Milošević and other accused to the Yugoslavia tribunal's custody. But I had already thanked General Powell, and, as for some others, I was growing weary of uttering empty gratuities to empty ears.

Tenet greeted me in the hallway just before our meeting. "Carla," he said, "my dear Madame Prosecutor." Next came the *bacini bacetti*, the cheek kissy-kissy that grates on my nerves. We entered a conference room with wood-paneled walls, cherry perhaps, and no windows. Tenet sat at the head of the table, after I had taken the chair beside him. He uttered a few words of nothingness in an informal tone. He said he could not tell me everything the CIA was doing. This was understandable. He said arresting our fugitives remained a high priority. He said unsuccessful operations had been conducted. And these statements made me feel comfortable enough to come to the point without resorting to flowery words and fulsome expressions of gratitude. Perhaps it was a mistake to figure that Tenet, the superpower's top spy, the man of the Mediterranean with a blunt, direct style, would not interpret candor as disrespect: "George, I saw you in September. You told me then that Karadžić was a top priority of the CIA. But here we are six months later, and, given the results, I find it hard to believe you."

Intelligence chiefs do not like outsiders telling them how to do their jobs, and many of them think they have nothing to gain and much to lose by chasing down war criminals in far-off lands. Maybe my words stung Tenet in front of his staff. But he knew I had not come to thank the United States for its financial support for the United Nations. He knew I was there to discuss how to secure the arrests of Karadžić and Mladić. I knew by now that he had thrown up the *muro di gomma* at our first meeting the previous September, telling me Karadžić was a priority on a par with bin Laden. But if the CIA director tells me that arresting Karadžić is a priority, I assume the CIA's operatives are competent enough to achieve its director's goals in a timely fashion. "What measures are being taken to ensure arrests?" I asked. "How can the CIA cooperate with the tribunal?" I told him the Office of the Prosecutor wanted to assemble a team to track fugitives. Then I suggested that we elaborate a new strategy on how to apprehend Karadžić. I thought that, within the bounds of United States law, we would be able to share information and work together with the intelligence agencies of other countries, especially France, Great Britain, and Germany. I said, "If you won't do anything, I think you should at least support our efforts."

"Look, Madame," Tenet replied. "I don't give a shit what you think."

CONFRONTING THE *MURO DI GOMMA* TO 1999

I hunted snakes with my brothers even before I had reached my teens. Asps and other poisonous species inhabit the forests and craggy thrusts of limestone surrounding the place where we grew up—Bignasco, a village of about 200 inhabitants near the high, closed end of a valley, the Valle Maggia, in the Swiss Alps above Locarno. Each week I had to take a small blue train down the valley to Locarno for piano lessons. Though I was nine when I began playing piano, my mother allowed me to go to the lessons alone, because it was only an hour's ride, and Switzerland was safe and efficient. My older brother, Flavio, soon discovered a zoo near the piano teacher's home. Next to the zoo was a medical lab that collected live asps in order to make antivenin, an antitoxin for treating people with snakebites. What interested us most was that the lab was willing to pay fifty Swiss francs for each of these copper and brown snakes. Fifty francs was a lot of money in the 1950s. My brothers and I had been pestering snakes for years, which was just as dangerous as hunting them.

To collect the bounty, we had to keep the snakes alive all the way to the lab in Locarno, and we could not let our parents know what we were doing. Our dog, a black *bastardo* named Cliff, was expert at tracking asps and not afraid of them even though he had once been bitten; Flavio injected him with a dose of antivenin we always brought to save ourselves, and Cliff had to fight for his life for two or three days. After he had recovered, my brothers and I would trudge up the mountainside behind him. Cliff would inevitably lead us to a snake, and we would pin it with a forked stick. Then one of us would grab it behind the head and, as it wiggled, drop it into a bag to carry home.

I was the one traveling to Locarno regularly. So I delivered the snakes to the lab, using a shoebox with a small air hole. We hunted all summer, and our secret stash of francs grew. We bought a snare and a special glass container to keep the snakes alive under Flavio's bed. And as the weeks passed, I felt my brothers accepting me as an equal. Once, while I was on the train, one of the asps started poking his upturned snout through the air hole and attempting to escape from the shoebox. It was a big specimen. I kept slapping it back with my music book or something. But it kept struggling to slither out. I was concerned, but not afraid, and I managed to deliver it to the lab and pocket the fifty francs. I knew it was forbidden to bring poisonous snakes aboard the train. During one delivery, the train conductor became suspicious. He asked what I was carrying. I knew I could not lie. So I told the conductor it was an asp. He laughed, at first: "Do your parents know what you are doing?"

"Why no," I said, trying to make this fact seem irrelevant.

After each station, the conductor passed through the train to stamp tickets and asked how my snake was doing. He must have run into my mother a few days later, because she came home angry and punished us and outlawed further snake hunting. We missed those fifty-franc bounties.

I knew I could not lie to the train conductor out of respect for my mother. The lessons from childhood that have guided my choices in life are so simplistic that remembering them is effortless, so simplistic that it seems trite to raise them here. I recall, for example, my mother teaching me good manners. She was a proud, free-spirited woman named Angela, who never bubbled over with emotion but did raise eyebrows in the villages up and down our valley in Switzerland when we raced by in her MG roadster, top down, hair flying. When I was six or seven, she stood me at one end of a long hallway in our house and sat on the stairway at the opposite end; then she had me stride toward her, upright and proper, and greet her with a curtsy as if she were a complete stranger. And I remember her telling me that, if ever I got into trouble, if ever I had to struggle, so long as I knew I was in the right and true to myself, she would support me. She assured me of this many times. Remembering her words has filled me with strength over the years. Whenever I have come under pressure, sensed danger, or felt the sting of criticism, I have asked myself whether, in my heart, I was in the right and whether I was being truthful. And if so, I felt her backing. It gave me fortitude. I persevered. Simplistic? Admittedly. Cliché? Of course. But honest.

Without my mother's support and the confidence it instilled, I might have taken a different path down from Bignasco. I might never have dared to hunt snakes or become a lawyer, an examining magistrate, or a public prosecutor. I might never have left Ticino, our Italian-speaking canton, or learned to assert my will. I felt no sense of ever having been wronged early in life. So I cannot say that some subconscious drive to compensate pushed me along a career that led into courtrooms to argue the guilt of people I was convinced were criminals. I came from a prosperous place in a prosperous, multicultural country whose neutrality, wealth, political stability, and respect for local autonomy have underpinned its identity and shielded it from the ravages of war for so many decades. Perhaps, instead, my comfortable childhood and the ordered society in which I grew up gave me a sense of equilibrium, and I wanted to apply my talent and energy to the criminal-justice system in order to restore the balance other people had lost in their lives through some wrong. Perhaps I simply inherited some deep-seated drive to vanquish evil. Perhaps some part of me is ambitious, perhaps some part craves attention and excitement, like the attention my mother gave me as a little girl and the excitement we felt while roaring through the Swiss Alps in her roadster. Now, however, I know that the quest has become something more than a search for attention or excitement or a drive to vanquish evil. It is at a higher level. It is a desire to help remove the impunity that has for so long allowed the powerful to bring woe to millions upon millions of people, from shop owners forced to pay extortionists weekly protection money to people forced by soldiers from their homes and raped and butchered.

Generations of Del Pontes have inhabited Bignasco and owned land around the village. My ancestors resided for so long beside the village's old stone bridge that they drew our surname from the structure. My uncle owned a general store that carried everything from eggs to explosives. My father owned a small hotel, held the post of village secretary, and managed the local hospital; he was distributing ration coupons during World War II, when he met my mother, a twenty-year-old pediatric nurse who had come to Bignasco to care for the children of a wealthy family. My birth came during the winter all of Europe shivered, 1947, on February 9. I was the second of four children, and the only girl. My brothers inadvertently taught me to fight for my rights. They constantly reminded me that I was a girl and at first tried to keep me from coming along when they went trout fishing in the Maggia, the river that cuts through the bottom of our valley. They said the Maggia's currents were too treacherous for a girl to go wading in for the sake of a few fish, as if it would not sweep away little boys just as easily. It was my mother who taught me to fly cast, and she saw to it that I learned from an elderly man in the village how to tie a fly. So, of course, I tagged along. And I followed my brothers, despite more objections, when they went hunting in the highland forests and climbed to the tops of hardwood trees to gaze at the valley, the forests and craggy mountains, and the eternal river.

Bignasco and the nearby villages did not have a junior high school or high school. When I was eleven years old, my parents enrolled me in a boarding school at a Roman Catholic convent in the town of Bellinzona, which seemed far from Bignasco at the time. I did not return home every weekend, and I could no longer run free the way I had through our Valle Maggia. But the convent school did not seem like a jail, and I never suffered, perhaps because one of my aunts, my father's sister, was a nun there.

After my primary grades, I entered another convent school, in the town of Ingenbol, in the German-speaking region of Switzerland, where I completed my studies for the baccalaureate examination. This was a reputable school. Its students included girls from many different countries. On Mondays and Tuesdays we were obliged to speak only English; on Thursdays and Fridays, only French; and on the other days, German. I think you have to possess particular character traits to endure life in an all-girls boarding school without sustaining permanent damage. You must have a sense of independence and self-confidence, the kind my mother gave me, in order to cope with the regulations and rigid discipline. The nuns taught me to organize my time, and I took the best they had to give: academic studies, piano lessons, tennis, horseback riding . . . My friends and I would sneak away from time to time and head for the nearest town that had a Catholic school for boys. During my last two years, I was allowed to share an apartment with three other girls in Brunnen, a resort town on Lake Lucerne. We were completely free. No parents. No nuns, except at school. Nobody to nag us. It was a fantastic life for a teenager. But we had to pass our exams and, *of course*, strained our eyes studying night after night.

My father said he did not want me to attend a university. He said I did not need to continue my education. But perhaps he was testing my resolve. "You are a woman," he said. "You are going to get married. Don't make me spend money on you." I yearned to find something beyond the walls of a home filled with children. So I enrolled at the university in Berne out of spite and failed to become the cook Italian wives were supposed to be. At first, I wanted to follow my brother Flavio's example and study medicine. But I found out that a medical degree required seven years of schooling, and this was entirely too much classroom time for me. I decided instead to pursue a career in law. I lived under Flavio's supervision in Berne for a year. This turned out to be a positive experience. He had many friends coming over, and I wanted to get to know all of them. I would sometimes go with him to lectures and point out young future doctors I was interested in, and he would bring them home for me to meet.

After that year in Berne, I transferred to the law faculty in Geneva and, in 1972, I completed my degree. My life path could not have been more conventional. I married my college sweetheart, Pierre-André Bonvin, the son of a president of the Swiss confederation, Roger Bonvin. Our relationship was long distance. He stayed behind in Geneva to complete his law studies while I moved back to Lugano and entered private practice. Our marriage buckled after I fell in love with Daniele Timbal, an attorney who was engaged in commercial work in Lugano. Even before I married him, Timbal counseled me to concentrate on representing women in divorce cases. It was good advice—to a point. I was successful at it. The work paid well. Timbal and I opened a law practice. I bought my first Louis Vuitton bag, and would have bought my mother one but she had accumulated enough bags already. I learned to race sports cars at the circuit in Hockenheim, Germany, and drove my Porsche 911SC up to Bignasco to take my mother—and *her* mother—on rides at 200 kilometers an hour. But divorce work became tedious. I would sit in an office day after day, listening to clients describe the mundane details of their loves and lives gone awry, trying all the while to steer them to the point. From time to time, the local court would assign me to defend people indicted for crimes, burglaries and robberies mostly, which gave me some experience in criminal law. It is imperative for accused persons to have effective defense counsel. But this was not fulfilling work for me, especially under the civil law system in continental Europe. As defense counsel, you receive a dossier; you read the statement of the case; you examine the evidence; and you see that, almost always, the defendant is guilty. I would visit my clients in prison and they would whine, "Not me," but offer no compelling alibis. And I would lose my patience. It gave me a sick feeling to stand up in a courtroom and defend someone I knew should be behind bars. And I think my mother's lesson about being true to myself might have given me second thoughts, not only about whom I was defending but about defense work in general. In August 1977, my son Mario was born. For a time, I worked only half a day and had a nanny take care of him while I was away.

I n 1980 I applied for my first prosecutorial position, as a *juge d'instruction*, an examining magistrate, a member of the bar who conducts investigations and passes on the results in a file to a prosecutor who presents the case in court. In Switzerland at that time, almost all examining magistrates were men. I remember having to go before a panel of judges and lawyers to interview for the position. One of the questions the panel saw fit to ask was whether I wanted to have another child. I was married to Timbal at the time; I was not some entry-level candidate. My almond-brown hair had already begun sprouting strands of gray and, clinging desperately to my youth, I had begun bleaching it blond. And here the panel members were clearly implying that if I wanted to have more children, I would not receive the appointment. The question itself angered me, especially because the judge who had posed it was a woman. I fired back. I told the panel it had no right to inquire into such personal matters. My private life, I said, was my private affair, and it was improper and discriminatory to delve into it. So I answered them by attacking the question. They awarded me the job anyway.

During the years I worked as an examining magistrate, I developed a specialization in cases involving financial misdeeds. Lugano was an excellent place to probe financial legerdemain. The city lies just inside Switzerland's border with Italy, astride a main traffic corridor from Geneva and Zurich to Milan, Venice, Florence, Rome, and the other rich cities and ports of Italy. Border and customs controls between the two countries have been minimal since soon after World War II. Lugano is home to bank officials who speak Italian, the operational language of the Sicilian Mafia. And, most important, Lugano, like the rest of Switzerland, had a decades-old tradition of bank secrecy. Some Swiss take comfort believing the story that their laws protecting bank secrecy were passed in order to protect the assets of German Jews who were victims of blackmail by the Gestapo after Hitler's rise to power. The more compelling story, as I know it, anyway, is that, in the early 1930s, French authorities caught Swiss bankers in Paris visiting clients who were using banks in Switzerland to evade taxes; the bankers were carrying files with hundreds of account numbers and the names of their owners. The ensuing scandal prompted the Swiss parliament to pass the Banking Act of 1934. This law made it a criminal offense, punishable by sizable fines and imprisonment, for bankers in Switzerland to violate the privacy of their clients, unless the authorities could show that the bank accounts held funds derived from criminal activity, which did not, under Swiss law, include tax evasion and other acts Switzerland considered misdemeanors and not crimes. So, under the Swiss system, money laundering—the practice of executing financial transactions in ways that conceal the identity, source, and destination of money in order to evade taxes and cover a trail leading back to criminal activity—existed in a kind of legal Neverland. Banks in Switzerland effectively allowed anonymous accounts, and the country's bankers too rarely inquired about the origins of significant deposits or the destination of significant outgoing transfers. The utility of such a financial environment for drug dealers, illegal weapons merchants, corrupt government officials, and criminal organizations is obvious.

My involvement in financial cases began after an examining magistrate from Italy visited Lugano and requested assistance from our office in investigating crimes involving the Sicilian Mafia. The other examining magistrates in the Lugano office were already engaged in their own cases. They clearly did not want to waste time or jeopardize their careers by working alongside some foreigner who had come begging with tin cup in hand, especially since he was asking them to contend with the local banking community, which might jeopardize their careers, and the Sicilian Mafia, which might jeopardize their lives. I had just arrived in the office and was still the most junior of the examining magistrates. My only sense of the Mafia came from Italian detective stories and *The Godfather* novels and movies about the Corleone crime family. And now I found myself with an offer I could not refuse, an offer that would change my life and give it a sense of mission.

The examining magistrate from Sicily turned out to be one of the most formidable figures Italy would produce during the twentieth century. Giovanni Falcone was a handsome man driven by a monomaniacal urge to end the culture of impunity that organized crime had enjoyed for far too long in his homeland. He had come to Lugano in 1981 to inquire about funds transiting a local bank account. He brought evidence that the money was dirty, so even under Switzerland's banking laws I was able to freeze the account and obtain the records. Next, he asked to interview the bankers who managed the bank account; he wanted information on the account's owner and the people servicing it. Under Swiss law, Swiss examining magistrates have to preside over interviews involving magistrates from other countries. I formally asked the witnesses and their lawyers if they would allow Falcone to pose questions himself. Nobody objected. The first case Falcone brought to Lugano led to a second. The second led to a third and a fourth. Falcone had a charismatic personality. During the interviews we conducted together, I tried to absorb everything he said and to master as many of his techniques as possible, and I developed a detailed mental map of the Sicilian Mafia and its personalities and methods. I repeatedly visited Lugano's banks and demanded the balance sheets and transaction slips from tainted accounts. Time and again, bankers turned me away. Time and again I faced the *muro di gomma* and returned to demand the documents. And very often, I got them. This was a fulfilling job, and it taught me to assert my will in the cause of justice.

At about the time I began working on the Mafia cases, I learned again that I had a congenital weakness for Italian men, southern and macho and utterly opposed to the concept of a woman returning from work later than her husband, the concept of a cold kitchen and no waiting pasta. My second, and final, marriage ended by mutual consent. Mario came with me, and I engaged a live-in nanny. The divorces angered my father; but my mother was unfazed. In 1983, when Mario was about to begin school, my mother and I decided that, during the workweek, she would care for him in the home where I had spent my childhood. Bignasco would be much quieter than Lugano. Mario would attend a nearby school and have a more normal life with my mother than with a nanny. I would join him every Friday evening, making the one-hour drive up the Valle Maggia. We kept this arrangement up for three school years, until about the time my father suffered a stroke and passed away.

In 1982, I began working on financial aspects of the case involving Roberto Calvi, whose mysterious death in London that June would for years attract headlines and tease the imaginations of conspiracy theorists around the world. Calvi was chairman of Italy's second-largest bank, the Milan-based Banco Ambrosiano, which had links with the Vatican and the Sicilian Mafia. Regulators had for years questioned the integrity of Banco Ambrosiano. In 1978, Italy's national bank revealed that Banco Ambrosiano had illegally transferred abroad several billion lira. A court sentenced Calvi to a four-year jail term and a multi-million-dollar fine in 1981. He was freed on bail pending his appeal, and within a few months Banco Ambrosiano dissolved. Calvi disappeared from Rome and fled Italy, apparently through Yugoslavia, using a bogus passport. Eight days later, a mail carrier in London spotted his body dangling by a rope from scaffolding beneath Blackfriars Bridge over the River Thames. He was wearing a Patek Philippe wristwatch. His wallet was stuffed with Swiss francs and other currencies. The British authorities declared Calvi's death a suicide.

The police in Lugano arrested an Italian named Flavio Carboni in connection with the Banco Ambrosiano affair. I interviewed Carboni and conducted extradition proceedings with Italy. Carboni revealed nothing in our interrogation. He denied involvement in Calvi's murder, though he admitted meeting Calvi the night before he was found hanging by the neck above the Thames. It was October 2002 before an independent forensic report established that Calvi had been killed. Three years later, Carboni and four other defendants went on trial in Rome. They were acquitted in June 2007.

Falcone's investigations led to the arrests that revealed the famous Pizza Connection, which would produce one of the most complex criminal trials in Italian and American history. The Sicilian-based Pizza Connection distributed an estimated $1.6 billion in heroin and other illicit drugs through a network of pizzerias in the United States between 1975 and 1984. It began to unravel after the police at Palermo airport apprehended a number of men attempting to smuggle in cash. More than twenty defendants stood trial, all of them Sicilian; one was murdered before the trial began; two others were shot while the hearings were proceeding. A *pentito*, a former member of the Mafia who is collaborating with the police, agreed to testify after the Corleone crime family had killed members of his family and had attempted to kill him.

Just before the end of the Pizza Connection trial, the police in Lugano arrested a Mafia money man, Oliviero Tognoli, in connection with the laundering of millions of dollars in revenues derived from the sale of heroin and other illicit drugs. Both Switzerland and Italy had issued warrants for his arrest. Tognoli decided to surrender to us and did not want word to spread that he had done so voluntarily. He would eventually receive a three-year prison sentence.

Developing the case against Tognoli required me to travel to Palermo for the first time. Falcone initially told me not to come because it was too dangerous. Months later, in June 1989, he gave the green light. I met him at his office. Both of us had Italian bodyguards around-the-clock. I found the experience suffocating but was willing to put up with it for a few days;

I could not comprehend how Falcone could stand having it intrude on his life every hour, year after year. The day before I was to return to Switzerland, we visited a restaurant for dinner. Falcone told me we would finish our work early the next day, go to a house he had rented by the sea, and take a swim. I did not say yes or no. I did not want to go swimming. I was about to take a long seaside vacation, but, to be polite, did not say so. I switched the topic, and the conversation took a different tangent. When we met the next morning in his office, I told Falcone that I would rather visit the town of Palermo to see the sights and shop for some gifts. So we ended up not going to the beach house. This was a fortuitous change of plans. Someone at the restaurant—it was the only place in which we ever discussed going to the seaside—must have overheard our conversation and informed the Mafia about our plans. On that beach the next day, the police recovered a bag packed with 125 pounds of explosives wired to a radio-controlled detonator.

In about 1988, I became a prosecutor in the Ticino canton. The investigations my office undertook together with Falcone and other prosecutors in Italy led to the arrest of many people, including some bankers in Lugano. The Mafia started referring to me as *La Puttana,* The Whore. Perhaps the nickname was a sign of respect, an indication that we were getting to them. Later we learned that Swiss banks were hiring Italian-speaking account managers for their offices in Geneva, Zurich, and other cities to accommodate Italians who were shifting their transactions away from Lugano, because, as one *pentito* told us, the risk was too high that we would freeze their accounts.

I was proud when Falcone characterized me in a newspaper interview as the "personification of stubbornness." And I was proud that my mother was following the newspaper and television stories about what my office was doing. At times she would warn me not to be so unbending. At times she was afraid for me. My brothers and I had to call her regularly to say we were all right, and I did at least once a week. My mother and my son also forged a close relationship, and I do not regret the time he spent with her instead of with me. He was happier in Bignasco. He could run free. He had close friends. He lacked for nothing.

I was with my mother in Bignasco on Saturday, May 23, 1992. I do not remember what I was doing when the telephone rang at about six in the evening. A police officer was on the line. He told me Falcone was dead. Then I saw the television news reports from Palermo. Hit men had detonated a radio-controlled bomb that destroyed Falcone's car, killing him and his wife, Francesca Morvillo, who had been a juvenile magistrate, and three of their bodyguards. The explosion ripped a crater in the earth and reduced Falcone's car to bits of twisted, sheered metal scattered over a debris field. I could not believe my eyes, and I could not pull them away from the screen. I did not cry. But I did begin to burn with rage against the Mafia, especially after we learned that the attack was the work of the head of the Corleone family, Salvatore Riina, reputed to be the boss of bosses, or *capo dei capi*, of the Sicilian mafia. I wanted to attend Falcone's funeral. The security threat in Palermo made this impossible, and it brought home not only the loss of a friend and mentor but a deeper emptiness. I saw the fate that can befall anyone who dares fight openly against the impunity powerful criminals and political figures too often enjoy, and I sensed the uncertainty of my own circumstances and my responsibility toward my son. I considered quitting. I pondered going back to divorce work and those tedious conversations about love betrayed. I thought about making more money and racing Porsches. I thought about not having always to glance over my shoulder, about not having to encounter the *muro di gomma.* Then I spoke with Ilda Boccassini, a friend and prosecutor from Milan and another of Falcone's collaborators. She, too, was angry. But she said she would not give up. And this was a comfort to me.

I went to the office that Monday and spoke with a number of journalists. Italian police investigators visited the next day. And about three days later, my mobile telephone rang again. This time, a soothing voice with a Sicilian accent delivered a message from afar: "You see what happened to your friend." The line clicked dead. The message was clear: "You should be kind and gentle with us." A few weeks after my phone threat, another of Riina's bombs killed Falcone's ally, Paolo Borsellino, and five of his bodyguards. Since then, the Swiss authorities have kept me under guard. (This experience has warped my life in so many ways, some of them humorous. I would like to say, for example, that it was my mother who trained me to carry my handbag in a way that exudes self-assurance. But it was my Swiss bodyguards, and for a practical reason. Wherever I left my home or a building, the guards insisted on reducing as much as possible the amount of time I spent in the open, moving from the door to the car or from my car to the office or the airplane. Until then, I always fumbled with my own luggage and briefcases. Now, the bodyguards managed the luggage. My hand was free to carry the Louis Vuitton.)

The Falcone and Borsellino killings ignited public opinion in Italy and forced the Italian government, finally, to crack down on organized crime. Ilda Boccassini successfully conducted the investigation in Sicily. On January 15, 1993, a captain in the Italian police, Sergio de Caprio, a fearless man referred to at the time only by his code name, *Capitano Ultimo*, arrested the Mafia boss Salvatore Riina as he sat in Palermo traffic. Riina denied the Mafia's existence. He denied knowing that he had been Sicily's most wanted man for most of three decades. Naked before the eyes of the Italian people, leaders of the country's law enforcement agencies had to admit that for thirty years, Sicily's most wanted fugitive, this sixty-two-year-old diabetic, had been living peacefully at home in Palermo, his whereabouts known to practically everyone in the city for the entire time. Absent the public outrage at the killings of Falcone and Borsellino, the Italian authorities would never have summoned the will to arrest Riina and end the impunity he had enjoyed thanks to his money, his political influence, and the violence he was willing to use to defend his position.

I avoided traveling to Palermo for two years after Falcone's assassination. But I kept investigating Mafia cases. I also worked with Antonio Di Pietro, a magistrate from Milan, who was gathering evidence in the early 1990s to bring corruption charges against political leaders in an effort to introduce transparency and accountability to Italy. By the spring of 1994, he had identified a significant number of bank accounts in Ticino containing deposits of corruption money from Italy. I opened a money-laundering investigation in cooperation with Di Pietro, but the *chambre d'accusation*, a kind of court of appeals in Ticino, would not allow us to pursue the matter further. I do not know what lay behind this decision, but, from my vantage point, it seemed politically motivated.

Salvatore Cancemi, a *pentito* from the Corleone crime family, eventually squealed to a judge in Palermo about how he had once traveled to Lausanne to collect $10 million in cash but, to avoid the risk of having all the money confiscated by the customs officers at the border, did not want to cross back into Italy with all of the cash. He drove instead to a farmhouse that a married couple from Italy had rented near Lugano. He said the husband and wife were just friends and not connected with the Mafia, but he stayed with them for two or three days and, at some point, wrapped in waterproof packaging bundles of $50 and $100 bills totaling $6 million, stuffed the packages into a metal milk container, and buried it in the garden—all the time assuming he would return later to recover the cash.

The Italian police arrested him in the meantime. We brought him to Lugano from his prison cell in Palermo, and he led us to the farmhouse and the garden. We did not doubt Cancemi's story. But the idea of recovering a stash of $6 million buried for eight years was a bit much. We used a metal detector and dug up old spoons and cans and other trash several times before the detector beeped again. A few minutes later, a shovel struck the metal can. The owner of the farm told me he had planned to build a new house on the site and would have found the money. "You're lucky you didn't," I told him. "We would have found your body, and the investigators would never have discovered the motive."

Cancemi told us that he was transporting the cash on behalf of Salvatore Riina. And, without approaching the purported "owner" of the $6 million, we could not legally confiscate the money on behalf of the Swiss authorities. So I took the opportunity to travel to Palermo's Ucciardone Prison, the venue of Italy's famous Mafia trials during the 1990s, and interviewed the head of the Corleone crime family, the man who had ordered the hit on my friend and mentor, Falcone. Ucciardone Prison is an aging facility. Inside, engineers constructed a modern courtroom—bullet proofed, bomb proofed, and equipped with metal cages to thwart any escape attempt—so the police would not face the security problems associated with transporting the dozens of defendants each day through streets exposed to Mafia bombs and anyone thinking of abetting an escape. I sat down at the judge's bench with my counterpart, the Italian magistrate. The atmosphere was quiet and strange. The air conditioning provided a welcome relief from the stifling summer air outside.

The guards behaved with deference toward Riina as they led him in and sat him down, about six feet away from me. It was as if the guards were afraid that this man, attired in a tailored shirt, slacks, and fine leather shoes rather than the standard-issue prison jumpsuit, could make a single phone call to the outside world and ruin their lives. The Italian magistrate gave me the floor. I introduced myself. I said I had come from Lugano. Riina glowered at me as I described how we had recovered the $6 million and discovered its connection to drug trafficking. As I proceeded, Riina's face grew flushed. I could sense anger rising within him. And it quickly erupted: "Why have you come here? Why are you telling me this? I have nothing to do with this. You should go back to your town and stay there."

I did not react to his jibes. I had prepared myself to keep my poise. I had thought about it in advance. I knew I was facing the man most responsible for the death of my friend, the man who dared think that, by assassinating officers of the law, he might so intimidate the entire Italian government that the culture of impunity, the culture that creates so much fear that even law enforcement officers do not enforce the law, would be restored and surrounded by a *muro di gomma.* I wanted to confront him about Falcone, but this would have been outside my remit. I did, however, raise my voice: "I'm not going to stand for your attitude. I've got a job to do, whether you like it or not. I have a statement that implicates you." He refused to cooperate. And the meeting came to an abrupt halt. Before the guards led Riina away, however, he turned to me. "*Mi scuso, mi scuso,*" he said, apologizing in a fulsome way that I understood to be a threat. At about that time, Riina's thugs were attempting to spread terror through all of Italy by detonating bombs at tourist attractions, including the Uffizi Gallery in Florence. There was even a plot to topple the leaning tower at Pisa. Ten innocent people died and hundreds more suffered injuries.

I n 1994, I became the Swiss federation's attorney general, its top federal law-enforcement official. I directed a significant amount of my office's attention toward combating attempts by organized criminals to use Switzerland's banks to launder money. I also enlisted in a campaign to convince the country's parliament that it was in Switzerland's interests, and even in the interests of its banks, which had enjoyed years of windfall profits from such activity, to amend the laws governing financial institutions and halt money laundering.

A new law, which took effect on January 1, 1995, criminalized money laundering and made bankers criminally liable for failing to exercise due diligence when opening new accounts, accepting deposits, and making transfers. Switzerland's banking regulators subsequently issued a battery of detailed regulations, essentially forcing banks to employ teams of lawyers and managers to guard against money-laundering activities. The new laws enable the Swiss government to provide information to foreign law-enforcement authorities in cases covered by mutual assistance agreements.

Strict laws mean nothing, however, if the appropriate authorities do not implement them. I leapt at the opportunity to apply Switzerland's new laws. The first big case I recall arose in November 1995, when Swiss police officers arrested Paulina Castañon, the wife of Raúl Salinas, who is the brother of Carlos Salinas, Mexico's former president. At the time of her arrest, Castañon was attempting to withdraw more than $80 million from a Swiss bank using a bogus passport. My office received evidence that the millions of dollars Raúl Salinas had deposited under various names at a number of Swiss banks was related to drug dealing, and I responded by freezing these accounts. Defense lawyers argued that Salinas was running an "investment fund" for Mexican businessmen; we maintained that these funds were revenues from drug trafficking, and I told the press that if Raúl Salinas' bank transactions were related to an investment fund, then his management methods were unsound and contrary to customary business practice. A decision by Switzerland's Supreme Court forced us to withdraw our charges of money laundering against Raúl Salinas, and we were obliged to transfer all of our files to Mexico so proceedings could be launched against him there. The Mexican courts had already jailed Raúl Salinas for corruption and the murder of a political rival.

I took the opportunity to interview Raúl Salinas in December 1995, during a visit to a prison in Mexico with Valentin Rorschacher, head of the Swiss Central Office for Drug Trafficking. Raúl Salinas, of course, denied any wrongdoing, but his description of the transactions he had undertaken gave us a clear indication that the changes to Switzerland's banking regime were having desired effects. "We had trust in Swiss banking secrecy," Salinas told us with the despondence of someone who had assumed he enjoyed impunity.

Our enforcement of the new banking regime upset many people in the wood-paneled boardrooms and the fancy health spas and country clubs: men, mostly, who had fought to preserve the status quo and their institutions' profits. Some critics began calling me Pinko Carla or Red Carla; one banker apparently dubbed me an "unguided missile." And, again, these were signs that we were getting to them.

Later, I froze the Swiss bank accounts of the former prime minister of Pakistan, the late Benazir Bhutto, the daughter of Pakistan's former president. She returned to power after elections in October 1993 and remained in office until 1996, when her government fell for a second time after accusations of corruption. A commission of inquiry came to Switzerland from Pakistan seeking information on Bhutto's husband, who had been arrested on corruption allegations. The Pakistani commission provided enough information and evidence to require Switzerland to open an investigation. We located significant sums of money in Geneva and evidence that Bhutto had received a cut from government-controlled contracts. I froze each of the relevant accounts and remember receiving letters of complaint from Bhutto and several lawyers. I also remember Switzerland's ambassador in Islamabad complaining about demonstrations outside the embassy. He was laughing, but not really laughing, because he was confined to his official residence.

Another big case arose on November 17, 1997, but it had nothing to do with banks or big money. On this day, six armed men disguised themselves as members of the Egyptian security force around Deir el-Bahri, a famous archaeological site situated across the Nile River from the fabled ruins at Luxor. At about a quarter to nine in the morning, these men cocked their automatic weapons, descended from the Mortuary Temple of Hatshepsut, the first known queen regnant in history, and attacked a group of tourists. They killed about sixty of the sightseers, including thirty-five people from Switzerland. Some they beheaded; others they disemboweled; the women they shot in the head. During an ensuing gun battle with Egyptian police officers and military forces, the attackers were either killed or committed suicide. The gunmen, tearing pages from al Qaeda's modus operandi, were attempting to deprive Egypt of desperately needed foreign income by trying to frighten away foreign tourists.

My office opened an investigation into the Luxor attack. There was little we could do independently, because the Egyptian authorities undertook the primary investigative effort. We contacted the Egyptian prosecutor's office, and I traveled to Cairo once to meet with him. It was not a fruitful encounter. I think it surprised the prosecutor when I walked into his office and he realized I was a Carla and not a Carlo. He was reticent and curt and did not want to cooperate with me. At the ministry of internal affairs, however, things were different. And after I assigned a male investigator to handle the case, we received all of the information we needed.

By 1998 we became involved in the fight against corruption and the culture of impunity in Russia. The ranking justice official in Russia, Yuri Skuratov, had launched an investigation into Mabeteks, a Lugano-based construction company with sizable contracts in Russia during the 1990s, included agreements for renovation of the Kremlin and repairs to the parliament building damaged by tank shells during the attempted coup of 1993. Skuratov sent us a request for assistance to look into bank transactions in Switzerland. In January 1999 I issued a search warrant for the offices of the Mabeteks. In the company's files, police officers found photocopies of credit cards issued in the names of Boris Yeltsin, who was then Russia's president, and his daughter and personal adviser, Tatyana Dyachenko. The resulting scandal threatened to plunge Russia into a political crisis. I remember that on my second or third trip to Moscow I saw demonstrators carrying picket signs with my name on them. I thought they were protesting against me. It turned out, however, that these were people who had lost out in the lawlessness and corruption that was transforming Russia from a Communist Party kleptocracy into a secret-police kleptocracy, and they were calling upon me to run for president and clean up the mess. Unfortunately, the investigation of the Kremlin ended Skuratov's tenure as Russia's general prosecutor. Russian television soon afterward showed videotape of a man resembling Skuratov in a sauna with two prostitutes, and Skuratov, after a bitter fight, was forced to resign his position. I spoke afterward with Skuratov about the videotape, and I believed him when he told me it was a fake.

About Yugoslavia, I knew little more than I had seen on television or read in the press, because my job did not allow me time to learn more. At the time Yugoslavia was breaking apart, I was involved in investigating Mafia money flows. In May 1992, as the Serbs were launching their ethnic-cleansing operations in Bosnia and Herzegovina, the Corleone family assassinated Falcone. In January 1993, when Croatia was launching its proxy war against Bosnia's Muslims, I was captivated by the arrest of Salvatore Riina, the Corleone *capo*. In 1995, when Serb gunmen from Bosnia and Serbia were massacring thousands of Muslim prisoners near Srebrenica, I was attempting to apply Switzerland's new law on financial services to investigate dirty money in my country's financial institutions. But even as I watched from afar as these sad events unfolded, I could hardly believe that such wholesale crime could be committed in Europe at the dawn of the twenty-first century: ethnic cleansing, on television (sometimes live), only an hour's flying time from peaceful, well-groomed Ticino. I recall having been outraged enough by Radovan Karadžić that, when he traveled to Geneva for peace negotiations soon after I was appointed Switzerland's attorney general, I wanted to have him arrested and handed over to the United Nations war crimes tribunal in The Hague. My staff and I discussed it. I first wanted to see whether the tribunal had prepared an indictment against him; then I thought we could open an investigation ourselves. We concluded at the time that Switzerland, on its own, had no jurisdiction, because it had not ratified the international convention against genocide. And we learned that, at that time, the Yugoslavia tribunal had issued no indictment against him. So we did nothing more. Today, I regret not being more aggressive, though I do not know how I might have been. Srebrenica was still just a United Nations "safe area," and we might have helped change history if we had arrested him.

By 1998, an Albanian insurgency group, the Kosovo Liberation Army (KLA), was escalating attacks on Serbian police officers, and Albanian civilians were suffering retaliatory attacks by the Serbian police. I opened an investigation into Albanians in Switzerland who were collecting money like racketeers and using it to acquire weapons and send them to the Kosovo Liberation Army. We tailed two trucks full of weapons until the Italian authorities interdicted them on Italian territory. I had a few Albanians arrested in Switzerland in connection with this gunrunning. But I could not continue the effort because we received no assistance from Kosovo or Serbia and could not show where the weapons from Switzerland were going and how they were being used. I sent a deputy to Priština to investigate the matter. We received threats from Albanians, but too little information of evidentiary value.

By the end of the 1990s, the mood toward me within Switzerland's banking community had begun to change—at least on the surface. I think some people began to see the benefits to the banks of operating within a legal framework that did not allow for money laundering and other activities linked with the Mafia. Dealing with criminals destroys the credibility of legitimate businesses, especially banks and lawyers. And the Swiss banks were having their names besmirched with each new revelation of their association with drug dealers and other organized criminals. Today, Switzerland is one of the most advanced countries in the world in terms of fighting money laundering at the banking level. Continuing the struggle is only a matter of will.

In 1998, a journalist for *Time* asked me to describe my dream job. "I want to be the chief prosecutor of the International Criminal Court," I answered. The Rome Statute, the treaty that established the court, had just been adopted, but it would be years before the first permanent international court to try war crimes opened its doors. I never sought to become chief prosecutor of the tribunals the United Nations had established to try persons responsible for war crimes in Yugoslavia and Rwanda. I assumed that I would remain a prosecutor in Switzerland until retirement. In June 1999, while my team was assembling a corruption case against a high-ranking Swiss military officer, I received a telephone call from the country's federal secretary of state, Jakob Kellenberger, who is now president of the International Committee of the Red Cross. He asked me whether I would mind if the government of Switzerland submitted my name as a candidate for the post of chief prosecutor of the tribunals in The Hague. I had no objection. But I agreed only because I assumed I would never get the job and because Switzerland, a resolutely neutral country that had for decades resisted becoming a United Nations member state, was attempting to put forward a new effort to belong. Kellenberger was reassuring: "No, you don't have any chance, because Switzerland is not a member of NATO or the European Union."

In July, I was on vacation in Tuscany. I received a call from Berne informing me that Kofi Annan, the United Nations secretary-general, wanted to see me immediately in New York to discuss appointing me to the post of chief prosecutor in The Hague. I still assumed that I had no chance to get the job. In fact, I did not want the job. So I replied that I would not interrupt my vacation to fly all the way to New York for a meeting that was going to be without substance. I would be traveling to Mexico a month later on a mission related to the ongoing case against Salinas. I said I would stop in New York if Annan still wanted to see me. So for a few days in August, I laid over in New York. At Switzerland's mission to the United Nations, I learned that Annan really did want to appoint me to the post in The Hague. The NATO bombing of Serbia had just ended, and Russia and China did not want the new chief prosecutor to come from a NATO country; the NATO countries clearly did not want anyone from Russia or China or the former nonaligned states; the tribunal's first prosecutor had come from South Africa; so someone from Switzerland, which was not a member of NATO, the European Union, or the United Nations, was an acceptable compromise. "No, I cannot accept it," I said. "Absolutely not. I am Switzerland's attorney general. I have an important trial pending. Only I can do it. My deputy cannot to do this." The day before my meeting with Annan, I went jogging in Central Park. I thought, "*Bene*, I'll tell him, 'No thank you. No, no, no, and *grazie*.'" The next morning, before I went to United Nations headquarters, the ambassador to Switzerland's mission told me that my country's president,

Ruth Dreyfus, wanted to speak with me by telephone. Dreyfus told me it was important for Switzerland's prestige that I accept the position. She pressed hard. And, at the conclusion of our conversation, I told her I would think about it.

I had met Kofi Annan before, during his tenure as head of the United Nations Department of Peacekeeping Operations. My brother Flavio, the one who saved our *bastardo* by injecting him with antivenin, the one who brought me future doctors to meet during his days in medical school, was by now a surgeon and had met Annan during his days working in peacekeeping. While I was attorney general in Switzerland, I received invitations to the annual World Economic Forum in Davos. One year, my brother asked me to seek out Annan and pass along his greetings, and this was how I first met Annan. We discussed little except Flavio and one or two corruption investigations, and nothing at all about Yugoslavia. On the morning I met him in New York, he insisted on putting my name forward for the chief prosecutor position at the tribunals. He urged me to accept the job and reminded me that the Swiss government also wanted me to take the post. I asked him how long I had to decide. He gave me a week. In this life, one week is not enough time to know where you are or what you are doing. If I had had a month to decide, I surely would have declined. Knowing what I know now, I would have regretted it.

After returning to Berne, I met with Ruth Dreyfus as well as the ministers of foreign affairs and justice. I told them I did not want to work for the United Nations in Holland. I had important work in Switzerland. Salary was a factor; I wanted to be able to afford the Louis Vuitton bags I knew I would keep buying. Instead of using the week and talking with Louise Arbour, who was then the tribunals' chief prosecutor, I remained in Berne fighting to stay in Berne. I am certain that many members of the government wanted me to go to The Hague to raise Switzerland's profile in the international community. I am just as sure that there were Swiss bankers and persons in Switzerland's military and civilian bureaucracies who wanted me out. Maybe a Russian president did, too.

Two or three days passed before I informed Dreyfus that I would accept the position. On the next Thursday, August 12, 1999, Annan visited Geneva for the fiftieth anniversary of the signing of the Geneva Conventions, the international community's basic laws on war and human rights. After the celebrations in the Alabama Room at the city's town hall, I had a meeting with Annan to seal the deal. The ministry of foreign affairs sent a minder to ensure I did not back out at the last minute.

Annan immediately led me before several hundred journalists. I did not quite feel like the bride in a shotgun wedding, but I did feel more anxiety than on a flight to Palermo. My command of the English language—despite the Monday and Tuesday English-only days at the boarding school in Ingenbol—was rudimentary. I managed to say it was an honor for me and for Switzerland that the United Nations had chosen me to be the chief prosecutor for the two tribunals. I expressed heartfelt gratitude to Annan for having nominated me. I stressed that I would investigate crimes against women and children most energetically. "I have never been at the service of anyone except the law," I told the journalists. "I plan to continue to work in this way. It makes for many enemies, but that doesn't matter, that's what we are here for."

I hardly understood the gist of most of the questions. In fact, the meaning of one question escaped me completely. I think it was: "Are you concerned about the backlog waiting for you?" I looked to Annan for a timely rescue. He whispered an answer, and I repeated what he told me: "I am not afraid about future work. I will go to The Hague and show what we can do and if we need some help or some more personnel to work with. I will ask the secretary-general to give me the necessary instruments to go on, to make sure that what he says can be realized."

"And if it doesn't work, blame me," joked Annan like an experienced handler.

Afterward, there was a telephone interview in English with the BBC, and I have to admit that I had little idea what I was saying. Only for the German, French, and Italian media could I deliver a coherent message, but I knew nothing of Yugoslavia or Rwanda, so there was nothing much I could say. I told one journalist that I had received assurances from Annan that I would be able to work with complete independence and that I intended to pursue Milošević, Karadžić, Mladić, and the other accused aggressively, because every member state of the United Nations was obligated to cooperate in this respect. I said that I saw the tribunals on Yugoslavia and Rwanda as precursors of the International Criminal Court and that this was a move in the right direction, because organized crime was way ahead of governments simply because there is no international law-enforcement system for global crime suppression.

At the end of August or in early September, I received a telephone call from the Yugoslavia tribunal's chief of investigations, John Ralston, telling me that two tribunal staff members would be coming from The Hague to Berne to discuss an important issue. A day or so later, I met with Steve Upton, the leader of an investigative team, and Brenda Hollis, an American prosecutor. They said the office had just been in touch indirectly with Radovan Karadžić, who had by now been a fugitive from justice for about half a decade. They said Karadžić had expressed a willingness to surrender voluntarily. But, for a reason I could not fathom, he did not want to be transferred immediately to The Hague. He wanted, instead, for me to receive him in Switzerland, place him under arrest, and, subsequently, organize a transfer to The Hague so the Swiss authorities would ensure his security. The message was that Karadžić was even willing to pay a large amount in German marks for his security, suggesting that he must have been afraid of someone. Perhaps it was Slobodan Milošević, who for years had been ridding himself of personal liabilities like Karadžić. I answered, "Yes, of course." I was still Switzerland's attorney general. I still had the authority to have him arrested. I could have easily arranged his transfer to the Netherlands. And arriving in The Hague with Karadžić in tow would have made for a triumphant entrance I certainly would have relished.

Never is life this good. We eventually heard that Karadžić's wife had objected to the arrangement at the last minute. But the entire story might have been foolishness on the part of Karadžić or his supporters, who loathe the Yugoslavia tribunal's existence. Either way, it was my first encounter with war crimes prosecution, a challenge more complicated, frustrating, and heart-rending than any Mafia case I have ever seen, but a challenge as exciting as riding down the Valle Maggia in an MG roadster, top down, hair flying in the mountain air. I knew from the very beginning whose lessons would guide me. Simplistic? Admittedly. Cliché? Of course. But honest.

CONFRONTING YUGOSLAVIA'S WAR CRIMES

For most of eight years, I lived in a bomb-proofed apartment whose tall windows overlook a cobblestone street in the center of The Hague, capital of the Netherlands. This city has hosted professional and academic conferences proclaiming itself "World Capital of International Justice." The title might be deserved. The Hague is the seat of several international judicial bodies including the Yugoslavia tribunal, where I worked; the International Court of Justice, or World Court, the main judicial organ of the United Nations, which was created after World War II to settle disputes between sovereign states; and the International Criminal Court, the permanent tribunal established in 2002 to prosecute individuals for genocide, crimes against humanity, and war crimes. Even for members of the legal profession, who have a knack for flourishing under any conditions, The Hague is an acquired taste. I have often found its idea of order an irritation; cloudbursts wash out its sunniest days, and its restaurants have soured the best of my moods. But the rains scrub and scent the air. The North Sea winds did sometimes hurl my best tee shots onto the wrong fairways, but more often than not they saved me from disasters I would have brought upon myself. And from my office window, I have watched the sun cut like a blowtorch through rain-swollen skies and produce clouds of luminescent white, purple, and orange more beautiful than Vermeer ever dabbed onto a canvas. I also learned that a churchyard at the city's heart holds the mortal remains of Baruch Spinoza, a philosophical giant who championed reason and skepticism and identified the force that drives so many war crimes: the manipulation and exploitation by powerful leaders of popular bigotry, envy, stereotypes, and superstitions in order to seize and retain power and enrich themselves.

The North Sea winds also blow cold against Scheveningen prison's high, red-brick walls, which confine men who whipped the fears of

Yugoslavia's people into a frenzy that extinguished the lives of tens of thousands and ruined the lives of millions more. If the inmates in the cellblock for indicted war criminals from Yugoslavia can look to the north through their barred windows, they would see clumps of tall grass and brush that bend and strain as wind gusts tear through empty dunes that stretch on for a couple hundred miles. These sands remind me that the potential for human depravity follows humanity wherever it wanders. Just off the edge of the dunes, not far from my nearest golf course and a house where Spinoza mulled over his treatise on God and Man, archaeologists have unearthed remains of medieval villagers massacred by Viking raiders. Between mounds of sand a few minutes' march from the gates of Scheveningen prison, SS stormtroopers and their Dutch collaborators once executed Jews and other people they had condemned as traitors and *Untermenschen*. Just across Van Alkemade Street from the prison, there is a wooden house with tall gables. This was once the Wittebrug-Pompstation train depot; on its platform, the SS gathered Jewish families and jammed them into railroad cars for the first leg of their journey to the ash heaps at Auschwitz. The abandoned right-of-way became a bike path my bodyguards and I sometimes rode for exercise.

It seemed the beginning of an eternal rain when I arrived for the first time at the tribunal's headquarters, a few kilometers from the prison. The building is a masterpiece of mediocrity—the creation of architects clearly cowed by some committee of Dutch insurance company executives. The brick is the color of wet sand. A forbidding metal fence guards the perimeter. The air inside is dry and foul and seems bacteria infested, because the windows have been screwed shut and the ventilation system functions poorly. I eventually pried open my window so I could breathe the fresh air and enjoy my Marlboro Golds without poisoning the rest of the staff; and I once sat before an assembly of the entire staff and told them to pry their windows open, too.

I touched down in Rotterdam on September 15, 1999, after working deep into the previous night at my office in Berne. On the inbound flight, I had pondered the wars in Yugoslavia, the genocide in Rwanda, and the controversial NATO bombing of Serbia that would now fill so many of my waking hours. These events were but abstractions to me, vague memories of news stories that my mind, almost instinctively, began to deconstruct and fit into prosecutorial frameworks. For weeks on end, I pored over the latest political situation reports, learned the state of play in the trials and investigations of both tribunals, and absorbed the inner workings and intrigues of my office and the Byzantine ways of the United Nations bureaucracy. I immersed myself in the histories of Yugoslavia and Rwanda, because without a grounding in the antecedents to war crimes and the social milieu in which they occur one cannot grasp motive. Each night I would read myself to sleep, alternating between books on Yugoslavia's conflicts and the Human Rights Watch reports on the Rwandan genocide. The Yugoslav cases were most familiar to me and first occupied my attention. But it was the Rwandan genocide that later tore at my heart and stirred the depths of my passion to see justice done.

have enjoyed holidays and long weekends along the French Riviera and in Tuscany and Africa. I regret, however, that I never toured the former Yugoslavia or visited its Dalmatian coast before the wars of the 1990s. Like every educated European, I had gathered some knowledge of Yugoslavia from school textbooks, newspaper articles, and television broadcasts, especially reports that appeared during the fighting in Croatia and in Bosnia and Herzegovina. Many Europeans regarded Yugoslavia with a nostalgic eye. They saw it as a grand experiment, a romantic attempt by a raucous conglomerate of Slavic peoples to overcome their cultural and religious differences and build a multiethnic society—not unlike Switzerland's— so that they, and not some foreign potentate, would profit from the bounty of their lands and the fruits of their labor. Yugoslavia had emerged, like so many European countries, out of the ruins left by World War I. The country's western regions—Slovenia, Croatia, and parts of Bosnia and Herzegovina, as well as parts of Serbia—once belonged to the lost Habsburg Empire. Yugoslavia's eastern regions—Montenegro, Macedonia, Bosnia and Herzegovina, and most of Serbia, including Kosovo, an autonomous province—were components of another lost universe, the Ottoman Empire, a farrago of peoples, languages, and religions administered by slaves of a single, all-powerful sultan.

Like so many other Europeans, and, in fact, like people the world over, many inhabitants of the old Yugoslavia—the Serbs, Croats, Slovenes, Montenegrins, Macedonians, and Albanians; the Slavic Muslims of Bosnia and Herzegovina, Montenegro, and Kosovo; and every conceivable (literally) combination of them all—tend to view the Universe and its inhabitants through a prism of ethnicity and to define themselves, not by their accomplishments, but by their cultural and economic differences, their religious legacies, and their jealousies toward one another. The traumas of the Balkan wars of 1912 and 1913, World War I, and the threat of external domination after 1918 helped bind them within the borders of a single state. Nazi Germany invaded and dismembered Yugoslavia in 1941 and placed extremist nationalists in control of large swaths of the country, including a shrunken Serbia and an expanded Croatia. These extremists manipulated and exploited the animosities that divided Yugoslavia's peoples, and especially those passions that had set the Croats and Serbs and the Serbs and Muslims against one another. The result was a bloodbath, especially by Croats against Serbs; more than half of Yugoslavia's war dead perished at the hands of other Yugoslavs. The country's postwar communist government, under Josip Broz Tito, used a mix of political repression and economic reward to harmonize ethnic relations. For years many diplomats, scholars, and journalists in the West assumed that these methods had been effective.

I recall now how, during the wars of the 1990s, guests interviewed on Swiss, French, and Italian television argued that ancient ethnic hatreds—deep-seated, centuries-old animosities among Serbs, Croats, Muslims, and Albanians—had exploded to destroy Yugoslavia. My background reading, however, revealed to me what I had expected to find: that, in the final analysis, social conditions and culture do not produce war crimes. People commit war crimes, people egged on by political and military leaders. This reality was apparent even in 1914. In my prefatory remarks at the opening of the Milošević trial, I quoted a passage penned by the chairman of the International Commission to Inquire into the Causes and Conduct of the Balkan Wars, Baron d'Estournelles de Constant. In his introduction to the commission's report on the wars of 1912 and 1913, the baron wrote:

> The true culprits are those who mislead public opinion and take advantage of the people's ignorance to raise disquieting rumours and sound the alarm bell, inciting the country and, consequently, other countries into enmity. The real culprits are those who by interest or inclination, declaring constantly that war is inevitable, end by making it so, asserting that they are powerless to prevent it. The real culprits are those who sacrifice the general interest to their own personal interest which they so little understand, and who hold up to their country a sterile policy of conflict and

reprisals. In reality, there is no salvation, no way out either for small states or for great countries except by union or conciliation.[1]

In the same way, Yugoslavia was destroyed during the 1990s by a relatively small number of men, and women, many of them engaged in corruption, who were willing to incite their people to commit large-scale acts of violence. The main culprits were Slobodan Milošević of Serbia, Franjo Tudjman of Croatia, and their protégés: men and women who were embodiments of the kind of leaders Spinoza had disdained, men and women who had gained power and were striving to enhance and retain it by whipping up their people's fears into hysteria and turning them against one another.

Serb–Croat violence, most of it incited by police agents and members of irregular military units on both sides, escalated after Croatia declared its independence from Yugoslavia on June 25, 1991. By the autumn, the Yugoslav National Army had invaded Croatia ostensibly to protect its Serb minority from genocide. Within four months, nationalist Serbs had seized a quarter of Croatia, driven out hundreds of thousands of Croat natives of these lands, and convinced the United Nations to send in a military force to safeguard the territory they had "cleansed." Serb howitzers and mortars had rained shells upon the famous seaside town of Dubrovnik. Serb aircraft, artillery, and tanks had ground Vukovar, a town on the banks of the Danube River, into rubble and dust. Serb firing squads had shot hundreds of prisoners, including wounded men dragged from the town's hospital. Away from the killing fields, many Serbs were dumbfounded at how the entire world seemed to have turned against them. Sadly, some of them, and even some of their leaders, are still lost in a miasma of self-pity.

The war in Bosnia began in the spring of 1992, when a secret-police assassin from Belgrade sent his gang through the town of Bijeljina on a killing spree. In the weeks that followed, this Belgrade gang and other militias that were armed and funded by Serbia's secret police attacked one town after another in eastern Bosnia. They lashed out against the region's majority Muslims. The killers, some of them psychopaths sprung from mental institutions and prisons, worked for cash and plunder and sex. Any Serbs who protested or tried to protect their Muslim friends were risking death. Neighbors turned against neighbors. The horrors of Sarajevo, images of concentration camps, and even pictures of women and children herded aboard railroad cars and deported would fill television news shows night after night for three years.

Franjo Tudjman resented Bosnia and Herzegovina's very existence as an independent country. At a meeting with his closest advisers and a group of nationalist Croats from Bosnia and Herzegovina on December 27, 1991, Tudjman demonstrated that the subsequent division of Bosnia was not just a Serb affair; it was the result of a Serb–Croat land grab. At this meeting, Tudjman pointed out that an opportunity had arrived to expand the Croatian state at the expense of Bosnia and Herzegovina's territory: "[I]t is time," Tudjman said, "that we take the opportunity to gather the Croatian people inside the widest possible borders."[2] Croat attackers triggered Muslim violence in January 1993, and fighting continued for over a year.

Then came the denouement. The Bosnian Serb Army and police troops from Serbia attacked the tens of thousands of Muslims crowded inside United Nations "safe areas" in eastern Bosnia. In April 1994, when the Rwanda genocide should have been garnering larger headlines and more serious attention in Washington and the European capitals, the Serbs stole attention with their bombardment of Muslims trapped in the Drina River town of Goražde, one of the safe areas. So blatant was the Serbs' defiance of United Nations Security Council resolutions that the Secretariat in New York could no longer block calls for NATO air strikes. Undeterred, in July 1995, the Serbs overran the Srebrenica and Žepa safe areas. As the world stood by, Serb execution squads killed about 7,500 Muslim men and boys, some by club, others by knife and hatchet, most by bursts of automatic gunfire. Within weeks, Tudjman's troops had overrun Serb-controlled United Nations Protected Areas in Croatia, and hundreds of thousands of Serbs were fleeing for their lives.

The Dayton Peace Agreement of December 1995 halted the bloodshed in Bosnia and Herzegovina, but the violent break up of Yugoslavia did not end there. In 1997, Albanian gunmen of the so-called Kosovo Liberation Army (KLA) began attacking Serb civilians and retaliating against the Serbian police forces that had been the instruments of Milošević's repression in Kosovo since 1989. Milošević was eager to engage. He was facing a political upheaval at home and, once again, needed to whip up his people against an external enemy to deflect attention from his own responsibility for Serbia's domestic woes and the corruption of his regime. In late 1998, the NATO alliance warned Milošević that it would attack Serbia by air if it did not take effective measures to halt the violence by its police units against Albanian civilians. Bloodshed, much of it KLA instigated, continued. In the early spring of 1999, NATO air strikes began. Police and military forces under Milošević's control launched attacks clearly aimed at driving the Albanians from Kosovo. An exodus of biblical proportions took place before the eyes of television viewers the world over. The NATO bombing dragged on for months before Milošević relented.

One of my main duties as the tribunal's prosecutor was to seek justice for the victims of the violence. The Croatian war of 1991 had left 10,000 to 15,000 dead and many thousands more wounded. After years of wrangling by journalists and political leaders over the Bosnian death toll—estimates ranged from 25,000 to 329,000—my office's demographics experts produced the best accounting I have seen: 103,000 dead, 55,261 of them civilians.[3] In the Kosovo conflict of 1998 and 1999, the number of Albanian dead ranged from 9,000 to 12,100,[4] and some 3,000 Serb soldiers and civilians perished. The estimated 3,000 missing include 2,500 Albanians, 400 Serbs, and 100 Roma. NATO's bombing campaign claimed the lives of about 495 civilians, most of them Serbs.

In 1991, 1992, and early 1993, some United Nations member states and human rights advocates urged the United Nations Security Council to establish a war crimes tribunal to deal with the bloodletting in Yugoslavia. The Cold War was over. These advocates thought the time had come to follow up on the tradition of the Nuremberg and Tokyo tribunals, to create international justice institutions to document atrocities and hold individuals accountable for them, and thereby to end the culture of impunity that had made the twentieth century the bloodiest in human history. The tipping point came in the wake of an offensive by the Bosnian Serb Army during late winter of 1993. In defiance of the international community, it had herded about 40,000 Muslims, most of them hungry refugees fleeing through deep snow, into a tiny pocket of territory around the mining town of Srebrenica in eastern Bosnia. Council members were loath to intervene militarily to stop the bloodshed at Srebrenica. On April 16, they adopted the resolution naming Srebrenica and other besieged Bosnian towns and cities as United Nations safe areas. A little over a month later, with Resolution 827, the Security Council created the Yugoslavia tribunal to address the serious violations of international humanitarian law that had been committed in the territory of the former Yugoslavia from 1991; to prosecute and try persons allegedly responsible for grave breaches of the 1949 Geneva Conventions, violations of the laws or customs of war, genocide, and crimes against humanity; to contribute to the restoration of peace by promoting reconciliation in the former Yugoslavia; and to deter the commission of further violations of international humanitarian law. (Unfortunately, this diplomatic decision and the Yugoslav tribunal's early work did not deter Serbs under Karadžić and Mladić from executing those 7,500 Muslims from the Srebrenica safe area two years later.)

The Office of the Prosecutor, the division of the Yugoslavia tribunal that I managed for eight years, is but one of the organization's three components. The office of the Prosecutor investigates war crimes, drafts indictments, presents evidence at trials, and argues their guilt. The office, theoretically, is an autonomous body, which means I was supposed to be able to operate independently of governments, the United Nations Security Council, international organizations, and the tribunal's other divisions. The muscle tissue of the Office of the Prosecutor was composed of trial attorneys and jurists, forensic experts, police officers, and analysts of the history, culture, languages, and other aspects of the former Yugoslavia. Investigations require painstaking, tedious work, collecting and examining documents, identifying witnesses, gathering statements, exhuming mass graves, and gathering other physical evidence.

The United Nations main deliberative organ, the General Assembly, which is composed of delegates from all United Nations member states, elects the judges who serve in the tribunal's trial chambers. Permanent judges have four-year terms and can be reelected at the end of these terms. The General Assembly also elects up to nine *ad litem* judges, that is, judges appointed to serve only on particular cases for only a single four-year term. The judges' main responsibilities include hearing testimony and legal arguments, deciding whether to convict or acquit the accused, and passing sentence upon those found guilty. The permanent judges also have important regulatory functions. They draft and adopt basic legal documents of the tribunal, including the Rules of Procedure and Evidence and the Rules of Detention. The composition of the judicial chamber that hears appeals for the Yugoslavia tribunal and for the International Criminal Tribunal for Rwanda are identical. The third component of the tribunal, the Registry, is responsible for the organization's administration and judicial support services, including translation of documents and court proceedings. The Registry schedules hearings and trials, files and archives evidence, operates the legal-aid and outreach programs, provides assistance and protection to witnesses, and manages the detention unit at Scheveningen prison. The maximum allowable sentence is life imprisonment, and convicted prisoners can serve their sentences in any one of the countries that have entered into agreements with the United Nations to accept persons the tribunal convicts.

It is the chief prosecutor's discretion to initiate a criminal investigation, but a tribunal judge must confirm all the draft indictments the chief prosecutor submits. No trial can take place without the accused present. At his or her initial appearance, an accused person may enter a plea of not guilty or guilty. The tribunal's Rules of Procedure and Evidence are supposed to guarantee that its proceedings comply with internationally recognized principles of fairness, and they combine elements of both the civil law system, which sets out a comprehensive set of rules that judges apply and interpret, and the common law system, the system derived largely from English law, which gives considerable weight to precedents developed in court decisions through history. The tribunal recognizes the presumption of innocence, the right to a trial without undue delay, the right to examine witnesses, the right of appeal, and the right of indigent defendants to be provided with legal assistance. The Victims and Witnesses Section within the registry is responsible for ensuring that witnesses can testify freely and securely. Judges may also order that the names of protected witnesses not be revealed. All witnesses are provided assistance and protection before, during, and after their testimony before the tribunal.

Although it is judicially independent, the tribunal lacks the powers enjoyed by courts in sovereign states. Like most national courts, the tribunal has the power to issue subpoenas requiring persons and institutions to hand over documents and other evidence and to issue summonses and international arrest warrants. But unlike national courts, the tribunal has only the authority to request that its subpoenas, summonses, and arrest warrants be executed; it can only request that states cooperate voluntarily and in good faith, and this means that cooperation is dependent too often upon political criteria, and especially the political interests of the people governing these states. If the leaders of these states do not want the tribunal to discover critical evidence, recruit significant witnesses, or arrest individuals in their jurisdictions, they can simply choose not to cooperate. Evidence can be concealed, witnesses hounded, and fugitives hidden. The Office of the Prosecutor has no judicial police to carry out searches and arrests, and the tribunal lacks the authority to impose penalties if a state fails to cooperate. This lack of authority ineluctably forces the tribunal into the realm of politics. It can approach the United Nations Security Council, which has the power to impose sanctions. The imposition of such sanctions is unlikely, because the Security Council rarely takes significant action unless there is a crisis situation, and the Council is not likely to allow issues like those faced by the tribunal to factor into the diplomatic deal-making that goes on at the highest levels of the international relations. The best the tribunal can expect is a Security Council resolution. If the council's member states do not agree on action, it will do nothing. The only other leverage the tribunal has is to approach national governments and ask for their support to convince uncooperative states to comply with its orders. During my eight years in The Hague, I dedicated the bulk of my time to mustering political pressure upon states like Serbia and Croatia to comply with their international obligation to cooperate.

The tribunal's budget had risen from $10.8 million in 1994 to about $94 million at the time I arrived in The Hague. The Office of the Prosecutor had a budget of about $30 million and was employing about four hundred lawyers, investigators, analysts, and language assistants. The tribunal had by then issued sixty-five public indictments for alleged atrocities committed in the former Yugoslavia. The detention center in the Scheveningen prison was holding thirty accused, and thirty-five individuals named in public indictments remain at large. The fugitives living in Serbia included Slobodan Milošević and General Mladić. Two of the accused were residing in Croatia or Croat-controlled areas of Bosnia and Herzegovina. Radovan Karadžić and the other Serb accused were in hiding at least part of the time in Serb-controlled territory in Bosnia and Herzegovina. Milošević, Karadžić, and Mladić were the only high-ranking political and military leaders under indictment.[5]

My first opportunity to look the Balkans in the eye came on a Tuesday evening, October 26, 1999. Our Swiss government jet tipped its wings and traced a descending spiral in the sky to avoid Šar Mountain, a massive upheaval of rock, soil, forest, and legend that paints the backdrop to Skopje, the disheveled capital of Macedonia. The southernmost and least developed of the old Yugoslavia's republics, Macedonia was spared the ravages of war, but was important to the tribunal as a staging area for its investigative teams and as place for gathering information on events in other areas of the former Yugoslavia, especially Belgrade. My team and I spent the night in a villa on a hillside overlooking the lights of the city, and we held discussions the next day with the country's prime minister, a former rock musician named Ljupčo Georgijevski, and other officials. The conversation with Georgijevski was my first attempt to convince Balkan political leaders to meet their obligation to assist the tribunal in its efforts to investigate war crimes and apprehend persons indicted for committing them. Prime Minister Georgijevski and the country's interior minister, Pavle Trajanov, looked at me with blank expressions when I told them we had noticed media reports that Ratko Mladić had been spotted on Macedonia's territory. Georgijevski assured us that Macedonia would never, of course, inhibit the tribunal's work. "Mladić's wife is Macedonian," he said, before admitting that he had heard the stories about Mladić and making it clear that the reports predated the elections that gave him control of the government. Trajanov said Macedonia's intelligence service had no information on the whereabouts of Mladić or other tribunal accused. "They are very well known people," he said, trying to convince us that the police would have noticed Mladić if he had ever visited Macedonia. "Everybody knows what they look like."

"The arrest of such a person would have serious consequences, very grave consequences for us, possible terrorist attacks," Georgijevski asserted. Then Trajanov added that the Macedonians were not the only ones afraid to arrest the tribunal's fugitives. He pointed out the sad fact that NATO's forces in Bosnia and Herzegovina and in Kosovo were also reluctant. "Everybody wants somebody else to do the arrests," he said.

I urged the Macedonians to take action. "Just do it. We will send a plane. It is also important for us to seize assets. They are still working, so they need to move around to do business."

"You can be 100 percent sure we will check on their assets. We can freeze accounts with no legal problem," Trajanov promised.

"We are not very afraid to do this," Georgijevski said. "We will cooperate."

This refrain, this promise—"We will cooperate"—would ring like a noontime church bell toward the end of practically every official conversation I had in the Balkans, and beyond, during my eight years as chief prosecutor. Every government, every official, every NATO commander, every diplomat was always eager to pledge full cooperation, so willing that they had taken no significant action to arrest Karadžić and Mladić, who had already been at large for more than three years and would remain so until after my mandate had ended. So often toward the end of my conversations did I hear these words—these signposts toward the *muro di gomma*—that I took them to be a kind of signal that it was time to pick up my handbag and depart.

We departed Skopje the next morning, October 28, for a several-hour overland journey to Priština, capital of Kosovo, a mineral-rich region Serb nationalists consider the cradle of their nation and claim sovereignty over despite the fact that its population is almost entirely Albanian. I gazed through the window at the rolling hillsides. We passed high-walled family fortresses and boys tending flocks of sheep and goats. I recalled newspaper articles I had read about drug trafficking through Kosovo, about its poverty, illiteracy, malnutrition, disease, infant mortality, and criminal gangs who enslave women from all over Eurasia, force them into prostitution, and trade them like cattle. People of this region have never enjoyed the rule of law except for the tradition of blood vengeance—an eye for an eye, a life for a life. This is not passion-driven individual revenge, but an outcropping of a pre-Homeric form of maintaining social order. It requires men from one family to take the life of an adult male of another family if someone from the second family has killed, even by accident, a male member of the first.

After years of Serbian oppression and the massive ethnic cleansing campaign during the spring of 1999, the thirst for revenge was making life perilous in Kosovo. Serbs, especially elderly Serbs, had found themselves trapped in enclaves throughout the region. Road travel required passing through Albanian-controlled regions. KLA contingents were behaving like lynch mobs, kidnapping and killing Serbs and members of other ethnic groups, notably the Roma, simply for their ethnicity. Albanians had even attacked Serbs traveling in convoys under the protection of the NATO peacekeeping force in Kosovo, or KFOR. The force was holding four hundred suspects in prison in connection with a variety of crimes, fourteen of them with war crimes. No judicial system existed to try them. Even if a judicial system had existed, holding trials would have required assuming significant security risks. Rumors that the tribunal was preparing indictments against KLA leaders for the killings of Serbs had angered some Albanians, and KLA leaders were whipping up popular hysteria against the tribunal, just as Milošević was doing in Belgrade.

We arrived in Priština before noon and made our way toward KFOR's main base. I was astonished at the city's disorder, the piles of rubbish lining its streets, the scars left by the conflict on houses and buildings, the satellite dishes tilted skyward from so many rooftops and balconies. My first meeting was with KFOR's German commander, General Klaus Reinhardt. Using grim images to describe ethnic animosities in Kosovo, he voiced concern about war crimes prosecutions and warned that indicting the KLA's former chief of staff, Agim Çeku, would create problems for both KFOR and the United Nations Mission in Kosovo (UNMIK). General Reinhardt said he wanted the tribunal to give KFOR as much advance warning as possible of any such indictment. I made it clear that the tribunal would focus on trying only high-level perpetrators. I notified them that, regardless of the security situation and the hostility of the Albanian military leaders toward the tribunal, we were going to investigate crimes allegedly committed by the KLA and would therefore need more KFOR support and protection on the ground. General Reinhardt assured me he was genuinely committed to providing all necessary assistance.

In the afternoon, we met with the head of UNMIK, Bernard Kouchner, now the foreign minister of France and the cofounder of the international relief organization, Doctors Without Borders. Kouchner agreed that pursuing KLA targets was important for UNMIK and the international presence in Kosovo, and even the "politically crucial" thing to do. Members of his staff said they were interested in the crimes perpetrated after the end of the NATO air campaign, and we informed Kouchner that these crimes, including systematic killings and abductions, were a part of the tribunal's mandate.

In the evening, United Nations security guards and KFOR soldiers escorted us to our sleeping quarters at the tribunal's guest house in the KFOR compound. There was no electricity. The one toilet served a dozen people. I was shown to a single room with a bed whose sheets had not been changed. I complained that this was unacceptable, but learned that clean linens were unavailable. So I emptied my luggage and spread a layer of my clothes over the bottom sheet and tried to sleep. My skin seemed to crawl around me. I kept the window open to enjoy some fresh air, but someone outside began firing a gun. I lay there asking myself how I had come to be there, in this place that seemed beyond the far edge of Europe. Another gunshot sounded. I closed the window and sank into a fitful sleep. In the morning, the showers were cold.

It took less than an hour to realize that investigating war crimes and defending human rights involve more than enduring soiled sheets, restless nights, and waiting in line for a toilet. These tasks require taking personal risk, the kind of risk that tempers a soul like the one that glows inside Nataša Kandić, founder of the Humanitarian Law Center in Belgrade. Kandić is a diminutive Serbian woman. Her raspy voice, sanded down by years of chain smoking, exudes a deadly serious determination. Undeterred by Serbian police checkpoints and bands of vengeance-driven Albanians, Kandić had traveled into Kosovo by car during the NATO bombing to bear witness to the expulsions of its Albanians. Now, even months later, she looked physically devastated, and when I saw her for the first time I said to myself, "For me it is only one day." She lit a cigarette. I did, too. Then she described the miserable situation in Kosovo.

There was a need, she said, to put pressure on the Kosovo Liberation Army. In Peć, a town the Serbian forces had torched, the local KLA was clearly involved in organized killings. "It is very difficult for the Roma," she explained. "They are paying the price for everything." In June and July, the KLA had mounted efforts to kill Serbs around Peć, and in August and September, Albanian factions had been abducting Serbs from around the town. "We have had no success finding KLA prisons," she said.

Kandić also said finding witnesses willing to cooperate was especially problematic. Albanians feared KLA retaliation so much that they would not speak about its atrocities or even work with UNMIK or the tribunal. Serb witnesses were now speaking, but they had fled beyond Kosovo's borders, into Montenegro and Serbia, places that had been out of reach for tribunal investigators since just before the NATO bombing. She said Serbs were starting to admit to crimes. One witness, the commander of the guards at a prison, had even begun describing the killing of about a hundred prisoners. "He should be gotten out of the country," Kandić replied. "He is very afraid to speak even to my lawyers." My staff and I were all wondering when we would be able to visit Belgrade and restart investigative work there. We spoke of it at dinner two nights earlier. I blurted out, "Let's go to Belgrade now. Let's ask for visas. Let's get arrested." The Tribunal's deputy prosecutor, Graham Blewitt, looked uncomfortable, so I assumed I had said something wrong.

That afternoon, we boarded a military helicopter and visited a team of Austrian forensic anthropologists excavating a mass grave at Sičevo, a village next to a towering mountain known as "The Accursed." A hot sun beat down upon the gravesite and lifted into the air a pasty stench that invaded my nostrils and hair and clothes and attracted swarms of flies. Emerging from the earth were human shapes, figures like George Segal's plaster sculptures, only twisted, brown, and gray. Rodents, insects, and billions of bacteria had consumed the eyes and other facial features of a dead man spread over a table. A pathologist cut away at his ribs with a saw as the relatives watched. I asked the team members about the man and how he had died. Investigators said the man was eighty-six years old. Witnesses had alleged that Serb gunmen had entered his house, slit his throat, and shot him before executing two women, another civilian man, and a KLA fighter.

Experiencing this gravesite did not stir in me an emotional reaction, at least not one that I consciously noticed. The stench left a sour taste in my mouth. The bones and teeth sticking through rotting flesh were macabre. But for me, this was just physical evidence, more elements in a fact-base for building the case against Slobodan Milošević and the other men accused of the war crimes in Kosovo. I could have stood there all day inhaling that stench, just as the Austrian pathologists had been doing for days on end. I could have come back on the stickiest July afternoon. This was my job. I repressed whatever fear and trembling it might have excited in my subconscious mind. I shuddered, however, as I met one of the survivors of that old man whose body the anthropologists were examining on the table. His name was Jakub Berisha. I shook his hand, looked at him, and do not remember what I said. The handshake alone was enough to convey his loss and the trust he had that a tribunal somewhere far away was trying to administer a kind of justice that was different than any Kosovo had ever known.

Sarajevo is a famously wounded city, a city of Muslims, Serbs, Croats, and thousands upon thousands of people born of mixed marriages, a city of people who bear the scars of a war that began in March 1992 and dragged on for almost four years. The Dayton Peace Agreement ended the fighting in late 1995. Elections the following summer returned to power Muslim, Serb, and Croat nationalists—including many of the same men and women who had led the country into war—and gave them control of a federal government and the governments of two entities: Republika Srpska, the Serbs' national subdivision, and the Muslim–Croat

Federation. I began experiencing first hand some of the absurdities of post-Dayton Bosnia during my first meetings in Sarajevo on Monday, November 1, after a weekend of rest in Lugano. Two days later, I met the members of Bosnia and Herzegovina's collective presidency—a Muslim, a Serb, and a Croat, who insisted on being served three different kinds of coffee—at a sitting room in the Presidency Building in central Sarajevo, the same room where teams of peace negotiators and diplomats had tried for years to halt the fighting. I recognized at once Bosnia's wartime Muslim leader, Alija Izetbegović, and reminded myself that tribunal investigators were examining his activities during the war. Izetbegović's words of welcome were a brief repetition of support for the tribunal, without, of course, any reservations or limitations. Then there was the Serb, Živko Radišić, who questioned the tribunal's use of secret, or sealed, indictments. (These indictments clearly made persons who had taken part in war crimes uncomfortable because they had to wonder night and day whether they might receive a knock at the door.) Radišić also criticized the slow pace of the legal proceedings and trials, something I, too, found disturbing; and he called for investigation of crimes in Kosovo. I wondered who stood behind Radišić. Milošević, the indicted head of state? Karadžić, the fugitive in hiding? Other members of the mafia that had run Karadžić's Serbian Democratic Party?

Ante Jelavić, the Croat, was president of Bosnia and Herzegovina's collective presidency at the time I made my visit, and even I, the least experienced person at the table about Balkan affairs, knew that Croatia's president, Franjo Tudjman, was his *éminence gris*. As I expected, Jelavić made a statement, not on behalf of Bosnia and Herzegovina, but on behalf of the Bosnian Croats, and he too, as expected, promised full cooperation with the tribunal. Jelavić is a living embodiment of the problems I was facing when I went to ask local Bosnian officials to cooperate with prosecution investigations. At the very same moment I was meeting Jelavić, my investigators and analysts were collecting information for a possible indictment against him. He had been a colonel in the Bosnian Croat militia known as the Croatian Defense Council, an offshoot of the Army of the Republic of Croatia that Tudjman had explicitly tasked with seizing territory in Bosnia and Herzegovina to fatten his independent Croatia. Jelavić was also corrupt. He was appointed assistant chief of the Croatian Defense Council's Department of Defense and placed in charge of procurement. During the war, he acted as one of the paymasters of the Bosnian Croat militia and assisted in the transfer of money from Croatia's government coffers to the Croatian Defense Council's bank accounts. Jelavić would eventually be arrested on corruption charges; after being found guilty and sentenced to ten years in prison, he fled to Croatia and dropped off the face of the earth.

He filled a few minutes with pretty words like "harmony," "multiethnic society," "reconstruction," and "reconciliation" before getting down to the concerns of the Croat "community"—a loaded term meaning those Croats of Herzegovina who had launched the war against Bosnia's Muslims in January 1993. "CIA analyses," he said, "estimated that 10 percent of all crimes committed in Bosnia and Herzegovina were committed by Croats, but 50 percent of the detainees in The Hague are Croats, including two leaders of the Croat people, Dario Kordić and Tihomir Blaškić." The tribunal had indicted these men, among others, on charges stemming from a massacre of Muslim families at a village known as Ahmići in April 1993. "The Croat people," he continued, "are asking why only Ahmići? Why not other places crimes were committed against Croats?"

This kind of rhetoric—for which Americans have the best expression—always tests my patience. After thanking the presidency's members, I told Jelavić, "Do not play numbers games with me." There was no need to remind him or any of the others about Bosnia and Herzegovina's obligation to cooperate with the tribunal, but I did remind them that, until Bosnia and Herzegovina's judiciary had shown itself to be effective and independent of political influence, the tribunal's primacy in investigating and trying war crimes cases would be indisputable. "In the future," I said, "I am sure we will be partners with the local judiciary." Now was not the time.

Jelavić, as president of the presidency, concluded the meeting. I sensed in advance what was coming. Cooperation with the tribunal would improve, he promised. He insisted that he had not meant to focus on numbers but had only wanted to point out that there was an "equality of responsibility." This was an inept attempt at saving face, for I knew Serb and Croat leaders were doing everything they could to have foreign leaders, diplomats, and opinion-makers believe that the Muslim leadership was just as responsible as its Serb and Croat counterparts for the violence. I also knew that Bosnian Serb and Bosnian Croat leaders were working to undermine the tribunal and disrupt its work. Both the Serbian and Croatian media were indulging in tribunal-bashing, misrepresenting facts and painting the institution as if it were evil incarnate. They were also treating the Serbs and Croats under indictment as if they had been knights in shining armor and were now suffering persecution.

The next day, I flew over the rolling mountains of Bosnia and Herzegovina—ideal ski country, if it were not for global warming and thousands of antipersonnel mines—and landed in Banja Luka, the largest town of the Serb entity in Bosnia and Herzegovina, Republika Srpska. I had no preconceptions of the Republika Srpska. In fact, I must confess, I did not even know that the Republika Srpska existed as a legal entity until soon after I had taken up my position. This was Bosnia's ethnic-cleansing heartland. During the war, the Serb leaderships in Banja Luka and nearby towns—Prijedor, Čelinac, Kotor Varoš, and others—had shamed their nation by committing unspeakable acts of violence. Hundreds of thousands of Muslims were forced from their ancestral homes. Thousands were killed or penned up in concentration camps. In Čelinac, the Serb leaders had placed restrictions on Muslims that resembled the Jewish laws of the Nazi Reich. My first impression was that Banja Luka was a place fifty years behind the rest of the world, a place with a four-lane, divided highway on which badly tuned Mercedes Benz sedans went rumbling by horse carts clopping along at six miles an hour or less.

The man who held the office of Republika Srpska's prime minister was Milorad Dodik. His lips dripped with saccharine whenever he uttered the word "cooperation," but the pledges were empty because Dodik controlled neither the Republika Srpska's territory nor its police and military. I did not sense that he feared for his life and for this reason did so little on the tribunal's behalf. I believe he had made a simple calculation and concluded that cooperating with the tribunal would put a dent in the political future he was attempting to engineer for himself.

Dodik maintained that his government had been ready to cooperate with the tribunal from its inception and that his office had first suggested that some of the accused be persuaded to surrender voluntarily. He complained that the tribunal's detainees were waiting in jail for considerable periods and that political instability in Republika Srpska and the NATO bombing of Serbia had made the whole issue of cooperating with the tribunal difficult for any local political leader. "My government," Dodik said, "seeks to remove the main problem in the Republika Srpska, Radovan Karadžić, who must go to The Hague at any cost." He maintained that Karadžić and other persons indicted by the tribunal were in Bosnia and Herzegovina, but not under his government's protection. Dodik said Ratko Mladić had been in Belgrade for the past three years and had never crossed into the Republika Srpska. (This I assumed to be false, and later learned to be false.)

I told Dodik that I wanted to be frank with him. I stressed, first, that the Republika Srpska's government could demonstrate its willingness to cooperate fully with the tribunal by providing the information we required and by beginning to arrest our accused. I told him that our priority was apprehending Karadžić, who was appearing in Pale from time to time: "With your help and cooperation, with the right information, and with the help of [NATO], we can detain him." I urged Dodik to hand over sensitive information including recent photographs of our accused and their whereabouts. My team presented Dodik with a formal request for assistance. Our investigators wanted to interview seven individuals—some suspects, some prospective witnesses—in connection with the investigation into the Srebrenica massacre of 1995. We anticipated that these individuals would be reluctant to meet our investigators, so we presented Dodik with the seven summonses for interviews to take place in December. The deputy prosecutor, Graham Blewitt, assured Dodik that there would be no tricks and that the persons we wanted to interview were not wanted on sealed indictments and would not be detained. Dodik said that it was fine with him if we guaranteed that there was no deception involved, but he warned us that he could not guarantee results because he was leading a government that lacked the support of a majority in the Bosnian Serb parliament and that the police were still loyal to Karadžić's Serbian Democratic Party.

We listened with skepticism when Dodik predicted the fall of Slobodan Milošević during the next year. He said the opposition to Milošević in Serbia would turn the popular dissatisfaction against him to their political advantage, and he expressed dismay that the tribunal had not indicted Vojislav Šešelj, a rabid nationalist and militia leader who was the head of the Serb Radical Party. I could not go into details, but I told Dodik that Šešelj was not beyond the scope of our interest and that if he had any evidence about Šešelj and other leaders he should provide it.

Dodik said he suspected that Šešelj was behind recent bomb attacks in the Republika Srpska.

Vibrant but provincial, Zagreb is a city striving to forge its twenty-first-century identity even as it clings to the legacy of the Habsburg era, and especially Austria-Hungary. (I noticed that President Franjo Tudjman had dressed his honor guard in uniforms almost identical to those of its Hungarian counterparts.) On the day after our meeting with Dodik, I began meetings with officials of the Republic of Croatia's government in Zagreb. Ravaged by cancer, President Tudjman had but a month to live when I made my visit. Tudjman had been an early promoter of a war crimes tribunal for Yugoslavia, clearly because Croatia had been on the receiving end of most war crimes committed by the Serb-controlled Yugoslav National Army and rebel Serbs during the 1991 war. A few years later, however, he made it clear to his advisers and military commanders that Croatia, if it was going to become independent and expand its territory, required men willing to carry out the dirty work of war, and in so doing Tudjman rationalized their crimes.

Many Croats regard Franjo Tudjman as the father of their independent state. Just before my arrival in Zagreb, Tudjman spoke from his sickbed and declared that Croatia should never apprehend and transfer to The Hague military officers the tribunal had indicted for war crimes. Tudjman said, "Croatian men, who were liberating the country from evil, cannot be held accountable." Clearly, these words were as much an effort by a dying man to preserve his own legacy as they were an effort to guard Croatian military men from prosecution. I began my visit by releasing a statement describing how I was disappointed that Croatia had maintained a position of seeming to cooperate fully with the tribunal while failing in fact to cooperate with ongoing investigations into two operations the Croatian Army had undertaken in 1995 against the rebel Serb-held regions that had been under temporary United Nations protection. These operations, code-named "Storm" and "Flash," were a legitimate use of force on their face, but they produced a huge population transfer and killings of civilians, most of them elderly people who had chosen not to flee their homes. Croatia, I said, must acknowledge the tribunal's authority to proceed with all investigations of the armed conflict within Croatia, including Storm and Flash. I said that if Croatia did not comply with its obligations I would report this failure to the United Nations Security Council.

Tudjman and his protégés had been working systematically for years to stymie the tribunal's investigations. I knew none of the details of this operation when I sat down to meet with the highest official Zagreb managed to serve up on the day I visited, a deputy foreign minister named Ivo Sanader, who would later become Croatia's prime minister. Sanader, not surprisingly, began our session by promising to cooperate fully with the tribunal. "My country was the first to propose the tribunal's creation," he assured me. "Full cooperation is our policy in spite of the fact that sometimes we are not satisfied." He went on to ask why the tribunal had not indicted the commanders responsible for the destruction of Vukovar and the siege and bombardment of Dubrovnik. "We strongly support your work," Sanader said, pointing out that Tihomir Blaškić, Dario Kordić, and other Bosnian Croats indicted on charges linked with the Ahmići massacre of 1993 had been handed over to the tribunal thanks to Croatia's intervention.

I told Sanader I was surprised at Tudjman's call for Croatia not to turn over men indicted in connection with Operation Storm and Operation Flash. Tudjman's position, I said, was legally unfounded and unacceptable in principle. We had not yet even requested the transfer of anyone connected with Storm and Flash. We were only demanding that Croatia fulfill its obligation to cooperate with our investigations. "I can assure you that the tribunal in general and my office in particular is doing everything possible to investigate and prosecute the most serious crimes, at the highest possible level of responsibility. We have no bias toward any party. We are simply following our mandate."

I told him that Croatia's government should end its hostility toward the tribunal because cooperation was in the interests of Croatia's people. "You have to cooperate," I said, assuring him that we needed time and information to carry out our investigations of war crimes, including those that took place in Vukovar and Dubrovnik, and that we could not comment in any way upon them in order not to jeopardize them.

Sanader was clearly uncomfortable defending a position that might have soon prompted Security Council members to reduce assistance to Croatia. He was reading from a script handed down from on high when he told us that Storm and Flash were a delicate matter and that the government could not support the tribunal's position on it. His adviser chimed in: "We cannot give you archives and have you indict somebody. We cannot allow you to criminalize our legitimate action." He complained that the tribunal had indicted only four Serbs for crimes that had taken place during the 1991 Serb military campaign to carve up Croatia: "Let's be open why Storm and Flash now and not 1991. There were 14,000 people killed in Croatia." Sanader admitted that Croats had committed crimes on the margins of Operation Storm and that a lot of men had come into the war zone wearing military uniforms, implying that the Croatian commanders, and specifically one of Tudjman's favorites, General Ante Gotovina, might not bear responsibility for the actions of these men. But Sanader insisted that Croatia would not allow for the operation itself to come under tribunal scrutiny. Again, he launched into comparisons with Croatia's enemies. He was exaggerating when he said that every week people were discovering mass graves dug during the 1991 Serbian assault upon Croatia. Given what we know now about Croatia's efforts to hamper the tribunal's investigations, he was certainly lying about the extent of Croatia's cooperation and inaccurate in making implicit comparisons with Serbia's utter failure to assist the tribunal's efforts. But he was correct when he said the credibility of the international community was at stake on the issue of Karadžić and Mladić. "If you could state publicly that the aggression of 1991 is under investigation it would help," I recall Sanader saying. I assured him that I would.

In 1998, my predecessor, Louise Arbour, visited Montenegro, which had been Serbia's partner during the violence against Croatia in 1991 and at the outset of Belgrade's attempt to carve up Bosnia and Herzegovina. In May 1992, the United Nations imposed economic sanctions upon Serbia and Montenegro—the only two republics left in the rump Yugoslavia. As the war in Bosnia burned on and the sanctions began to smart, Montenegrins began having second thoughts. Some of their political leaders began working to distance themselves from Milošević and his protégés in Montenegro. By 1999, the opposition to Milošević had triumphed in Montenegro, and the two republics had practically become separate countries sharing a single army and a common currency. As Montenegro's government defied decisions handed down in Belgrade, emotions ran higher. There was widespread concern that violence might erupt between Serbs and pro-Belgrade Montenegrins living in Montenegro, on the one hand, and proponents of Montenegrin independence on the other. After the NATO bombing campaign, Milošević and the Yugoslav Army wanted nothing to do with the tribunal, for obvious reasons, and the security risk they posed made visiting even Montenegro impossible for tribunal investigators. We decided to invite Montenegro to send a government delegation to The Hague. On February 4, 2000, then-Prime Minister Filip Vujanović visited the tribunal's headquarters.

I told Vujanović we needed Montenegro's assistance. I said that we were placing a high priority on investigating war crimes with Serb victims in Bosnia, Croatia, and Kosovo, but that Belgrade had cut off our access to witnesses and documentary evidence in Serbia. My other obvious priority was detaining fugitives, first and foremost Karadžić and Mladić. Graham Blewitt added the name Veselin Šljivančanin, a native of Montenegro whom the tribunal was seeking on charges connected with the execution of 260 prisoners taken from a hospital following the fall of Vukovar in November 1991.

Vujanović smiled when he said Montenegro's relations with Belgrade had deteriorated to such a degree that cooperation with the tribunal could spoil them no further. But he asked that, for the sake of caution, the assistance remain confidential. Montenegro, he said, was ready to take part in operations, exchange information, and arrange interviews with victims and witnesses. Montenegro was also prepared to arrest our fugitives so long as they were on Montenegrin territory and so long as the targets were not persons at the highest levels of the command structure of the Federal Republic of Yugoslavia. In Vujanović's view, nobody could expect Montenegro to arrest high-profile figures like the head of the Yugoslav Army's counterintelligence service, General Dragoljub Ojdanić, or the interior minister, Vlajko Stojiljković, because arresting such people would give Milošević a pretext to intervene militarily and overthrow the Montenegrin government. Vujanović said the Montenegrin authorities were afraid that Milošević, a master at instigating and exploiting crises, would initiate labor unrest or civil strife in an effort to retain political power in Belgrade and eliminate potential rivals. Karadžić and Mladić, however, were another matter. The Montenegrin authorities were more than willing to arrest them, he said. But he cautioned us that Karadžić had not visited Montenegro for years. Mladić was not coming to Montenegro and had no family connection in the republic.

I assured Vujanović that we did not want to create trouble for Montenegro's government by calling upon it to arrest high-level officials from Belgrade. We did, however, want Montenegro to cooperate with our efforts to nab Karadžić, especially given that his mother lived in Montenegro and that Karadžić might attempt to visit her. Vujanovic said the

Montenegrin authorities were willing to maintain police surveillance, including video surveillance, on family members of the accused. He asked us to provide the Montenegrin authorities with a list of victims, contacts, potential witnesses, so the Montenegrins could contact them or place them under surveillance.

Several more months would pass before the authorities in Serbia chimed in, and it was in a predictable manner. Nationalist euphoria in Serbia had fueled the breakup of the former Yugoslavia. Milošević exploited the dissatisfaction of the Serb minority in Kosovo during the 1980s to maneuver himself into power. He took control of the Communist Party of Serbia, organized takeovers of the governments of Montenegro and Vojvodina, a province of Serbia, and made a botched attempt to seize control of Bosnia and Herzegovina by working through the intelligence services and the Communist Party. With this failure and a decision in early 1990 by Slovenia's communists to leave the Communist Party of Yugoslavia, Milošević had failed in his bid to take all of Yugoslavia and portray himself as a kind of reformist cross between Tito and Gorbachev. Now, the question became how to make his Serbia as strong as possible. The resulting wars had shrunk Serbia's influence to the borders of Serbia itself. Even Kosovo was lost. But still Milošević was clinging to power, effectively in a coalition with the ultranationalist Serbian Radical Party of Vojislav Šešelj, a man who was abused in jail under Yugoslavia's communists and emerged from prison, with Milošević's help, to found the party, organize a party militia, and beckon his partisans to use rusty spoons to scoop out the eyes of Croats and, presumably, Serbia's other enemies. Milošević's propaganda outlets were blaming the entire world for Serbia's woes. Louise Arbour had issued an indictment against Milošević during the NATO bombing campaign of 1999. After that, we made fruitless attempts to obtain Belgrade's assistance with investigations.

On April 26, 2000, I sent a letter to the federal minister of justice in Yugoslavia, Petar Jojić, a Radical Party true believer. My letter began with the usual diplomatic obeisances, though reading them aloud left a foul taste in my mouth. "Excellency," my letter began, "the Office of the Prosecutor has the honour to request the co-operation of the Government of the Federal Republic of Yugoslavia . . ." I went on to request assistance in serving a summons upon a certain Yugoslav army colonel whom we wanted to question concerning violations of international humanitarian law during the takeover of the Srebrenica "safe area" in July 1995.

On May 24, more than a week after the date we had set aside to speak with this colonel, Jojić signed and stamped his reply on Ministry of Justice stationery. He began the letter thusly: "To the Whore Del Ponte, Self-Proclaimed Prosecutor, Criminal Hague Tribunal." What followed was a rant that carried on for twenty-five single-spaced pages. "I want to inform you that I am aware of your perfidious intentions," Jojić began. "[U]nlike you, I pay due respect to international law, particularly to responsibility for international criminal acts; also, I want to show you clearly that there are people who do not sell themselves for money, do not debase themselves by stepping all over the sciences they have studied, who believe in God, and have no blood of innocent victims on their hands.

"The dungeon that you manage, the dungeon where, like the lowliest whore, you have sold yourself to the Americans, the dungeon where, even by using murder to do so, you forcibly drag innocent Serbs, the so-called Hague Tribunal, is an illegal institution, founded contrary to the provisions of the Charter of the United Nations and international law as a whole. . . . Sooner or later, even you will have to face the truth; your actions will be subject to investigation and the last part of your rotten life you will spend behind prison bars." The words continued screaming and shouting, and then he challenged me to meet, in a Moscow hotel room, General Dragoljub Ojdanić, Yugoslavia's Minister of Defense, a man who, Jojić assured me, had "Serbian and not perverted tastes." In the end, Jojić's letter, whatever else it was, amounted to an impassioned appeal to indict military officers and political leaders of the bombing campaign NATO carried out against Serbia and Montenegro from March 24 to June 9, 1999.

This letter marked the end of my first effort to look the Balkans in the eye. Ironically, after encountering so many empty promises about cooperation and a *muro di gomma* stretching from Zagreb to Skopje, someone was at last telling me what he genuinely thought. After a night of background reading in my apartment, between clean sheets and behind bomb-proofed windows, I recalled all those leaders I had met from Macedonia to Croatia. "*Ma dio*," I thought. "How are we going to be able to deal with them?"

My inbox had filled with letters from all over the world calling for investigation of NATO's bombing campaign against Serbia in 1999. Many of these letters, some from the United States, France, Canada, and other NATO countries, provided information on the bombing operation and the civilian casualties and damage it had inflicted. Delegations from Russia and Italy delivered documents. The government of Yugoslavia published materials showing convincingly that about 495 civilians had been killed and 820 civilians wounded. Some letters argued that NATO's bombing campaign violated international law and that NATO aircraft had deliberately attacked civilian targets and disregarded the rule of proportionality. Other letters maintained that, in an attempt to wage war and sustain no casualties of its own, NATO had ordered its aircraft to operate at altitudes beyond the reach of Yugoslavia's air defenses, which made it impossible for the NATO personnel controlling the weapons to distinguish between military and civilian targets. Still others alleged that NATO officers and their political taskmasters were guilty of crimes against humanity and genocide.

I had followed televised news bulletins about the air operation while in Berne during those months before I assumed my position at the tribunal. Back then, I was no pacifist. I welcomed NATO's decision to use force against Serbia and Montenegro. After ten years of useless bloodshed, after the bombardment of Dubrovnik, the leveling of Vukovar, and the winters and summers of shelling and sniping in Sarajevo, after the ethnic cleansing and concentration camps in Western Bosnia, the mass deportations and killings in the Drina River valley, the attack on Goražde, the thousands of massacred men and boys at Srebrenica, and the moral bankrupting of the United Nations—after all of this, I felt that now, finally, somebody was acting to end the madness Milošević had unleashed and was now turning against Kosovo's Albanian majority. The killing had to cease. The wanton destruction of communities had to cease. Nobody was willing to deploy troops to do the job. Empty rhetoric had only emboldened Milošević and Serb extremists who sought to cleanse Kosovo. Finally, I thought, it was going to stop. And it did stop. But at what cost?

Soon after my arrival in The Hague, I asked my deputy, Graham Blewitt, whether my predecessor, Louise Arbour, had launched an inquiry into allegations of NATO misdeeds. Arbour had warned all sides, including NATO, to respect the laws and customs of war and had specifically notified NATO leaders that the tribunal had jurisdiction over all war crimes committed by any side on the soil of the former Yugoslavia. On May 14, 1999, she established a working group to assess the allegations against NATO and to advise her whether or not there was evidence of sufficient weight to merit a full investigation. Despite my support for the bombing campaign, my instincts told me to pursue this effort. My interest in the case was not only drawn by the demands of my mandate. Reports of one particular incident, an air attack on a passenger train that was crossing a railroad bridge, piqued my prosecutorial interest. Why, I wondered, would a pilot try a second time to down a bridge when he knew that his first bomb had struck a passenger train as it was on the bridge?

My staff formed a committee to assess whether the available evidence warranted a full investigation. I needed to know whether the train attack and other specific incidents, including attacks on Serbia's main television station and the Embassy of China in Belgrade, constituted crimes for which responsibility could be traced up the chain of command to persons in leadership positions who would fall under the tribunal's authority. I needed crime-base evidence in order to prosecute. This was the first step. Then I required evidence linking the crimes to higher military and political leaders. In an interview with *The Observer* of London, I was asked whether my office was preparing to press charges against NATO. I answered: "If I am not willing to do that, I am not in the right place. I must give up my mission."[6]

I forwarded the material mailed to my office to the chairman of this committee, William Fenrick, a Canadian who was one of the Office of the Prosecutor's staff attorneys. Despite criticism in the United States Congress that a tribunal committee was examining the NATO operation—political leaders in the Balkans are not the only ones who exploit nationalism to score cheap points with the voters—I sent a long letter to John Lord Robinson, NATO's secretary-general, including a battery of interrogatories on a number of incidents that occurred during the bombing campaign. We needed details. What we received instead was a three-page missive containing little more than vague assurances that NATO had taken every precaution to limit civilian casualties and to strike only targets that were militarily significant. Perhaps, I thought, Lord Robinson had tried to respond in a forthright manner. But it was clear to me and to my staff that NATO either was withholding crucial information the tribunal was seeking about targeting and other decision making or that this information lay only in the hands of NATO member states whose governments would not release it. China gave us nothing. Even Belgrade refused to cooperate with us in any meaningful way. I asked the authorities there to provide us access to files and documents. They agreed, but never provided the information we were seeking.

No one in NATO ever pressured me to refrain from investigating the bombing campaign or from undertaking a prosecution based upon it. But I quickly concluded that it was impossible to investigate NATO, because NATO and its member states would not cooperate with us. They would not provide us access to the files and documents. Over and above this, however, I understood that I had collided with the edge of the political universe in which the tribunal was allowed to function. If I went forward with an investigation of NATO, I would not only fail in this investigative effort, I would render my office incapable of continuing to investigate and prosecute the crimes committed by the local forces during the wars of the 1990s. Security for the tribunal's work in Bosnia and Herzegovina as well as in Kosovo depended upon NATO. The tribunal's forensics teams were able to exhume mass graves only because they enjoyed NATO escorts. Arrests of fugitives depended upon NATO-country intelligence as well as NATO ground and air support.

The debate in my office on the NATO bombing was open, sometimes heated, but ultimately overshadowed by a sense of futility. I remember once discussing NATO's use of cluster bombs—aerial bombs that, before impact, disperse a hail of smaller shells that do not explode and subsequently function like landmines. "These cannot be legal," I argued. Fenrick came to me a few days afterward with compelling legal authority demonstrating that cluster bombs were, in fact, lawful. He also brought authority saying that no specific treaty ban on the use of depleted-uranium projectiles existed. And my advisers warned me that investigating NATO would be impossible.

I understood this to be true, but was nevertheless disappointed when I received the committee's report. The committee never reached the question of the overall legality NATO's use of force against the Federal Republic of Yugoslavia because, even if the campaign were found to be unlawful, it would constitute a "crime against peace," a category of law over which the tribunal has no jurisdiction. The committee split over whether to press for further investigation of the NATO personnel who intentionally launched the second bombing run against the rail bridge on which the passenger train had been struck. It found that the bridge was a legitimate military target and that the train was not deliberately targeted in the first strike. Some members thought the pilot displayed recklessness in launching the second attack. Nevertheless, the committee members agreed that no further investigation was warranted, because no information before it led the members to suspect that further investigation would ever lead to prosecution of persons higher up the chain of command.

I felt the committee members had drawn restrictive interpretations to avoid being obliged to go on. I must confess, however, that I knew going on was impossible, both technically and professionally. We had no cooperation, none, from anybody—this was the technical problem. And it was impossible to go on politically without undermining the rest of the tribunal's work. I could discount the political considerations, because of the technical impediment. This was the reason I went public with the committee's report. Nobody from my staff complained, but the president of the tribunal, Judge Antonio Cassese, did express his dismay at the result. "You could have indicted the pilot," he insisted.

"I cannot," I answered, "It isn't my jurisdiction. A pilot is just too far down the chain of command." We should have been allowed to visit the NATO bases at Aviano and Naples, in Italy, as well as NATO headquarters in Brussels to investigate whether the pilot had received orders to launch his second bombing run even though they knew of the damaged train on the bridge he had been tasked to destroy. Years later, during his trial, Slobodan Milošević introduced into evidence a transcript of a conversation that purportedly had taken place between this pilot and the controllers at Aviano. I went to Brussels and asked NATO to produce their records of the communication between the pilot and Aviano; NATO responded by saying the records could not be found.

In an address to the United Nations Security Council on Friday, June 2, 2000, I publicly announced my decision not to open a full-fledged criminal investigation into NATO's air campaign. About ten days later, I released the committee's report. The document drew the following conclusions based upon the information in the committee's hands, including some information provided by strange bedfellows, the government of the Federal Republic of Yugoslavia and Human Rights Watch:

• The NATO attacks on industrial facilities, chemical plants, and oil refineries did damage the environment in Serbia and Montenegro. But the environmental damage caused during the NATO bombing campaign did not reach a threshold necessary to constitute a violation of the applicable law; and a United Nations report suggested that much of the environmental contamination in Serbia and Montenegro could not unambiguously be attributed to the destruction NATO had inflicted.

• The bombing of the Radio-Television Serbia headquarters in central Belgrade, which claimed the lives of some seventeen people, had been a component of an effort to disrupt and degrade the Yugoslav military's command, control, and communications network, of which the television center was part. [I later discussed the television station bombing with NATO officials over cocktails at their headquarters in Brussels. I learned that NATO had informed Milošević in advance of an imminent attack on the building and that Milošević had intentionally removed some staff members from the building but left others inside.]

• The missile attack on the Chinese Embassy in Belgrade, which killed three Chinese nationals and injured about fifteen others, was, based upon available information, a mistake. [I hope that Clinton Administration defense department officials and United States military officers someday reveal all they know about this attack and whether it was related to Serbia's success in downing stealth aircraft.][7]

Despite my announcement to the Security Council, I never closed the book on the NATO bombing. We had found it impossible to conduct an effective investigation at the beginning of my tenure; but I was more than willing to reopen the case if we received evidence or access to records that would allow us to conduct a full investigation. I thought we might be able to accumulate evidence slowly, without publicity, and issue an indictment toward the end of my mandate, meaning toward the end of the tribunal's lifetime as an institution when it would no longer be so dependent upon NATO's support. As time passed, however, the tribunal received no compelling evidence, and no access that warranted opening an investigation against high-ranking NATO officers or political leaders. I was later told I was *persona non grata* at the Pentagon. I did not get an interview there again until 2005.

A few years later, General Wesley Clark, the former supreme commander of NATO forces in Europe, testified in the Milošević case. On cross-examination, Milošević began questioning General Clark about the NATO bombing. I listened with attention, hoping that Clark's words might yield some kind of revelation that would allow me to reopen the inquiry into the bombing campaign. The presiding judge, the late Sir Richard May, hastened to stop Milošević from pursuing this line of questioning. I was disappointed. It was the only moment during the entire trial that I found myself pulling for Milošević. After the hearing, I approached a court-appointed defense adviser from Belgrade and asked him to inform Milošević that I wanted to discuss the NATO bombing with him in order to find out what more he knew of the NATO operation and the air attack on the train. The defense adviser agreed. Many weeks later I approached him to find out how Milošević had responded. The answer was no.

3

CONFRONTING RWANDA'S GENOCIDE

Tourist brochures promote Rwanda as the "Switzerland of Africa," but I had never visited the country before my first mission as a war crimes prosecutor. Rwanda is a land of volcanoes, a land whose cinnamon-colored soil bursts forth with banana palms and fields of sorghum and corn and lush jungles, a land whose human voices fill the evenings with hypnotic songs that move to the rhythms of the native Kinyarwanda language and an accented French that made me feel more at ease than I have ever felt in Holland. Before Rwanda, however, I never imagined that one brief visit to a Catholic church could shake my confidence in humanity's capacity to keep the basest of passions from dictating its behavior. Before Rwanda, I had never met a genocide survivor who regretted surviving, or a rape victim cast into a jungle by her kin for bringing the child of her molester into this world. Before Rwanda, I never thought it possible that a tribunal might free a man accused of genocide on a procedural question alone.

I was gratified to learn that so many African states, including some of the world's poorest countries, in terms of material wealth but certainly not in terms of human pride and determination, had cooperated with the Rwanda tribunal, arresting and transferring to its custody leaders of the genocide. According to an American nongovernmental organization, the Coalition for International Justice, by the end of 2000, Benin had transferred two accused, Burkina Faso one, Cameroon nine, Ivory Coast two, Mali one, Namibia one, South Africa one, Togo two, Tanzania two, and Zambia three. Kenya had transferred thirteen of the accused; in one arrest operation engineered by Louise Arbour, the Kenyan authorities apprehended seven indicted Rwandan leaders on a single day and subsequently transferred them to the tribunal; the Kenyans knew, however, that they could have arrested and transferred several more; one of the fugitives in

Nairobi was Félicien Kabuga, a wealthy businessman who allegedly helped finance Hutu militias and plan the genocide. In contrast, at the close of 2000, NATO, the most powerful military force the world has ever known, had been patrolling Bosnia for five years, and, within its borders, eighteen of the Yugoslavia tribunal's accused war criminals, including Radovan Karadžić, were still roaming free. As I made my rounds of world capitals seeking assistance to secure the arrest of the Yugoslavia tribunal's fugitives, I recalled the African states' cooperation. I brought it up during private meetings with Western leaders. At the time it seemed that, thanks to these African countries, the Rwanda tribunal, much more than the Yugoslavia tribunal, stood to rival Nuremberg in its success at bringing surviving members of the top leadership to the dock.

Too many news commentaries I read and watched about Rwanda during the genocide and war of 1994 attributed the mass killing there to historical animosities, this time "ancient hatreds" between the country's Hutu majority and its Tutsi minority, as if these peoples, like the various peoples of the old Yugoslavia, had some kind of genetic predisposition to engage in the ultimate interethnic zero-sum game. Through my briefings from Catherine Cissé, the Rwanda Tribunal's French–Senegalese legal adviser, and through background reading on Rwanda and its genocide and war, notably the Human Rights Watch reports compiled by Alison Des Forges, I discovered the more complex background I had expected to find. "Ancient animosities" do not precipitate genocide in Africa any more than they do in Europe. People organize and incite genocide. In Rwanda, an explosive mixture of poverty, overpopulation, lack of economic opportunity, anarchy, bigotry, jealousy, and other factors made genocide possible, but military and political leaders intent upon seizing and retaining power and reaping wealth controlled the detonator.

The background narrative crucial to understanding the culture of impunity in which the Hutu leaders mobilized vast numbers of people to carry out the genocide in 1994 began decades earlier, when European colonial rulers originally drove the Hutus and Tutsis asunder. After World War I, Belgium took control of Rwanda and relied upon an elite drawn from the minority Tutsi population to crack the whips that kept the majority Hutus in line. By the end of the 1950s, political and economic power in Rwanda had shifted from the Belgians and their Tutsi favorites to an emerging Hutu êlite. Belgium granted Rwanda independence in July 1962. In 1963, a rebel army of Tutsi exiles marched back into Rwanda and attempted to overturn the emerging Hutu-dominated order. In an eerie foreshadowing of what would come in 1994, Hutus killed more than 10,000 Tutsis and drove another 300,000 into exile in Burundi, Uganda, and other neighboring countries. No one was held accountable. For years thereafter, Hutu leaders used their protégés to control the populace, just as Tutsi leaders had once used theirs to dominate the Hutu majority.

For the next thirty years, Hutu political leaders tightened their grip on power by stoking Hutu fears of a return to Tutsi hegemony. Hutus killed thousands more Tutsis in massacres, for which, again, no one was held accountable. Stories filtered into Rwanda about Tutsi massacres of Hutus in neighboring Burundi, whose border is just several hours' drive south from Rwanda's capital, Kigali. Again, no court or tribunal, no political leader, no party took steps to hold anyone personally responsible for the violence.

There were perhaps a million Rwandan Tutsis living in exile by 1990. Militants among them, including one Paul Kagame, organized an insurgency, the Rwandan Patriotic Front (RPF), whose aim was to pry Rwanda's Hutu president, Juvénal Habyarimana, from power and clear the way for Tutsi exiles to return to their homeland. Guerrillas from the RPF infiltrated Rwanda's territory and blended in with its Tutsis to carry out attacks, and the RPF's own propaganda compared these fighters to *inyenzi*, the local word for "cockroaches," because they had managed to infest the country just as cockroaches infest a house. In another eerie foreshadowing of the horrors to come in 1994, Habyarimana's supporters massacred hundreds of Tutsi civilians in retaliation for attacks by the RPF. None of the killers, and none of their political backers, faced prosecution. But within a few months, an eruption of popular discontent forced Habyarimana to abandon his monopoly on political power.

New Hutu parties and groups began competing against Habyarimana's circle for popular backing. During this political struggle, Habyarimana and other Hutu leaders resorted to fear-mongering to garner support, and they exaggerated the threat posed by the RPF as a way of wooing disaffected Hutus. Habyarimana's circle and other radical Hutus stirred up memories of Tutsi domination in decades past. They warned that Tutsis were preparing to enslave the Hutus once again. Hutu parties marshaled young men into militias and began training them to fight to defend partisan interests. By early 1992, Habyarimana's party had founded a militia that came to be called the *Interahamwe*, a word that means "those who fight together." As clashes between Rwandan government forces and the RPF erupted, members of Hutu militias carried out massacres of Tutsi civilians.

Slaughtering defenseless Tutsi women and children did little to sharpen the combat skills of the Rwandan military and the Hutu party militias. And successes by the RPF forced Habyarimana to enter into negotiations on a power-sharing arrangement. Hutu extremists began planning to subvert the peace effort and eradicate the RPF's base of support within Rwanda: the Tutsi population itself. These Hutu extremists believed a campaign of genocide would solidify the fractious Hutu community under their leadership and enhance the chances of defeating the Tutsi-dominated RPF. By early 1993, one Rwandan army colonel had reportedly opened his *agenda* and jotted down elements of an extermination program; his name was Théoneste Bagosora; he would be charged with leading the genocide of 1994.

On August 4, 1993, the Habyarimana regime and the RPF signed a power-sharing deal. In an attempt to buttress a cease-fire, the United Nations Security Council voted to deploy a peacekeeping force—the United Nations Assistance Mission for Rwanda—but failed to provide this force with sufficient troops, funding, or staff to fulfill its mission. By now, Hutu extremists were working to spread fear of the Tutsi *inyenzi* through Radio Télévision Libre des Mille Collines, a new broadcast outlet that would one day become a focal point of a precedent-setting tribunal judgment that incitement to genocide through the mass media is a crime. Tutsis presented Hutu propagandists with abundant material to instill the terror that helped fuel the massacres of 1994. In October 1993, Tutsi soldiers in neighboring Burundi assassinated that country's newly elected Hutu president, Melchior Ndadaye, which touched off a spate of killing in Burundi that claimed as many as 50,000 Hutu and Tutsi lives. Radio Mille Collines could also draw upon accounts of earlier Tutsi massacres of Hutus in Burundi. In 1965, Burundi's Tutsi-dominated army had killed 5,000 to 10,000 Burundian Hutus. In 1972, upward of 100,000 Burundian Hutus had been killed. In 1988, Burundi's army had killed another 20,000 Hutus; and in 1991, another 3,000. The culture of impunity reigned supreme.

By early 1994, Hutu political and military leaders had for months been distributing firearms, machetes, and knives to Hutu militia members. Now Hutu extremists in Rwanda were threatening to assassinate President

Habyarimana and arranging street demonstrations in Kigali against the power-sharing arrangement. Kagame and other leaders of the RPF readied their Tutsi-dominated forces for further clashes, clearly knowing that Hutus had taken vengeance upon Tutsi civilians for earlier RPF attacks and that a breakdown of the cease-fire and power-sharing agreement would leave vast numbers of Rwandan Tutsis exposed to massive Hutu retaliation.

On the evening of April 6, 1994, President Habyarimana was flying into Kigali after a round of negotiations on implementation of the power-sharing agreement. The French pilot had already maneuvered the aircraft onto its final approach when someone launched surface-to-air missiles that blew the plane from the sky. Mystery surrounds the identity of the persons who fired the missiles, but the sound of the presidential plane exploding in the air suspiciously coincided with the beginning of genocide. Hutu extremists rushed to blame the Tutsis for Habyarimana's assassination. A small group of the assassinated president's closest associates now began executing the organized slaughter of Tutsi civilians that Colonel Bagosora had allegedly roughed out in his *agenda* more than a year earlier. Military units backed by the Hutu militias combed neighborhoods of the capital with death lists, murdering Tutsis along with Hutu government officials and leaders of the political opposition. Military officers and administrators in districts and towns far from Kigali began sending off soldiers and militiamen with orders to kill local Tutsis as well as moderate Hutu leaders. The Tutsi-dominated units of the RPF sprang back into action against the Hutus. Radio Mille Collines beckoned its listeners to do more than strike against the enemy RPF; it called for eradicating all of the *inyenzi*, which by now referred to every Tutsi man, woman, and child.

Pondering the violence that now spread across Rwanda crodes my faith in the power of human reason over human irrationality, so astonishing was its speed, so widespread was the participation, so intimate was the slaughter, the rape, the hacking of children to death . . . I can only imagine the sound of the metal blades tearing through healthy bodies, the screaming in the night, the children crying, angry orders of crazed voices, but I know that the real horror outstrips my powers of imagination.

The Hutu extremists cowed the commanders of the United Nations peacekeeping force with such ease that it caused an international scandal. The United Nations Department of Peacekeeping Operations ordered the United Nations force to take no provocative action against the Hutu extremists, which amounted to abandonment of the unarmed portions of the Tutsi population to machete-wielding Hutu gangs. Elite French, Belgian, and Italian troops landed at Kigali airport, but only to help evacuate foreign nationals; units of United States Marines stood by in Burundi, but they withdrew after the evacuation of American citizens. Bagosora's troops discovered Belgian peacekeepers guarding the home of the country's moderate Hutu prime minister, Agathe Uwilingiyimana; the troops murdered Uwilingiyimana and her children; then they tortured and killed ten of the Belgians, an act that prompted Brussels to withdraw the entire Belgian peacekeeping contingent.

In May and June, military defeats and the first significant expressions of international disapproval for the killing had undermined the position of the Hutu extremists in the government. By June 1994, the Tutsi-dominated RPF was advancing toward Kigali. In July, the Hutu extremists abandoned the capital and joined an exodus from Rwanda more massive than the flight of people across the country's borders in April. The fleeing Hutus included thousands of people who had taken part in the killing of some 500,000 to 800,000 Tutsis and moderate Hutus.

The Rwandan Patriotic Front's victory ended the genocide, and brought Paul Kagame and other Tutsi leaders into power in Rwanda. But RPF troops had also committed massive crimes against humanity, killing some civilians during military action and executing many more after fighting with the Rwandan army had ended. In some areas, Tutsi troops killed unarmed women and children after luring them with promises of food or transportation to other areas.

The United Nations Security Council created the International Criminal Tribunal for Rwanda on November 8, 1994. This act was not just an effort to end the culture of impunity that had developed in Rwanda for generations before the genocide. It was a diplomatic *mea culpa*, an act of contrition by the world's major powers to make amends for their gross failure to prevent or halt the massacres. The council gave the Rwanda tribunal jurisdiction over the war crimes that occurred in Rwanda and its neighboring states between January 1, 1994, and December 31, 1994. The Rwanda tribunal's structure mirrors the Yugoslavia tribunal's: twenty-five judges, sixteen permanent and nine *ad litem*, sit in four "chambers"—three to conduct trials and an appeals chamber shared with the Yugoslavia tribunal. The Office of the Prosecutor at the Rwanda tribunal is split into two sections: the Investigation Section, headquartered in Kigali, is responsible for collecting evidence; the Prosecution Section, based at the tribunal's headquarters in Arusha, Tanzania, has responsibility for prosecuting all cases before the tribunal. The Registry is responsible for the overall administration and management.

I do not know why the United Nations Security Council chose to give the chief prosecutor of the Yugoslavia tribunal responsibility for the prosecution effort at the Rwanda tribunal. I have read that some council members believed the prosecution efforts in the tribunals would benefit from the development of common strategies and procedures. I have also heard that the Security Council had had so much trouble choosing a candidate to fill the chief prosecutor post at the Yugoslavia tribunal that it spared itself the pain of a similar selection process for Rwanda by opting to merge the two positions. To my mind, combining the two positions was a good option, because, among other things, it allowed for the development of uniform approaches to investigations and helped develop a body of international case law. I was happy to accept the challenge offered to me. I could only do my job as well as I knew how, blind to the racial realities, and to ensure that my subordinates did their jobs as well. I know the Rwanda catastrophe gripped the member states of the Security Council. I know it ripped at the hearts of the diplomats who represented these nations. And I know they gave the Rwanda tribunal and the Yugoslavia tribunal equal weight.

The Rwanda tribunal had little choice but to establish its operations in Arusha, a town in Tanzania. But even by air, the town is two hours away from Rwanda's capital, Kigali, which was ruled out as a site for the tribunal for security considerations. The nearest gaggle of the international press is in Nairobi, Kenya, a five-hour overland journey away; so the tribunal could count on nothing but desultory coverage from the major papers and broadcast networks. (A few freelancers and a number of nongovernmental organizations working over the Internet did a yeoman's service for their readers, the tribunal, the victims, and the cause of international justice.) The Rwanda tribunal's headquarters, Arusha's International Conference Center, is a musty, concrete structure whose flow of electricity seems to wax and wane with Tanzania's shifting moods. Telephone service is whimsical. The guards used to snap to attention and saluted me each time I entered the building, which made me feel enough like a colonial magistrate to arouse pangs of guilt. As the chief prosecutor of both tribunals, I suppose I could have chosen to reside in Arusha. But as a base for work, Arusha would have been impractical. So much of the chief prosecutor's activity depends on almost constant communication with major capital cities in Europe and North America, with the European Union and NATO, with the United Nations headquarters in New York, and with nongovernmental organizations, and so much of the diplomatic work was still to be done on the Yugoslav cases, because there were so many accused still at large.

The face of a single *génocidaire*, Jean-Bosco Barayagwiza, glowered over the offices and corridors of the International Criminal Tribunal for Rwanda on November 23, 1999, my first day in Arusha, as I spent the time acquainting myself with the prosecution teams. By this time, the Rwanda tribunal had indicted forty-eight persons in connection with the genocide, and its detention unit was holding twenty-nine persons awaiting trial. Jean Kambanda, prime minister in the extremist Hutu government, had already pleaded guilty to genocide. On that first morning, I gathered the team together in a small office to discuss how we would continue Louise Arbour's efforts to convince the trial chamber to merge our cases thematically, so we could prosecute multiple defendants more efficiently. The office had already filed a motion to merge into a single trial the cases against defendants indicted for genocide through, among other things, their connection with Radio Mille Collines and other media outlets. Another trial team was preparing to argue a motion for joining in a single trial the highest-ranking Hutu military leaders, including Théoneste Bagosora, the colonel who had reportedly jotted down the genocide plan in his *agenda*. But the backdrop to our procedural strategizing was the looming face of that one *génocidaire* who almost escaped justice: Jean-Bosco Barayagwiza.

Born in 1950, Barayagwiza is a slight, tranquil-looking man. His gold-framed spectacles give him the studious look of an insecure first-year law student. He trained as a diplomat after taking a degree in international law at the State University of Kiev in the Soviet Ukraine. He authored a book on human rights. The Rwandan government seconded him to a senior position in the Organization of African Unity. But Barayagwiza's looks and his diplomatic and legal résumé are deceptive. The tribunal's investigation turned up compelling evidence that, during 1993 and 1994, he had played pivotal roles in the planning and execution of the massacres. This evidence indicated that he had founded the Committee for the Defense of the Republic, an extremist party that worked to rally all Hutus, regardless of their political affiliation, to the common struggle against the Tutsis. He allegedly ran the committee and developed its ideology. At mass rallies, Barayagwiza had allegedly joined party members in chanting "*Tubatsembatsembe!*" or "Let's exterminate them!" Barayagwiza had allegedly supplied weapons to the party's youth wing and issued orders for its members to set up roadblocks and kill Tutsis who happened by. In addition, the evidence indicated that Barayagwiza was a member of the steering committee of Radio Télévision Libre des Milles Collines.

Barayagwiza fled Rwanda after the genocide. On March 28, 1996, the authorities in Cameroon arrested and detained him in response to a warrant the Rwandan government had issued. Three days later, the Rwanda tribunal's first prosecutor, Richard Goldstone, wrote a letter expressing the tribunal's interest in proceeding against Barayagwiza. At one point, an appeals court in Cameroon rejected the Rwandan government's request for extradition and ordered Barayagwiza's release. He was taken into custody again in February 1997, transferred to the Rwanda tribunal's detention facility in Arusha on November 19, 1997, and given an initial hearing on February 23, 1998. Barayagwiza's attorneys soon filed a motion with the Trial Chamber requesting his release from pretrial detention on the grounds that he had been held for an excessively long period in Cameroon and at the tribunal's detention unit without being brought before a judge for an initial hearing. (In many states, such hearings must be held within twenty-four or forty-eight hours.) The Trial Chamber rejected Barayagwiza's argument, but he appealed. On November 3, 1999, the Rwanda tribunal's Appeals Chamber, presided over by an American judge, Gabrielle Kirk McDonald, sided with Barayagwiza, citing the duration of his pretrial detention in Cameroon and the three months that had elapsed between his transfer to Arusha and his initial hearing. McDonald and the other judges dismissed the charges against Barayagwiza "with prejudice," meaning that they barred the prosecution from ever again raising the same charges against him.

This decision outraged the Rwandans. Demonstrators took to Kigali's streets. The government, under the control of Tutsi veterans of the RPF and survivors of the genocide, suspended its cooperation with the tribunal. I, too, was disturbed that Barayagwiza would escape justice on this procedural question and not face a full trial. But I was more concerned with the real danger that, because of the Barayagwiza fiasco, the Rwandan government would retaliate against the Rwanda tribunal itself by permanently refusing to cooperate with its work; this would deal a major setback to the cause of international justice in general. I spent that Saturday poring over the case file and the decision. How could we keep Barayagwiza in custody? How could we prevent his return to Cameroon? How could we overcome the words "with prejudice" and obtain his trial there in Arusha? I recall some of my advisers saying we could do nothing. I disagreed. My instincts told me that this decision could not stand, simply because it was so inherently unjust. I ordered my team to rush to bring a motion before the Appeals Chamber. We would request a review of the chamber's decision before Barayagwiza was released from the tribunal's custody.

First, we got lucky. Barayagwiza himself requested that the tribunal delay his transfer from Arusha to Cameroon. He was terrified that Cameroon would extradite him to Rwanda to answer charges. In Rwanda, Barayagwiza would find himself just one of more than 100,000 accused *génocidaires* awaiting trial in inhuman conditions; in the end, he might find himself facing an executioner. On November 19, my team filed with the Appeals Chamber a notice of intention to present a motion for a review of the ruling handed down on November 3. We argued, among other things, that new facts—facts that could not have been discovered earlier with due diligence—would have had a decisive impact on the ruling. It was a long shot—a very long shot. On November 22, 1999, Barayagwiza's defense team filed its response. They argued that we did not intend to produce any new facts, and they maintained that the Rwandan government had pressured me to fight the ruling and that I was doing so for political reasons that sullied the judicial process, something no United Nations tribunal required to protect the rights of the accused should tolerate. The Appeals Chamber accepted our notice of intention. Its members gave us permission to file a request for review of the November 3 ruling. Better still, pending the outcome of the review decision, they suspended the order to release Barayagwiza.

Nervous preparations for filing the request for review were under way when I arrived in Arusha on Tuesday, November 23, 1999, and met the staff for the first time. So angry were the Rwandan authorities that they refused to grant me a visa for my planned first trip to Kigali, which was supposed to take place in conjunction with this first trip to Arusha.

Two days later, I appeared before the Rwandan tribunal for the first time to help my team present arguments for a joint trial of two defendants linked to the genocide by their incitement to violence through the mass media: Ferdinand Nahimana, former director of Radio Télévision Libre des Mille Collines, and Hassan Ngeze, former editor of an extremist newspaper, *Kangura*. It irritated me that Barayagwiza was not sitting beside them in the bulletproof dock. I instructed the deputy prosecutor, Bernard Muna, to come from Kigali to Arusha. I asked the Rwandan authorities to issue me a visa. I told Muna, "You stay with me here in Arusha until I am allowed to go to Kigali." Two can play the cold-shoulder game, I thought. I knew that Muna had intimate contacts with the government in Rwanda. I also knew that he enjoyed Kigali more than Arusha. Kigali was a real town, lively and throbbing. Muna was living there in a wonderful villa. So, by holding him in Arusha, I knew he would do everything he could to get me my visa. "You're staying here," I instructed him. "You deal with the government from here."

I was still waiting for a visa on November 30, the day the judges issued their decision to allow us to hold a joint trial of Nahimana and Ngeze. Three days later, we filed our motion for the Appeals Chamber either to reverse its decision to release Barayagwiza or to remove its provision that the release should be "with prejudice" so we could rearrest him. I wanted Barayagwiza in the courtroom to answer charges as part of the media trial. I wanted him, with his suit and gold-framed eyeglasses, sitting next to Nahimana and Ngeze. In the end, the Appeals Chamber agreed to consider the matter. A hearing date was set for mid-February 2000.

In the end, thanks to Muna and pressure by the United States government and others, the authorities in Kigali granted me a visa for Rwanda. Flying northward from Arusha to Kigali takes just two hours aboard the Beechcraft prop plane the United Nations provides the Rwanda tribunal for its personnel and witnesses. Over the years, I enjoyed this final leg of my journeys to Kigali. The Beechcraft does not climb so high or fly so fast. A magnificent slow-moving landscape stretches before you. Kilimanjaro, with its disappearing glaciers, seems like a watchtower guarding all of Africa. Herds of zebra, elephants, and other wildlife dot the plains. And as you approach Kigali, as President Habyarimana did, so lush is the jungle below that it seems nature has placed a green filter over the airplane's windows.

My first visit to Rwanda was friendly enough. During courtesy calls to the country's ministers and the prosecutor general, I took care not to probe any sensitive nerves. I knew the Rwandan authorities were displeased with the tribunal in the wake of the Barayagwiza ruling, and I had technical issues to resolve so our teams could carry out investigative work, approach witnesses, and visit crime sites. I never raised the issue of investigating another thematic case I wanted to bring before the Rwanda tribunal, a joint case against government officials and military commanders who were criminally responsible for the widespread killings that the mostly Tutsi contingents of Kagame's Rwandan Patriotic Front had committed during the genocide. We knew the government was opposed to helping us on that score, and had even broken into our headquarters to spy on our activities. Given the emotional turmoil after the Barayagwiza ruling, I wanted to do what I could to achieve full cooperation and squeeze everything we needed out of it to pursue Hutu defendants. I did not meet Kagame on that first trip, but I did send him a personal greeting. Before dinner on my first evening, I was in my room at the Hotel des Mille Collines, of *Hotel Rwanda* fame, when I heard fantastic drum beats and voices singing. It was a stage drama put to music, a benefit performance Kagame's wife, Jeannette, had organized to collect money for drought victims. I strayed into the hall, and was invited to take a seat at the front next to her. A tall, beautiful woman, Mrs. Kagame explained to me a bit of what was going on. I ended up staying for the entire performance, much to the dismay of the waiting Muna, who was hosting me for dinner. After the finale, I passed my regards to Kagame through her.

On my second trip to Kigali, I ventured into the field. I wanted to see something of the real Africa. Beyond Kigali's outskirts, the roads and dirt tracks lead you into a realm of abject rural poverty that could have been anywhere. The landscape shifts from jungle to cornfields to mango groves. Mud and grass huts cluster to the sides of the road. Girls carry water jugs. Long-horned cows amble by. Chickens dart and dash. Men ride rickety bicycles. Sanitation, electricity, and telephones are nonexistent. Many of the inhabitants have probably known no footwear other than flip-flops. And there, atop so many hilltops, were churches, most of them Roman Catholic. I remember asking myself the same questions many people were asking after the genocide: "What has organized religion accomplished in Rwanda? What have these missionaries accomplished with so many church buildings? Why didn't they help the poor build better houses and live better in this life? Why did some members of the clergy and church-going people participate so willingly in the genocide?"

The Rwandan government had security escorts trailing us wherever we went, and, particularly at the beginning, this was important. But it was also, I understood later, to monitor our operations, to make sure we were investigating Hutu attacks upon Tutsis instead of Tutsi attacks upon Hutus. During our meetings, the minister of justice and the prosecutor general always made it clear that they knew where we had been, what we had been doing, and with whom we had spoken. I once traveled into the field with Alison Des Forges, and somewhere along the road she asked our driver to stop. We got out and walked to the edge of a sewage pit. There, at the bottom, was a mass of human bones, the remains of dead Tutsis. Flies were buzzing all around us. The sun was shining with utter indifference. I wanted to remove them, these victims. I thought we could use the remains from this site as a part of our crime base investigation and rescue the dead from the pit of waste into which their killers had thrown them. Frankly, I could not believe the government had not already done so. During my next meetings with the prosecutor general and the minister of justice—even before I had raised the issue—both men informed me that exhuming the bones in that sewer was not possible. It would create, I was told, disorder in society. Exhumations and burials had gone on for years already, they said, and it was not necessary to do any more. Rwanda, they said, was now looking toward the future. Rwanda, they said, needed a quietus.

One late morning in early February 2000, the sun had baked the ground into a crumbly crust that the vehicles in our convoy kicked into a pastel-pink cloud. The air conditioner whirred without complaint. I gazed through the windshield at the lead vehicle, an open truck with a squad of Rwandan soldiers who bounced up and down in unison at each dip in the road. An hour or later, we turned onto a shaded, red-dirt track. The leaves of plants swiped at the fenders and doors and side windows. Then we halted at a clearing and walked into the compound of a rectangular brick building with a corrugated-metal roof. This had once been a Roman Catholic church. I am sure that birdsong filled the air. Car doors had to have slammed shut. Curious kids had to have been poking fun at one another. There had to have been words of greeting and explanation, words posing questions and providing answers. But the visual sensations were so intense that my memory seems to have registered not a single sound.

A throng of Tutsi families—extended families, with their little girls and boys, their mothers and fathers and aunts and uncles, their grandparents and great grandparents—had gathered in the compound of the Ntarama church by the afternoon of April 14, 1994, when Hutu militiamen arrived—here, right where I was standing in the silence. The gunmen ordered the people to summon all the other Tutsis from the surrounding villages, ostensibly so they, too, could be provided protection. More families arrived, and perhaps some of the adults among them believed the promises of safety. But by the time the troops reentered the compound the next morning, the throng had been concerned enough about survival to withdraw into the church. Voices were praying and singing behind the locked doors. Inside were women with their purses. There were children with toys. There were old people with canes and bottles of water. Someone was wearing eyeglasses with white plastic frames. There were plates and spoons and Bibles and images of saints. At one instant, sledgehammers began thumping at the walls. Mortar crumbled and bricks fell onto the church floor allowing sunlight to burst through the dim light inside. Then the militiamen began throwing hand grenades through the holes in the walls. The concussion and shrapnel killed and wounded and stunned people in the crowd. Hammers broke open the doors. Men rushed inside and launched themselves into the tangled, stunned throng with rifles, bats, machetes, and clubs with protruding nails. Several of these attackers spoke years later to a French journalist, Jean Hatzfeld.[1] One of them, who had been a volunteer deacon at this same church, said people inside screamed as the men lowered the clubs and blades down upon their heads and limbs. Another recalled combing through the piles of dead bodies the next day in an effort to kill any survivors twitching among the twisted mass of dead. Cocksure they had completed their task, the militiamen left the bodies to the farm animals and dogs and the rodents and insects and maggots.

In the silence of the yard, I looked at the skulls of these people, hundreds of them, arrayed on makeshift tables, warm in the noontime sun. Ranks of skulls with no mandibles, adult skulls, child skulls, skulls with missing teeth, skulls with baby teeth, skulls that were intact, and skulls crushed and dented by impacts of machetes and clubs. I studied them, and *memento mori*, a penetrating awareness of one's own mortality, stirred in me a kind of courage and determination. It was not horrifying. It was not revolting, at least on a conscious level. It was saddening. Some of these relics seemed to want to speak.

The caretaker, an old man in a T-shirt and dust-covered shoes, urged me to enter the church building. I was hesitant. But he urged me again. I entered through the same side entrance the killers had poured through. It was like entering a cavern, pitch black and filled with ear-muffling silence. My eyes needed a minute or two to adjust. Then I saw. At the opposite end of the room was an altar standing on a brick base. Across the floor was a chaos of bones and wooden benches, thousands of bones, curved, brittle, and odorless, with pieces of stained and dusty clothing tangled among them—pants, shirts, shoes, leather sandals, and flip-flops. I was afraid to step further. There were the purses. There were the eyeglasses with white frames. There were the toys and the water bottles, the dishes and spoons, the Bibles, the images of saints. I did not want to disturb this scene, to step on a piece of the dead, to touch the clothing. The caretaker explained what had happened. I gave his words my rapt attention. This was more than a crime scene, but it was my habit to treat it as one. I wanted to know exactly what had happened, clinically, unemotionally. At one spot, there at the back of the church, I felt something break with a crackle beneath my shoe. I had stepped on one of them, one of these dead. I moved, and it crackled again, a rib, perhaps, or a small vertebra, like the crunch of a pretzel stick under foot: "*O dio*, this is not some soup bone. *O dio*, how cheap life is." In Lugano, the murder of a single victim will generate a comprehensive investigation—interviews with witnesses, dusting for fingerprints, forensic analysis, DNA testing, and binders filled with paper. And here, confronting me at this instant, were thousands of dead whose names were lost in the silence of the mayhem spread out over the floor between the pews and the altar. The numbers—the number of femurs and tibias, the number of names, the number of lacerations, the number of causes of death, all a tangled confusion that would take years to untangle, if anyone were to untangle it—and no one would.

I walked out of the church into a light so bright it seemed to burn my eyes. I was perspiring, though it had been cooler inside the building. Our guide led us over to two people who were looking at me. I approached with the Kinyarwanda translator. They appeared to be fifty or sixty years old. One of them explained that he had been inside the church during the massacre. He had been twitching there, lying wounded among the dead, unconscious and unnoticed by the killers. Two or three days passed before someone arrived and noticed that he was still breathing. His head bore a scar from a machete blow. Now, he was living alone in a shack with no family, too little food, and scant hope. He repeated several times that he was not grateful to be alive. He kept repeating that he was not happy about surviving. He said curiosity had driven him to come see *the prosecutor*—or at least this is what the translator said. This made me feel something like the guilt I sensed when the guards at the tribunal's building in Arusha snapped to attention as I entered. There was a kind of ego-gratification and a sense of responsibility, as if I could help bring them peace, or at least peace of mind.

I suffer through conversations with victims and survivors. I prefer to keep these people at a distance. What can you say to them about the kind of suffering they have endured? Nothing except a few words whose meaning falls somewhere beyond the banal. What can you do to improve their lives or ease the burden? Nothing significant, nothing lasting. I recall meeting one Tutsi woman who described how Hutu soldiers had raped her repeatedly. They wounded her and left her for dead. But someone had saved her life. She had become pregnant during the rape. Her family wanted her to leave their village, because her child was half Hutu. They sent her and the infant into the jungle to live. And there she was, with her child, living in the wild. Tell me what to say—I'm sorry?

Memento mori is a life-altering force. In me, it does not trigger an urge to mourn, and certainly not an urge to weep. But in this instance it did trigger an urge to do something to right a wrong, to do right by those mute skulls I saw on the makeshift tables, by the man who would rather have died with his kin, by the mother and child living in the jungle because their kinfolk would have them no longer. Overcoming the Barayagwiza ruling seemed even more important to me.

Two weeks of preparing for the hearing before the Appeals Chamber revealed a lot about the caliber of some of my team's legal professionals. During one meeting, the sun seemed to have stood still in the African sky. One of the lawyers lectured us on and on, apparently in support of reversing the ruling dismissing the case against Barayagwiza. I could not follow his train of thought. I did not know where he had started his theorizing or where he was going with it. And I knew that if I allowed him to present the arguments in this way, the Appeals Chamber would never reverse its ruling. The tedium had dragged on for more than an hour before I grew impatient, blurted out "*Ma tête est pleine*" and "*Basta*," and thanked him for his contribution. In the United Nations system, you cannot simply dismiss people, because this will produce seasons of wrangling and complaints and piles of paper, and you will lose; you can, however, shunt the less competent onto a side track and give them nothing to do, and thereby mitigate the damage. I turned to another of my legal advisers, and suggested that he take up the case. This one hesitated and objected. He seemed to fear getting up before the court and presenting the arguments that had a chance to prevail. Finally, I turned to Norman Farrell, former counsel for the International Committee of the Red Cross in Geneva. "You're going to argue the legal issues," I said. Farrell is a Canadian, from Ontario, a common-law jurisdiction. He had no idea I was going to drop this on him. I hardly knew him personally, but I had noticed him speaking out a lot during our strategy sessions and he clearly had one of the best legal minds in the office.

The challenge we faced prior to the Barayagwiza hearing was how to convince the judges to strike a balance between the two dominant systems of justice in the Western world, the common-law system, like the system Judge McDonald knew in the United States, and the civil-law system that exists in continental Europe. Necessity forces these two systems to confront one another in the new international justice institutions. Under the common-law system, if the court finds that an egregious violation of an accused defendant's rights has occurred, it can order exactly what Judge McDonald's bench ordered: a halt to the proceedings and dismissal of the case with prejudice. Under the civil-law system, the court will take a violation of the defendant's rights into consideration only after a trial of the issues. If Barayagwiza were found guilty at trial, the court might reduce his sentence; if Barayagwiza were found not guilty, the court might order that he receive monetary compensation.

The Appeals Chamber's ruling under Judge McDonald made sense under the common-law system that exists in the United States, Canada, and other countries. From the perspective of the civil-law system, however, the result was almost incomprehensible. How do we reconcile these different systems to reach a just result? How do we bring together legal minds from these different systems and find a common ground based upon shared principles? Like other aspects of my job, it is about balance, but not at the cost of justice.

The first element of our strategy was to present arguments in a way that did not deny that Barayagwiza's rights might have been violated, but to show that the gravity of any violation of Barayagwiza's rights was not so extreme as to warrant dismissal of his case with prejudice. The second element of our strategy was to argue the differences in the two legal systems, which would allow the common-law judges in the Appeals Chamber to accept that the appropriate outcome would be a lesser remedy for Barayagwiza than striking out the entire indictment against him. A month and a half before the hearing we had filed a brief that outlined several new facts. First, we had obtained an affidavit from David Scheffer, United States ambassador at large for war crimes issues, indicating that, for political reasons, Cameroon had delayed Barayagwiza's transfer to Arusha. Then we followed up with a motion that dealt with the delays in holding a hearing before the tribunal until several months after Barayagwiza's arrival at the detention facility in Arusha.

Four days before the oral hearing, I told Farrell that I would argue the civil-law aspects at the hearing. He had four days to prepare his oral arguments to deal with the common-law side, with reconciling the two systems in order to achieve a just outcome. One factor had tipped in our favor since the Appeals Chamber had handed down its unanimous ruling on November 3. The original Appeals Chamber ruling had been Judge McDonald's last as a member of the court. The remaining members of the chamber were the same, but McDonald's successor, Judge Claude Jorda of France, had, like me, come from a civil-law background.

As I recall, the skies over Arusha were gloomy on the morning of the hearing. I remember feeling anticipation during the ride to the tribunal and thinking about the churchyard, about those five thousand skulls arrayed upon the tabletops, about that bone crumbling under my shoe like a pretzel and the face of the survivor who told me he would rather have died. I remember feeling, in a tactile way, the meaning of the words "miscarriage of justice."

The room was filled with attorneys and photographers anxious to get their pictures of the courtroom just before the hearing began. (I remember Farrell showing up last with all of his binders and finding no seat at the prosecutor's table until after the photographs were all taken, when the ranking staff members, people who were trying to grab attention even though they were not going to argue the case, had to get up and leave.) The room seemed to glow with tension and an ominous sense that if our argument did not go well, Barayagwiza was going to walk and Rwanda was going to walk out. Then the judges entered. The room fell silent. After a few minutes of procedural housekeeping, Judge Jorda yielded me the floor.

I stood and positioned myself behind a wooden podium. In my opening words, I attempted to take the rhetorical high ground. I said that, by dismissing the case "with prejudice," the court had stripped me of my power to prosecute: "I was surprised because, at the time that I assumed my new role, I was told that the prosecutor is completely independent, completely at liberty to prosecute. . . . [W]ell, the Appeals Chamber in its decision prohibited me from prosecuting Barayagwiza, a prohibition never before seen.

"I realized that, in the system I worked in for over twenty years, a civil-law system, such a possibility did not exist, such a sanction could not be meted out. Let us be clear. The release, a release based upon procedural defects, procedural failures, is provided for. But the fact of prohibiting a prosecutor from further prosecution . . . I have never seen that." With this, I was bringing to the forefront the realities of the civil-law system, realities Judge Jorda and other members of the panel who came from the civil-law system would grasp. I was counting on them to empathize with my sense of shock and that this might restore the balance between the common-law and civil-law approaches and lead them to overturn the appeal decision and allow us to bring Barayagwiza to justice.

Then I argued that new facts provided sufficient grounds for them to overturn the ruling of November 3. I denied that the prosecutor had committed any error that had violated the rights of the accused. And then I stressed that allowing Barayagwiza to go free would be a travesty. "I am the only person here to represent the victims, and on their behalf I pray you to allow the prosecutor to institute proceedings against Barayagwiza, who has committed crimes against humanity, who has committed genocide, and his indictment has been confirmed. He is no longer a suspect. He is an accused. This accused is responsible for the death of over 800,000 people in Rwanda, and the evidence is there. Irrefutable, incontrovertible, he is guilty. . . . In the name of justice, genuine justice, for the sake of the victims, for the sake of the survivors. There are victims who are still suffering for what happened in Rwanda. I will always continue to say that Barayagwiza is guilty."

In hindsight, these words might have gone over the line. I allowed my zeal on behalf of the victims to carry my rhetoric beyond the bounds required by the presumption of innocence and respect for the tribunal's own independence. Perhaps I should have stressed that Barayagwiza had only been *indicted* for genocide and crimes against humanity, that he stood *accused* of these crimes. I anticipated that the judges would comment upon my rhetorical flourish. But I decided that if I did not stress as starkly as possible the fact that, if the Appeals Chamber did not overturn the previous ruling and allowed a guilty man, a man who had participated in genocide at the wholesale level, to go free, then it would be on their conscience and not mine. I was almost daring the judges not to overturn the ruling of November 3. And I chose to trust Farrell to roll back my hyperbole in his detailed legal arguments and presentation of the new facts.

"What are the rights of the victims?" I asked rhetorically, conjuring up images of the churchyard. I recalled the unburied dead, the rows of skulls, the bones scattered across the church floor, the face of the despairing survivor. I told the chamber that the dead in that church had the right to be identified, but never would be. I told them the people who had survived these dead had the right to see autopsy results and to know how their kin had perished. I told them that the dead had the right to a humane burial. And I told them that all of these rights had been violated. "The victims, most of them do not have a name," I said. "We do not even know their names; therefore nobody talks about them. . . . If Barayagwiza cannot be tried, that will amount to a violation of the rights of the victims. . . . Let us also talk about the survivors, because we don't only have victims, corpses, but there are also survivors who are involved in these proceedings, who are interested in these proceedings. . . .

"Genocide is the most serious crime known to humanity. [The] penalty for genocide is life imprisonment. . . . What I, as prosecutor, cannot accept is, where it is stated in the judgment that no account is taken of the seriousness of the crimes. In other words, crimes against humanity and genocide are not duly considered because it is felt that three months of delay between the transfer to Arusha and the initial appearance—that is a lot more serious than genocide and crimes against humanity . . . [a]nd as a result to say that three months was clearly a violation resulting in a refusal to allow a trial on [the] merits, and in view of the fact that there was a decision that that delay was unduly lengthy. And here again I do not understand."

Then, in the most controversial of my assertions, I dragged the real world into the rarified air of the courtroom. I focused upon the political ramifications the ruling would have if it were allowed to stand: "It was the prosecutor [who] had no visa to travel to Rwanda. It was the prosecutor who was unable to go to her office in Kigali. It was the prosecutor who could not be received by the Rwandan authorities.

"In November after your decision, there was no cooperation, no collaboration with the Office of the Prosecutor. In other words, justice, as dispensed by this tribunal, was paralyzed." I noted that one trial had to be adjourned because the Kigali government did not allow sixteen witnesses to leave Rwanda and make the Arusha-bound flight aboard the Beechcraft to appear before the tribunal. "Whether we want it or not, we must come to terms with the fact that our ability to continue with our prosecution and investigations depend[s] on the government of Rwanda. That is the reality we face. What is the reality? Either Barayagwiza can be tried by this tribunal . . . or . . . for Barayagwiza to be handed over to the state of Rwanda to his natural judge. . . .

"Otherwise, I'm afraid, as we say in Italian, *possiamo chiudere la baracca.*" We could put the key in the lock, shut the tribunal's doors, and open up the prison doors and let him go free. "In that case, the Rwandan government will not be involved in any manner. . . ."

My point was hardly subtle: "[T]he law must not be interpreted beyond what is reasonable, so that it not become harmful. . . . I am asking you . . . not to allow . . . Barayagwiza . . . to decide on the fate of this tribunal. It is my hope that he will not be the one to decide the fate of the tribunal after he . . . decided on the genocide in Rwanda in 1994."

Sometimes my instincts lead me astray. Sometimes I misread my audience. But in this instance, I trusted them completely. I trusted that I was appealing to the right ears. I knew that if we failed, there would be hell to pay. Farrell and my other team members did not let me down. They presented the finely honed legal arguments. They presented new facts showing that Barayagwiza had known of the nature of the charges against him during his detention in Cameroon and that the tribunal's former registrar, Andronico Adede, had undertaken multiple efforts to obtain Barayagwiza's transfer from Cameroon to Arusha. Officials in Cameroon had, in March 1997, submitted to Cameroon's president, Paul Biya, a draft decree ordering Barayagwiza's surrender to the Rwanda tribunal; that Cameroon had issued no decree until October 1997, apparently because of the political sensitivity of the issue at a time of presidential elections. President Biya signed the decree only after the United States government asserted pressure upon him to do so. David Scheffer's affidavit stated that he contacted the United States ambassador in Cameroon's capital, Yaounde, and requested that the ambassador intervene with President Biya. Shortly thereafter, Biya issued a decree authorizing Barayagwiza's transfer. We argued that this diplomatic intervention, and its role in securing Barayagwiza's transfer, demonstrated that Cameroon had resisted the tribunal's judicial orders.

Barayagwiza's defense counsel, Carmelle Marchessault, argued that the Appeals Chamber had no jurisdiction to review the ruling of November 3, because such an appeal would apply only to a convicted person, and not someone like Barayagwiza, who had neither been tried nor convicted. She also pointed out that the prosecutor had submitted no new facts to justify the reversal of the decision. The prosecutor general of Rwanda, Gerard Gahima, appearing as an *amicus curiae* to the Appeals Chamber, openly threatened that the Kigali government would no longer cooperate with the tribunal if the Appeals Chamber did not rescind its original ruling.

On March 31, 2000, the Appeals Chamber rendered its decision in our favor. I had been right in assuming that the judges would not take kindly to tough rhetoric and argumentation that introduced unpleasant facts of life into judicial proceedings. "Prosecutor Ms. Carla Del Ponte made a statement regarding the reaction of the government of Rwanda to the Decision. She stated that: 'The government of Rwanda reacted very seriously in a tough manner to the decision of November 3, 1999.' Later, the Attorney General of Rwanda appearing as representative of the Rwandan Government, in his submissions as 'amicus curiae' to the Appeals Chamber, openly threatened the non-cooperation of the peoples of Rwanda with the Tribunal if faced with an unfavourable Decision by the Appeals Chamber on the Motion for Review. The Appeals Chamber wishes to stress that the Tribunal is an independent body, whose decisions are based solely on justice and law. If its decision in any case should be followed by non-cooperation, that consequence would be a matter for the Security Council.

"The Chamber notes also that, during the hearing on her Motion for Review, the Prosecutor based her arguments on the alleged guilt of [Barayagwiza], and stated she was prepared to demonstrate this before the Chamber. The forcefulness with which she expressed her position compels us to reaffirm that it is for the Trial Chamber to adjudicate on the guilt of an accused, in accordance with the fundamental principle of the presumption of innocence."

These raps on the knuckles were expected, and easily withstood. I am, after all, a survivor of Catholic boarding schools. The media trial began on October 23, 2000, with Barayagwiza, in a suit and glasses, among the defendants. In an unprecedented decision issued on December 3, 2003, the Trial Chamber found all three of the accused media *génocidaires* guilty as charged. Nahimana and Ngeze were sentenced to life imprisonment. The court noted that Barayagwiza, who was found guilty of genocide, conspiracy to commit genocide, direct and public incitement to commit genocide, as well as extermination and persecution, would also have been sentenced to life imprisonment. But, in consideration of the Appeal Chamber's decision of March 31, 2000, the judges reduced his sentence to thirty-five years minus time served. He can be held behind bars until 2030. By then, he will be eighty years old.

4

CONFRONTING BELGRADE
2000 AND 2001

Years of pent-up frustration, years of accumulated anger and desperation and personal trauma, the years of Slobodan Milošević's misrule drove crowds of demonstrators into Belgrade's streets in early October 2000. Thousands of voices jeered and shouted. Flames and smoke rose from the city's center. And it was exhilarating to think that, finally, a political upheaval was about to create conditions for the Yugoslavia tribunal to arrest and bring to trial the man who, together with the late Franjo Tudjman of Croatia, had engineered Yugoslavia's bloody dismemberment. Slobodan Milošević had suffered an election defeat but was refusing to relinquish power. On October 5, 2000, agitated crowds besieged Yugoslavia's parliament building, the majestic domed structure where representatives of the South Slavs had for decades after World War I struggled and failed to legislate a framework to manage their multinational state.

On that autumn day, my advisers and I were in Macedonia, stopping over at the Hotel Alexander Palace in Skopje in preparation for a foray into Kosovo. In the sitting room of my suite, we watched live televised images of the events in Belgrade. We heard determined shouts calling for Milošević to step down. We saw clouds of tear gas. We saw a mob storm the parliament building. Smoke began pouring from windows. Demonstrators seized the state radio and television station. Riot police stood by. And everyone knew that, somewhere in Dedinje, the hilltop neighborhood inhabited by Serbia's political elite, the man the *New York Times* had dubbed the "butcher of the Balkans," the man who was the object of an international criminal warrant, could feel his power waning. It was my job to decide how the Office of the Prosecutor could best take advantage of this sea change and bring Milošević and a significant number of his generals, intelligence chiefs, and political protégés to answer before the law for what they had done in Croatia, Bosnia and Herzegovina, and Kosovo.

The next morning, October 6, a Ukrainian helicopter reeking of aviation fuel shuttled us to Priština, where we met with Bernard Kouchner, who was still leading the United Nations Mission in Kosovo (UNMIK). Tribunal investigators and forensic anthropologists had spent more than a year in Kosovo exhuming corpses that Milošević's troops had dumped into mass graves. By now, I told Kouchner, the tribunal had amassed sufficient crime-scene and mass-grave evidence for its prosecutions. It was time that UNMIK or some other organization took over the humanitarian mission of excavating the region's other grave sites. I also told Kouchner that the Office of the Prosecutor understood that UNMIK and the NATO military force in Kosovo, known as KFOR, were alarmed by speculation in the local press that the tribunal had issued secret indictments against a number of leaders of the Kosovo Albanian militia, the Kosovo Liberation Army (KLA). I told him that tribunal investigators were probing allegations of KLA war crimes against Serbs, Roma, and others, because my mandate required mounting these inquiries. I was happy to take on this task, despite the fact that I was facing criticism for pandering to the Serbs and complicating the efforts of UNMIK and KFOR to carry out their missions. I was determined to present indictments against KLA leaders implicated in criminal activity. The tribunal's credibility depended upon this. A war crimes tribunal that tries the accused from only one side of a given conflict is dispensing only a victor's justice. This alone cannot help end the culture of impunity.

Our Ukrainian helicopter touched down again in Skopje later on the afternoon of October 6. By this time, the decorative columns, cornices, and lintels that feigned to support Milošević's rule had come crashing down. He now appeared to control only a few die-hard commanders in the army, his police commando units, and the palace guard surrounding his residence in Dedinje. My mobile telephone sounded. United States Secretary of State Madeleine Albright was on the line from Washington. The events in Belgrade, she said, had delighted the United States. Milošević was about to plummet into an abyss. But the situation was delicate. She warned me that this was not the time to call for Milošević's arrest. She asked me to maintain a low profile. Belgrade's streets would be awash in blood if Milošević attempted to escape by sending in tanks, water cannon, and riot police with clubs, gas, and automatic weapons to quell the demonstrators. I told Albright that I agreed with her assessment of the situation. I agreed to refrain from seeking Milošević's transfer. But, I added, "Once the danger has passed, the strategy will change."

Later the same evening, Milošević conceded defeat. He congratulated his successor, Vojislav Koštunica, Yugoslavia's new president. My advisers and I were en route from Skopje to The Hague when we received word of the handover. I remember feeling certain that, sooner or later, Milošević would fall into our hands. I knew that a tortuous transfer process lay ahead, and I chose to ignore signs suggesting that Milošević had stepped down only after Koštunica had promised that he would not surrender Milošević to The Hague. Just a day earlier, Koštunica had announced on television that he opposed the "extradition" of Milošević and considered the tribunal to be a political creation of the United States, and not a truly international institution. This was a harbinger of things to come from Koštunica. But several months would pass before I took heed of my advisers' warnings about him, before I learned that, for Koštunica, it was as if there had been no ethnic cleansing in Bosnia, as if there had been no massacre at Srebrenica, as if hundreds of thousands of Kosovo's Albanians had not been forced across the borders into Albania and Macedonia in 1999. His worldview was, and remains, rigid, dogmatic, and nationalistic.

Upon our return to The Hague, I raised the Milošević prosecution to the top of my agenda. In April 1999, my predecessor, Louise Arbour, had hurriedly signed an indictment against Milošević predicated only upon crimes committed in Kosovo. The charges were primarily rooted in the fact that Milošević, as Yugoslavia's head of state and its military's commander-in-chief, had criminal responsibility for the acts of the police and army troops in Kosovo who were carrying out ethnic cleansing even as Arbour's team, led by Nancy Patterson and Clint Williamson, were drafting the indictment. Arbour worked fast. She sought to demonstrate that the tribunal—and therefore international criminal justice institutions in general—had the capacity to respond effectively in real time to a pressing emergency on the ground. She also wanted to preempt any possibility that the United States and the other NATO member states, who were desperate to find a way to declare victory and halt the bombing of Serbia and Montenegro, would do a deal and exempt Milošević from prosecution in exchange for withdrawal of Serbian forces from Kosovo. Arbour's indictment had been a groundbreaking event. It was my task to direct the effort to follow up.

Investigators in the Office of the Prosecutor had worked for years to amass witness statements and other credible evidence of the crimes committed in Croatia and in Bosnia and Herzegovina. Soon after my arrival at the Yugoslavia tribunal in the autumn of 1999, I had ordered efforts to collect additional evidence on Milošević's complicity in the crimes committed in Kosovo and to complete indictments linking Milošević to crimes committed in Croatia and in Bosnia and Herzegovina. In the summer of 2000, I had called upon the lawyers and investigators working on the Milošević indictments to deliver progress reports. To my surprise, I learned that the investigations had produced scant progress in linking the crimes in Croatia and Bosnia with Milošević and other high-ranking military and police officials in Belgrade. The best evidence in the tribunal's possession flowed from a few lower-ranking witnesses of dubious credibility and from transcripts of radio and telephone conversations between members of the Serbian military and police that the Bosnian military and intelligence service had intercepted during the war. At that time, the tribunal had not recruited a single, credible high- or mid-level insider witness against Milošević, even for Kosovo, and many of the intercept transcripts had gone unread. The fact that Milošević's Serbia was off limits to tribunal investigators hampered this aspect of the effort to build a case against him—this I understood. The powers in Belgrade were still refusing to surrender documents, minutes of meetings, or any other evidence showing responsibility for crimes. These factors, however, did not change the reality that instructions I had issued in 1999 were, to a significant degree, ignored. My management style is to set goals and to let my staff, in this case the senior trial attorneys and, especially, the investigators, achieve them as they see fit. Perhaps I should have been more hands on; perhaps I should have required frequent progress reports and applied pressure more often. I could not accept that evidence of linkages between Belgrade and the violence in Croatia and Bosnia did not exist. The press reporting on the war had shown clearly that Milošević bore significant responsibility for the crimes in those two republics. This deserved a better investigation effort, and I was determined to have it undertaken.

My deputy at the time, Graham Blewitt, and the chief of investigations, John Ralston, had not considered Milošević a priority even after my instructions in the autumn of 1999. In their judgment, my office had neither sufficient time nor resources to chase evidence on Milošević when it was so unlikely he would ever end up in The Hague. They explained that other cases had taken priority. So I again ordered them to focus immediately on preparing the Croatia and Bosnia indictments against Milošević. I told them to redeploy investigators to this effort, because Milošević was coming our way and we had to be prepared. Even after his fall from power, however, it was difficult for many staff members to comprehend the urgency of the work on the Croatia and Bosnia indictments. I had to motivate my subordinates who did not share my optimism. It seemed that only my closest advisers were ready to follow. But I think the others—Blewitt, Ralston, leaders of the investigation teams, and personnel further down the chain—did not believe me. And as time passed, I became more convinced that I could not trust some of them to execute my instructions. The time was approaching when I would have to make personnel changes as well as fundamental adjustments to how the Office of the Prosecutor functioned.

On the evening of October 10, 2000, I received a new appeal from Secretary of State Albright. "Please," she asked, "continue to refrain for the moment from speaking to the press about Milošević and the necessity of transferring him to the tribunal." I agreed once again. I did not yet have new material to support an amended indictment for the crimes committed in Kosovo, and I still had no interlocutor in Belgrade willing to respect a summons for Milošević's arrest. I trusted that the international community would not remain silent for long on the question of Milošević's transfer to The Hague. There were, however, portents of a softening toward Serbia after Milošević's fall from power. Just a day earlier, the European Union had decided to ease economic sanctions upon the Federal Republic of Yugoslavia. The European Union had made its announcement without mentioning the necessity for Yugoslavia to arrest Milošević and the other accused and transfer them to the tribunal for trial. Within a few weeks, General Ratko Mladić would feel comfortable enough about his security in the post-Milošević Serbia to attend a wedding in Belgrade and pose for a picture.

Secretary of State Albright also specifically asked me to remain silent about Radovan Karadžić. She had good reasons. Never before, it seems, were we so close to capturing him. The French government had informed me that Karadžić was now in Belgrade. The United States, Great Britain, and France had succeeded in identifying an apartment where he was hiding in the Serbian capital. They had even spotted his wife, Ljiljana, making visits. On the same day, Hubert Védrine, the foreign minister of France, had flown to Belgrade and congratulated Koštunica on his victory over Milošević. Védrine's visit was more than just a bilateral backslapping session, however, because at that time France was holding the presidency of the European Union. Upon his return to Paris on October 11, I called Védrine. He refused to speak about a possible arrest of Karadžić. Perhaps he had not received word that the French intelligence service had spotted Karadžić in Belgrade, and, over an open telephone line, I did not point this out; I thought it fair, however, to assume Védrine knew what his own intelligence service was reporting. For his part, Védrine informed me that Koštunica did not consider the tribunal a priority. Koštunica's main aim, Védrine explained, was to establish political control of the country's institutions. After this, Védrine said, Koštunica wanted Milošević to be tried in Belgrade for crimes committed in Serbia. Koštunica had asked Védrine that this question not be raised until after parliamentary elections scheduled for December.

I had agreed to respect the calls by the United States and the European Union for silence regarding Milošević. But my prosecutorial instincts told me to press immediately and aggressively to make Milošević the first head of state ever to answer charges before an international tribunal. We were pressuring Croatia to comply with its obligations under the United Nations charter to cooperate with the tribunal. We were pressuring Bosnia to do the same. Why should we not pressure Belgrade to act? I certainly did not want to be seen making concessions to Serbia. My advisers, Jean-Jacques Joris and Florence Hartmann, insisted that I show patience. "Don't be a killjoy now," Joris said. "Don't be seen to be rocking the boat. Use this time to build your case." They began urging me to set deadlines for the investigation teams to complete the indictments of Milošević for the crimes committed in Croatia and in Bosnia and Herzegovina. For the time being, I held off from setting a target date for my teams, but I did agree to remain quiet. Winter had descended over Europe. The December parliamentary elections in Serbia were likely to bring to power men and women willing to surrender Milošević. And I was still nurturing the illusion that Koštunica might play a constructive role. It was up to me and my immediate advisers to prepare ourselves to implement a strategy in January 2001.

The parliamentary elections on December 23 confirmed the victory of Serbia's opposition over Milošević's Socialists and the ultranationalist Radical Party. The next prime minister of the Republic of Serbia would be Zoran Djindjić, a spry, pragmatic, German-educated man, who understood the positive effects the tribunal could have for his homeland and its people. In Djindjić and his supporters, I would have people in positions of authority in Belgrade who might respond to the tribunal's requests for assistance. Now was the time to seek the arrest and transfer of the twenty-four fugitives on Serb territory and to draw up indictments of more leaders. Now was the time to press for cooperation in obtaining interviews with hundreds of witnesses and access to thousands of documents. The time had come to travel to Belgrade.

I knew my reception would be chilly. Milošević had for years used his newspapers and radio and television stations to spread propaganda about the tribunal. They had asserted that the tribunal was a component of a Western conspiracy bent upon destroying the Serbs. And it was easy for Serbs to believe these messages. People in any state that comes under attack—as Serbia had come under attack from NATO, as the United States had come under attack from al Qaeda, and, later, as Iraq had come under attack from the United States and its allies—are susceptible to the siren call of official propaganda to defend the homeland and national honor, no matter how brutal or beneficent the regime. My first visit to Belgrade was a venture whose risks were worth assuming despite the many unknowns. The new authorities did not exercise full control over the security apparatus, whose ranks still harbored cadre loyal to Milošević. Tribunal investigators were carrying out inquiries into the same middle-rank security officers whom we were entrusting with our security, and these suspects were still under the influence of high-ranking individuals who were right to assume that we would soon prominently display their names atop fresh indictments.

Tuesday, January 23. Graffiti shouted "Karla *puttana*" from a billboard looming beside the highway from Belgrade's airport to the center of the city. A kilometer later, another billboard, "Carla is a whore." Our plane had touched down about half an hour before noon. Black limousines awaited us on the tarmac. I had never before visited the city, which was still, in early 2001, capital of both the Republic of Serbia and the Federal Republic of Yugoslavia. My first impressions confirmed how correct my compatriot, the architect Le Corbusier, had been when he lamented that, of all the cities in the world situated in beautiful locations, Belgrade is the ugliest. There is a beaten-down grayness to the place; even newer buildings seem to look sad, like women aged by hardship long before their time. Looks, however, are deceiving when it comes to Belgrade. For a vibrant, defiant heart beats in this city; and defiance attracts me—to a point. The car covered another half a mile, and passed another billboard that read "Carla is a whore."

It was already mid-afternoon on January 24, when we entered an office inside one of Belgrade's crumbling-stucco buildings to meet two of Serbia's most defiant and courageous people, Nataša Kandić and Sonja Biserko. I was there to listen, for these women and their associates had done much more than the Serbian government or any other organization in Serbia to bring the tribunal evidence, and especially the statements of Serb victims. Biserko runs the Helsinki Committee for Human Rights, which championed protection of minority rights at a time when so many of Serbia's majority Serbs were rabid with nationalist hatred. Biserko stressed that our visit to Belgrade marked an important milestone. Recent surveys, she said, had indicated that about 36 percent of Serbia's people—a surprisingly high number, given the years of Milošević's propaganda—favored cooperation with the tribunal. It was obviously important to increase this support, as the tribunal was now in the local news every day. I had met Kandić in Priština during my first visit to Kosovo in November 1999. Since then, I had developed only deeper trust in her judgment. Kandić cautioned me not to have any illusions about Koštunica. She pressed me to work to extend the tribunal's mandate beyond the armed conflict in Kosovo, so we could investigate and prosecute crimes by the Kosovo Liberation Army against Serbs and others, including alarming reports that the KLA had kidnapped Serbs under NATO's nose.

The darkest shades of gray fell like drizzle over Belgrade when my team and I arrived a few hours later at the *Palata Federacije*—the Palace of the Federation—to meet with Vojislav Koštunica. This sprawling office building was once the heart of the bureaucracy Tito had engineered to manage postwar Yugoslavia. The heart, however, was no longer beating. An eerie silence filled the building's hallways and chambers. And here, with a chilling, nervous handshake, was Koštunica, a man who, when adoring crowds were calling upon him to claim his rightful election victory, balked for a time because, he explained, everything had to be "constitutional." Koštunica is a nationalist in the Karadžić mold who wears the fleece of a postcommunist reformer. To this day Koštunica is angling for parts of Bosnia to be assumed into the Serbian state; and, about Kosovo, he is obdurate: it is Serbia and nothing else. From Koštunica, there is little admission that Serbs ever did anything untoward during the wars, and much insistence that Serbs were, are, and always will be victims and only victims. A few days before my visit, Koštunica had written in a newspaper that forcing Serbia to honor its international obligations and hand Milošević over would strengthen extreme right-wing political parties and that, if someone wanted to destabilize Yugoslavia, he should behave like Carla Del Ponte. This cry-wolf argument had gained currency in some capitals. I knew that Secretary of State Albright had based her warnings during Milošević's downfall upon prudent risk assessments. But Koštunica's effort to ward me off was aimed at achieving something different. It was an attempt to exploit the political situation for as long as possible to avoid taking hard decisions required under international law. This was an attempt to conceal the full reality of the wrongdoing of his fellow Serb nationalists in order to preserve the Serb nationalism that structured Koštunica's worldview and political fortunes.

After Nataša Kandić's warnings, I presumed that my face-to-face with Koštunica would not be pleasant. I paid him the customary diplomatic obeisance. I congratulated him on his election victory and expressed hope that the situation in Yugoslavia would improve for its people. The point of my visit, I told Koštunica, was to express my desire to help him and the other new leaders and members of the government in the difficult task of initiating full cooperation with the tribunal. I pointed out that the United Nations Security Council had created the tribunal and that it was the Federal Republic of Yugoslavia's obligation, not its option, to cooperate. I asked Koštunica to outline his understanding of cooperation and how it might begin. I told him that my priorities in the Federal Republic of Yugoslavia included investigation of war crimes and crimes against humanity that the Albanian militia in Kosovo, the KLA, had committed in 1998, investigation of the Milošević government's financial misdeeds, the arrest and transfer of fugitives to The Hague, and access to Serb victims of war crimes in Croatia, Bosnia, and Kosovo. Each of these priorities, I said, offered Serbia and the Serbs many benefits.

Koštunica, despite the diplomatic English that clad his opinions, was as hidebound as my aides had warned. He began by passing the buck, saying that he could not provide complete responses to my inquiries about cooperation, because it was up to others in the government to elaborate the details of cooperation. He recognized that cooperation with the tribunal was an international obligation and said the new authorities accepted the necessity of cooperating with the tribunal. It was, he said, only a matter of when and how.

This was an attempt to erect the *muro di gomma*. It took only a few minutes for the real Koštunica to step out from behind it. He began griping about the tribunal, as if arguing with me was going to render the institution nonexistent. He claimed that the law governing the tribunal had been imperfectly conceived. He complained that the tribunal had amended its rules too often on its own authority—something it had the power and responsibility to do, especially as it tried to find its legs during its start-up phase. He complained about the tribunal's practice of issuing sealed indictments and about some of the arrests NATO had undertaken before my arrival in The Hague. The conflicts of the former Yugoslavia, he said, were too complicated for one ad hoc tribunal, even if it were to receive additional resources. He argued that a truth and reconciliation commission—something I consider a toothless entity that would collect accounts of the war but undertake no prosecutions—would be a more academic, systematic, and analytical approach to reconciliation.

Next, he explained that Yugoslavia's national assembly and government had to approve new laws on "extradition" and cooperation with the tribunal before the government could hand over any fugitives. It would be possible to exchange evidence with Yugoslav courts, he said, insisting that these courts would have the final word on concrete issues of cooperation and could try any crimes. He complained that the tribunal's indictments against some Bosnian Serbs had mentioned, as if it were a crime, the fact that they were members of the Serbian Democratic Party—the nationalist Serb party in Bosnia and Croatia, whose program clearly squared with Koštunica's thinking. (This was a gross misreading of the indictments.) He complained about the tribunal's unwillingness to investigate the NATO bombing and the use of depleted-uranium ammunition. He claimed that the NATO bombing had been entirely unjustified. He said my office was applying a standard of collective guilt against the Bosnian Serbs, pointing out that the tribunal had indicted almost all Republika Srpska leaders. These were the reasons, he asserted, that Serbs were viewing the tribunal in a negative light. He insisted that the tribunal not pretend to be a judge of history, as if he feared that adjudicated facts of what had happened in Croatia, Bosnia, and Kosovo would disturb his view of history, as if adjudicated facts would become obstacles to efforts by Serb nationalists to continue to propagate a view of history that presented Serbs as victims, and victims only.

I attempted to squeeze a word in edgewise. I told Koštunica that I was surprised at how ill informed he was about the tribunal and its authority. "If the president is ill informed," I said, "then what can one expect of the people?" Blewett and I tried our best to make clear to Koštunica the realities of the sealed indictments, the rules and procedures of the tribunal, the need to conceal the identities of some witnesses, the facts of the NATO bombing and the depleted-uranium issue, the realities of international obligations under Chapter VII of the United Nations charter, and other issues. Additional explanation, however, did not budge Koštunica. When asked why the Yugoslav authorities had not surrendered some accused Bosnian Serbs and Croatian Serbs—among them Karadžić, Mladić, and Milan Martić, the man alleged to have fired rockets indiscriminately into Croatia's capital city—he said that this question was not for him to answer, but for the government. After assurances that I had teams of investigators preparing indictments based on crimes committed against Serbs in Croatia, Bosnia, and Kosovo and that these teams needed the Yugoslav authorities' complete cooperation to gather evidence, he gave no positive reaction. It seemed that, for Koštunica, it was too dangerous to allow us to investigate crimes against Serbs, because this would mean allowing us to investigate crimes Serbs had committed.

Koštunica interrupted us time and again, accusing the tribunal of nurturing an anti-Serb bias, of being a political court, of serving the interests of NATO by indicting Serb leaders and acting in a political manner. I wondered, in all this, whether I was actually speaking with an expert on constitutional law. Instead of citing facts, he was basing his opinions on disinformation and regurgitating propaganda. Twenty minutes of his rhetoric was enough to exasperate me. I realized we would achieve nothing. "*Basta*," I thought. I stood up, reached for my handbag, and said, "Mr. President, I think we should end our conversation." I concluded this frustrating exercise by saying it was a very inauspicious beginning for cooperation. I said that, from my viewpoint, cooperation was not possible for the time being. I asked how long it would be before the new national assembly and government adopted the legislation to underpin cooperation. Of course, Koštunica and his advisors insisted that they were not saying "no" to cooperation, though they were certainly not saying "yes." They pointed out that they merely needed to remove the obstacles to cooperation and to create the means for cooperation through the necessary legislation, which were technical questions. In their view, such changes would require "a reasonable time," not years of parliamentary debate. I had nothing to say to the press after our meeting, because it had achieved nothing.

The sky was still gray over Belgrade when I awoke the next morning. The Sava River looked like cold lead. We encountered demonstrators shouting "Carla is a whore." We met with representatives of Serbs missing in Croatia and Kosovo. We held talks with various government ministers. Then, at about 3:30 that afternoon, we met Zoran Djindjić, soon to be Serbia's prime minister. "Milošević has finally lost," he exclaimed. "There is a huge need to bring those responsible for war crimes to justice. People need to see what happened."

"What a relief," I thought.

"We are still not in complete control," he cautioned. The police, the secret services, and the army were not fully responsive to the government. There was a need to purge the entire criminal justice and court system. "To begin with the tribunal would be disastrous," Djindjić said.

Nevertheless, Djindjić insisted that he would be able to begin cooperation with the tribunal in only two or three months. He assured me that Milošević would be in prison within a month and that Serbia might try him for war crimes as well. I asked Djindjić how cooperation might begin. He responded by dropping a bombshell. He alluded to secret reports he had received that Serb police forces, in their pains to destroy evidence of the killing of civilians in Kosovo, had shipped the bodies of some of their victims, including women and children, to Belgrade, and secretly buried them within the confines of the Yugoslav Army airfield at Batajnica, just outside the capital city. This revelation was stunning. The order for such a cover-up operation had to have originated high in the chain of command. It had to have involved the police. It definitely implicated the army. And it raised the question: Who were these dead men, women, and children? Where were they from? How were they killed? Who had killed them? Djindjić said the tribunal should start immediately by sending investigators to speak with Serbian police officers who knew of these cover-up operations. He said it would be beneficial to reveal this information to Serbia's people. He was waiting for the proper moment.

Djindjić expressed confidence that Serbia's parliament would adopt a law on cooperation with the tribunal even if the federal parliament, which was full of Milošević's supporters, did not. Blewitt and I explained aspects of the investigation into the KLA and the need for the United Nations Security Council to amend the tribunal's mandate in order to probe the abductions and killings that took place subsequent to June 1999. I then mentioned that tribunal investigators had managed to trace $2 billion from Yugoslavia and explained that we needed the government's assistance to complete our investigation into Milošević's finances. "Give me a billion," Djindjić laughed, "and you can have Milošević."

I told Djindjić that the Serbian government, the government he would soon control, should not tolerate indicted persons residing on the republic's territory. It should arrest or expel them, even to Bosnia. Mladić was in Belgrade, I told him, and we had brought with us the original of the indictment against him, the arrest warrant, and every other document he needed to take action. I gave him clear notice that the international community was monitoring the attitudes of the new Yugoslav and Serbian leaders toward the tribunal. Again, I pushed for our investigators to have access to victims and witnesses of KLA violence and intimidation: "It will be interesting to see your court files."

One of my aides, Anton Nikiforov, was carrying the indictments, more than ten of them, in a bulky briefcase when we walked into the office of Momčilo Grubač, Yugoslavia's federal minister of justice, later that day. Grubač said that the ministry would be coordinating work with the Yugoslavia tribunal and that a special governmental body for cooperation with the tribunal would soon be formed. After a few more minutes of small talk, Grubač accepted the documents, but said he would pass them on to the Republic of Serbia's Ministry of Justice for action, because it was Djindjić's republican government, not Koštunica's federal authorities, that was responsible for taking action on them. After we asked Grubač how it had been possible for the former regime to hand over two fugitives without implementing legislation, the minister replied, "Milošević never respected the law."

On our way home from Belgrade, Joris and I attended the World Economic Forum in Davos, Switzerland. Here was a chance to hobnob with Olivero Toscani, the photographer famous for his Benetton ads; Elie Wiesel, the Nobel Laureate who wrote so eloquently of the Holocaust; and Paulo Coelho, author of *The Alchemist* and other novels translated into Serbo-Croatian, who offered to provide the tribunal whatever support he could to explain to his readers in the former Yugoslavia how important it is to achieve reconciliation. I also recall that Israel's prime minister decided to go skiing, apparently for the first time, and how his bodyguards kept falling down. In between the laughter, it seemed, everyone on the slopes and in the reception halls was raving about Koštunica of Serbia, as if he had been the one to bring down Milošević. I heard all about Koštunica the visionary, Koštunica the moderate, Koštunica the man of peace. Carl Bildt, the Swedish political *wunderkind* who had cochaired a failed peace effort during the Bosnian war, was not the only one to chastise me and warn that my efforts would destabilize Yugoslavia. I thought we had shown enough understanding of Belgrade; diplomatic soft-pedaling was not going to help us apprehend men wanted for mass murder, and a Yugoslavia with accused mass murderers lurking within the government, the military, and the police would not enjoy stability. After all this praise of Koštunica, I almost sympathized with the antiglobalization demonstrators who were blocking the train line and the roads. I wanted to escape Davos and get home to Ticino. The only way down the mountain was by Swiss army helicopter. The weather was brutal. Wind gusts tossed the aircraft as if it were a golf ball. Snow was blowing horizontally. The pine forests and craggy limestone of the mountain walls closed in upon us from right and left. I glanced at Joris. "Look at this diplomat," I smirked. "He is afraid to smile." A few minutes later, however, the turbulence forced the pilot to steer beneath a set of high-voltage electricity lines. Our bodyguard made the sign of the cross. And I, too, stopped smiling.

We traveled from The Hague to Brussels a few weeks later to visit Lord Robinson of NATO and Javier Solana, the foreign minister of the European Commission. Thereafter, we worked on a daily basis with Solana's people to ensure that the new cuddly attitude toward Serbia would not lead the European Union to lift its demand that Belgrade demonstrate its willingness to cooperate with the tribunal. The arrival of the Bush administration in 2001 seemed to portend trouble for international justice. One of President George W. Bush's first acts would be to withdraw the signature President Bill Clinton had placed on the Rome Statute, rescinding, for the time being at least, the United States' commitment to the world's first permanent war crimes court, the International Criminal Court. Now Washington was preparing a campaign to cajole other states either to withdraw their signatures on the Rome treaty or sign bilateral agreements ostensibly to protect Americans from the International Criminal Court's clutches. Many people in Brussels were arguing that it was futile for the

European Union to continue to apply pressure upon Serbia if the United States was not going to do so. Why, they asked, should Europe make Serbia's relationship in the European Union conditional upon cooperation with the tribunal?

Thus, the prerequisite for European Union support was United States support. The tribunal, and especially the Office of the Prosecutor, had enjoyed the backing of Secretary of State Madeleine Albright. It was now critical that I forge strong ties with her successor, General Colin Powell, a Bush appointee who, thanks to his stature as the former top officer of the United States military, the commander of the joint chiefs of staff, would enjoy broad discretion on a wide range of questions, including, I hoped, issues related to war-crimes prosecutions. I happened to read in a newspaper that, on February 27, Secretary Powell was going to make his first trip to Brussels, to meet with NATO and the European Commission. I was desperate for a face-to-face with Powell before President Bush had time to appoint a new head of the State Department's office on war crimes, because I assumed that whomever Bush appointed would not be able to overcome the White House inner circle's apparent aversion to international war-crimes prosecutions. After finishing the newspaper article, I called the United States ambassador to the Netherlands, Cynthia Schneider, and requested a meeting with Powell during his visit to Brussels. "Carla," Ambassador Schneider answered, "the Secretary is going to be there for only one day. . . . It will be impossible." It was now a question of will. So we intrigued and had an appeal presented to Powell personally. An answer came back through the United States embassy in The Hague: "The Secretary will receive you in Brussels for exactly three and one-half minutes. Are you still interested?"

"Yes," I answered.

On the morning of the meeting, Dutch security men escorted my team and me to the Belgian border. I urged the driver on, faster, faster. We switched cars at the frontier. The Belgian driver reminded me of my automobile racing competition back at Hockenheim, so I settled back as Joris repeated to me what I had to say to Secretary Powell:

> You need to make economic assistance to Yugoslavia conditional upon Belgrade's beginning cooperation with the Tribunal. . . .

> I am not asking for Milošević's immediate transfer to The Hague. But procrastination is no longer acceptable. . . . Mladić is a case in point. . . .

> Democratization in Serbia is too important to be put at risk. . . . But the international community will best serve its purpose of fostering democracy by finding compelling incentives for Belgrade to cooperate with the tribunal. . . .

> There is no will to cooperate whatsoever on Koštunica's side. . . .

> If war crimes go unpunished, there can be no regional reconciliation, and no healing of Serbia's body politic. . . .

> People of Serbia are exhausted and want to live in a normal country, one that no longer serves as a safe haven for war criminals. . . . They tell us that, without pressure now, nothing will be done. . . .

We timed it out. Three minutes and forty-five seconds. "No, Carla," Joris said, "you have to say it in a different way." We drilled the pitch over and again. We subtracted seconds. "Remember," Joris insisted, "you want to have the last word."

In the end, I had my opportunity to look General Powell in the eyes and established the direct link I had been seeking. I made an end run around the State Department's war crimes bureaucrats. No chit-chat. No fluff. Three and a half minutes. And Powell understood. He always kept his word.

Prime Minister Zoran Djindjić contacted me just a few days later and requested a secret meeting. I suggested we see each other on March 3, 2001, in Lugano, where I would be spending the weekend. In the middle of that afternoon, Djindjić and his wife, Ružica, landed in Lugano. I met them at the city's airport and suggested that Ružica head to the shops in town to take advantage of some sales. After she drove off, Djindjić and I went to the office of the canton's police chief. Djindjić, energetic and enthusiastic, did not come all the way to Lugano to waste my time. We spoke for two and a half hours in German about Serbia and its problems.

Djindjić explained that Milošević was continuing to direct the Socialist Party of Serbia and attempting to survive politically by transforming himself into the head of the opposition. Djindjić understood that Milošević had to be neutralized. Djindjić explained that he needed the support of the United States and delivery by the end of the month of economic aid earmarked for Serbia. The United States had made this economic aid contingent upon cooperation with the tribunal. But Koštunica was delaying cooperation, Djindjić explained, and the adoption of a law on cooperation would not come soon enough to meet Washington's demands. Djindjić was seeking a way to overcome Koštunica's stalling tactics and accomplish something before the end of March to demonstrate his commitment, and Serbia's commitment, to cooperate with the tribunal. Djindjić informed me of attempts by Koštunica and his entourage, notably Ljiljana Nedeljković, his chief of staff, to overthrow him. Djindjić said he was under surveillance. His telephones were tapped. He said Koštunica had concluded some kind of an agreement with Milošević on the night before he had stepped down, but Djindjić did not know what this agreement entailed. When I asked Djindjić why he had agreed to back Koštunica's run for Yugoslavia's presidency in the first place, he answered that he could not have done otherwise, even though it was like making a Mephistophelian pact.

Then Djindjić surprised me. He had requested this meeting to propose a plan of action. His strategy would begin with the adoption of a law that would allow for the Serbian government to offer incentives for the tribunal's accused to surrender voluntarily, something Koštunica would not be able to block. Djindjić told me his government had already done a deal with one of the accused, Blagoje Simić, who was wanted on charges of persecution and deportation in connection with the ethnic cleansing of the northern Bosnian municipality of Bosanski Šamac. (The tribunal would eventually sentence Simić to fifteen years in prison.) The Serbian government had agreed to pay Simić's family 500 German marks each month in exchange for his voluntary surrender. I found, and still find, such payoffs revolting. Among our accused were men alleged to have massacred thousands of prisoners, and, beginning with the Simić surrender, families of accused killers and rapists started to receive payments while survivors of massacre victims, the women of Srebrenica, for example, not to mention tens of thousands of Serb refugees who had lost their homes, had been left barely able to feed themselves. Despite the obvious inequity and immorality of this practice, it is legal. Serbia can give money to whomever it wishes. It was up to its government to bring the accused into custody and transfer them to the tribunal's jurisdiction. I was willing to accept the fruits of any legal means the governments used to lure our accused into custody.

Djindjić said he was trying to convince other indicted fugitives to give themselves up, but few were willing. Djindjić also wanted the tribunal to make public the indictments it had kept sealed in order to make arrests easier, especially in Bosnia where we notified only NATO that these secret indictments even existed. The practice of issuing sealed indictments, Djindjić explained, allowed the tribunal's detractors in Serbia to spread paranoia by saying every Serb who had gone to fight was a suspect.

Next, Djindjić spoke of the pending arrest of Slobodan Milošević. A new prosecutor general would be named and given responsibility to launch an investigation of high-level members of the Milošević regime. Milošević would be examined for several days for his implication in corruption, abuse of power, electoral fraud, and the attempted assassination of Vuk Drašković, a nationalist firebrand who despised Milošević as a communist. Djindjić explained: "Everything depends upon the evidence we are able to assemble before March 15, when we think to request Milošević's arrest. For sure, he will be arrested for other crimes that will be of interest to you. But he will make it difficult for us to hold him in detention for too long. I will deliver Milošević to The Hague, even if it means kidnapping him."

Djindjić also spoke about Ratko Mladić, who was still residing in Serbia and collecting a salary from the Yugoslav Army. Djindjić confirmed that it was impossible, for the moment, to arrest Mladić, because he enjoyed the army's protection. But, as with Milošević, Djindjić promised that he would take up this question in time and that an arrest of Mladić would probably take place on the border between Serbia and Bosnia and he would be handed over to the forces of NATO.

Djindjić understood exactly what he had to do. I had no need to repeat yet again the arguments I had been making for months. He assumed responsibility for Serbia's future. He knew that it was not a viable option to put Milošević on trial in Belgrade, where the court system was full of pro-Milošević judges. I had no doubts about the will of the Serbian prime minister, but could he fulfill his promises? In some ways, Djindjić reminded me of Giovanni Falcone. Each of them was a risk-taker; each knew no fear. Falcone, a judge, was working to impose law and order upon a land infested with organized crime whose leaders were sure they had a right to impunity, and Djindjić, a politician, was attempting to engineer compromises and survive in a treacherous political environment against leaders, and their executioners, who had assumed that they, too, were immune from criminal prosecution.

Three days after my meeting with Djindjić, I received a letter from the secretary-general of the United Nations, Kofi Annan. Word had gotten back to New York that I had asked the United States to continue making financial assistance to Yugoslavia contingent upon Belgrade's cooperation with the tribunal's efforts. Annan was critical of my methods to gain Milošević's transfer. The letter reads:

Dear Ms. Del Ponte,

My attention has been drawn to a number of statements that have appeared in the press over recent weeks and which have been attributed to you regarding the transfer of Mr. Milosevic to The Hague for trial before the International Tribunal for the Former Yugoslavia.

I fully recognize that, as Prosecutor of the International Tribunal, you have a direct and immediate interest in ensuring that warrants for the arrest of persons who have been indicted by the Tribunal and orders for their transfer to The Hague, are duly executed by the States to which they are addressed.

I recognize also that it accordingly falls within your competence to make public statements regarding the indictment of Mr. Milosevic and the discharge by the Federal Republic of Yugoslavia of its obligation to execute the warrant for his arrest and the order for his transfer to the International Tribunal.

At the same time, I note from recent reports in the press that you would appear now to have broadened the scope of your remarks and to have entered into the discussion of more general political issues, such as the granting and withholding by States and international organizations of economic assistance to the Federal Republic of Yugoslavia.

In view of the very sensitive situation prevailing within the Federal Republic of Yugoslavia and the delicate position in which Mr. Kostunica finds himself as the head of a multi-party coalition government, you may wish to give further thought to whether statements of such a kind are likely to prove productive or to promote the achievement of the goal that we all seek.

While naturally wishing to respect your independence as Prosecutor, I would accordingly encourage you in future to confine your interventions to matters that are more directly within the sphere of your lawful concern.

Yours sincerely,
Kofi A. Annan[1]

Whenever I receive a letter of this kind, whether it be from Kofi Annan or ministers of state governments, I simply ask myself whether I have broken any law. The answer, inevitably, is no. Did I exceed my authority? No. Did I behave within the bounds of my competence? Yes, I did. So I deposited this letter in my file and effectively ignored it, because this was political interference, and I would resign rather than accept this kind of interference in our work. I wondered who had complained to Annan. I also noted that Koštunica was not the head of government of a multiparty coalition; Koštunica was a popularly elected head of state. The leader of the government of a multiparty coalition, the man who was in a treacherous position, was Zoran Djindjić.

On March 20, Djindjić and I met again at Schiphol Airport near Amsterdam during a stopover on an official visit he was making to Washington. When I arrived at this sprawling airport with three terminals spreading out over hundreds of miles of reclaimed land that lie below sea level, the Dutch police informed me that they could not provide a private room for us to meet. Djindjić arrived with his bodyguards, and I stood there with mine and had to explain the situation. It was his suggestion to leave the security contingent behind and simply take a walk. (We were, after all, inside the concourse shopping mall and everyone there had, I hoped, passed through a metal detector.) So we set off alone, conversing in German as we meandered through the crowds of travelers and the duty-free stores. We stopped sometimes before displays, as if we were window-shopping. Perhaps we even stepped inside a shop or two.

Djindjić began by telling me that he had arranged for a new surrender: Milomir Stakić, the former mayor of the Bosnian town of Prijedor, whom the tribunal would eventually find guilty of murder and persecution and sentence to forty years behind bars. Djindjić said the Serbian authorities would transfer him to the NATO forces in Bosnia and Herzegovina, and NATO could arrange the transfer to The Hague.

Then Djindjić delivered the best news: "We are close to arresting Milošević, not only for fraud but for very grave crimes, too. We have a problem with the United States ultimatum. We do not want it to seem that we are acting under American pressure. So it might be better for us to arrest him during the first week of April instead of before March 31. We are closing in on him and his allies. If, after the elections in Montenegro, the federal government refuses to proceed with the law on cooperation, then we will act on the level of the Republic of Serbia. Koštunica will oppose it."

I reminded Djindjić that Mladić and Karadžić and the other accused were also important. "The French and the United States can help you," I said.

Djindjić replied with an update on possible arrests: Mladić was still a high-ranking officer of the Yugoslav Army and, like the other 1,800 Yugoslav Army officers who were serving in the Bosnian Serb Army, was still on the Yugoslav Army's payroll. General Nebojša Pavković, the Yugoslav Army's chief of staff, had agreed to put an end to this situation by the end of May. The Republic of Serbia and the Yugoslav Army would agree to this and Yugoslavia's federal government would likely oppose it. Mladić was not only still an active officer, he was also heavily protected, probably by more than twenty troops. "As for Mladić," Djindjić said, "we have not seen him for one week now. But this case will soon be ripe. We will arrest him and hand him over to [NATO's peacekeeping contingent in Bosnia]. Koštunica must not know about this, as he was already quite upset with Blagoje Simić's surrender. He knows Simić personally."

"Karadžić is hiding in Belgrade," I said. "I know that Karadžić has written to Koštunica asking for his assistance and protection but that Koštunica refused."

"Koštunica probably doesn't know that Karadžić is in Belgrade," Djindjić replied.

I pressed him further. I asked him whether he could hand over the three Serbs who had been indicted for war crimes that occurred during the attack on Vukovar in 1991.[2] "I'm ready to help you with the financial investigation," I said, "And I told you I would give you access to my files and we have just found money also in Singapore, $14 million. But cooperation must work both ways."

He responded: "One of the Vukovar three is retired, and we can start by approaching him. The other two are active officers in the Yugoslav Army. We must first speak with the army and have them start investigating them. They are protected for the time being." He said the atmosphere in Belgrade was difficult. There had been an outbreak of Albanian unrest in Macedonia, Kosovo, and southern Serbia, which had made it increasingly difficult to discuss the subject of war crimes with the army.

Djindjić then brought up the names of men who were accused with Milošević of having committed war crimes linked with the ethnic cleansing in Kosovo. He mentioned Serbia's former president, Milan Milutinović, and its former deputy prime minister, Nikola Šainović: "Milutinović is very close to surrendering. But the case of Šainović is more difficult. He was Milošević's key person for all logistic and financial questions in Croatia and in Bosnia. He was involved in all operational matters. He is a good case for you. He was Milošević's Eichmann, and he is not popular in Serbia. But the timing is delicate."

After our walk around the Schipol Airport, Djindjić flew on to Washington. Since January 2001, the major powers had been demanding that Belgrade cooperate fully with the tribunal. The results, however, had been meager. Djindjić knew that his country had not persuaded Washington of its willingness to fulfill its obligations. Secretary Powell was not convinced. Thanks in large part to lobbying efforts by Nina Bang-Jensen and her associates at the Coalition for International Justice, Stefanie Frease and Edgar Chen, the United States Congress had demanded that Belgrade demonstrate concretely its willingness to cooperate fully with the tribunal before it would authorize financial assistance the Bush administration had earmarked for Yugoslavia. The decision on "certification"—whereby the State Department determined whether a country was or was not fulfilling prerequisites for receiving financial aid—fell that year on March 31. The United States was demanding the detention of Slobodan Milošević, the arrest and transfer of at least one accused by March 31, access to archives, and the adoption of a law governing cooperation with the tribunal. In all, there were eleven conditions. Djindjić was far from satisfying them.

In the days before the United States decision on whether to certify, I sent Joris to Washington to establish contact with members of the new, Republican administration as well as with members of Congress and others. Joris made it clear during his stay in Washington that, of course, I did not want to interfere in any way with the ongoing decision-making on certification, which was solely a concern of the administration and Congress. But Joris also made several crucial points during his meetings with senior officials of the Department of State, the National Security Council, and the Department of Defense, as well as with members of the Senate and House of Representatives. He mentioned encouraging signals from the Belgrade government, including the transfer of Stakić to The Hague, assurances given about a "coordinated" expulsion of one other accused before adoption of a law on cooperation, and the fact that the tribunal received approval to reestablish a presence in Belgrade.

Caution, however, was still in order. "Comprehensive and firm policy commitment to cooperation on behalf of Yugoslavia as a state is lacking," Joris told these officials and elected representatives in meeting after meeting. "The impression arises that each step of cooperation must be negotiated with Belgrade—as if this were some kind of a bazaar." For example, he explained that the Serbs promised piecemeal cooperation in exchange for investigation of the Albanians for crimes in Kosovo or for reopening the investigation of the NATO bombing. "The international community must call the bluff of the Serb leadership," Joris advised, otherwise Milošević would never be transferred or effectively tried, Mladić would continue to receive his salary from the Yugoslav Army instead of being handed over, Karadžić would run free, and the tribunal would become farcical. "All the positive steps—such as they are—have occurred thanks to the March 31 deadline," Joris said. "Without consistent pressure from outside, the Federal Republic of Yugoslavia's government will drag its feet."

"Koštunica remains a serious obstacle," Joris told them. "He even put out a negative statement on the arrest of Stakić and has a negative influence on parliamentary discussion of the draft law on cooperation. . . . Cooperation should be nonnegotiable and cannot be defined by the Federal Republic of Yugoslavia according to its preferences." Joris reminded the Americans of another key deadline in June, a donors conference at which the United States, the European Union and its member states, and others would make commitments on aid to Yugoslavia. "If the United States maintains a firm line on conditionality, the European Union will eventually strengthen its stance." Joris reported back to me that Bush administration officials emphasized their commitment to the tribunal and stressed that they would continue to make United States support to the Federal Republic of Yugoslavia, including support at the June donors conference, conditional upon cooperation with the tribunal.

On Tuesday, March 29, I was in Macedonia, near the end of another four-day tour of the Balkans. Djindjić called me on my mobile telephone and said he was sending his chief adviser, Vladimir Popović, whom everyone called "Beba," with an important message. Popović arrived early that evening at the Hotel Alexander Palace in Skopje. The message was succinct and highly sensitive. Serbia's probe into Milošević's corruption and abuse of power had begun just a few weeks earlier, but a judge magistrate had already determined that there was sufficient evidence to order a hearing. "Milošević had not responded to the judge's order," Popović told me. "He will be arrested. . . . Tomorrow we will launch the operation." He left immediately. No dinner. No coffee. No cigarettes. No *muro di gomma.*

"Finally," I thought.

The next day, in the late afternoon of Thursday, March 30, Serbian police officers surrounded the villa that Milošević and his family were occupying in Dedinje, protected night and day by members of his personal guard. Gunfire erupted, then petered out. A standoff ensued. Djindjić later told me that Koštunica knew in advance of the arrest operation but chose to depart for a summit in Geneva, where French president Jacques Chirac asked him whether Milošević's arrest was imminent and Koštunica denied it. Returning to Belgrade on Saturday evening, Koštunica tried in vain to intervene before acceding to the arrest in exchange for an agreement that Milošević not be handed over to The Hague. For his part, Milošević imposed this same condition before he surrendered before dawn on April 1, 2001. At 4:45 a.m., Milošević crossed through the gates of the central prison in Belgrade escorted by Serbian special-forces troops. In the end, Djindjić had acquiesced to Milošević's demand that he not be transferred to The Hague. Djindjić, however, soon assured me that this agreement, so useful for ending a standoff, would not affect what was to come. The double-cross was on. Milošević found himself locked in a prison cell. Djindjić had kept his promise to take him into custody. Serbia reacted well to the news of Milošević's arrest. Only a few diehards demonstrated their support for their former head of state. The rest of the population seemed relieved. This convinced the Americans and Europeans that the next phase—transfer to The Hague—would not destabilize the country. Nevertheless, Koštunica and his camp accused me at every turn of imperiling Serbia's "democratization process."

Securing Milošević's transfer to The Hague was no simpler than obtaining his arrest. We were concerned that international support for the tribunal would wane now that Milošević was behind bars. The United States had rewarded Belgrade for the arrest, but Koštunica and many more Belgrade politicians were still dragging their feet on cooperation with the tribunal. The political situation in Serbia was fragile. Montenegro was angling for independence. Pro-Milošević forces remained within the police and military and the Belgrade underworld. It was uncertain how long the Serbian authorities could detain Milošević in custody, or whether they could put him on trial. I feared that the process might take two years. And the tribunal did not have this kind of time to wait.

The head of the tribunal's Registry, Hans Holthuis, traveled to Belgrade to serve the indictment and other documents on Milošević and to press the authorities to hand him over. This effort yielded nothing. Milošević refused to accept the documents or to surrender himself to the tribunal's custody. We concluded that another new international deadline was necessary to pressure Belgrade to hand him over. At the same time, I tried again to push my staff to have the indictments for Croatia and for Bosnia and Herzegovina ready before Milošević's transfer. I warned my people that he would arrive before the end of the year—though I do not remember why I mentioned this time frame—and I gave the teams until the end of September 2001 to produce the indictments. It was still April. Five months.

The tribunal had opened a new office in Belgrade, directly across a narrow sidestreet from a residence of the army's chief of staff, General Pavković, one of our key suspects. Now our investigators were able to launch fieldwork in Serbia. But Koštunica's supporters and the right wing in Yugoslavia's federal assembly and in Serbia's parliament were fighting to delay passage of a proposed law on cooperation that would allow for the transfer of fugitives and access to archives and key documents, including the minutes and transcripts of government bodies whose very existence was a secret. Then, thankfully, the United States announced that it would not participate in the June donors conference unless Belgrade began to cooperate with the tribunal. This was the work of Colin Powell, among others, and it presented us with a window of opportunity to turn to the European Union countries to increase the pressure on Belgrade to honor its obligations.

On May Day 2001, *Le Monde* published an interview in which I demanded that Serbia transfer Milošević and the other accused immediately and that the international community—read "France," for I was speaking to *Le Monde*—assert additional pressure upon Belgrade to do so. The interview set the stage for a meeting I had the next day in Paris at the Quai d'Orsay with Foreign Minister Hubert Védrine and Defense Minister Alain Richard. Both of them were angry. Védrine, the host of Koštunica's coming out before European Union leaders, was condescending. He insisted that Milošević be tried in Belgrade before a local court, and was saying so publicly. "France has a mission to bring Yugoslavia back into the community of European nations, into the family of European nations," Védrine said. "In so doing, France has to keep a perspective that is much broader and farsighted than the little patch of the international Tribunal. . . . I, as a minister of France, have a vision of the future. And you have your little tasks you have to fulfill, your shortsighted limited thing." The two ministers, Richard no more courteously, insisted that Europe in general did not want to impose a deadline upon Belgrade for an international trial against Milošević because they thought such pressure might destabilize the country. This position was a reiteration of Koštunica's cry-wolf line, and it irritated me. Europe should have stood up in the early 1990s and dealt with the causes that were fueling the Yugoslavia violence, and it had failed time and again by not insisting on resolute action, by allowing the lack of will to triumph.

A week later, I traveled to Washington and met with Secretary of State Powell. I had to convince him that the United States had to continue to play a proactive role in pressuring Belgrade to cooperate with the tribunal. This was not the moment to backtrack. This was not the moment to speak of local courts trying the likes of Milošević, because everyone, perhaps even Koštunica, understood that Belgrade had no capacity for such trials and that holding this out as an option was the equivalent of tacitly granting Milošević immunity. Without conditionality, the Serb nationalists who were obstructing the work of the tribunal could play a waiting game and win. The United States had to continue to make financial assistance conditional upon cooperation with the tribunal.

I explained to Secretary Powell that Djindjić had told me it might take two or three years to try Milošević in Serbia on evidence of abuse of power, political assassinations, and corruption. I told Powell that the tribunal would have three indictments ready by September and that I would submit a motion requesting the joinder of these indictments for a single trial. Once Milošević was convicted and sentenced in The Hague, the tribunal would be willing to transfer him back to Serbia to be tried for other crimes.

President Koštunica happened to be in Washington at the same time, clearly attempting to buy time and lobby for trying Milošević in Belgrade. According to one report we received, during a meeting at the Cato Institute, neoconservatives told Koštunica that the Bush administration would eventually dump the Yugoslavia tribunal, which it regarded as a Trojan horse of international justice. Perhaps this opinion of the tribunal and its work was the reason the director of the CIA, George Tenet, was not so tolerant of my frankness during this trip. But Colin Powell clearly commanded more leverage. During our meeting, I told the secretary of state: "It is important for Belgrade to announce when Milošević will be transferred, because there is no discussion possible on transfer. It is a legal obligation. You should ask Koštunica to give you a date tomorrow, when you meet him. The transfer of Milošević is a test case."

Powell spoke with no hesitation. "We will keep the pressure on," he assured me. "We will not be satisfied, nor will Congress be satisfied, until they cooperate." Powell reminded me that the United States had only conditionally certified Serbia's cooperation with the tribunal in March. "We have not seen much since April 1," he added, "and their progress is not acceptable." I do not know the exact words of the message the United States government passed to Vojislav Koštunica. But I do know that the message he received was clear and robust: If Belgrade did not cooperate with the tribunal, it would receive no more international financial aid.

During my meetings that day with Secretary of State Powell and other United States government officials, including George Tenet, Paul Wolfowitz at the Pentagon, and President Bush's national security adviser, Condoleezza Rice, I requested support for the creation of a coordinated effort to pursue and arrest the tribunal's fugitive accused. Before leaving Washington, I discussed this effort with the man I had wanted to direct it: NATO's former supreme allied commander Europe, General Wesley Clark, who was now a private citizen. I knew I was overreaching. But I also knew that General Clark, despite the problem with NATO's cooperation over the 1999 bombing, felt a deep commitment toward the tribunal and that he was a man who enjoyed the thrill of throwing himself into water from bridges, hotel balconies, and other high places and might just accept a thankless, quixotic mission like the one I had in mind. You never know.

During our conversation in Washington, General Clark declined my offer to come and hunt Karadžić and Mladić, just as Sergio de Caprio had declined. "I'd love to do it," Clark smiled. "But you can't afford me." I'm sure Clark was already contemplating a run for the White House in 2004. He agreed, however, to testify against Milošević and made good on his commitment. Then he warned me that Mladić and Karadžić had been protected by Russian agents during his tenure at NATO: "The Russians don't want you to succeed. They are with the Serb nationalists. They play a dirty game. They read all your mail. And they listen to all of your telephone conversations."

The next day, May 10, I was at the United Nations Headquarters in New York to meet with Secretary-General Kofi Annan. He was still displeased with my efforts to urge the United States and, especially, France, Germany, and the other the European Union countries to link their financial assistance to Yugoslavia with Belgrade's cooperation with the tribunal. Annan recalled the letter he had sent me in March concerning certain remarks I had made in the press. I told him the letter had disturbed me. Then Annan explained that he had wished to encourage me to reflect upon the fact that there were limits I had to observe in campaigning for Yugoslav cooperation with the tribunal. He said he did not consider it to be within the chief prosecutor's remit to enter into questions of economic assistance to Yugoslavia.

"You're not happy with European Union," Annan asserted. "You're not happy with the secretary-general. But all of us cannot be wrong. . . . You cannot tell the member states that they should suspend cooperation with Yugoslavia. This kind of conditionality is political. It's politics."

Also sitting in the room was Hans Corell, the United Nations undersecretary for legal affairs. He mentioned that there was a perception in "certain quarters"—Koštunica, I recalled once again, had been touring the neighborhood—that the Yugoslav tribunal was politicized and that if officials of the tribunal made remarks of a political nature that were not squarely within their competence, it made it more difficult for the secretary-general to defend the tribunal against such charges. "You cannot go around criticizing Koštunica," Corell instructed. "You are allowed to be forceful as a prosecutor. But do not undermine your position."

Annan continued: "I'm in touch with all member states, and they complain all the time."

I thought for a moment: "The obligation of states to cooperate with the tribunal had the force of law flowing from a Security Council resolution already on the books, and I served the Security Council and was supposed to enjoy complete independence." I responded by saying that engaging in a transparent discussion of Yugoslavia's failure to cooperate was one of those prerogatives that came with the independence of my position. It was within the scope of my authority. Pressure by certain states was the only way to coax the Federal Republic of Yugoslavia and other successor states of the former Yugoslavia to cooperate with the tribunal. How else was I going to achieve the tribunal's aims if I were to refrain from calling upon relevant governments to apply financial and diplomatic pressure? If I failed to make such an appeal, Milošević would likely die a free man in Serbia, and the tribunal would be a sham. The criticism I faced made it clear to me why the United Nations had gotten itself into such trouble in Srebrenica and so many other places by refraining from wielding the authority and political clout it had in its hands.

In Belgrade, the internal debate over adoption of the crucial law on cooperation with the tribunal had reached an impasse. The allies of Milošević, who enjoyed a majority in the federal parliament, opposed cooperation. The opposition was divided. Djindjić advised me that the transfer would take time, but I was impatient. The tribunal's time was running out. I wanted to visit Belgrade again to increase the pressure on Koštunica, Djindjić, and the others. But Djindjić dissuaded me from going. He warned me that a visit would strengthen resistance to cooperation. Now, I began to mistrust Djindjić's intentions. Instead of traveling myself, I sent Joris to ask Djindjić whether he had abandoned his plans to hand Milošević over.

This was the moment, on May 28, that Djindjić revealed to the world, and especially to Serbia, documentary evidence of the link between the Milošević regime in Belgrade, including the Yugoslav Army, and Serb crimes committed in Kosovo. The interior minister, Dušan Mihajlović, announced the discovery of eighty corpses of Albanians that the Serbian police—the police Milošević had controlled—transported in refrigerator trucks from Kosovo to the grounds of a military airfield just west of Belgrade. After this announcement, I believed Djindjić might have abandoned the tribunal and conceded to the idea of trying Milošević in Belgrade for fraud as well as crimes of war.

Joris asked Djindjić to set a firm date for Milošević's transfer to The Hague. "Serbia has no hidden agenda, such as a local indictment for war crimes, to avoid his transfer to The Hague," Djindjić replied. "Before the law is adopted, no transfer can be carried out. It would jeopardize the whole process. . . . After adoption of the draft law, which I expect next month, the transfers will resume, not only for those whose names are under seal. . . . But a commitment on Milošević's transfer, like a date, is difficult. Milošević is a special case. I can only say, for the moment anyway, that all parties are aware that adoption of the law is not sufficient and that concrete action must be taken before the donors conference."

This message reassured me only by half, but at the beginning of June I was very concerned. Djindjić had said, "Milošević must first answer in his own country for his actions. . . . It would be too simple to send him to The Hague like a package." I still thought the transfer of Milošević was destined to take place, but I questioned whether Djindjić would have the capacity to overcome the resistance in Serbia. A few days later, his government shocked Serbia again with even more revelations about the bodies of Kosovo Albanian civilians discovered in the mass grave hidden on the outskirts of Belgrade. For the first time, Milošević appeared before the eyes of the Serbs as a war criminal. For the first time, public opinion was being prepared to accept his transfer to The Hague. Djindjić never told me whether this was serendipitous or the result of a public-relations strategy.

It was by now mid-June. The Yugoslav parliament had still not voted on the proposed law on cooperation with the tribunal. The country was desperate for financial help. Washington was standing firm: no cooperation with the tribunal, no financial assistance. Djindjić tried to reassure me. "Carla, Milošević will soon be transferred. You must have confidence in me. I have a plan to get around the federal parliament. You will see. We will do what is necessary."

A few days later, I learned that Djindjić had asked the United States whether its forces in Bosnia could transfer Milošević to The Hague. Djindjić wanted to do everything he could to avoid a failure of the donors conference scheduled for June 29, because his country was in such dire need of financial support. He promised Washington he would transfer Milošević to the tribunal before the conference. Now, the man who for more than ten years had spilled so much blood and lit so many fires in the southeastern corner of Europe was set to be delivered only because of the robust stance taken by the United States and, more quietly, Great Britain, and, regrettably, not by the leading European Union countries on the continent, Germany and France. Continental Europe's absence from this process shocked me. Europe had marched at the forefront of the effort to collect signatures on the Rome Statute, which, by creating the International Criminal Court, might someday remove the impunity thugs in leadership positions all over the world were enjoying. Now, Milošević was practically on his way to become the first head of state ever to go on trial before an international tribunal on European soil, and Europe itself, especially France and Germany, had yet to lift even its pinky finger. This, I could not comprehend. And it was necessary to urge the Europeans to get into the game, if only to save face.

On Thursday June 21, a Swiss government airplane was waiting for us at Valkenburg, the Dutch military airport near The Hague, to fly us to Berlin. The Germans, like most Europeans, resented the pressure of the tribunal and Washington's decision to make its participation in the donors conference conditional upon the transfer of Milošević. They feared this might destabilize the new authorities in Belgrade. I tried to explain to them that the continuing presence of Milošević in Serbia was a destabilizing factor. And what stability would Serbia enjoy if some Belgrade judge ordered Milošević released from custody?

In Berlin, I urged Chancellor Gerhard Schroeder to intervene with Koštunica in Belgrade and oblige him to transfer Milošević to The Hague. The thrust of my argument was simple: In the end, Milošević would be transferred. The United States was applying sufficient pressure, and Djindjić would see to it. And if this happened while the Europeans were twiddling their thumbs on the sidelines, the United States would, once again, garner all the credit. "You are Europe," I told Schroeder. "And Milošević is Europe. Are you really going to let the United States do this alone with no contribution from you?"

"I will not stand for being a prosecutor for some tribunal that is only an alibi," I said, and by alibi I meant a farcical attempt by the international community to make itself feel better because it had stood by idly watching genocide unfold in Bosnia and Herzegovina. "If I don't get Karadžić and Mladić, I won't continue."

Schroeder listened politely. I could see in his face that the "European prestige" argument had struck a consonant chord.

"You are not the person for an alibi court," Chancellor Schroeder said. "We will tell Koštunica that he has to jump over his shadow, that he has to take a real step."

After our meeting, Schroeder took my advisers and me upstairs for a private tour of his official apartment overlooking the brilliant lights of the new, undivided Berlin that was the return address on the letter he would soon send Koštunica. Amid the small talk there, overlooking the skyline of Berlin, one of his aides laughed that members of their security detail had fallen into the habit of drifting up here on sunny summer days to peer down at the wife of the Swiss ambassador, who had taken to sunbathing topless on the embassy's rooftop.

On June 25, I spoke by telephone with Jacques Chirac. Here was a more difficult challenge. There are limits to the powers of the French president; and Védrine, in the Socialist government, was pro-Koštunica. "Don't allow the credit to accrue only to the Americans," I told Chirac, adding, "The Germans have agreed to intercede." Then I reminded Chirac— he hardly needed it—that Karadžić and Mladić, the masterminds of the Srebrenica massacre, were still at large. Srebrenica's fall to the Serbs in 1995 had shocked Chirac. Even before reports had spread that the Bosnian Serb Army were executing thousands of prisoners; Chirac had gone out of his way to call for retaking Srebrenica. Chirac also has a genuine concern for minorities. He agreed to make Koštunica listen to reason. So now, the two main continental powers positioned themselves behind the demand to try Slobodan Milošević in The Hague. For the first time in history, France and Germany had agreed to join their efforts to see to it that a head of state did not escape justice. The new authorities in Belgrade were under unprecedented pressure to transfer Milošević.

The feast day of Saint Vitus, or Vidovdan in the Serbo-Croatian language, is a day pregnant with symbolism for Serbs. On Vidovdan in 1389, an Ottoman army defeated Serbia's medieval king at the Battle of Kosovo. This was the day in 1914 when a teenaged Serb nationalist, Gavrilo Princip, assassinated Archduke Franz Ferdinand; the day in 1921 when a Serbian king, Aleksandar I, proclaimed the ill-fated constitution of the interwar Kingdom of Serbs, Croats, and Slovenes; the day in 1948 when Stalin announced the Soviet bloc's abrupt split with Tito's communist Yugoslavia; the day in 1989 when Slobodan Milošević rallied hundreds of thousands of Serbs gathered on the Kosovo battle site; and the day in 1990 when Franjo Tudjman angered Serbs everywhere by revealing draft amendments to the Constitution of Croatia that eliminated the status of that republic's Serbs as a constituent nation.

On the Thursday that was Vidovdan in 2001, the Serbian government turned over Slobodan Milošević to face trial. A little after seven in the evening, the Belgrade government made a public announcement that Milošević had been placed in the tribunal's custody. Kevin Curtis, a British police officer and former Olympic-caliber swimmer, was shown to an area behind a government building where three helicopters awaited. After a few minutes, Milošević arrived in a prison van. The sight of the helicopters appears to have alarmed him, as if he did not know that any deals he might have struck with Koštunica no longer held. He raised his arm. He asked the prison warden what was going on. And the warden explained that he would soon be departing for The Hague. Milošević protested. He complained that he did not recognize the tribunal's authority. He said he would not leave. The warden led him toward Curtis, who read Milošević his rights and formally placed him under arrest.

Milošević refused to acknowledge or accept any of the paperwork offered to him. A security officer searched Milošević's person. Then the security officer, Curtis, their translator, and Milošević boarded a helicopter that set off toward Bosnia and Herzegovina and the NATO military base outside the city of Tuzla. Against the engine scream and beating chopper blades, Milošević attempted to converse with Curtis in English. Stepping off the aircraft at Tuzla, he asked Curtis to put a handkerchief on the ground so he would not have to set foot on Bosnian soil; and he tried without success to exchange small talk with the soldiers who were guarding him. Sometime after ten o'clock, handcuffed and ordered to remain silent, he boarded a C-130 transport aircraft and flew to Eindhoven, a small airport east of Rotterdam. There he boarded a Dutch helicopter that flew him to a landing pad inside the penitentiary at Scheveningen, where he would reside until his dying day.

In the hours that followed, I received misdirected messages of congratulations from all over the world. The people who deserved most of the credit were Zoran Djindjić and others in Serbia who had, at significant personal risk, handed over the head of the mafia that had run so much of their country and its institutions. Colin Powell, too, deserved congratulations, for it was clearer than ever at the moment of Milošević's transfer that, without the decisive pressure from Washington, the tribunal would never have taken Milošević into its custody. One of the letters that touched me most was from Secretary-General Kofi Annan.

I heard later, from a source who was in a position to know, that another passenger had almost flown with Milošević to the Netherlands on that Thursday night. An official of the federal ministry of interior had proposed, to a friendly embassy, the arrest of Mladić. The source said that Mladić was in or around Belgrade and that, at the time, he did not enjoy heavy protection. The NATO base at Tuzla was apparently asked if it could handle another "package." It replied that planning would require four additional hours. Time ran out, and Mladić may never have known how close he had come to being arrested. This left Vojislav Koštunica to complain that only Milošević's transfer was illegal and unconstitutional. Mladić's absence would have no bearing on the donors conference that took place in Brussels on the day after Milošević's transfer. Yugoslavia received pledges totaling $1.3 billion.

The initial appearance in Case Number IT-99-37-I, *The Prosecutor v. Slobodan Milošević*, took only twelve minutes on the morning of the first Tuesday in July 2001. I donned my black, prosecutorial robe and walked into a courtroom whose gallery was filled with journalists and onlookers. Milošević, in person, did not square with the image of Milošević, the "Butcher of the Balkans" the media had presented. The full-bellied, supercilious figure who lumbered into the courtroom was no strong man, though he did look at me defiantly. Judge Richard May of Great Britain, who presided over the Trial Chamber, opened the hearing by noting that no defense counsel were present on Milošević's behalf and by advising him that the trial would be long and complex and that he would need defense counsel. Milošević answered in English with the now-famous words, "I consider this tribunal a false tribunal and the indictment a false indictment. It is illegal being not appointed by the UN General Assembly, so I have no need to appoint counsel to illegal organ."

When Judge May asked Milošević whether he wanted to exercise his right to hear the indictment read aloud in court, Milošević replied, "That's your problem." I had been pressing for the indictment to be read aloud, but it was not. This was an historic moment—the first trial of a head of state before an international tribunal. Reading the indictment aloud, live on television in Serbia, would have provided the public with a dramatic, definitive statement of the charges against the man who had once been their leader. It would have rendered homage to the people who had died or had suffered during his ethnic-cleansing campaign in Kosovo in 1999, and given the victims of his military campaigns in Croatia and Bosnia a foretaste of the indictments that the lawyers on my staff were preparing against him.

Asked to enter a plea, Milošević replied: "This trial's aim is to produce false justification for the war crimes of NATO committed in Yugoslavia. . . .

That is why this is a false tribunal . . . an illegitimate one." Judge May then entered a plea of not guilty on Milošević's behalf and adjourned the session.

Before the hearing, I had asked the registrar, Hans Holthuis, to arrange an opportunity for me to speak privately for a few minutes with Milošević. I was, for a while, making it a point to meet all of the tribunal's accused. Under the rules of procedure, the prosecutor has the right to ask the accused to cooperate with the investigation and submit to an interview in the presence of defense counsel. For security reasons, the face-to-face with Milošević took place in the courtroom after the judges and the other parties had left. A kind of card table found its way into the center of the room. I sat down on one side and waited before two or three security guards brought in Milošević. For a few moments, he glanced around, avoiding eye contact. I introduced myself as the chief prosecutor. I began explaining the rules of procedure and my right to request an interview. "I am ready to hold this interview immediately," I said, "because you have much to say."

Now Milošević looked me in the eyes. He tried to make a strong impression, to dominate the conversation, as if he were still a president, still a head of state, still a military commander-in-chief, still a *capo dei capi*, and was receiving me only because he could not avoid it. "I perfectly understand the rules of procedure," he said in English. "I can refuse to answer your questions." I sat up straight, stone faced. Then Milošević turned his head and began to speak in Serbian. He began repeating his canned denunciations of the tribunal and the Office of the Prosecutor. He became agitated. His voice resonated with anger. He looked vigorous, sharp, not at all infirm. But he was no longer the man whose charm and cool and self-confidence had deceived so many diplomats and political leaders. He seemed a spoiled child whose ranting quickly became annoying.

I had exercised my right to ask him to cooperate with the investigation. He had exercised his right to refuse. I did not have to listen to him any more. "Take him away," I told the security guards. They signaled Milošević to stand and escorted him from the room. We never shook hands. We would never again meet alone, face to face.

5

CONFRONTING THE TRIBUNAL BUREAUCRACY
2000 TO 2002

I had barely begun to grasp the intricacies of my mandate before it became apparent that time for the tribunals was running out. The United Nations and the states funding the tribunals were making it clear that they were not going to back them indefinitely. The prosecution teams were not achieving their goals fast enough, and, despite the successes of my predecessors, Richard Goldstone and Louise Arbour, in organizing the offices in The Hague and Arusha, some of the teams had been working for years and had expended untold resources without producing a confirmable indictment or even a definitive statement that they could not make a case. Correcting the problems required taking tough decisions. And for many good reasons, people who had worked at the tribunals far longer than I had, some of them competent and hard working, others not, were going to find themselves seeking jobs elsewhere or complaining to the United Nations bureaucracy in New York. The first personnel issue I encountered in Arusha arose with a lie I heard uttered during my first hearing before the Rwanda tribunal; but the operational problems at the Yugoslavia tribunal posed the more daunting challenge.

By the end of August 2000, it was clear that some investigation teams in The Hague were targeting the wrong suspects. Too many of our investigators were spending an inordinate amount of time and travel money exhuming bones, interviewing witnesses to individual criminal acts, and gathering evidence applicable only for cases against low-ranking individuals and not for indictments against the persons the Security Council had intended the tribunal to pursue: those persons most responsible for the crimes who had inhabited the higher political, military, and security echelons during the years Yugoslavia was at war. Moreover, many effective staff members had become frustrated in their efforts to gather the evidence linking the criminal activity with the leadership figures. After consultations with several trial attorneys and my political adviser, Jean-Jacques Joris, whom the Swiss foreign ministry in Berne had seconded to the Yugoslavia tribunal, I decided to shift the direction of the prosecution effort, and this required, among other things, shifting the locus of power in the management of investigations. Florence Hartmann, the former Belgrade correspondent for *Le Monde* who had become my spokesperson, also encouraged me to make this change.

The Office of the Prosecutor's operational model, applied for valid reasons during the Yugoslavia tribunal's formative years, had not evolved sufficiently by 2000 to fulfill the requirements of the tribunal's mandate in the limited time still available. This model was largely, though not exclusively, the creation of Deputy Prosecutor Graham Blewitt, an Australian. In an interview with a Dutch newspaper years later, Blewitt described his professional background and the experience he drew upon in designing the Yugoslavia tribunal's operations. Before coming to the tribunal, Blewitt had headed an Australian government prosecution unit charged with bringing to justice former Nazis and other persons in Australia suspected of having committed war crimes during World War II. The suspects were primarily concentration camp guards and other low-ranking individuals. After a decade or so in operation, the unit managed to produce only three court trials and no convictions.

In February 1994, U.N. Secretary-General Boutros Boutros-Ghali hired Blewitt to be deputy prosecutor at the Yugoslavia tribunal. The Security Council had yet to appoint Judge Goldstone as chief prosecutor, so Blewitt was left to deal with wresting a sufficient budget from New York and hiring sufficient staff. According to his interview, Blewitt faced a crisis soon after he arrived in The Hague. A potential witness had come forward and needed protection; Blewitt had insufficient resources to deal with the situation. The war in Bosnia was still generating headlines. The United Nations Headquarters in New York was pressing the tribunal to prove its worth by bringing charges against somebody as soon as possible. The tribunal's judges, already occupied for months drafting rules of procedure, were grumbling. So Blewitt wisely informed New York that he had to hire staff as quickly as possible and requested that the United Nations Secretariat waive its hiring formalities. Dispensation was granted. Blewitt brought the tribunal's corridors to life by hiring a significant number of prosecutors and investigators, including many from Australia, Scotland, England, and Canada who had backgrounds similar to his own. The United States soon seconded a few dozen lawyers and investigative staff to The Hague.

By happenstance, in February 1994, police officers in Germany arrested a Bosnian Serb named Duško Tadić, who had been a guard in a notorious concentration camp set up at a mining facility in Omarska, a village not far from the city of Banja Luka. Tadić's arrest and transfer to The Hague handed the Yugoslavia tribunal a defendant alleged to have taken part in gruesome criminal acts, including rape and sexual mutilation. But Tadić's transfer to the tribunal also attracted criticism. Despite the heinous nature of the charges filed against Tadić, some judges considered the case a nuisance. They and other staff members complained that it was a waste of scant resources to chase camp guards, policemen, and other military grunts like Tadić. They wanted indictments against leading politicians, generals, and spy chiefs. Blewitt disagreed. His opinion was that the tribunal needed a case to test its organizational integrity and procedures and to build up morale and momentum. And his assessment was sound. The tribunal desperately had to get a case through its untried system, and it had to build its body of evidence from the ground up and begin by working its way from the bottom to the top of the chain of command. Indicting heads of state, prime ministers, military commanders, political leaders, and secret police officials is a complex challenge, especially when the tribunal in question lacks sufficient resources. (At its beginnings, I heard, the Yugoslavia tribunal was hard pressed to subscribe to Belgrade newspapers.) I wonder whether the diplomats who drafted and voted for Security Council Resolution 827, the act that created the Yugoslavia tribunal in 1993, were aware of how complicated and labor-intensive presenting such indictments is or how difficult it would be to secure the arrest and transfer of the accused. When Tadić fell into the tribunal's hands, both Karadžić and Mladić were already facing indictments, and the NATO states had already demonstrated a reluctance to arrest the fugitives.

Problems with the investigative efforts into Milošević's participation in the crimes committed during the wars in Croatia and in Bosnia and Herzegovina gave rise to new complaints in my office during the autumn of 2000. I learned that some members of the investigation teams were doing little more than collecting and registering crime-scene evidence and stacking it on shelves and in refrigerated storage rooms rather than designing and building a sustainable leadership case. The managers of these investigations were reporting this evidence-collection process as progress. Some of the investigators were even rationalizing their own lack of knowledge and curiosity about Yugoslavia and its political and military leadership by saying that the less they knew, the better, because it allowed them to undertake their inquiries with an "open mind." Joris told me that one of my deputies had even explained to him that Milošević—the man who, together with Tudjman, had engineered the destruction of the old Yugoslavia—could not be indicted for crimes committed in Bosnia or Croatia because Bosnia and Croatia were countries separate from Serbia. Gradually, I began to sense that some staff members were blocking my access to accurate information about what was really going on in the investigative efforts for which I was ultimately responsible. And I noticed that some of them were not carrying out my instructions.

Soon, one of the trial attorneys from Great Britain, Andrew Cayley, confirmed to me much of what Joris and Hartmann had been saying. Another attorney, an American, Brenda Hollis, complained that investigators had collected stacks of documents but had failed to scan them into the tribunal's computer database so they could be electronically searched for key words and phrases and properly evaluated for their significance and evidentiary value. "How can we put together indictments without even knowing what is in the documents in our possession?" Hollis asked. The answer to her question was obvious. We could not. And we did not even know whether the mounds of documents in our custody held exculpatory evidence against the potential accused. For a prosecution effort, this was an information-management nightmare come to life. The first draft indictment to come across my desk had a meticulous presentation of crime-scene evidence, but a flimsy fact-base linking this evidence with the political leader the indictment was supposed to be targeting. I cannot remember how many draft indictments I sent back to the staff attorneys because the linkage evidence was inadequate. I cannot remember how many meetings I had with attorneys and investigators to explain this problem. I know Louise Arbour rejected many draft indictments for the same reason.

Sometime in late 2000, I had a chat in the hallway outside my office with Clint Williamson, one of the trial attorneys who had helped draft the Milošević indictment. Joris told me Williamson had shared with him some constructive criticism of the investigation efforts, and I invited Williamson to come to my office to discuss these issues in detail. After several abortive attempts, we sat down together in March 2001, a few weeks before he left the tribunal to take a position with the United Nations Mission in Kosovo. It was supposed to be a forty-five-minute conversation. Williamson ended up talking for two hours. He did not overstay his welcome.

"The best of intentions can be undermined if the concept of operations is faulty," Williamson warned me. The most significant problem with the Office of the Prosecutor, he said, is that it was geared to prosecute low-ranking perpetrators of war crimes. The Office of the Prosecutor was organized, he said, along the lines of the Australian war crimes unit, which had followed the model of criminal investigation and prosecution in Australia: The police have sole responsibility for investigating a crime; they turn over a finished case file to a lawyer who drafts an indictment; and, when a case is deemed ready for trial, a senior trial attorney carries the file into a courtroom to present the facts and arguments. In the different phases of this prosecution effort, each of the players has exclusive responsibility and expects no interference from the others. This operational model, however, proved to be inadequate for complex war crimes investigations of presidents, generals, and security chiefs far removed from the actual murders, rapes, and forced expulsions.

The Office of the Prosecutor had grown and evolved significantly since the days of Duško Tadić, and the structural framework that Goldstone and Arbour, along with Blewitt, had engineered was still sound. But the investigative engine attached to that framework sputtered and choked. In a memo I am drawing upon freely to describe this situation, Williamson pointed out that, since the Office of the Prosecutor's investigations section had enjoyed exclusive responsibility for the investigative process, the investigations section largely drove the work of the entire office. Decisions made by the investigation managers had largely predetermined which cases would be brought and in what form. The prosecuting attorneys had to suffer the results of the investigators' work. Since the chief prosecutor and deputy prosecutor were generally uninformed about the factual minutiae of the specific cases, they were left at the mercy of the chief of investigations and his immediate staff for guidance on strategy, policy, and operational matters. A rigid division of responsibilities among the prosecuting attorneys, investigators, and analysts meant that there was no effective check on the output of the investigations until it was too late in the process to remedy mistakes. When a case reached the courtroom, the lawyers too often had to struggle to adjust their arguments to fit evidence collected under misdirected theories they had no hand in fashioning. In essence, the investigators held all of the power over the investigations but no accountability for the results, and the prosecuting attorneys who had to try the cases had no power over investigations but all the accountability.

The challenge was to redirect the thrust of the investigations and make them more efficient in collecting evidence appropriate to leadership prosecutions. This would require shifting power from the investigators to the prosecuting attorneys and better engaging the military and area experts who spoke the local language, who knew the background to the conflict and the key perpetrators, and who understood the business of armies in wartime situations. Executing this shift required overcoming resistance from investigators who opposed the idea of prosecutors actively supervising cases and their work. I could not let them prevail. My experience in Switzerland had made it clear to me that a prosecutor responsible for taking a case into court must be able to guide an investigation from its inception and direct the police investigators. The prosecutor must engineer the indictment. The prosecutor must decide what needs investigating and when the evidence is sufficient to present an indictment to a judge for certification.

Most of the investigators were fully capable of contributing to the effort to prosecute leadership targets, so long as these investigators were willing to carry out specific instructions and submit to supervision by the prosecuting attorneys. But some of the investigators lacked the skills and experience to carry out the investigative tasks necessary to collect evidence on high-ranking individuals. As an international organization working under United Nations rules, the tribunal had to construct efficient teams of investigators and attorneys from around the world, people with different cultures, different languages, different values, people who relate to authority in different ways, people who might not be capable of questioning witnesses and suspects who hold or have held positions of authority. Personnel problems in such a situation are unavoidable. And this in no way means that investigators from Western countries were more or less competent than their counterparts from Asia or Africa or the lesser-developed countries.

In making their personnel decisions, the men managing the investigations division appear to have favored detectives with years of "street experience" in apprehending murderers, rapists, and other perpetrators of violent crimes. These detectives had skills in extracting information from witnesses about such crimes, and this was one reason the Office of the Prosecutor had become so proficient at developing crime-base evidence. But demanding investigators with these skills to build cases against members of a political or military hierarchy that functioned far from the scenes of the actual killing and raping proved in too many instances to be asking too much. Only a few investigators had education beyond secondary school. Only a scant number could utter a word of the Serbo-Croatian language, not to mention Albanian. Few could write effective English or French, even when English or French, the tribunal's official languages, were their native tongues. As a result, investigators were churning out stacks of witness statements and too many of them were proving to be worthless for prosecuting high-level perpetrators. I cannot even cite an example, because the information so many of them contained was so off target that it slid through my brain into nothingness. Once I identify a crime-base witness, I do not need to know his or her whole life story—like those of the poor divorcees I interviewed so long ago in Lugano. I need facts pertinent to the crime, facts that lead to evidence linking a political leader, a general, or a secret police chief. I found that we were conducting trials with two hundred witnesses, and 150 of them were for the crime base.

The detrimental impact of investigators lacking background knowledge about the wars in Yugoslavia was most apparent when they were assigned to interview potential insider witnesses: persons in a position to provide crucial, high-grade information about political and military decision making, because they had witnessed events at close proximity to the decision makers. Gradually, I began to hear credible stories about how some investigators had demonstrated ineptitude with sensitive-source witnesses like diplomats, internal-security officials, and politicians and about how the investigation managers in the Office of the Prosecutor had failed to recognize the damage such botched encounters were doing to the institution's credibility.

I learned, for example, of two attempts to interview the former chief of Croatia's secret police, Josip Manolić. This elderly man had the potential to be an especially valuable witness against high-ranking Croats who had participated in the military campaign Tudjman had launched to partition the territory of Bosnia and Herzegovina for a Greater Croatia.

During the first attempt to interview Manolić in the mid-1990s, an investigator lashed out at him, accusing him of committing war crimes, as if Manolić, a man who had been a secret police operative for decades, were a common street punk and the investigator was trying to pressure him to rat out some neighborhood thug. "That's it," Manolić interrupted. Then he threw the investigators out. The next attempt to interview Manolić, in the late 1990s, involved two different investigators who knew next to nothing about the former Yugoslavia and not a syllable of his native language. Five minutes into the interview, Manolić mentioned something about the Yugoslav National Army's military-intelligence service, known locally as the *Kontraobaveštajna služba* (KOS). Anyone who has spent more than a month reading about the wars in the former Yugoslavia should have nightmares about the KOS. Nevertheless, these investigators asked Manolić to explain the acronym "KOS," because they did not know what it meant. Manolić said, "Why are you wasting my time here?" And he ended the interview. Imagine if a former head of the KGB had defected to the West during the Cold War and a CIA interviewer asked him to explain the letters "KGB." A professional intelligence officer like Manolić, someone who is coming forward voluntarily as a witness, will neither tolerate an investigator who is so ignorant nor entrust his future prospects as a living human being to this investigator or the institution he represents. The persons who finally convinced Manolić to testify were attorneys and analysts who spoke his language and knew the background. But it took until 2005, which meant that most of a decade had been lost. Would that Manolić were the only potential insider to have suffered such encounters.

Problems were also prevalent among the attorneys. Relatively few of the lawyers hired in the Office of the Prosecutor were capable of overseeing complex investigations or processing mountains of raw information in the local language to distill a prosecutable case. Fewer still had invested the time or effort to understand the global issues or to seek assistance from analysts or other area specialists, and the shallowness of many draft indictments reflected this. Williamson and others warned me that qualified people in the office had become frustrated and were finding work elsewhere. The personnel recruitment process was still not yielding individuals with the skills the office required: knowledgeable political and military analysts, persons with backgrounds in intelligence work or in organized-crime investigations. There was a tendency among personnel of the Office of the Prosecutor to form opinions about the overall Yugoslav conflict based upon what witnesses from one particular village, one region, or one side were telling them. As a result, many staff members were incapable of assessing the relative importance of particular incidents, documents, and targets in terms of how they fit into the overall context of the wars. They were also susceptible to manipulation by interested parties, because they lacked criteria for assessing the witnesses' credibility or the plausibility of the accounts they provided.

Finally, the managers below me were doing nothing effective to correct these deficiencies. And they were certainly not reporting anything negative. Instead of hiring better-qualified persons or encouraging persons in the office to educate themselves, there seemed to be a bias against people with education and in favor of people who exhibited "street savvy." Individual investigative teams were left to create and implement their own strategies. Management had been incapable of seeking consistency or in ensuring the sustainability of resulting indictments because, on too many occasions, it had been reliant upon representations made to them by investigative team members who had lost perspective and advanced cases that were not sustainable in court. Lack of effective guidance from above made the tribunal's results dependent upon the quality of the investigative teams. The idea of prioritizing resources based upon the relative importance of the cases was missing; as a result, resources were misdirected into relatively meaningless cases, while significant cases were delayed or ignored. The way in which prosecutions were brought reinforced the perception that the tribunal was a political puppet, reducing the institution's credibility in the former Yugoslavia and making it more difficult to bring the region "peace through justice."

Thus, the Office of the Prosecutor's capacity to pursue complex leadership investigations was diminishing at a time when—thanks to political changes in Croatia and Serbia—there was increasing potential for investigating and indicting those leaders most responsible for the crimes committed during the wars. The Office of the Prosecutor had fewer and fewer people capable of seeing to it that the cases being produced would withstand scrutiny and be sustained in court.

My staff members and I discussed, among other things, forming a support staff of individuals who were experienced in all aspects of complex investigations and prosecutions and who would have meaningful input from area specialists. We discussed developing a strategy to ensure that all investigations were conducted with clear objectives and within the framework set down by the responsible attorneys. We discussed establishing a threshold level of crimes and perpetrators for the investigators and lawyers to pursue and to apply this threshold level to all sides involved in the conflicts. (Thus, instead of working up from the bottom of a command structure, we would work, as much as possible, from the top down.) We discussed deploying investigators to take simple statements and collect physical evidence, but not to allow the investigators to control the strategy-making process. We discussed hiring investigators who had been engaged in organized-crime cases and other complex investigations and who were capable of working with documents. We discussed requiring a review process with input from lawyers and analysts before submission of an indictment.

After considering these and other proposals, I gave the senior trial attorneys supervisory authority over all investigations, making one senior trial attorney responsible for investigating and constructing each new case. I took steps to increase the number of attorneys, and especially the number of senior trial attorneys, in order to meet the increased load of leadership cases we anticipated. I informed New York that we were fully capable of evaluating our own people and wanted a system of internal promotion, and we succeeded in introducing a system of promoting our trial attorneys to senior trial attorney posts. One of the idiotic constraints we had had to contend with was a requirement that a senior trial attorney have fifteen years of experience. I had good trial attorneys who had half that much experience; so we changed this requirement, and I cannot say how many times I had to break through the *muro di gomma* of the United Nations Secretariat. Kofi Annan gave me significant support, but in some instances even his backing was not sufficient to prevail against the bureaucracy.

I also took greater control of case management. As I have said, my management style is to allow the senior trial attorneys to run their own cases. But from this time forward, I required them to inform me regularly about their investigations and preparations for trial. I relocated the senior trial attorneys to offices on my floor, so it would facilitate greater contact. They in turn met with me every morning and updated me on significant developments and received updates on activities and problems and what they might need from me in terms of support vis-à-vis national governments. Perhaps I should have walked the halls and visited the rooms of the investigative teams more often.

I neither demanded nor expected blind obedience. Attorneys are notoriously ego driven, and I, obviously, am not an exception. Sometimes the senior trial attorneys ignored my instructions and did what they thought best. I would, of course, become angry when I noticed what was going on. In some instances I let the matter drop, because the attorneys in question came back and convinced me that their position on a particular issue had been correct; in other instances, I was not shy about stating my objections and they were not shy about stating their points. It took until 2005 to get New York to allow us to create a new position to ensure consistency in the Office of the Prosecutor's approaches to its most thorny legal issues; Norman Farrell took up this job, and more than once over the years acted as an effective peacemaker. We also attempted to organize an effort to coordinate the various investigations in order to avoid duplication of work and enhance information-sharing.

The Office of the Prosecutor hired more military analysts and area researchers to serve the senior trial attorneys. We also hired more nationals from the successor countries of the former Yugoslavia, more Serbs, Croats, Bosnians, and Albanians, who had intimate knowledge of the factors and individuals who had torn their country apart; this had been frowned upon earlier, apparently for security reasons. My spokesperson, Florence Hartmann, became my personal encyclopedia on all things Yugoslav and gave me support I needed when insisting that investigations pursue higher ranking individuals and link them with cross-border crimes, even when investigators came back from missions reporting they had not found any evidence. I also hired a new chief of investigations, Patrick Lopez-Terres, a French examining magistrate who had been a senior trial attorney. Soon, disaffected staff members began to complain about a French mafia in the office.

In many ways, the Rwanda tribunal's investigations of the *génocidaires* were more straightforward than the investigations at the Yugoslavia tribunal. But still there was trouble in Arusha. The Rwandan government was criticizing the tribunal for its slow work. Few genocide suspects had been successfully prosecuted. I responded to these critics by initiating changes in the Office of the Prosecutor.

The challenges I encountered in Arusha and Kigali lay in the realm of personnel and incompetence. As I mentioned above, these problems first became apparent to me during a hearing in Arusha in November 1999. A senior trial attorney stood before the court and uttered a statement that both he and I knew to be an untruth. The judges apparently took no notice. But I confronted him after the hearing: "What are you doing? Why did you lie to the court?"

"Oh, Madame Prosecutor, why do you worry yourself? It doesn't matter."

"No," I answered, hardly able to believe he was telling his new boss that lying in court was immaterial. "It does matter, and it is unacceptable."

I removed him from the trial team and deposited him in another section where he would never again have an opportunity to appear in a courtroom for any prosecution under my control. He did not complain because he managed to remain, for a time, in the legal adviser's section. Later, I dismissed him because he was not performing satisfactory work. He complained and eventually received a job in the Rwanda tribunal's Registry, where I was no longer responsible for him.

The Rwanda tribunal's chief of investigations resigned soon after I arrived, and I had to fill the position quickly. In late 1999 or early 2000, I learned that Louise Arbour had offered the chief of investigations position at the Rwanda tribunal to one of my old acquaintances from Switzerland, the former police chief of Geneva, Laurent Walpen, with whom I had once argued about the prosecution of one of his police officers on espionage charges. Walpen is a first-rate police chief and had managed security for the Swiss military. The United Nations hiring procedures had dragged on for so long that, by the time Arbour's offer arrived, Walpen had accepted another job. I was desperate to find someone whom I could trust to fill the chief of investigations post in Kigali. So, I did not hesitate to call upon him.

"*Bonjour*, Laurent," I said, "and how is the weather in Geneva?" He suspected something was afoot when I started making inane pleasantries, half in French, half in Italian. Then I made my pitch. "By the way, I heard you were candidate for chief of investigations and that you turned it down. Well, I'm going to need you in Kigali and want you there by May 1." Walpen clearly understood that he now had as much choice as I had had when Giovanni Falcone came to Lugano looking for someone to investigate the Mafia's bank accounts.

Kigali was home for Walpen on May 1. He soon reported back that the office was in need of reorganization after his predecessor's long absence. Investigators were going everywhere and looking into everything for some two thousand suspects, which suited the investigators fine, because they, like their counterparts at the Yugoslavia tribunal, were collecting fat *per diems* for their travel and thus had a financial interest in staying on the road as many days as possible. But there was no strategy, no centralized archive, no effective evidence-processing unit. A few ineffective investigators did not have their contracts renewed. And, following up on the work of my predecessors, Walpen decided to focus most of the investigations on three main areas: a government team responsible for building cases against members of Rwanda's Hutu government, a military team responsible for cases against members of the Hutu military, and a media team to take on persons suspected of inciting people to genocide through the radio and newspapers. In addition, Walpen added an evidence unit and organized a tracking team to seek out fugitives and witnesses. To each unit he assigned a criminal analyst and a specialist on crimes against women and children. This improved the level of technical efficiency.

I needed several more months to realize that the competence problem was more widespread. By comparison with the Office of the Prosecutor at the Yugoslavia tribunal, the prosecutor's office in Arusha was fully staffed with attorneys. But when I discussed legal and factual issues with them, I discovered the inexperience and incompetence of about a dozen of them, which was making the workload on the others all the more burdensome and was significantly detracting from the quality of cases the Office of the Prosecutor was presenting. I went to Arusha once every two months for three weeks at a time. I used these opportunities to sit in court and observe my lawyers perform, because, even then, I had no way of monitoring the proceedings on closed-circuit television in my office. I found some of the courtroom performances to be so lacking that I sensed a real possibility that serious killers were going to win acquittal. I remember one white Westerner, an academic, who had found his way onto a prosecution team having neither practical knowledge of procedure nor experience in the courtroom. Another attorney was clearly not meant for prosecutorial work because he lacked the capacity to grasp the essence of cases on which he was working. Some of the attorneys had trouble showing up for work. I remember asking to see one of them early one afternoon. The door to his office was open. The lights were on. But he did not return until the following day and did not have a compelling explanation. After this, I had to organize an attendance system to make sure the professionals were actually in their offices. At a news conference in Arusha on December 13, 2000, I announced that three or more prosecutors would soon be replaced.

If I made a decision that a staff member was incompetent, I would first call him or her into my office to discuss the matter. Some of them acknowledged that they were out of their depth and resigned immediately. I informed others that I would not be renewing their contracts, and this prompted them to resign voluntarily. Actual nonrenewal of persons who refused to resign, however, was more problematic because the United Nations bureaucracy imposes cumbersome procedures, including a complaint process that sometimes leads to investigations by officials from New York and entails wasting time I could not waste. If the investigators asked me to respond to questions in a written form, I had someone else in my office do it. Seven members of the prosecution team, six African lawyers and one Indian lawyer, eventually complained that race was a factor in my decisions. This was ridiculous.

I traveled to New York and reported that I would need to appoint new senior trial attorneys for the Rwanda prosecution effort if it was going to complete its mandate in a timely manner. Secretary-General Annan asked what prevented me from replacing them. I answered that the current appointment process was excessively slow and cumbersome. Annan listened, and then asked his legal affairs department to allow us to accelerate and simplify the appointment process for senior trial attorneys.

I later moved to replace Deputy Prosecutor Bernard Muna. I did not see a problem with him during my first visits to Arusha. After a year or so, however, I discovered that Muna was not following my instructions. I wanted him to reside in Arusha, where trial preparations needed supervision, and not in Kigali; it was enough to have Walpen, the chief of investigations, in Kigali. Muna, however, did not want to stay in Arusha. I learned that whenever I was in Arusha, he would be there happily going through the motions. But after I had left for The Hague, he would close the door and go back to business as usual in Kigali. Muna is a pleasant, intelligent man. He is also a natural politician. He socialized with the ministers of the Rwandan government and, working his contacts, did a good job at obtaining the Rwandan government's cooperation on a wide range of issues. But Muna had no experience as a prosecutor and insufficient knowledge of the cases to contribute much to what the trial attorneys were doing. These were significant problems. In November 2000, Muna protested my decision to remove trial attorneys on the grounds of incompetence. I told Muna, "Your problem is that you have a woman as a boss. Do you agree?" And he answered, "Yes."

At the beginning of April 2001, I announced that I would not be renewing Muna's contract. During a conversation in New York early that May, I told Kofi Annan that Muna and I had reached an agreement that he would not seek renewal of his contract when it expired in another week or so. I learned, however, that Muna had, behind my back, written to Annan seeking renewal of his contract. Under the Rwanda tribunal's statute, the deputy prosecutor was appointed by the secretary-general on the recommendation of the chief prosecutor, and I told Annan that I had lost confidence in Muna. Work began on identifying candidates to replace him. My goal was to find someone experienced and competent, and I wanted someone from Africa, because I thought it was important to have Africans doing the job. It took significantly longer than I anticipated.

As the effort went forward to solve the personnel problems, we had to prioritize our targets and choose which investigations to pursue and which to leave to the Rwandan criminal justice system for prosecution. We organized our investigation effort using the same model we were applying at the Yugoslavia tribunal. Each senior trial attorney received responsibility for a case, or a cluster of cases on a similar theme. The senior trial attorney was to be fully informed of the facts and have daily contact with his or her team of investigators in order to coordinate their activities. I saw to it that each investigative team would have one trial attorney in Kigali to act as a conduit to the senior trial attorney in Arusha responsible for the case. I asked the trial attorneys to go on missions with the investigators when there were especially important witnesses to interview or evidence to collect.

The prioritization of suspects was particularly painful, because in Rwanda, the numbers of victims each person was allegedly responsible for killing were astounding. When I first arrived, the investigators were gathering information on about two thousand individual *génocidaires*. We quickly reduced that number to two hundred—calling it our Gamma List—and we would soon have to cut this number significantly due to pressure from outside the tribunal.

Such is the absurdity of the reality you face working with the United Nations. Not because of any fault in the organization itself, but because of the political battering the organization must suffer. For example, you have a suspect who may have killed six thousand people, but you decide not to prosecute him because his rank is not high enough, and you wonder whether he would ever be tried, because the backlog of cases in Rwanda's criminal-justice system is so great it will require a century to process everyone.

The tribunal's prison facility in Arusha presented another absurdity. I visited it once, arriving at an hour when the prisoners were at classes. This was a surprise. A woman was teaching the prisoners English, and sitting there in neat rows was an entire class of school pupils, each an accused *génocidaire.* Word spread, "Madame Prosecutor is coming." And they all stood up like children welcoming the principal into the classroom. One at a time they shook my hand, so meek, so mild. One at a time they said, "So nice to meet you." I recognized some of their names. I recalled the gruesome killings and other crimes described in the indictments these accused were facing and found the incongruity surreal, and pathetic. These same accused *génocidaires* had also organized a kind of shadow Rwandan government and were meeting, there inside the prison, to organize their return to power.

On the wall of the prison kitchen I saw sheets of paper listing food items. "What are these?" I asked. Someone explained that they were individual menus for each detainee, because the prisoners were monitoring their calorie intake and having special meals prepared, as if they were on a trans-Atlantic flight on the old Swissair. One wanted low-fat milk, another whole milk; one wanted meat and no fish, another fish and no meat. Made-to-order meals for accused *génocidaires.*

This was beyond insipid. Life did not present a choice of chicken or beef to the surviving victims of the crimes these men—and one woman— had allegedly committed, or to the ordinary Rwandans, be they back in Rwanda or among the hundreds of thousands of refugees in neighboring countries. They did not have access to health care or AIDS medicines or English classes. The most courageous of our witnesses were living on next to nothing. I asked how we might be able to take better care of the people who had shown the courage to step forward to testify. I immediately met criticism. The defense lawyers even argued that I was attempting to corrupt witnesses.

The location of our office, in Arusha, a two-hour plane flight from Kigali, also presented problems. Several times I spoke with New York, with Kofi Annan and his legal advisers, about moving the entire Rwanda tribunal to Kigali. I know the Rwandan government was willing to accept the move. I even think the Registry and the judges were willing to go. But it was not possible. At first, the rationale had been security. But as the security threat waned, there was another issue. The Rwanda tribunal had become an economic asset for Tanzania. Arusha, before the tribunal's arrival, had not been much more than an oversized village; now it was becoming a bustling town. More than a thousand people worked at the tribunal in one capacity or another. Landlords were earning rents. Domestic servants and drivers were earning wages. Builders were constructing new houses. Entire families were moving into the town. I kept asking, however, to transfer the venue of certain trials to Kigali, and obtained funding from the European Union to support this. Even this failed to gain approval.

CONFRONTING BELGRADE
2002 AND 2003

I have no idea how much the world beyond the tribunal's walls knew or understood the challenges that arose during the preparation and presentation of the Milošević trial. The complexities of the case, Milošević's tactics and antics, clashes of personality and culture within the office, difficulties recruiting insider witnesses and securing the testimony of high-ranking foreign leaders and diplomats, the obstruction by Koštunica and his supporters—Milošević's protégés, the Yugoslav Army, and Serbia's police and intelligence organs—all of these tested the mettle of the team's members.

Foremost among the legal challenges was proving the link between Milošević and a multitude of criminal acts committed hundreds of miles from his office, including the act of genocide committed at Srebrenica and crimes associated with the siege of Sarajevo. These acts occurred in three different jurisdictions: the Republic of Croatia; the Republic of Bosnia and Herzegovina; and Kosovo, a region that was still *de jure* part of Serbia but had been outside the Belgrade government's control since July 1999. Collecting key linkage evidence and recruiting meaningful insider witnesses required investigative and diplomatic work in a fourth jurisdiction—Serbia, where men who had ordered and committed war crimes were still working in the state security and intelligence services, the Yugoslav Army, and the criminal networks with which these government organs interlocked. The initial indictment against Milošević, presented by Louise Arbour in the spring of 1999, covered only his responsibility for crimes committed in Kosovo; it was the autumn of 2001 before the Trial Chamber had confirmed indictments against him for the crimes committed in Croatia and in Bosnia and Herzegovina.

Dirk Ryneveld, an attorney from Canada, was already in charge of the Kosovo elements of the Milošević case. I placed Dermot Groome, a former prosecutor from New York City, in charge of the components of the case arising from the conflict in Bosnia and Herzegovina, and Hildegard Uertz-Retzlaff, an experienced German prosecutor, in charge of investigating links between Milošević and crimes committed during the conflict in Croatia in 1991. The lead investigators for the Milošević cases were Kevin Curtis for Kosovo, Bernie O'Donnell for Bosnia and Herzegovina, and John Cencich for Croatia.

The statute governing the Yugoslavia tribunal, which describes ways in which accused participate in crimes, also posed a problem. The statute's provisions worked well enough for the immediate perpetrators of the crimes, generally the lower-ranking trigger-pullers, but these provisions were not well suited to deal with the way senior political figures participated in the crimes. The statute did not, for example, include the crime of conspiracy, apart from conspiracy to commit genocide. The prosecution did not maintain that Milošević personally ordered individual atrocities; rather, the prosecution argued that he devised a broad criminal plan at the strategic level and implemented it using his authority, initially as president of Serbia and later as president of Yugoslavia. In October 2000, Groome and Cencich sent me a memo on how the Office of the Prosecutor might present cases against senior political figures more effectively. They recommended that I apply the doctrine of "common purpose," first employed after World War II at Nuremberg and Tokyo, in cases where multiple perpetrators worked in concert to achieve a goal that involved criminal acts. The Appeals Chamber in the Tadić case determined that this concept was implicit in the word "commit" in the Yugoslavia tribunal's statute and proposed that this legal principle be employed in cases in which senior political leaders participated in a criminal enterprise to commit international crimes. This later became known as the concept of "joint criminal enterprise" and proved an effective method of prosecuting high-level perpetrators who participated in crimes at a strategic level.

Lack of time exacerbated the pressure on the prosecution team. A period of seven months separated the evening of Milošević's departure to The Hague from the morning the trial opened, and, for a case as complicated as Milošević's, seven months provided only a narrow opening to recruit witnesses and pressure the authorities in Belgrade to provide critical documents and grant permission for investigators to interview sensitive witnesses and convince them to testify. The Trial Chamber also restricted the prosecution's time to present its case. Then, clearly in an effort to diminish even this limited time, Milošević announced that he would defend himself in court. The trial's presiding judge, Richard May, tried to convince Milošević that the case would involve voluminous documentary evidence and testimony, making it impossible for him to mount an effective defense alone. Milošević remained obdurate. The prosecution team filed a motion requesting the Trial Chamber to require that Milošević retain defense counsel or to appoint counsel to defend him. The Trial Chamber decided instead to allow Milošević to defend himself, and the prosecution team appealed, in vain. Milošević clearly knew he could not defend himself successfully in a legal sense, because he did not bother to mount a legal defense. He chose instead to present a political defense, to speak through the window to his nationalist constituents in Serbia, to exploit each trial day as an opportunity for political diatribe. It did not have to be this way. Switzerland and other jurisdictions recognize that an accused does not have the necessary distance to mount an objective defense and, if a defendant cannot provide himself or herself defense counsel, the court is required to appoint one. If, from the beginning, the judges had shown resolve in this regard and required defense counsel, Milošević would have had to concede and surely would have resorted to some fallback strategy to politicize the trial. In my opinion, the Trial Chamber's judges exaggerated concerns over a fair trial and created a situation that was unfair to everyone, including Milošević. The judges' lack of resolve was a weakness Milošević exploited immediately. And once Milošević had passed through this looking glass, other accused—notably Slobodan Praljak, a Croat general facing charges linked with Tudjman's attempt to partition Bosnia and Herzegovina; Momčilo Krajišnik, who was appealing a twenty-seven-year sentence for persecution, extermination, murder, deportation and other charges; and Vojislav Šešelj, a rabid Serb nationalist and ally of Milošević who allegedly led a notorious paramilitary unit— would also exploit it. (In the Šešelj case, the Trial Chamber would make the sound decision of not allowing him to defend himself; after Šešelj announced that he was going on a hunger strike, the Appeals Chamber would reverse this decision.)

Milošević's "defense" consumed inordinate amounts of courtroom time, not only because it enabled him to present a stream of irrelevant political and historical questions and arguments, but also because the prosecution found itself with no interlocutor, no objective counsel with whom to stipulate undisputed facts or sort out technical questions. This left it to the trial judges to handle mundane issues, including the minutiae of Milošević's treatment in the detention unit, in open court rather than outside. The Trial Chamber's decision to appoint three "friends of the court," or *amici curiae*, attorneys to provide a defense of sorts did not help matters. This was a bastardization of the customary practice that allows *amici curiae* to advise a court. The three attorneys—one each from the Netherlands, England, and Serbia—primarily provided support to Milošević.

As the days in trial dragged on, the court found itself placing new limits upon the prosecution to present its case. Milošević's high blood pressure would soon prompt the Trial Chamber to ease the burden upon him by limiting the number of hours of testimony each week and often by recessing the trial for days at a time. Later Milošević began disregarding the advice of his doctors and tampering with his medicines, which drove up his blood pressure and on occasion prompted his doctors to advise the judges that he would be temporarily unable to withstand the rigors of open court. The prosecution trial team noted that Milošević's blood pressure seemed to rise just before the appearance of witnesses who had the potential to be especially damaging.

Disagreement over the structure of the prosecution's case posed yet another challenge. The trial team's aim was to merge the three indictments against Milošević into a single process and present the case chronologically. If the trial team could begin by presenting evidence related to the war in Croatia during 1991 and proceed to the war Bosnia and Herzegovina from 1992 to 1995 and the crimes in Kosovo during 1998 and 1999, it could demonstrate how Milošević's criminal intent developed and evolved through changing circumstances. In late 2001, we filed a motion with the Trial Chamber to merge the three indictments. We had several reasons to seek this joinder, in addition to the desire to present the material chronologically. First, there is a basic principle in criminal law that an accused person has the right to be confronted immediately with all the crimes he or she is facing. Second, victims have a right to expect equal justice; for example, the victims of Bosnia and Herzegovina, where the most heinous crimes were committed, deserved treatment equal to that received by the victims in Kosovo and Croatia. Third, the team wanted to buy time, because the Kosovo element of the indictment was the least prepared of the three, simply because the available time for the investigative efforts, especially in Serbia itself, had been so limited. The Trial Chamber judges denied the prosecution's motion and ordered that the trial begin with presentation of our case for Kosovo. The prosecution appealed the denial of the motion, and the Appeals Chamber reversed the original decision and ordered the joinder of the three indictments in a single trial. Perturbed I am sure, the judges of the Trial Chamber—Judge May, Judge Patrick Robinson of Jamaica, and Judge O-Gon Kwon of South Korea—immediately ordered that the single Milošević trial begin with the Kosovo elements, defeating the entire purpose of the prosecution's motion. My opinion is that the Trial Chamber's judges decided to punish the prosecution because it had appealed their denial of the motion to join the indictments. This would have significant ramifications later on.

During the autumn of 2001, Deputy Prosecutor Graham Blewitt and Chief of Prosecutions Michael Johnson, an American, traveled to London to recruit Geoffrey Nice, a British barrister who had been a senior trial attorney at the Yugoslavia tribunal, to join the Milošević trial team. Upon returning to The Hague, they informed me that Nice had accepted. I learned only later that they had agreed to make Nice, at his insistence, the *principal* senior trial attorney on the case with authority to coordinate the three senior trial attorneys who were responsible for the three indictments, Ryneveld for Kosovo, Groome for Bosnia and Herzegovina, and Uertz-Retzlaff for Croatia. Nice's record suggested that he was a solid choice, but he is also overbearing and tends to surround himself with people who do not challenge his thinking, which perhaps made clashes with the other senior trial attorneys inevitable. He also has trouble having his views challenged and his decisions overruled by a superior he does not respect. In this situation, his superior, who came from a different culture and a different legal system than Nice, was me. I do not know whether I could have foreseen the clashes that eventually took place between us. Even if I had foreseen them, I think there was nothing I could have done to avoid them.

The usual scramble to prepare briefs and statements and voluminous spreadsheets of evidence and binders bursting with documents preceded the opening of the Milošević trial. We expected the media carnival that spread out around the reflecting pool in front of the tribunal on the opening day. I used the first session of the trial to make prefatory remarks before the Trial Chamber. I called for reflection. I asked the court to consider the scenes of grief and suffering that had characterized the conflict in the former Yugoslavia, a conflict that had enriched the lexicon describing man's inhumanity to man by adding the term "ethnic cleansing." The law, I said, is not merely an abstract concept. It is a living instrument for protecting our values and regulating civilized society. It was up to us to assert the will to demonstrate that no one is above the law, that no one is beyond the reach of international justice:

> I bring the accused, Milošević, before you to face the charges against him. I do so on behalf of the international community and in the name of all the member-states of the United Nations, including the states of the former Yugoslavia. The accused in this case, as in all cases before the Tribunal, is charged as an individual. He is prosecuted on the basis of his individual criminal responsibility. No state or organization is on trial here today. The indictments do not accuse an entire people of being collectively guilty of the crimes, even the crime of genocide. It may be tempting to generalize when dealing with the conduct of leaders at the highest level, but that is an error that must be avoided. Collective guilt forms no part of the prosecution case. It is not the law of this Tribunal. . . .
>
> An excellent tactician, a mediocre strategist, Milošević did nothing but pursue his ambition at the price of unspeakable suffering inflicted on those who opposed him or who represented a threat for his personal strategy of power. Everything, Your Honors, everything with the accused Milošević was an instrument in the service of his quest for power. One must not seek ideals underlying the acts of the accused. Beyond the nationalist pretext and the horror of ethnic cleansing, behind the grandiloquent rhetoric and the hackneyed phrases he used, the search for power is what motivated Slobodan Milošević . . . not his personal convictions, even less patriotism or honor or racism or xenophobia. . . .
>
> The trial which commences today will evoke the tragic fate of thousands of Milošević's Croatian, Bosnian, Albanian victims. . . . Yet the accused, Milošević, also [victimized another group of people] . . . the Serbian refugees from Croatia, from Bosnia, from Kosovo abused by Milošević, whose fears were fed and amplified and manipulated to serve Milošević's criminal plans. Many paid with their lives; most lost their homes and their futures. These men and women must rightly be counted among Milošević's victims, just as the citizens of the Federal Republic of Yugoslavia, who now must reconstruct the . . . country which Milošević, the accused, bequeathed to them. . . .
>
> [H]ere . . . it is Slobodan Milošević's personal responsibility which the prosecution intends to demonstrate for the crimes ascribed to him, noth-

ing but that, but all of that. This is the contribution of justice, and we wish to make it dispassionately, recalling the words of Ivo Andrić [Yugoslavia's Nobel Laureate] pronounced at the Jewish cemetery of Sarajevo, and I quote: "If humanity wishes to be worthy of that name, it must organize its common defense against all international crimes, erect a barrier which is sound and sure and truly punish all those who murder individuals and people."[1]

Nice, Ryneveld, Groome, and Uertz-Retzlaff, and their teams of lawyers, police investigators, analysts, language assistants, and administrative staff now set out on a what would become a four-year marathon, presenting thousands of pieces of evidence, document by document, transcript by transcript, photograph by photograph, preparing and examining witnesses, and rushing to collect new evidence even as the trial ground forward. From the first day and consistently thereafter, Milošević spoke to the judges, and especially Judge May, in a disrespectful tone, ostensibly to underscore his refusal to recognize the tribunal's jurisdiction over him. He famously kept referring to Judge May as "Mr. May" instead of "Your Honor." I remember once catching Judge May's eye in the corridor. Without engaging him in any exchange that might be deemed inappropriate, I asked him, "Why, Judge May, didn't you immediately inform Milošević that you would not accept his disparaging treatment?" Judge May chuckled, "Oh, Madame Prosecutor, other things are much more important."

"You're right," I answered. "But appearances are important, too."

The first witnesses the prosecution team called were victims of crimes committed in Kosovo by Serbia's police and paramilitary units and units of the Yugoslav Army. This, as I had forewarned the prosecution team, was a tactical error, mostly because it wasted time. It also took an event billed as a "trial of the century" and doused it with anticlimax. Viewers across the world, and especially people in Serbia and Kosovo, were expecting to see Milošević, the man most responsible for the destruction of the old Yugoslavia, face witnesses who were of his stature: diplomats, international negotiators, and, especially, former protégés who were prepared to testify against him. Instead, there appeared a series of victims, some of them barely literate peasants and working people who were utterly disoriented outside of their home villages and neighborhoods and had no idea how to respond to the browbeating Milošević served up as "cross-examination." Within a few weeks, the people who needed most to see the trial, the people of Serbia, Kosovo, and the rest of the former Yugoslavia, had tuned out. Journalists went looking for other stories, and, in the world that developed after the September 11, 2001, terrorist attacks, they quickly found more compelling topics of interest.

I convened a meeting with Nice, Ryneveld, Groome, Uertz-Retzlaff, and other members of the team. "This," I told them, "is not the trial we wanted to present to the world." I did not want to see Milošević beating up on our witnesses. I recall one of Milošević's cross-examinations that was particularly disconcerting. An elderly Kosovo Albanian, who was not only a victim but a political leader, was so weak that, in response to Milošević's questions, he embellished his story in ways that undermined his credibility. Milošević was trying to paint the Albanians as terrorists, and, most likely, the witness had been involved in some kind of antigovernment activity and wanted to avoid any admission of it. Whatever the reason, his performance reflected badly upon the prosecution and its case and allowed Milošević to score political points in Serbia.

We discussed how to improve the presentation of the prosecution case. I wanted to see insider witnesses. I wanted to see ranking diplomats and leaders from the international community who had dealt with Milošević during the war. I did not want to see evidence of shootings and rapes and other crimes; I wanted to see evidence *linking* Milošević with the shootings, rapes, and other crimes. I said we did not need to bring on a seemingly endless series of crime-base witnesses and agreed with a proposal that we present the testimony of crime-base witnesses to the court as written statements and allow Milošević to cross-examine these people on that basis if he so chose. "We're giving Milošević an opportunity to show his strength," I said, and we had to alter our approach. My stepping in certainly bruised some egos. Managing teams of attorneys inevitably requires managing ego-driven people. How does one do this, especially in an institution where professionals trained in two different legal systems, the civil and common law systems, function side by side? I am not sure. But it is a crucial problem those who support war crimes tribunals must solve.

After the arrest and transfer of Milošević to The Hague, we had begun, slowly, to receive signals that insider witnesses were prepared to speak with us. It was a period of intensive work. The senior trial attorneys and I dispatched lawyers and investigators to Serbia and Montenegro to knock on the doors of military, police, and political figures who, our research showed, would have had knowledge about key events; a surprising number agreed to provide information and eventually many of them testified at trial. We were able to capitalize on a growing recognition among many people in Serbia that Milošević was a criminal and had caused great damage to the country. The witnesses the team recruited began to reveal the existence of crucial documents and provide advice on where to find them. And finally, on Friday March 15, Milošević faced off against his first formidable witness, Lord Paddy Ashdown, a member of the House of Lords of Great Britain, who had been engaged in peacemaking efforts in the former Yugoslavia. He described how Franjo Tudjman had sketched for him a map of a Croatia and a Serbia enhanced by territory carved from Bosnia and Herzegovina. He described the scene of a massacre of Serbs in Kosovo. He gave crucial evidence on the nature of the armed conflict in Kosovo in 1998, including an eye witness account of a Yugoslav Army operation to burn Albanian villages:

> What we were presented with was an entire amphitheatre of hills in which every village was ablaze, and we saw and heard the reports of shell-fire, saw the explosions. I said to [Milošević] that what I had witnessed could only be described as the actions of the main battle units of the Yugoslav Army in an action which could only be described as indiscriminate, punitive, designed to drive innocent civilians out of their properties, could not be explained by any targeting military operation, that this was, in my view, not only illegal under international law, damaging to the representation of the Serbs and his nation, but also deeply counter-productive. . . .
>
> [Milošević] first of all denied that these things were going on and said that they were not happening, and I informed him that they were because I was there on the previous day and saw them with my own eyes. . . . I recall specifically saying that the actions that he was taking were, in my view, clearly in breach of the Geneva Convention.[2]

This, I thought, was a welcome relief.

Over the next few months, recruiting witnesses for the Milošević trial and obtaining sensitive documents, especially records of Milošević's discussions with his ranking military commanders and his intelligence and police chiefs, occupied the highest slots on the agenda I carried into meetings in Washington, D.C., New York, and the European capitals as well as in Belgrade, Podgorica, Zagreb, Sarajevo, and Priština. But maintaining pressure to arrest fugitives was never ending, because the need for pressure was never ending. I had evidence of it over dinner in October 2001 with the United States ambassador to Belgrade, William Montgomery. He raved about the efforts of the United States and Great Britain to arrest Karadžić. His next suggestion made me wonder about his credibility. "I think Koštunica would agree to obtain the voluntary surrender of Karadžić," Montgomery said, but only if the tribunal would agree to give Karadžić provisional release pending trial after his arrest. "He is a hero for Koštunica." More evidence came during a meeting in November at the Hôtel de Brienne. France's minister of defense, Alain Richard, was still enamored with Koštunica, and did not bother with diplomatic niceties. "I know your position," he said, chastising me. "I've read it in the press. . . . Koštunica is the key to transforming Yugoslavia. . . . Your investigations and indictments are endless. There is a point where you have to draw the line."

"Yes," I thought, "but not on the wrong side of impunity."

In the early spring of 2002, my advisers and I were back in Washington, D.C. The time had again come for the United States Department of State to determine whether Serbia and Montenegro had been cooperating sufficiently with the tribunal and could therefore receive United States financial support as well as Washington's diplomatic backing for international aid. The first meeting was with our staunchest supporter within the Bush administration, Secretary of State Colin Powell.

I told General Powell that cooperation with Belgrade was practically at a standstill. Were it not for the transfer of Milošević, we would have achieved almost nothing in an entire year. The only cooperation we received came when Belgrade felt the sting of acute international pressure; but now, with the talk of the tribunal winding down its work, Koštunica and others in Belgrade were clearly calculating that stalling and stonewalling would pay off. Yugoslavia's federal government, including ministers who complained of Koštunica's browbeating, were reluctant to take any action. And the tribunal was receiving only limited cooperation from the Serbian government under Prime Minister Djindjić. I had received no responses to requests for selective access to relevant archives. "Instead," I explained, "we have been offered unsolicited access to much less important archives. In most cases, the Serbian and Yugoslav authorities only provide access to material of little sensitivity. Needless to say that Milošević's associates in Belgrade do not encounter such difficulties." I told Powell that, for the Milošević trial, the Belgrade authorities had granted only one of seventy-seven requests for interviews with prospective witnesses. We were aware that Koštunica had personally discouraged at least one crucial high-level witness from talking to prosecution staff: Zoran Lilić, who had been Yugoslavia's president and one of three members, with Milošević, of the Supreme Defense Council, the most powerful political entity overseeing Yugoslavia's defense organs. I was sure other witnesses were discouraged from talking to us. Moreover, federal and Serbian authorities were fully aware of the whereabouts of about half of our fugitives accused on the territory of either Serbia or Montengro. Until a few weeks earlier, Ratko Mladić had enjoyed the official protection of the Yugoslav Army, with the blessings of the federal presidency. I urged Secretary of State Powell not to certify Belgrade's cooperation and to know that Belgrade would view any effort to allow Serbia and Montenegro to join the Partnership for Peace—NATO's program to prepare Eastern European and former Soviet states for membership in the alliance—as an indication that *Realpolitik* would eventually prevail among the international community and that a policy of procrastination would succeed.

Once again, Secretary Powell stood foursquare behind the tribunal. He agreed to pressure the Belgrade authorities. "Last year, the United States and I took the certification process seriously," he said. "I personally attach a great importance to it, and I continued to communicate this to [the Belgrade authorities]. I told them that we are disappointed, that we've been disappointed since last year, and that it makes certification more difficult." He said Partnership for Peace was a different matter: "We must remain sensitive to the Yugoslavia tribunal's interests. But there can be no absolute link as far as Partnership for Peace is concerned. Other considerations play a role. . . . Be sure that the United States won't stop pressing for the arrest of Karadžić and Mladić, but that their arrest will not put an end to our support. And I'll make sure it won't end it."

Later in the day, I urged William Taft, the secretary of state's legal adviser, to support the appearance of former United States diplomats, government officials, and military officers as prosecution witnesses in the trial of Milošević. I guaranteed that we would bring before the Trial Chamber any legitimate concerns they had and help find ways to ensure the safety of their confidential sources. Our roster of prospective witnesses at this time included the former vice president, Al Gore, who agreed to testify but was eventually not permitted; the former secretary of state, Madeleine Albright, who was disinclined to testify; the former ambassador, Richard Holbrooke, the architect of the Dayton Peace Agreement, who agreed to appear but was eventually not called by the trial team; and General Wesley Clark. Taft replied that the United States would decide on each request on a case-by-case basis after the Office of the Prosecutor had submitted questions for these witnesses. "For the time being," he said, "we're leaning against public testimony for any of our witnesses. . . . The risks cannot be assessed without the questions being analyzed. . . . What we want is an understanding with you as to the scope of examination. Confidentiality is an essential element of diplomacy. We worked in coordination with our allies and we must take into account their sensitivity and interests."

Finally, we met with Greg Schulte, the senior director for Southeast Europe of the National Security Council. Schulte apologized for having had once promised that Radovan Karadžić would be in custody by November 2001. The terrorist attacks on September 11 had required the United States to shift its resources, he said, but now the United States had reassessed the situation and, together with its allies, renewed its focus on the need to have Karadžić arrested. "We're very active, again," Schulte announced. He described two unsuccessful attempts to apprehend Karadžić and indicated that Washington had increased its pressure to make life on the run more difficult for him. "As for Mladić," Schulte said, "it is more of a diplomatic challenge. We try to expose his whereabouts to embarrass Koštunica." A few weeks later, Washington announced that it had decided to delay until the end of June a determination of the Federal Republic of Yugoslavia's cooperation with the tribunal. This figured to increase the pressure on Belgrade to cooperate.

I was seeking to capitalize on this leverage when I traveled to Belgrade on April 18, 2002, in a bid to convince the government to arrest the tribunal's fugitives, provide documentary evidence the Office of the Prosecutor had requested, and allow investigators to recruit and interview sensitive witnesses. Only a week earlier, Yugoslavia's federal parliament had finally approved a law on cooperation with the tribunal. This should have been a red-letter day. But the law contained an article allowing the authorities to arrest only those persons whom the tribunal had indicted *before* the law took effect. (The United Nations Security Council had passed a resolution four years earlier declaring that just such a domestic law could not impede cooperation.) On the same day the parliament had approved the law, one of our key accused chose to commit suicide on the front steps of the parliament building: Vlajko Stojiljković, Serbia's former minister of internal affairs and a key leader of Milošević's operation to drive ethnic Albanians from Kosovo in 1999, was linked by documents with the transportation of the corpses of executed Kosovo Albanians, including women, to mass graves hidden on military bases and other facilities in Serbia.

Driving from the airport to the Serbian government's offices, I caught sight of the now-weathered *puttana* graffiti on the billboards. Tension seemed to fill the air, or perhaps someone wanted to make it seem that way. Police officers blocked the cross streets. My car and the escort vehicles had the main street to themselves, which was unusual. I learned later that there had been a threat against me, that someone was supposedly going to drive a car into mine and make it appear to be an accident.

Recruiting insiders, and especially political, military, intelligence, and police insiders, required the approval of the Belgrade authorities, who were adamant that such witnesses not reveal information they deemed to be "state secrets." Belgrade sat down with our prospective insider witnesses before their interviews with the tribunal and reminded them that divulging state secrets was a crime punishable by law. Most of these witnesses were debriefed after their interviews. (On one occasion, investigators gained access to a police archive and an elderly librarian helped them navigate their way through the documents; the librarian said she was afraid of being prosecuted for helping investigators locate documents.) Belgrade did not go to these lengths because revelation of "state secrets" would be so detrimental to the security of the Federal Republic of Yugoslavia. Any potential enemy already knew the country's security weaknesses, and the NATO air strikes in 1999 had so degraded the Yugoslav Army's fighting capabilities that, arguably, it hardly mattered what anybody revealed about events before the bombing. The federal authorities in Belgrade, and even leaders who had no reason to fear indictment, had another reason to be concerned that witnesses might provide the tribunal information revealing the complicity of the Milošević regime in the war in Croatia in 1991 and the genocide in Bosnia and Herzegovina from 1992 to 1995. The Republic of Croatia and the Republic of Bosnia and Herzegovina had filed lawsuits before the International Court of Justice seeking damages from the Federal Republic of Yugoslavia—and effectively against its constituent republics,

Serbia and Montenegro—based upon the damage caused by the wars. Evidence before the tribunal revealing Milošević's complicity in the events in Croatia and in Bosnia and Herzegovina could be presented as evidence by Croatia's and Bosnia's lawyers to support these lawsuits. When we asked, for example, to interview various generals—including General Momčilo Perišić, who had broken with Milošević over Kosovo and had recently been arrested on suspicion of spying, and General Nebojša Pavković, the Yugoslav Army's chief of staff—the federal authorities in Belgrade balked. Perhaps even more dangerous from their point of view was documentary evidence of Milošević's complicity in the crimes in Croatia and in Bosnia and Herzegovina, evidence like records of discussions that had taken place in the Supreme Defense Council, where Milošević had discussed policy with the country's highest military, police, and intelligence officers.

My efforts to help recruit witnesses and obtain access to documentary evidence took place in parallel with a campaign to pressure Belgrade, yet again, to surrender the fugitives facing tribunal indictments, including Ratko Mladić and Radovan Karadžić. I wanted results within a matter of days or weeks, not months or years. Just weeks earlier, during a meeting in The Hague, representatives of a friendly intelligence service informed me that Serbia was ready to transfer Mladić to The Hague if a deal could be made to protect General Pavković from prosecution and if Serbia could join NATO and the European Union. During a meeting with tribunal representatives in Belgrade, the minister of interior, Dušan Mihajlović confirmed that it was possible to have Mladić transferred and that I "knew how and held the key to make this happen." A few weeks later, Djindjić informed the Office of the Prosecutor that he supported the transfer of Mladić but that this action would require Koštunica to issue instructions to Pavković to do it. A week later, on February 28, 2002, Mladić was officially discharged from the professional military service of the Yugoslav Army and given a severence payment. Another week passed, and Djindjić reported to us that Mladić had fled to Bosnia and Herzegovina. For at least the next five years, Belgrade would insist that this was the last confirmed sighting of Ratko Mladić on Serbian territory.

My meetings on April 18, 2002, with the federal justice minister, Savo Marković; the federal foreign minister, Goran Svilanović; and Serbia's interior minister, Dušan Mihajlović, yielded official assurances that the authorities, of course, knew nothing of the whereabouts of Ratko Mladić.

These men quickly turned our conversations into briefings on the new law on cooperation. But it was obvious to me that nothing would come of it unless someone in Belgrade, beside Zoran Djindjić and his allies, summoned the will to cooperate. Marković even found the gall to state that the Federal Republic of Yugoslavia had "fulfilled all conditions for cooperation with the Office of the Prosecutor" and to chastise me for failing to file indictments against Albanians and other non-Serb perpetrators.

During the meeting with Mihajlović, we presented a list of twenty-three accused whom Belgrade was required to arrest and transfer to the tribunal's custody. We learned that General Dragoljub Ojdanić, the Yugoslav Army's chief of staff during the Kosovo cleansing operations in 1999, would be the next accused to surrender voluntarily. We discussed the possibility of meeting with Sreten Lukić, who had headed the Serbian ministry of interior's staff for Kosovo in 1999. We were told that Colonel Vinko Pandurević, whom the tribunal wanted on charges of genocide and other crimes related to the Srebrenica massacre, was no longer traveling to Serbia from Bosnia; that Stojan Župljanin, who had been indicted in connection with the ethnic cleansing of Western Bosnia and the persecution of Muslims in infamous concentration camps during the summer of 1992, had "disappeared"; that Dušan Knezević, who was also wanted for crimes connected with the cleansing of western Bosnia, had paid a visit to the Serbian police wearing dynamite strapped around his chest; that Veselin Šljivančanin, a former Yugoslav Army major implicated in the executions of wounded men and other prisoners taken from Vukovar hospital, had announced that he would not surrender alive; that Mile Mrkšić, a former Yugoslav Army colonel implicated in the Vukovar executions, was sick; that Miroslav Radić, a former Yugoslav Army captain also implicated in the Vukovar killings, happened to be married to a judge in the Belgrade court; that General Momčilo Perišić had tried to locate Mladić and persuade him to surrender; and that Radovan Karadžić was not in Serbia. At the end of this *macedoine* of truths, half-truths, and lies, Mihajlović asked if we "really needed" to arrest Milan Martić, whom the tribunal had indicted for, among many other things, cleansing Croats from Serb-held swaths of Croatia and firing rockets into the crowded center of Zagreb.

It was a relief to escape this meeting, and I took some malicious satisfaction at leaving behind my advisers to suffer more of these empty promises and excuses. I went with my aide, Anton Nikiforov, to the office of

Serbia's prime minister, Zoran Djindjić, who was absent from Belgrade on that day. I passed through his personal office, where Djindjić had set up a treadmill to keep himself fit, and entered a small salon for confidential tête-à-têtes. And there, sitting in an armchair and dressed in a suit, waited General Perišić. This was to be a secret meeting. Djindjić had arranged it to give me an opportunity to make a personal appeal to Perišić to testify against Milošević. "I want only one thing from you," I said, "the truth before the court." Perišić was clearly nervous. He spoke slowly, without emotion, but with the calculating demeanor of a general. He denied being involved in the events in Croatia in 1991. He said that he would be speaking in Milošević's defense about Bosnia, because "Milošević was much tougher toward the Bosnian Serbs than toward the Bosnian Croats or Muslims," and that he had no knowledge about the events in Kosovo. Perišić explained that participating in the Milošević trial in The Hague would violate his political and moral code, because Milošević should have been tried in Serbia, not in The Hague. He stated that he would be willing to testify against Milošević during a trial in Serbia "for what he had done to the Serbs." I asked Perišić whether his arrest on spying charges had been linked in some way to the tribunal or whether he had indeed provided a United States diplomat with documents relevant to the tribunal. Perišić denied any link between his arrest and the tribunal. He said that it was the result of a political game played by people surrounding President Koštunica and within the Yugoslav Army, whom he likened to Milošević's people.

A second secret meeting arranged by Djindjić took place in the same room soon after Perišić had departed. In strode General Pavković. I had three questions for him: Where was Ratko Mladić? Would Pavković be willing to undergo an interview as a suspect witness—that is, a witness who is informed in advance that he or a she might eventually face an indictment? And would Pavković be willing to testify for the prosecution in the Milošević trial? Pavković gave me the company line on Mladić, saying Mladić had disappeared two months earlier and that he had had no subsequent contacts with Mladić or Mladić's intermediaries. Pavković maintained that the Yugoslav Army had never protected Mladić or provided financial support to Mladić or his bodyguards, whose numbers he estimated at 30 to 130. Pavković said that, upon becoming the Yugoslav Army's chief of staff, he had banned Mladić from making public appearances at army events. Pavković added that, six months earlier, he had canceled a special identification pass that had allowed Mladić unrestricted access to Yugoslav Army facilities. Now, Pavković said, Mladić did not trust many people in the army. Pavković, like many people who agree to undergo questioning in order to gauge what charges and what evidence the prosecution might include in an indictment against them, had no objections to the suspect interview. He said he was ready to answer all prosecution questions related to charges laid out in the Milošević indictment for Kosovo. Pavković, however, was clearly hesitant about the idea of testifying in the Milošević trial. He said he would probably not be a good witness against Milošević as he "would be speaking more in Milošević's defense." As I sat there, I remembered the role Pavković had played in the removal of ethnic Albanians from Kosovo in 1999. I jotted in my notebook: "Pavković—indict."

Later that evening, we spoke with yet another potential insider witness, a man Koštunica had discouraged from testifying, a man who would eventually enable the prosecution to introduce before the Trial Chamber a set of documents that clearly incriminated Milošević and, by extension, Yugoslavia, in the war in Bosnia and Herzegovina. This man was Zoran Lilić, the former president of the Federal Republic of Yugoslavia during part of Milošević's tenure as president of Serbia. Lilić, who was dressed in a fine Italian business suit and bore a resemblance to the actor Robert Mitchum, met me and Nikiforov at the Hotel Hyatt.

Our conversation, sitting in armchairs around a coffee table in the hotel's lobby, was not Lilić's first meeting with tribunal officials. Initial contact began with a ring of the bell at the gate outside his house on a rainy morning a year earlier, in the autumn of 2001. His wife had appeared. A tribunal employee softened her up by commenting that his little girls used to walk by the Lilić house on their way to school and loved the winter mornings when they saw Lilić's bodyguards walking her poodle dressed in a knitted red sweater and booties. The tribunal employee gave Mrs. Lilić a business card. Lilić called an hour later and agreed to meet for a get-acquainted interview.

At about the same time as this first meeting, the prosecution team proposed cuts to the draft of the indictment against Milošević containing charges based upon crimes committed in Bosnia and Herzegovina. Members of the team felt uncomfortable. They were looking for links between Milošević and the violence in Bosnia and Herzegovina but felt the evidence discovered, though enough to establish a prima facie case and therefore include in the indictment, was not of sufficient quality to win a conviction for the crime of genocide.

Genocide is the most difficult of international crimes to prove. It requires the prosecution to show beyond reasonable doubt that the accused intended to destroy a group of people physically; and persons contemplating genocide, particularly those as shrewd as Milošević, do not express a genocidal intention in public. My closest advisers, including Jean-Jacques Joris and Florence Hartmann, who knew the conflict in Yugoslavia better than the attorneys drawing up the Milošević indictment, had advised me not to back down, to press to have Milošević to answer for the war in Bosnia and Herzegovina and all of its ramifications, including the Sarajevo siege and shelling, the massacre at Srebrenica, and, through these and charges related to violence in other regions, genocide. I received a draft indictment, and found it faulty. The crimes were too narrow. The historical context was potted. I demanded and received a new draft that included the genocide charge and other charges related to events at Srebrenica and Sarajevo. When we presented it to the Trial Chamber, the judges certified it—effectively agreeing that we had sufficient evidence to proceed to trial.

In the autumn of 2002, however, Geoffrey Nice began arguing that the evidence for genocide and the crimes connected with the events in Srebrenica and Sarajevo was not of sufficient quality to win a conviction of Milošević. At one point at least, Nice lost his temper about this issue. Joris told me that Nice had screamed at him after one meeting with me. Joris said Nice had referred to me as a "bitch" and said: "She calls herself a lawyer with her limited understanding of the law." He, and Graham Blewitt, the deputy prosecutor, went on to question my ethics, and Blewitt eventually did so publicly. Joris, Hartmann, and others pushed again for keeping Srebrenica, the Sarajevo siege, and genocide in the Milošević indictment. Nice was clearly looking for counterarguments. While I was away from The Hague, he summoned a meeting to discuss Srebrenica and Sarajevo with the Office of the Prosecutor's area analysts: staff historians, linguists, area specialists, and others who had more experience in Yugoslavia than anyone else in the building, though they may not necessarily have been working on cases related to Bosnia and Herzegovina or Milošević. Nice instructed the analysts not to prepare for the meeting, and when it convened, he ordered the chief of investigations, Patrick Lopez-Terres, to leave the room. The analysts, with almost unanimity, insisted that the Srebrenica and Sarajevo counts had to remain in the indictment if the tribunal was going to retain any credibility and that if the investigation had not yet turned up sufficient evidence, then it was a problem with the investigation, because evidence to this effect certainly existed.

Once again, in common-law systems, prosecutors enjoy considerable discretion with respect to the charges they bring against an accused. This differs for prosecutors in the civil law system, who are duty-bound to present the court with all charges supported by prima facie evidence. Dermot Groome, the senior trial attorney responsible for the Bosnia component of the indictment against Milošević, advised me again that after reviewing the evidence there was a prima facie case of genocide against Milošević. But Nice and Groome, who came from common-law backgrounds advised me that, given the very difficult burden of proving genocidal intent beyond reasonable doubt along with everything else we had undertaken to prove against Milošević, dropping the genocide charges would be a prudent exercise of my discretion and would have allowed them to focus the office's resources on the other serious crimes we had charged.

I felt more comfortable within my civil-law milieu. We had prima facie evidence of genocide, and I was therefore duty-bound to present the charges to the Trial Chamber to decide. I appreciated the concerns Nice and Groome expressed, but the decision was mine, and I respectfully disagreed with dropping genocide or Sarajevo or Srebrenica. I made the decision regardless of any disrespect I endured. I explained to all my senior trial attorneys that I would not allow a prosecutor to make the final decision that Milošević was not guilty of genocide or of complicity in the events at Sarajevo and Srebrenica. We had sufficient evidence obliging us to put the question before the Trial Chamber's judges, whose duty it was to make the determination of guilt. If I did not see to it that these charges were presented, I would be shirking my responsibility as a prosecutor. "Let the judges evaluate the evidence," I said. "The judges have the responsibility to determine whether he is guilty, not the prosecutor."

Moreover, I did not want some Al Capone–style, tax-evasion indictment against the likes of Milošević. I did not want Milošević to find himself in jail for a few years on some minor offense and allow partisan historians to use this as an excuse to minimize his crucial leadership role in acts that brought suffering to so many millions of people. We all knew that the evidence in our possession during the autumn of 2002 was going to make the judges' decision close. If Milošević were to find countervailing evidence and we were unable to find any new facts, then he might be able to show reasonable doubt and win an acquittal on the charge. "It is extremely important that we put all our evidence in court publicly," I said, "so it will be seen that we have done all we could do." We would also continue to collect evidence, because we knew compelling material linking Milošević with these events did exist in Belgrade. If we dropped the genocide count and subsequently obtained the evidence for genocide from Belgrade, we would no longer be able to submit it to the same effect. In the end, to his credit and despite the animosities that marred our relationship thereafter, Geoffrey Nice fought his hardest to make the genocide charge stick.

The significance of maintaining the genocide count and the Sarajevo and Srebrenica elements of the indictment returned to me during my meeting at the Hotel Hyatt in Belgrade with Zoran Lilić. He expressed enthusiasm about testifying, though I wondered how deep his ardor ran. He praised the prosecution personnel, including Geoffrey Nice and the persons closest to him on the trial team, for their professionalism and rectitude. He requested protection for himself and his family, advance notice of at least ten days before his appearance, and an official summons from the tribunal to the government calling him to testify. During subsequent conversations with prosecution personnel, he revealed the existence of the Supreme Defense Council's minutes. Within a matter of weeks, analysts working on the case, Nena Tromp, Julija Bogoeva, and Alexandra Milenov, had discovered that the Supreme Defense Council's records included not only the cursory minutes of the meetings, but a detailed stenographic summary of the actual dialogue of a given session. This was potentially high-grade evidence that promised to reveal the linkages between Belgrade and the events in Croatia and in Bosnia and Herzegovina. But first we had to obtain it. Within a few weeks, the Office of the Prosecutor had filed an official request for assistance, seeking from the Belgrade authorities access to these and other documents. This request, linked with a request to obtain a waiver for access to Zoran Lilić, who had been a witness to Milošević's meetings with his military and intelligence heads, would present us with a significant challenge to overcome the Belgrade government's reluctance to cooperate, especially when it risked exposing information that would militate against Yugoslavia in the lawsuits before the International Court of Justice. After finishing our business, Lilić told me he was writing a book about Milošević and his wife, Mirjana Marković, who had fled to Russia and was wanted in Belgrade on criminal charges.

Lilić said that Koštunica was conducting the same policy as Milošević, but in "different packaging," and that Djindjić had done nothing effective to remove or isolate Milošević-era criminals. This, Lilić explained, was why many people, including Lilić's friends, were afraid to cooperate with the tribunal. "These criminals," he warned, "represent the primary threat to persons who were willing to cooperate."

In many ways, the opening of the trial against Slobodan Milošević in February 2002 marked the beginning of the end for the Yugoslavia tribunal. By then, the Office of the Prosecution was planning to complete at least sixteen investigations, targeting fifty high-level perpetrators by the end of 2004. Trials were supposed to end in 2008. On July 23, 2002, I addressed the United Nations Security Council and warned the ambassadors that the tribunal would not meet its targets unless their governments continued to press Serbia and Croatia and the Republika Srpska to arrest the tribunal's fugitives and cooperate in other areas. "There has been some recent movement by Belgrade," I said. "But . . . the attitude of the authorities continues to be one of extending the barest minimum in terms of cooperation. They will do just enough to please the international community, and on several long-standing issues they will give no ground whatsoever."

Zoran Djindjić tried to lift my spirits during a conversation on July 19. "It is better than it looks from the outside," he said. But then he gave an unconvincing assessment of Koštunica and the Army. "Koštunica has men in the army," he said. Pavković, the army's chief of staff, was afraid of the tribunal. The military intelligence service was undermining the rule of law. "They deal with Mladić through Aco Tomić," Djindjić said, referring to the general heading the Yugoslav Army's intelligence branch. He went on to speak sociologically about the wars: "The killing was not systematic, like during Hitler's war. Thousands of people, psychopaths, were willing to kill for one thousand German marks. . . . This war is a big atrocity made of a thousand small atrocities. . . . Milošević wanted to clear the Albanians from Kosovo. There was no specific order to kill, but orders to do whatever needs to be done. After two years the minds have changed. People don't want to recall. And they've started believing their own lies. All we can hope for is for you to get the main ones. We can get sixty or seventy executioners. And we'll leave ten thousand killers to go free. But this is all we can do. Milošević loosed the accumulated hatred of five hundred years. Very negative energy is still around."

Koštunica in the meantime was doing his utmost to convince the United States and European Union that he was the West's best hope in Serbia. In mid-September, I had a telephone conversation with Lord Robinson, NATO's secretary-general. I had heard that Yugoslavia's foreign minister, Goran Svilanović, and the acting chief of staff of the Yugoslav Army would be paying the NATO head office a visit. Their aim, clearly, was to gain Yugoslavia's inclusion in the Partnership for Peace, NATO's program to prepare prospective members for entry.

"You promised no Partnership for Peace if there were no arrests," I reminded Robinson. "There have been no arrests since the elections. If Koštunica gets encouragement about Partnership for Peace, the tribunal will never get Mladić. So you have an opportunity now to play a role for justice. Tell them that Mladić is the price for Partnership for Peace."

Robinson was a charming man. "You speak so sweetly, Carla. Do you do that with all the men?" Then he answered my concern: "No, they won't get into Partnership for Peace. They won't get a free ride, I can assure you. I'm revising the talking points to make them tougher. It won't be just Mladić. It will be Mladić and the Vukovar Three." He was referring to the three Yugoslav National Army officers[3] indicted in connection with the murder of prisoners seized in Vukovar in November 1991, including wounded dragged from the town's hospital.

Robinson kept his word. But, despite my calls for making cooperation with the tribunal a prerequisite for allowing normalization of relations with the Federal Republic of Yugoslavia, on September 24 the assembly of member states of the Council of Europe, an international organization whose member states in the European region work to protect democracy, human rights, social rights, linguistic rights, and media rights, voted to admit Yugoslavia. Perhaps this vote had something to do with a European effort to promote moderate candidates in the upcoming federal presidential election. If so, the strategy failed. On September 29, Koštunica tallied the most votes.

On October 2, 2002, Biljana Plavšić announced her guilty plea. This should have been a fantastic opportunity. The tribunal had indicted Plavšić for genocide, crimes against humanity, and war crimes. She had been a close associate of Radovan Karadžić and Momčilo Krajišnik. She had participated at the highest political levels in the campaign to dismember

Bosnia and Herzegovina and ethnically cleanse large swaths of its territory. She had sat in the presence of Slobodan Milošević. She had heard the discussions between Karadžić and Mladić. And she was in a position to know critical details about the links between Milošević and the Bosnian Serb political, if not military, leadership. I wanted her to be a key witness against Milošević, Karadžić, Krajišnik, and other accused Serbian and Bosnian Serb leaders.

Plavšić had originally contacted us from Belgrade in late 2001 saying that she had learned about a sealed indictment against her and was willing to surrender voluntarily. I met with her shortly after she arrived in The Hague. We sat in my office smoking cigarettes. I recall giving her a pack of my American-made Marlboro Golds, figuring that she might have trouble obtaining authentic Marlboros in a Dutch jail and that the gesture might yield dividends. She tried to talk to me woman to woman. Dressed in a stiff tweed skirt, like a proper British lady, she informed me that she was a doctor of biology and proceeded to describe the superiority of the Serbian people. Her nonsense was nauseating, and I brought the meeting to an end. I wanted to seek life imprisonment against her.

After Plavšić had been locked up for a few months, we were suprised to hear from her defense counsel that she was willing to plead guilty, but not to the count of genocide. Two excellent prosecutors, Alan Tieger and Mark Harmon, negotiated a plea agreement, and I agreed to it. We dropped the genocide charge and she admitted to the facts laid out in the indictment. My fundamental error was not obliging her to agree on paper to testify against the other accused. I accepted verbal assurances and was deceived. I had felt that my personal contact with Plavšić, despite her racial-superiority claptrap, had been so cordial that I could trust her. Again, this was my error. She got up during her sentencing hearing and read out a statement full of generalistic mea culpas but lacking compelling detail. I listened to her admissions in horror, knowing she was saying nothing. In the end, the prosecution sought a sentence of twenty-five years, and she complained after the Trial Chamber sentenced her to eleven.

Later, the prosecution called Plavšić to testify against Momčilo Krajišnik, probably the third most powerful figure in the Serb-controlled areas of Bosnia after Radovan Karadžić and Ratko Mladić. She refused. Dermot Groome insisted that Plavšić be compelled to testify against Milošević. I sent Groome and Bernie O'Donnell, the lead investigator on the Bosnia case, to a prison in Sweden, where Plavšić was serving her sentence. She disavowed knowledge of the crimes, characterized herself as a victim of circumstance, and provided self-serving statements that admitted moral culpability but denied legal responsibility for the crimes committed by Serbs in Bosnia and Herzegovina. I subsequently flew Plavšić to The Hague under guard to interview her with Dermot Groome in my office. But she stepped back even from the statements she had made in the plea agreement and began protesting her innocence. If this was the case, I told Plavšić, she had been ill-advised by her attorney to plead guilty. As I saw it, she was now in violation of the plea agreement. I went to my team and said, "We must advise the Trial Chamber of what Mrs. Plavsic is now saying. Let's present a motion to the court to put Biljana Plavšić on trial." My senior trial attorneys said this would be impossible. What's done is done, they said.

"No, no, no," I said. "File it." I sent the motion to the tribunal's president, but he returned it saying he lacked jurisdiction to decide the question. I then submitted it to the Trial Chamber that had accepted the plea. I still await the response.

On October 21, 2002, just before a trip to New York to address the United Nations Security Council yet again, I returned to Belgrade to urge federal and Serbian republic officials to cooperate fully with the tribunal's work. Svilanović, the foreign minister and head of the committee for cooperation, took exception to my characterization of his government's efforts at cooperation. The shopping list of problems was painfully similar to the last one I had brought to Belgrade: arrest of fugitives; obstruction by the Yugoslav Army; restricted access to witnesses, including Zoran Lilić; threats to witnesses; and statements by politicians trying to score cheap political points by bashing the tribunal. (Koštunica had even declared that there had been entirely too much cooperation with the tribunal.)

"My impression is that Koštunica's position is close to Milošević's and that the will for cooperation is decreasing," I said. Exasperation fell over the Serbs' faces when Patrick Lopez-Terres, the chief of investigations, served copies of new indictments and arrest warrants for four men implicated in the Srebrenica massacre: Ljubiša Beara, Vujadin Popović, Ljubomir Borovčanin, and Drago Nikolić. How, I thought, were the Yugoslav authorities, under the controversial Article 39 of the Law on Cooperation, going to refuse to arrest accused who had bloodied their hands in the way these men had done? I also informed the authorities we had received word that documents we had been seeking were being destroyed.

Svilanović poured forth warnings. If I informed the United Nations Security Council that Yugoslavia was not cooperating, he said, it would not improve cooperation. He said the Yugoslav government would present the Security Council with its own version of reality. He assured me that Koštunica had nothing to do with the fact that we had not yet received a waiver for Zoran Lilić to testify in the Milošević trial. Svilanović went on to announce that there were no more political problems with the arrests of fugitives.

We now had twenty-four openly indicted fugitives, and the Yugoslav authorities had in their possession four indictments more than they had when our airplane had touched down. We were informed that arresting fugitives was problematic only because of difficulties in locating them; they said some of the accused were beyond Serbia's borders, some were in Montenegro, and some were in Kazakhstan and other Soviet republics. Of course, there was no knowledge of the whereabouts of Karadžić and Mladić. Our investigators would be free to visit the former headquarters of the Red Berets, the paramilitary organization Milošević had created within Serbia's state security apparatus. We were told that we would have no direct access to the state security archives, and that there were disgruntled personnel in the service because of imminent plans to downsize it by half. We were finally told that there was no information about the investigation of the mass graves at Batajnica.

I felt no qualms about voicing sharp criticism of the Yugoslav authorities during my appearance before the United Nations Security Council on October 30, my third appearance before the council since the spring. The nature of my complaints was the same. I was concerned only that the council's ambassadors would suffer "tribunal fatigue" as they listened to my repetitive complaints. But one thing was for sure, if "tribunal fatigue" led to a lifting of the pressure on Belgrade, then Belgrade's procrastination strategy was going to prevail, and there would be no justice for the victims of Bosnia and Herzegovina, Croatia, and Kosovo.

The [Federal Republic of Yugoslavia (FRY)] does not show the slightest inclination to comply with any requests relating to the Yugoslav Army. Indicted military personnel are untouched. Notorious figures such as Ratko

Mladić are protected. You will undoubtedly have heard and continue to hear the strongest assurances that Ratko Mladić is not in the [Federal Republic of Yugoslavia]. While constantly denying that Mladić is in Serbia, the authorities have always conceded, in private meetings, that he had been in Serbia, "until recently." . . . We have had enough of this, and at my request President Jorda has now formally seized the Council of the failure of the [Federal Republic of Yugoslavia] to meet its obligations under the Tribunal's Statute.

Military archives are closed to us, even in investigations where Serbs are the victims. *The pattern is clear, and it may well be explained by an admission, made at one time but not since repeated, that nothing would be provided to the Tribunal if it might compromise the position of the FRY before the International Court of Justice, where Bosnia and Croatia seek the payment of war reparations. A quite improper consideration. . . .*

To make matters worse, having been told many times in the past that access to certain military documents would not be possible before the enactment of the Law on Co-operation, we have recently been informed that some requested documents have now been destroyed under a provision of the domestic law requiring the automatic destruction of documents after ten years. If the consequences were not so serious, this kind of blatant defiance of international obligations would be almost comical. It cannot be allowed to continue. . . .

We are beginning to be able to present what I might call crucial "insider" witnesses or "sensitive sources." But fresh hurdles are being erected and placed in the way of such people: they are being told that talking to my staff brings with it the risk of prosecution under domestic law protecting official and military secrets.

Formal waivers must therefore be granted by the Yugoslav authorities before these witnesses can be allowed to give their statements. Because certain waivers for key witnesses are incomplete, they do not provide the necessary reassurance to the individuals concerned. Worse, a very important witness in the Milošević trial has recently been threatened with actual prosecution by the Federal authorities, merely for having spoken with our investigators. The signal sent to others similarly minded to cooperate with the Tribunal is most sinister. But this, I'm afraid, does not deter the [Federal Republic of Yugoslavia from claiming] that it co-operates with us in providing all needed assistance to our witnesses. If these practices are allowed to continue unchecked, a great deal of critical evidence will be lost to the Tribunal. . . .

... [O]ne thing must be clear: We cannot be asked to complete soon our indictments and trials of top leaders and, at the same time, be told to be patient and not to rock the boat. This is an obvious contradiction.

The Council itself has stressed that States may not invoke provisions of their domestic laws as a means of avoiding their international obligations. That principle must be driven home to the [Federal Republic of Yugoslavia] by the Council and by the international community at every possible opportunity, in words and by actions.[Emphasis added.][4]

A month later, we received information that Secretary-General Kofi Annan would be visiting Belgrade. I have forgotten why Annan made this trip, but it clearly involved a transparent attempt by the federal authorities to help Yugoslavia insinuate itself back into the international community without having shown sufficient good faith in its cooperation with the United Nations' own tribunal. I took it upon myself to announce that I would be visiting Belgrade on the same day. I invited Annan to visit the tribunal's field office in the city and told him this gesture would boost the staff's morale and send a clear signal to the local authorities. He arrived at the office in a convoy of vehicles and a special security escort. We received him ceremoniously in an unceremonious basement meeting room and briefed him on our activities and the Belgrade government's failure to meet its obligations to cooperate with our efforts. I also recall that, to help make the visit an occasion Annan and I would never forget, the Bulgarian head of the field office, Deyan Mihov, presented us with coffee mugs bearing the United Nations logo and the words "ICTY Field Office Belgrade." (My dishwasher erased the inscription in one cycle.) I wondered during the briefing how many city blocks separated our field office from the hiding place of Ratko Mladić, and I recalled that Annan had headed the United Nations Department of Peacekeeping Operations at the time Mladić ordered his forces to overrun the United Nations peacekeepers in the Srebrenica "safe area" and proceed to execute those thousands of Muslim prisoners.

I had a free evening in Belgrade after Annan's departure and used the time to meet with the leaders of the organization that, more than any other, was frustrating our efforts, the Yugoslav Army. This series of monologues—air so thick with lies cannot sustain genuine conversation—took place in a tiny conference room somewhere inside a Yugoslav Army building in the center of Belgrade. I do not remember whether there was a shadow on the wall where the obligatory framed portrait of Tito once hung. But I did check for images of Mladić and wondered again, "How close is he?"

Around the table were crowded General Branko Krga, the acting chief of staff appointed by Koštunica; General Zlatoje Terzić, head of the Army's commission for cooperation with the Yugoslav tribunal; retired General Radomir Gojović, a long-time military prosecutor and president of the military court; and General Aco Tomić, a portly man who headed the general staff's security department and, reportedly, enjoyed Vojislav Koštunica's ear and acted as General Mladić's guardian angel.

Ranking government officials had informed us that the Yugoslav Army was protecting Ratko Mladić and that arresting Mladić was a matter for the Yugoslav Army, not the civilian authorities. So I cut straight to the point and handed Krga a copy of Mladić's amended indictment. I told him I wanted a clear response to two questions: What, if anything, had the Yugoslav Army done to locate Mladić? Would the general reveal Mladić's whereabouts and arrest him?

From officers of the Yugoslav Army, men steeped in the communist tradition, simple questions rarely yield simple answers. General Krga launched into a lecture on the role the Yugoslav Army plays in the state structure of the Federal Republic of Yugoslavia and the army's authority under "relevant regulations." (I knew the Yugoslav Army, along with the country's security and intelligence services, had long functioned as a state within a state, and that its leaders had and could find the "relevant regulations" to do practically anything they wanted, including, I heard, profit from black-market sales of weapons, ancient artifacts, and silver.) General Krga asserted several times that the Yugoslav Army was not sheltering any fugitives, not even Mladić. He noted that this "had been communicated" to certain "foreign representatives" together with an invitation to inspect suspected hideouts so they could see for themselves that Mladić was not present. Then, a minute after the general said that it was in the Yugoslav Army's interest to determine individual responsibility for crimes committed and that the army had initiated several war crimes cases, he stressed that the army was not responsible for arresting retired officers, including generals, because they now had the status of civilians.

General Terzić added that indicted former military personnel were the responsibility of the civilian authorities. He said the army had cooperated with the tribunal by granting waivers to General Nebojša Pavković,

General Aleksandar Vasiljević, and other retired generals to speak to investigators, but he criticized Vasiljević for having cooperated with the Office of the Prosecutor before receiving the waiver.

I had to get to the point. I presented my questions again: Where was Mladić? Did the army consider itself competent to find him? General Gojović said retired officers do not fall under the Yugoslav Army's jurisdiction for any kind of criminal investigation, including an effort to locate them in order to expedite serving arrest warrants. This, he said, was the responsibility of the police.

"General," I retorted, "the interior minister, Dušan Mihajlović, has told me that the police cannot arrest Mladić because he is under the protection of the Yugoslav Army. . . . We have information from reliable sources that Mladić has been visiting military compounds, for which he had a special access pass. . . . Even Pavković has confirmed this. . . . And we have information that Mladić has received medical treatment at the [main military hospital in Belgrade] and occasionally stayed at the country home of a retired general."

General Krga and, now, General Tomić stressed repeatedly that locating and arresting Mladić was Mihajlović's problem and responsibility as minister of the interior. Tomić pointed out that the police might be able to arrest Mladić when he entered or left the military hospital in Belgrade, assuming he is going there, which Tomić rejected with barely disguised glee.

Chief of Investigations Patrick Lopez-Terres made the point that the tribunal had indicted some fugitives while they were still in the Yugoslav Army, and the army had failed to arrest them. He added that the army should possess information that could assist in identifying their whereabouts. Was the army prepared to assist the police in this activity? Tomić avoided a clear response. He repeated for the umpteenth time that it was not the army's responsibility to search for fugitives. Then he commented that our information about Mladić and his activities, including a reliable account that Tomić had traveled with Mladić, was incorrect. "It would be impossible for Mladić to receive treatment at [the main military hospital in Belgrade] as he could not gain access without being checked," Tomić asserted. But he evaded my specific request to verify, with documents, whether Mladić had received treatment at the military hospital over the past few months.

Again, I pressed the generals for information: "Do the army's intelligence and counterintellingence services have any information about

Mladić's past whereabouts in Serbia? Could they develop such information now?" I made it clear to them that the Yugoslav Army could not even dream of joining NATO's Partnership for Peace so long as Mladić remained at large and the army did not engage itself seriously in locating him. "If there is a positive response, however, I will support Yugoslavia's goals before the relevant international bodies."

Krga and Tomić stuck to their fiction. I asked Krga whether he was denying that Mladić had seen fit to dine at a Belgrade restaurant—Milošev Konak—on the night of my last visit to Belgrade. Now, Gojović, the military prosecutor, wove a tale about the centuries-old "hajduk" tradition in the Balkans, the tradition of outlaws and rebels and freedom-fighters hiding in the mountains. "Mladić can survive for a long time in the mountains with help from the local population," he said, adding that Mladić did not recognize the tribunal and would certainly resist any attempt to arrest him.

"Is the army still paying the pensions of fugitives from the Military Social Fund?" asked Lopez-Terres. Terzić and Gojović responded that, such information would not be useful for locating the fugitives because the pension payments are deposited in accounts kept by the national postal service and could be collected by anyone who possessed power of attorney. They next asserted—in a bold-faced lie—that Mladić was receiving no pension from the Yugoslav Army because he, like Vinko Pandurević, one of the accused wanted in connection with Srebrenica, was a retired officer of the Bosnian Serb army.

They said too much. Lopez-Terres produced a copy of a formal answer to the tribunal from the Yugoslav Army and Yugoslavia's foreign ministry detailing the army's payment of Pandurević's pension. The room seemed to grow colder with each passing minute. Terzić denied that, after his discharge from the Bosnian Serb army, Pandurević had been an instructor at the Yugoslav Army's staff college; instead, Terzić expected us to believe that Pandurević had only been a student. It was as if the generals could not tell the difference between a world of verifiable facts and the fantasy universe they were inhabiting. They tried next to complain about the costs of responding to the tribunal's requests for assistance, including the cost of photocopying. It was too bad these words had not been captured on tape so all of Yugoslavia could see their top soldiers complaining about the high cost of photocopying. "*Madonna santa*," I thought. After a few minutes more, General Krga ended this idiocy by terminating the conversation. Before the generals left the room, however, I informed them that I expected the Yugoslav Army to assist in locating Mladić.

The next day, the Serb press attacked me for spoiling Belgrade's day in the sun with Secretary-General Annan.

Needless to say, the meeting with the generals produced nothing except a first-hand experience with the kind of people who rise to the top of the Yugoslav Army. On the government side, too, frustration was high. Our efforts to obtain the Supreme Defense Council minutes yielded nothing. On December 13, 2002, patience ran out. It was time to involve the judges. Geoffrey Nice filed with the Trial Chamber presiding over the Milošević case a motion, known as a Rule 54 bis application, to compel the Belgrade government to hand over these and other critical documents. Nice wrote:

> [T]he breadth and depth of material and assistance requested go to core issues of the case against the Accused. For example, documents being held in [Federal Republic of Yugoslavia]-controlled archives are expected to provide evidence of the involvement of the Republic of Serbia and [Federal Republic of Yugoslavia] political, military, and police organs in the conflicts in Kosovo, Croatia, and Bosnia and Herzegovina. Furthermore, documents such as official orders, reports, military and police rosters, meeting minutes, supply requests, inventory records, payment records and correspondence provide the critical linkage in a case that involves every level of the political, military and police hierarchy. . . .
>
> On 11 September 2002, the prosecution informed this Trial Chamber that there is no doubt that the documents requested exist and are in the possession of the [Federal Republic of Yugoslavia] authorities, and there is no excuse for the [Federal Republic of Yugoslavia's] failure to provide such documents. In addition, on 27 November 2002, Vladimir Djerić, Advisor to the Foreign Minister and President of the National Counsel for Co-operation with the [Yugoslavia Tribunal], confirmed the existence of a number of the documents during a meeting with [Office of the Prosecutor] officials.

Nice used a footnote to explain that, during this November 2002 meeting, Djerić had informed the Office of the Prosecutor that, while the Federal Republic of Yugoslavia did have some of the requested documents, these documents would be handed over to the Office of the Prosecutor only if the prosecution agreed with the Federal Republic of Yugoslavia on measures to keep the documents out of sight of the public. Djerić said such an agreement would require that all documents provided by the Federal Republic of Yugoslavia to the Office of the Prosecutor be submitted to the Trial Chamber in closed session. Djerić noted that the prosecution must undertake to initiate and support a request for such protective measures, on all documents provided, even before the prosecution would be allowed to examine the documents. Nice concluded that the prosecution was open to applying protective measures for individual documents on a case-by-case basis, but could not move to apply protective measures for all documents. Such an approch would run counter to the tribunal's goal of having open and transparent trials and violated the Office of the Prosecutor's policy.

This motion angered Foreign Minister Svilanović, because it made public the content of talks between the Office of the Prosecutor and his office and because it revealed the fact that Belgrade was holding back the records of the Supreme Defense Council so their content would not become known to the International Court of Justice. To add insult to injury, on Wednesday, December 18, the United Nations Security Council issued a presidential statement on noncompliance, reminding all relevant states, first and foremost, the Federal Republic of Yugoslavia, to cooperate fully with the tribunal.

Svilanović reacted with a degree of bitterness that was unjustified, and he clearly attempted, once again, to exploit a disagreement to cast Serbia in the role of victim. Svilanović told one Belgrade newspaper, *Nacional*, that the tribunal was a yoke around the country's neck and presented a serious obstacle to its entry into international organizations. "Without clarification of that part of our past, it is impossible even to imagine membership in the European Union," he said, correctly. Elsewhere, however, Svilanović resorted to uttering untruths, saying the prosecution was demanding unlimited access to the archives, which was a veiled reference to the Supreme Defense Council documents and other critical records the prosecution desperately needed. Svilanović said cooperation with the tribunal had never been worse, and, with vindictiveness dripping from his words, advised the tribunal to look back and see how much it had achieved by making public criticisms of Belgrade.

I waited until December 20 to make another public statement about the unsatisfactory cooperation of the Federal Republic of Yugoslavia. I described how Svilanović had refused even to speak with me and that he had said my office had "betrayed the confidence of the authorities in Belgrade."

"So much for a dialogue," I said, explaining that the prosecution teams received limited time to present their evidence in each trial. "The difficulties faced by the prosecution in the Milošević case with access to documents and witnesses came to the point where it was not possible to wait any longer, while the Trial Chamber had to be informed about the problems faced by us. I want to repeat, in the limited time given by the Trial Chamber in the particular case, the prosecution team must bring the most important witnesses and most important documents before the court."

In late February 2003, I made my first visit to the "State Union of Serbia and Montenegro," the state union that had succeeded the Federal Republic of Yugoslavia. I carried with me information from a friendly intelligence agency that General Krga, still the acting chief of staff of the country's army, had acknowledged to this agency that Ratko Mladić was living in Serbia, protected by members of his former staff, and enjoyed access to the army's premises and facilities. President Koštunica, I was told, was fully aware of this situation.

I traveled first to the disaffected junior partner of the new "State Union." I wanted to recruit Montenegro's prime minister, Milo Djukanović, to testify against Milošević, the man who had lifted him to power in the first place. Djukanović complained that Koštunica and the army were thwarting reforms and blocking Serbia and Montenegro's cooperation with The Hague. "Montenegro will suffer the consequences of Serbia's failure to cooperate with the tribunal," he lamented, clearly indicating that the confederation would be a short-lived entity. "Montenegro does not want to be a hostage to Serbia any longer," he insisted.

Djukanović refused, however, to appear as a witness. "Milošević never allowed me to be too close to him and know serious matters," Djukanović said. "Milošević never trusted me and involved only a few people in Belgrade in his real plans." Djukanović whined about how his testimony would damage him politically in Montenegro. He explained that he wanted to reform the country and had only limited time and a narrow majority in the parliament. He asked me to understand his predicament and his efforts to preserve stability in Montenegro. "Even among my supporters there are people who oppose the tribunal," he said, promising, nevertheless, to assist the Office of the Prosecutor in its work and provide it any information that might become available to him.

The Montenegrin officials we met denied the assertions of Dušan Mihajlović and others in Belgrade that tribunal fugitives, including Karadžić and Mladić, were residing in Montenegro or visiting the republic. The Montenegrin leaders said that "someone" was trying to shift the blame onto Montenegro, and that Montenegro's police and state security service were monitoring border crossings and other places Karadžić might appear. They lamented the fact that the intelligence services of different countries, and specifically the United States and France, were not cooperating with one another. Even more depressing was their assessment of the political stagnation in Belgrade, which would not allow a single politician to risk making a serious step forward, much less a move on arresting the tribunal's fugitives. The Montenegrins predicted that Djindjić would run for president of Serbia, form a council of ministers, and proceed with reforms, first and foremost of the Yugoslav Army, which would help solve the problem of Ratko Mladić.

My meetings in Belgrade took place on February 17. I used them to urge, once again, the authorities of the "State Union" and republican levels to comply with their international obligations. I began my meeting with Svilanović, now foreign minister of "Serbia and Montenegro" and chairman of its National Committee for Co-operation with the Tribunal, by saying: "Once, just once, I would like to come to come to Belgrade and report that I was satisfied with its cooperation. This, however, will not be the time." There were so many outstanding issues and the prosecution case in the Milošević trial was winding down. Where was the waiver for Zoran Lilić to testify against Milošević? Why was the waiver process so excruciatingly slow? Why were approvals only now arriving for the Kosovo element of the Milošević trial, which had been going on for months? Where were the police reports we had requested on the fugitives known to be living in Serbia? Why was Article 39 of the law on cooperation still on the books despite a United Nations Security Council resolution declaring that such laws were irrelevant to cooperation with the tribunal? Why had Dušan Mihajlović assured the national parliament that the police would not arrest new indictees? When would we receive adequate access to the archives? Where were the Supreme Defense Council minutes and similar documents that would link Milošević with the war in Bosnia and Herzegovina and support a count of genocide? Where was the military's complete personnal file for Ratko Mladić?

I anticipated that Svilanović would make a preemptive demand for balance and informed him that the first indictment against members of the Albanian militia in Kosovo, the KLA, would soon be forthcoming. In fact, the arrests of Fatmir Limaj and two other KLA commanders were only days away; they had been indicted for, among other things, the murder, inhumane treatment, torture, and beatings of Serb civilians and Albanians imprisoned at a KLA prison camp.

Foreign Minister Svilanović griped about the prosecution's motion for a binding order to hand over the Supreme Defense Council documents and other records. He complained that the motion presented the facts incorrectly and revealed the content of delicate consultations between Geoffrey Nice and the Belgrade government's negotiators. He said that if Milošević were convicted of genocide, it would militate against Serbia and Montenegro in the lawsuits the Republic of Bosnia and Herzegovina and the Republic of Croatia had filed before the International Court of Justice.

"Listen," I said, "I need these documents. I need to see them, immediately, the originals. . . . You can ask the Trial Chamber for protective measures."

Svilanović trumpeted Belgrade's approval of 113 of the 126 waivers the Office of the Prosecutor had requested, and he said that only Lilić was complaining. Svilanović recommended that the prosecution not object to a provisional release of Milan Milutinović, who had been arrested on charges related to the ethnic cleansing of Kosovo, because, in Svilanović's view, it would help build "confidence" and a "positive climate" and respect for the guarantees the government had given the accused who had agreed to surrender. Svilanović concluded the meeting by hinting that Belgrade might change its "cooperative" policy toward the tribunal. He said that "key people," and he was clearly referring to Zoran Djindjić, were under pressure not to cooperate any longer.

A few days before our meeting on February 17, 2003, Zoran Djindjić had suffered a foot injury. He had been playing soccer. I found this strange: The prime minister of a country playing soccer, his legs undercut so hard that it fractured his ankle, an injury that would slow him down. Dressed in a business suit, he propped himself up with crutches to greet me in his office. A plaster cast encased his foot.

I was eager, as always, to hear Djindjić's news of the tribunal's fugitives. Šljivančanin, the Serb commander who had overseen the fall of Vukovar: the police were closing in. Vojislav Šešelj, the head of the Serbian Radical Party and self-proclaimed "duke" who once advised his black shirts to scoop out the eyes of Croats with rusty spoons: soon to be in the tribunal's custody. (Šešelj, in fact, surrendered voluntarily a week later and promised to "destroy the evil tribunal." Djindjić had only one request concerning Šešelj: "Take him and never send him back." And he warned me that Šešelj's antics would disrupt the courtroom more than Milošević's obstinance.) Mountain folk were continuing to harbor Karadžić along the unguarded borders between Montenegro and Bosnia and Herzegovina. There were rumors that Mladić was hiding somewhere near Serbia's frontier with Romania and that the authorities were still trying to persuade him to surrender voluntarily. Djindjić, dismissing as "impossible" allegations that General Pcrišić might be in contact with Mladić, said that a "certain friend" had informed him that Mladić was surrounded, and probably held captive, by the people who were ostensibly protecting him but would kill Mladić to prevent his arrest. These people—Djindjić characterized them as "very sick"—were linked with criminals and were close to certain police officials and military officers. One friendly intelligence service had provided a tip on Mladić's whereabouts, backed up by overhead imagery, but it had yielded no positive result. The police said they had been monitoring Mladić's wife and son and their apartment for the past ten days to no avail, but Djindjić complained that the police had never given him accurate information about Mladić. "With Mladić there is no element of surprise," he said. "There is still too much pressure, too much attention on him." Djindjić suggested leaving Mladić alone for the time being, to start characterizing him as a small-time criminal and a coward, to throw him off-guard by showing no interest, and then to arrest him when he least expected it. Still, Djindjić promised he would hand over Mladić before the summer.

Serbia had to resolve the difficult issues of the tribunal as soon as possible, Djindjić said. The time was auspicious for cooperation with the tribunal, though some members of the government did not want to deal with it because it required taking political risks. The demise of the Federal Republic of Yugoslavia had left Vojislav Koštunica without an office. Soon, the new parliament of Serbia and Montenegro would amend the laws governing relations with the tribunal to make it easier to cooperate.

I then gave Djindjić news that I knew would test his enthusiasm for cooperating with the tribunal. I informed him that the Office of the Prosecution would soon submit indictments against four generals involved in the violence and ethnic cleansing of Kosovo, including a massacre at Meja, whose victims were among those transported in the refrigerator truck to the mass grave concealed within the Batajnica air force base near Belgrade. I told Djindjić that one of these indictments would name Sreten Lukić, a senior police commander on the ground in Kosovo who had subsequently played a crucial role in overthrowing and arresting Milošević. Djindjić responded viscerally. He said these indictments would pose grave political problems. He asked me to delay them, but I refused. "Kosovo is a real problem for the country," he said. "It is slowly drifting toward independence, day by day. The international community is pushing Serbia not only to accept it, but also to take care of Kosovo, so that this province will depend on Serbia's resources and budget." Nobody in Serbia, he continued, was willing to risk speaking openly about a solution. He then said that if the tribunal were to pursue indictments based upon chain-of-command responsibility for Kosovo, his government would openly refuse to cooperate, because to do otherwise would cost the government the support of the police. Djindjić was adamant. The government would act upon any indictment based upon "direct responsibility," that is, direct orders to commit war crimes; it would not accept indictments naming officers in the chain of command—men like Lukić.

When they helped topple Milošević in October 2000, Djindjić and other opposition political leaders had made compromises with Lukić and other officers within the Yugoslav Army and the police and intelligence services, whose cadres had developed a symbiotic relationship with the mafia underworld that had sprung from the criminal nature of the Milošević regime and the criminal means it resorted to while waging the wars in Croatia, Bosnia and Herzegovina, and Kosovo. Djindjić said he wanted to cut away the rot. He said that he and Djukanović, the Montenegrin prime minister, were about to assert the government's control over the army and purge its officer corps. "The army is the problem for the tribunal," he said. "The army is the main obstacle for reforms. It was protecting socialism and Tito's Yugoslavia. Now it is protecting itself from any reforms and civilian control. Reform will help move cooperation forward." Djindjić also said he was planning to assault the tangled network of organized criminals and members of the state security service. Djindjić told me that he had already dismissed the head and deputy head of state security because they had failed to produce actionable intelligence on Mladić.

I warned him to be careful. I handed him a two-page internal tribunal report describing a conspiracy to assassinate Djindjić. My eyes and ears in Belgrade had produced the document. It listed the names of persons who were allegedly working to kill him.

"I know this," he said, smiling. "They don't want me undertaking reforms. . . . But don't panic, I'll take care of myself."

"You know, I answered, "you should not brush this aside. You should take this threat seriously. . . . Experience has taught me that you never know. Most of this might be untrue. But there might be enough truth in it."

Four days later, an assassin tried unsuccessfully to kill Djindjić by driving a truck into his car. A few minutes after noon on March 12, 2003, in a building across from the seat of Serbia's government, two hands trained the barrel of a sniper rifle onto the back of Zoran Djindjić, and a finger pulled the trigger.

I was in my office when my aide, Anton Nikiforov, brought word that Djindjić had been shot. A short time later, we learned he was gone. This was a shock, but not a surprise. And it did not strike me in the same way as Falcone's murder. Falcone had been a colleague, someone from the same team. Djindjić had been the only politician in Serbia I knew who was willing to assume risks to cooperate with the tribunal. I recalled how he had revealed the news that the bodies of Albanians killed in Kosovo had been buried in hidden graves on the grounds of a Yugoslav Army base. I recalled how he had worked to begin the voluntary surrenders of the tribunal's fugitives. But Djindjić would always remain for me someone with whom I had to negotiate, someone I had to press to obtain arrests, the handover of documents, and permission to interview witnesses. I thought of his children. I remembered his wife, Ružica, and how I had sent her bargain-hunting in Lugano. I remembered Djindjić describing how, for the good of his country and his people, he would transfer Milošević to The Hague even if it meant kidnapping him. I remembered Djindjić laughing: "Give me a billion, and you can have Milošević."

CONFRONTING KIGALI

2000 TO 2001

Long exchanges with the Office of the Prosecutor's investigators marked my first trips to Rwanda, and the subject matter, pored over hour after hour, day after day, tested my mind's capacity to absorb the macabre. These meetings seemed always to begin with mounds of Tutsi dead, and the trail of testimony and forensic evidence led almost inevitably to Hutu *génocidaires*. During one of the early conversations, however, I heard about the other side of the Rwanda tragedy. In early June 1994, I was told, Rwanda's highest-ranking Catholic clergymen had found themselves surrounded inside the orange-brick cathedral complex in the town of Kabgayi. Thousands of terrified people, Tutsis and Hutus, had jammed into huts, tents, and buildings in and around the Kabgayi complex. The rooms of its hospital had filled with Tutsis and Hutus slashed by machetes and ripped through by bullets. Each night, Hutu troops and *génocidaires* would come into the complex and snatch Tutsi victims to execute. Bodies, dead for days, twisted and bent, lay around the grounds and beyond. Catholic priests found themselves among the victims and the perpetrators. One of the wounded in the hospital was a priest who was reportedly shot while attempting to prevent Hutu militiamen from killing people who had sought refuge in his churchyard; one of the alleged *génocidaires* was a Hutu priest named Emmanuel Rukundo.

The Hutu soldiers and machete-wielding militiamen had fled Kabgayi before the gates to the cathedral complex were closed on Thursday, June 2, 1994, as Tutsi soldiers of the Rwandan Patriotic Front (RPF) approached. By late morning, the RPF had surrounded the complex: the cathedral itself, the hospital, the school and seminary, and the residential buildings. Just before the midday meal, RPF troops scaled the walls. Some of them found the archbishop of Kigali, two bishops, and several priests who had come with them. The soldiers led these clergymen into an open area facing the cathedral, and held them there at gunpoint to bake under the afternoon sun. In the dead of that night, the soldiers drove these captives about fifteen kilometers toward the south, to Ruhango, and confined them there until Sunday, June 5. On that morning, the soldiers took the clergymen to Gakurazo, to a monastery, where they reportedly celebrated holy mass. Tension filled the afternoon. Troops questioned and searched the clergymen. Two soldiers threatened to kill the captives. In the early evening, the clergymen were grouped together one last time. The guns opened fire sometime between seven and eight o'clock. The archbishop of Kigali, two bishops, an abbot, nine priests, and three girls lay dead. One priest managed to flee.[1]

These clergymen were not *génocidaire* priests. Hutu *génocidaires* had not shot the archbishop and the others to death for resisting the genocide. The killers were members of the Tutsi-dominated RPF, which had cast itself as Rwanda's savior. Diplomats, journalists, and human rights investigators would characterize the RPF as a well-organized and well-disciplined force. A few days after the Gakurazo killings, the RPF announced that members of its ranks were responsible for this crime; it said the authorities were pursuing soldiers suspected of involvement and had killed one soldier who had participated. The official story, the story I would hear from Rwandan government officials, was that the slayings were a rash act of reprisal, unauthorized by any ranking officer, and not the result of a deliberate command. I was skeptical. These victims, including the highest-ranking churchmen in Rwanda, were held for four days, long enough for high-ranking commanders of a well-disciplined militia to know of their capture and whereabouts, long enough for the killings to have been premeditated or ordered from above.

During the campaign against the Hutus in 1994, troops of the RPF committed other grave violations of international humanitarian law by attacking and killing thousands of unarmed civilians. The United Nations High Commissioner for Human Rights, the United Nations Commission of Experts, Human Rights Watch, and the International Federation of Human Rights Leagues documented these violations of international humanitarian law. According to Human Rights Watch, these crimes were so systematic, so widespread, so numerous, and so dispersed in time that the militia's commanders had to have known about them; even if the militia's commanders did not specifically order these acts, the commanders had failed to take effective action to halt them or to discipline the soldiers and officers responsible. The RPF reported in early November 1994 that it had arrested twenty-five soldiers suspected of such crimes; eight of them were accused of killing civilians between June and August 1994. By the end of the year, military prosecutors had supposedly completed investigations of twenty such instances. A major, a corporal, and four soldiers indicted for these crimes were reportedly tried and convicted in 1997 and 1998; the major reportedly received a life sentence, the others two to five years.[2]

By the time I arrived in The Hague in 1999, the Rwanda tribunal had helped cast light upon the inner workings of the Rwandan genocide, but the institution was facing harsh, and justifiable, criticism for administering only victor's justice and allowing itself to become little more than a means for the international community to absolve itself of its responsibilities for failing to act to prevent or limit the genocide. Despite the credible reports of massacres by Tutsis, the tribunal had indicted only Hutus implicated in the genocide, along with the one so-called white Hutu, Georges Ruggio, a Belgian-Italian former journalist with Radio Télévision Libre des Milles Collines, who would eventually plead guilty to incitement to genocide. In Resolution 955 of 1994, the United Nations Security Council established the International Criminal Tribunal for Rwanda to prosecute not just the 1994 genocide but also "other systematic, widespread, and flagrant violations of international humanitarian law," which applies equally to those crimes alleged to have been committed by members of the RPF inside Rwanda during 1994. Thus, the tribunal's mandate was to investigate war crimes *on all sides* of the conflict in Rwanda and, if the evidence warranted, prosecute the most responsible individuals *on all sides.* Its task was also to establish a record of events that would contribute to reconciliation of the Hutu and Tutsi communities. Failure to investigate the RPF would send an unambiguous signal that Tutsi leaders enjoyed impunity, that they were above the law, that the innocent victims of their violence did not count. This failure would not bode well for the future of Rwanda or for the Rwandans scattered across east Africa and beyond.

In November 1999, I read in a newspaper that a French examining magistrate, Jean-Louis Bruguière, had launched an inquiry into the breathtaking act of violence that immediately preceded, and seemed to ignite, the Rwandan genocide: the mysterious missile attack that brought down the French airplane carrying Rwanda's president, Juvénal Habyarimana, a Hutu, and the president of Burundi, Cyprien Ntaryamira, as it approached the airport at Kigali on April 6, 1994. Three French crewmen had perished in the attack, and Bruguière had opened the investigation after their family members filed an official complaint in France.

I have known Bruguière since the mid-1990s. He had gained notoriety for prosecuting terrorists, including of one of the world's most notorious, Carlos the Jackal, a Venezuelan who, as a member of the Popular Front for the Liberation of Palestine, had carried out the infamous hostage-taking at the Vienna headquarters of OPEC and other brazen attacks; Carlos, whose real name was Ilich Ramirez Sánchez, was eventually apprehended in Sudan and flown to Paris, where, in 1997, a court sentenced him to life in prison on murder and other charges. I was conducting an investigation in Switzerland of supporters of Carlos's terrorist activities, and Bruguière cooperated with me in arranging an interview. After reading about Bruguière's investigation of the incident in Rwanda, I asked my aides whether the Rwanda tribunal was investigating the attack on the French aircraft. The answer was no, and for a good reason. My predecessor, Louise Arbour, had done an analysis of the attack and decided that, even if the prosecution could show that Tutsis had shot down the plane, it would be difficult to make a case before the tribunal against the persons responsible, because assassinating a president, while a crime, is not necessarily a war crime, and the tribunal's jurisdiction, roughly put, was limited to war crimes.

I concurred with Arbour's assessment. The prosecution, I thought, could only prove that assassinating President Habyarimana amounted to a war crime if it could show that the persons who shot down his plane had calculated that this act would trigger a genocide from which they could benefit politically. This scenario is almost too Machiavellian to imagine. Almost. Many Rwandans, and especially many Hutus, were clamoring for an answer to this mystery. Journalists and human-rights advocates had for years been demanding an inquiry. I was not so willing to make a decision to forgo a thorough investigation and write off prosecuting the persons responsible for blowing up President Habyarimana's airplane; I would rather have examined the evidence in detail and presented it to the Trial Chamber to decide whether or not to prosecute, but I was also not ready to divert investigators and scarce resources to examine the incident. Now the French had taken it upon themselves to do the investigative work. I called Bruguière and told him I was ready to cooperate fully with his inquiry. I said the Office of the Prosecutor had obtained documents relevant to the air attack and that, if he wanted to obtain copies or to interview any of the Rwanda tribunal's accused about this matter, he should submit a written request for assistance. Bruguière sent an official request. And in later discussions, he and I decided that the French authorities would take the lead on the investigation and share the evidence; then we would decide whether the French authorities would prosecute the matter or whether the Rwanda tribunal's Office of the Prosecutor would take up the task. By May 2000, one of the tribunal's accused, Hassan Ngeze, the former editor of a hate-mongering newspaper, was shouting from his jail cell that he had information about the air attack. I authorized Bruguière to interview Ngeze in Arusha. We made the fact of this visit public, which took some of the heat off the Rwanda tribunal.

My first discussions with Paul Kagame, the man who had commanded the RPF and become the dominant political figure in postgenocide Rwanda, did not hint at any investigation of him or his former comrades-in-arms. I first met Kagame on February 10, 2000, after having viewed the bone-filled church at Ntarama. Our conversation took place at the last minute before my departure from the Rwandan capital. Kagame was nominally Rwanda's vice president, and I was trying my best to smooth over the hard feelings in the Rwandan capital after the tribunal's Appeals Chamber had decided to free Barayagwiza. All I could do was assure Kagame that I would do my utmost in three days' time to argue the prosecution's case to reinstate the charges against Barayagwiza. Kagame pledged the Rwandan authorities' full cooperation with the tribunal, but he clearly wanted to see results from the genocide trials, as did I.

My second conversation with Kagame came on Friday, May 12, a month after he officially became Rwanda's president. This audience, too, took place at the last minute, despite the fact that my office had requested it weeks earlier. A driver took me and the tribunal's new chief of prosecutions, Laurent Walpen, to the protected cluster of houses that were Rwanda's presidential compound. Kagame's office was a modest workplace, and I appreciated this, because it implied he was in solidarity with the people outside the compound's walls who were suffering abject poverty while they struggled to cope with the trauma of the genocide. By then, Barayagwiza was again facing genocide charges, so I invested some of my accumulated capital to press for cooperation. I exploited the opportunity to present Walpen to Kagame. I underscored how important it was for Rwanda not to create bureaucratic obstacles for witnesses traveling to Arusha to testify. I briefed Kagame about the Office of the Prosecutor's efforts to investigate new suspects and to expedite trials by grouping the accused thematically—the media *génocidaires*, the military *génocidaires*, the government *génocidaires*—so we could try multiple accused at once. Tracking fugitives was another topic. Kagame never tired of telling us that key *génocidaires* were still at large in Africa and Europe. I mentioned Félicien Kabuga, the richest and one of the most wanted of the Rwanda tribunal's fugitive accused. Kabuga was living in Nairobi, protected, thanks to his vast wealth, by the Kenyan president, Daniel arap Moi. We could never get to Kabuga, but we knew President Kagame enjoyed good contacts with President arap Moi. "Why don't you ask arap Moi to give up Kabuga?" I suggested with more than a hint of sarcasm. Kagame replied that Kabuga was our priority, not his. "I have other matters to attend to," he said. (A year or so later, I heard that Kabuga's property in Rwanda's capital was returned to his family. The United States eventually offered a $5 million reward for information leading to Kabuga's arrest; the tribunal's tracking unit put up wanted posters all over Nairobi announcing the reward. As of 2007, Kabuga was still at large.) I also told President Kagame that I would ask the Rwanda tribunal's judges to hold trials in Rwanda in the near future. Kagame thanked the prosecution for contesting the Appeals Chamber's decision to release Barayagwiza. And Kagame again assured me that Rwanda would meet its obligations toward the tribunal.

Three weeks later, I reported to the United Nations Security Council that cooperation between Kigali and the Rwanda tribunal was now excellent. The tribunal's detention facility in Arusha was holding forty-two detainees, including eight former ministers, four senior military officers, and three journalists. Thirteen fugitives were still at large. Eight accused had been sentenced, three of them after having pleaded guilty. And thirty-five detainees were awaiting trial. All were Hutu, if you include the white one.

During my work in Arusha and Kigali that autumn, Laurent Walpen again raised the fact that the investigative team tracking fugitive accused had received more credible reports from witnesses in Europe and Africa about crimes members of the RPF had committed during and after the genocide. Estimates of the dead stood in the tens of thousands. Walpen had opened dossiers on thirteen massacres, including the killings of the archbishop and other churchmen at Gakurazo. We knew that opening an investigation of the RPF would strike a raw nerve in Kigali, because President Kagame and the other Tutsi leaders had staked so much of their claim to political legitimacy upon the RPF's victory over the *génocidaires* in 1994. They were marketing their takeover of the country as a righteous struggle to halt the genocide. After the war was won, ranking RPF officers had become ranking officers of the Rwandan army. Kagame and others who moved into the political realm relied upon the backing they enjoyed from their comrades-in-arms in the officer corps. Kagame and the others also depended upon this support as the Rwandan army continued to wage war against Hutus, including *génocidaires*, who had rearmed and were intermingled among the hundreds of thousands of refugees in eastern border regions of Zaire, now the Democratic Republic of Congo.

Walpen advised conducting a secret inquiry into the RPF and did not want to notify the Rwandan authorities. He was concerned that, if President Kagame and the other Tutsi leaders learned of the "Special Investigation," as he named the inquiry, they would stymie the investigative work and make it riskier. The Rwandan authorities, however, were already monitoring our investigators' every move. (Walpen entertained us with tales about how he would hustle around blind corners, stop, pretend to tie his shoes, and laugh as his Rwandan police minders would come rushing around the corner in pursuit.) We knew the Rwandan intelligence service had received monitoring devices from the United States and was using them to compromise our telephone, fax, and Internet traffic. We suspected that the Rwandan authorities had also infiltrated our computer system and placed agents among our Rwandan translators and other staff members in Kigali. Walpen also knew that the United States did not, for obvious reasons, want the tribunal's investigators to obtain state-of-the-art, Swiss-made encrypting cell phones. So, in other words, the Rwandans already knew, hour by hour, what the tribunal's investigators were doing.

In order for the Special Investigation to succeed, we had to obtain documents available only in Kigali and we had to recruit witnesses, including insider witnesses, accessible only in Rwanda. In my opinion, it would have been impossible to conduct such an investigation successfully without the cooperation of Rwandan authorities, and, after all, a resolution of the United Nations Security Council required the Rwandan authorities, like the authorities in Serbia, in Croatia, and in Bosnia and Herzegovina, to cooperate fully with the tribunal's work. The decision was mine, and I decided to notify the Rwandan government about our Special

Investigation and demand that the government cooperate. Within the next few weeks, the Office of the Prosecutor sent the government of Rwanda an official request for assistance seeking information relevant for the Special Investigation.

On December 9, 2000, I informed President Kagame personally that the Office of the Prosecutor had begun an investigation of allegations that the RPF had committed war crimes even as the Hutus were committing genocide. The meeting began in his modest office in the presidential compound. After the discussion turned to his former militia, however, Kagame invited me into an adjoining room, a sitting room with a pair of couches. I sat on one, and Kagame, so thin, sat on the other. None of our advisers were present. We spoke in English. I told him that the tribunal's investigators had collected evidence on thirteen incidents in which members of the RPF had allegedly massacred civilians during its advance across Rwanda in 1994. Kagame made no attempt to deny that these incidents had occurred. He told me that Rwanda's military prosecutors were conducting some investigations, but he clearly knew that I knew that the Rwandan authorities had already had almost seven years to investigate these incidents and bring charges. Kagame also knew that he could not explicitly refuse to cooperate in the tribunal's investigations of these allegations. His agreement to cooperate seemed genuine. But he advised me not to open investigations of all thirteen cases, because this would create problems for him with Rwanda's army. I was almost relieved to hear this, because the Rwanda tribunal lacked the investigative capacity to take on these thirteen cases simultaneously. "We will start with three," I said. The first case would focus upon the killings of the archbishop, the other clergymen, and the girls in Gakurazo. I tried to occupy the high ground. I tried to explain to Kagame how important an investigation of Tutsi wrongdoing would be for Rwanda. I tried to explain that this investigation would demonstrate that Rwanda's Hutus and Tutsis could reconcile their differences and live in peace, prosperity, and democracy. It would demonstrate that no side enjoyed impunity. I was sure, however, that Kagame's worries about problems with the army were legitimate. Whether he feared being indicted, I cannot say. In the end, I asked Kagame for the files of the investigation the Rwandan military had supposedly conducted on the Gakurazo killings and the other two cases. He said I had to obtain the files from Rwanda's chief military prosecutor.

Once I had obtained President Kagame's agreement, I wasted no time in arranging for Walpen and me to meet with Rwanda's military prosecutor, Lieutenant Colonel Andrew Rwigamba, at his office. Rwigamba was in uniform, and exceedingly polite. Instead of agreeing to hand over the files, however, Rwigamba informed us that he was conducting the investigations and that these investigations would not be the work of the tribunal. I notified him that President Kagame had agreed to cooperate with the tribunal's investigation of the RPF. Lieutenant Colonel Rwigamba was still reluctant to provide us access to files, documents, archives, and witnesses. I explained that the tribunal had primacy in prosecuting the cases arising out of the 1994 violence in Rwanda and that Rwanda was required by international law to cooperate. Finally, Rwigamba seemed to agree. But he advised us that he would have to speak with Kagame before he handed over any files. It was as if he was assuming that I had dropped Kagame's name without really having received Kagame's backing. Walpen and I were skeptical of Rwigamba as we emerged from his office. I assumed that, even before he made a call to President Kagame's office, if he ever did, Rwigamba would speak with his military superiors, including former commanders of the RPF who had reason to fear seeing their names on international arrest warrants.

I did not want Kagame to backtrack. During a press conference in Arusha four days after our meeting, I made a point of announcing publicly that the Rwanda tribunal had passed a watershed. By opening an investigation into crimes allegedly committed by members of the RPF, the tribunal was now working toward fulfilling every aspect of its mandate and might even have an indictment ready within a year. I commented on my meeting with President Kagame: "We discussed problems of cooperation in detail. We talked about investigations into massacres committed by the other side, that is, by soldiers from the [RPF]. I am completely satisfied Without the help of [Rwanda], we will have no results in these investigations. We need access to documents and testimonies. Let's be realistic: without cooperation, I'll get nowhere. I'm moving forward, step by step. I make no presumptions. I work from facts." The latter part of the press conference was a balancing act designed to demonstrate to the Rwandan authorities that they were not the only government obliged to cooperate with the tribunal. I complained that two African countries were harboring most of the Rwanda tribunal's dozen or so fugitive accused. Though I did not reveal them, these countries were Kenya, the refuge of Félicien Kabuga, and the Democratic Republic of Congo. "I depend on the good will of the governments in the search, arrest, and transfer of these subjects," I said, complaining that some of the accused had even been issued passports with new identities and nationalities.

My announcement seemed to strike a consonant chord in Kigali. Rwanda's prosecutor general, Gerard Gahima, told the press that international law required the Kigali government to cooperate fully and that the government would fully cooperate. The RPF's secretary-general, Charles Murigande, told an African newspaper, "We could not have attained the level of discipline in the army today without such actions. It's not an army of angels but human beings capable of committing a crime."

Despite these uplifting sentiments, we received no response to our request for the military's files. No commentary, no reaction, nothing. Months passed, and as they did, through the Rwandan mists I could make out the clear image of the *muro di gomma*. The reality became something worse: Rwanda again began making it difficult for prosecution witnesses to travel to Arusha to testify in trials against the accused *génocidaires*.

On April 6, 2001, the seventh anniversary of the missile explosion that blew President Habyarimana's plane from the skies over Kigali, the seventh anniversary of the beginning of the genocide, about three hundred demonstrators, most of them Hutu, gathered outside my office in The Hague and complained that the Rwanda tribunal was biased. The demonstrators presented a petition urging the Rwanda tribunal to investigate alleged war crimes by Tutsis as well as Hutus. Three days later, I was in Kigali for talks with President Kagame and other Rwandan government officials about Rwanda's failure to cooperate with the genocide trials and the investigations into the RPF. The military prosecutor had given us nothing. Prosecution witnesses had shown up at Kigali's airport to fly on the Beechcraft to Arusha, and Rwandan passport controllers had refused to allow them to board, saying they lacked some document nobody had heard of before. The venue of our meeting was again inside the presidential compound, a conference room near the same modest office where Kagame and I had met three months earlier.

"What are you doing?" I asked Kagame after completing the diplomatic niceties. He was dressed in a fine blue-gray suit. His gestures were firm and confident. He seemed to be making every effort to be accommodating. He told us that some new law was affecting all Rwandans going abroad, and not just witnesses the tribunal had summoned to Arusha. He assured us something would be done to take into consideration the special needs of the tribunal's witnesses. The entire problem with this red tape was so petty, so ridiculous, and apparently so easily resolved that I thought for a while that it had nothing to do with the investigation of Tutsi commanders. The connection became evident only later.

Next, we came to the main issue of our conversation. "Your military prosecutor is not cooperating," I said, explaining that Lieutenant Colonel Rwigamba had not answered our request for assistance. Rwigamba was sitting quietly in the room.

Kagame acted surprised. He turned to the lieutenant colonel and in strong words said: "Please cooperate with Prosecutor Del Ponte. Give her what she wants." Kagame was categorical. It was not a discussion. The military prosecutor uttered not a word. "I decide," Kagame said, "and I have decided that we cooperate in this investigation."

The military prosecutor nodded, meekness incarnate.

"*Bene*," I thought, "*problema risolto.*" Problem solved.

We had a press conference under the afternoon sun on that Monday. President Kagame, Prosecutor General Gahima, Lieutenant Colonel Rwigamba, and I spoke with the Rwandan press, the BBC, Reuters, and other agencies. The Rwandans told the world that they had agreed to cooperate with tribunal investigations of allegations of war crimes committed by the RPF during 1994. Lieutenant Colonel Rwigamba chose to keep his comments within the bounds of ambiguity: "We reiterated our determination to cooperate in dealing with suspects of genocide and other crimes against humanity." I said I was pleased with the cooperation the tribunal had received from the government of Rwanda particularly in the area of investigation of RPF officers who may have been involved in violations of international humanitarian law. Gahima said the government supported the work of the tribunal's prosecutor and that there was ongoing dialogue to resolve all issues of mutual concern.

A week or so later, I received a secure fax from Walpen, who had met yet again with Rwigamba. He was no longer ambiguous. He was refusing to cooperate. "You have misunderstood what the president wants," Rwigamba told Walpen.

During the spring and summer of 2001, the Rwanda tribunal's investigators continued to follow leads in the Special Investigation while they gathered evidence on the genocide and tracked fugitives accused in Africa and Europe. It was obvious that none of the tribunal's Hutu accused were in Rwanda. They were terrified of the Rwandan authorities, who were already holding at least 115,000 genocide suspects in squalid prisons; Rwandan courts had handed down about three thousand sentences since December 1996, including five hundred death penalties and seven hundred acquittals. Twenty-two persons had been publicly executed in April 1998.

The Kenyan government may not have arrested Félicien Kabuga, but this did not mean it was insensitive to the tribunal's complaints about its failure to apprehend fugitives accused on its territory. On April 25, 2001, Kenyan police in Nairobi arrested a Rwandan bishop of the Anglican Church and transferred him to the tribunal's custody to face charges of genocide, conspiracy to commit genocide, and extermination. The indictment against the forty-seven-year-old bishop, Samuel Musabyimana, alleged that he had participated in the genocide in the Gitarama region of central Rwanda by paying Hutus who carried out the killings and ordering a subordinate to list refugees arriving at his Shyogwe diocese according to their ethnic groups; this list was allegedly used later to select Tutsi refugees who were taken to nearby sites and killed. Rwanda's government welcomed the arrest. "We have enthusiastically hailed the arrest of Bishop Musabyimana," Justice Minister Jean de Dieu Mucyo said. "This is just one of the many genocide criminals of different denominations who are scot-free in Western countries, notably Belgium, France, Italy, and Switzerland."

He was right. And we decided to correct this matter. The tribunal had not listed its accused fugitives with Interpol, the world's largest international police organization, which works to facilitate cross-border cooperation. Walpen met twice in Lyon with Interpol, and it agreed to place the persons named in the tribunal's international warrants on their most wanted list. Walpen also suggested that, since the Office of the Prosecutor was attempting to organize thematic trials, for journalists, soldiers, and political leaders, we might want to do one for priests and other clergymen.

With Interpol's help, the tracking team discovered four Rwandans who had allegedly taken part in the genocide and had fled to Europe. Two of them were Roman Catholic priests living under assumed names, one in Switzerland, the other in Italy. Another was Rwanda's former finance minister, who was in Belgium, and yet another was a famous singer, who was living in The Netherlands, about a ten-minute drive from my favorite golf course. Walpen and the authorities in Europe engineered a plan to make a series of coordinated, simultaneous arrests, so we could capture as many accused as possible without spooking the others. Part of my intention was to use this operation to demonstrate to Kagame and the Rwandan military that the tribunal was doing its best to apprehend accused *génocidaires*.

The arrest operation took place on July 12, 2001, in three locations. In Switzerland, the authorities captured a former Rwandan army chaplain, Emmanuel Rekundo, the Catholic priest alleged to have taken part in the killings of Tutsis in Kabgayi. He faced an indictment listing four counts of genocide, complicity in genocide, murder, and extermination, and became the first Roman Catholic clergyman the Rwanda tribunal had taken into custody. In Belgium, the police arrested a former Rwandan finance minister, Emmanuel Ndindabahizi, on charges of genocide, inciting genocide, crimes against humanity, and murder. And in the town of Leiden, in the Netherlands, the Dutch police arrested Simon Bikindi, a popular Rwandan musician, who allegedly participated in the slaughter of Tutsis and helped organize *Interahamwe* militia groups.

A fourth arrest had been planned. But the authorities in Italy refused to execute the warrant, saying they did not have the proper authority. For the next several months, Walpen and I pressed both seats of authority in Rome, the Vatican, and the Italian government, to help the tribunal apprehend its accused. The fugitive was another Roman Catholic priest, Athanase Seromba, who had worked in the parish of Nyange, where, according to the indictment, Seromba played a role in the killing of about two thousand people gathered inside his own church. Bulldozers were used to bring down the walls and roof of the church upon the people huddled inside while *Interahamwe* members killed everyone who tried to flee. Seromba fled to Congo and, apparently making use of a network of nuns and priests, managed to obtain an offer "to study" in Rome. Under an assumed name, Seromba served as deputy parish priest at a church in Florence before moving to San Mauro a Signa in 2000. I signed his indictment on June 8, 2001. Seromba denied having anything to do with the massacre at Nyange and called the accusations against him politically motivated lies. Seromba, predictably, said he wanted to be left in peace, but announced that he wanted to explain himself at a sermon on the Sunday after he was to have been arrested. The church was packed with parishioners who, according to an article in *The Guardian*, were wondering whether marriages and other sacraments performed by Seromba would be considered valid if he did in fact participate in the Rwandan genocide. Seromba did not give them an explanation. He never showed up. Church officials sent him into hiding.

I was, to put it mildly, furious. I told the press: "Apparently, Italy doesn't know that the obligation to execute our arrest warrant is an international obligation without need of an internal law. In the light of the charges brought against the accused, I fervently hope that Italy will prove itself able to meet its responsibilities." Slobodan Milošević had arrived in The Hague only a few weeks earlier. I drew the obvious parallel: "It's a scandal. Belgrade has handed over Milosevic, but Rome won't grant me this arrest."

The Italian media suggested that the real reason why the government did not execute the arrest warrant was pressure from the Vatican, which had been seeking ways to understate the role some members of the clergy had taken in the Rwanda genocide. In mid-June 2001, the Vatican was questioning the objectivity of a Belgian court that had found two Rwandan nuns guilty for crimes connected with the genocide. Sister Julienne Kisito and Sister Gertrude Mukangango received twelve- and fifteen-year prison terms, respectively, for their involvement in the killing of thousands of civilians who had sought refuge in their convent. Witnesses testified that the two nuns had actively directed death squads to places where Tutsis were in hiding and had supplied gasoline to burn down a building with civilians inside. The Vatican spokesman, Joaquín Navarro Valls, reportedly said: "The Holy See cannot but express a certain surprise at seeing the grave responsibility of so many people and groups involved in this tremendous genocide in the heart of Africa heaped on so few people."

I met with the Vatican in an attempt to convince the Church authorities to persuade Seromba to surrender. It came to nothing. The Vatican's representative said Seromba was doing good works in San Maura a Signa and that the Church would do nothing, because the priest's arrest was a matter for the civil authorities. The Catholic Church was very interested, however, in the murder, in Gakurazo, of Rwanda's archbishop and the country's other ranking Catholic clergymen.

I had two meetings about the Seromba arrest with Prime Minister Silvio Berlusconi, the latter one in October 2001. He assured me that he would issue an executive decree if the matter was not resolved otherwise within a few months. This was a relief. Still, after our meeting, Berlusconi called me aside for a private chat. Of course, I agreed. He brought up the past and began discussing the investigations Ilda Boccassini, the magistrate from Milan, had undertaken in the early 1990s to bring corruption charges against political leaders in Italy in order to improve transparency and accountability. "You were helping these Italian magistrates, and they are communists. They are red, and they have no evidence. They are inventing things. . . . Why were you helping them? It must stop." He had criticized me openly in the press while I was still in Switzerland. Now he made it seem that I had acted in good faith, but had been a dupe for Boccassini and the other Italian magistrates.

We waited a few months more before Seromba finally boarded the aircraft that brought him to Arusha and the United Nations detention unit. The Diocese of Florence issued a statement saying that Seromba's decision to surrender sprang from a desire to "shed light on the grave accusations against him, which he learned only through the press." The Trial Chamber eventually found Seromba guilty of genocide and extermination and sentenced him to fifteen years imprisonment.

By the autumn of 2001, the Rwandan government and military had still given us no files on killings allegedly carried out by the RPF in 1994. During late 2001 or early 2002, I was in Kigali and spoke with Rwanda's prosecutor general, one of the Tutsi officials who had assured the entire world that his country was going to cooperate with the tribunal's investigations. As we were speaking, it became clear to me that Gahima knew everything about our investigative efforts, including their results. He knew where our investigators had gone and the testimony we had collected. This raised both witness-protection and investigator-security issues. Now, I withdrew three of the investigators from Kigali to Arusha in order to pursue the Special Investigation beyond Rwanda's borders.

By late 2001, we knew Bruguière's investigation of the shooting down of President Habyarimana's airplane had succeeded in assembling a critical mass of evidence and that he would eventually issue arrest warrants against a number of officers of the RPF who were now high-ranking members of Rwanda's military. Bruguière forewarned us that we might encounter trouble from Kagame and other members of the Rwandan government. On May 17, 2002, I met Bruguière at a military airport outside of Paris. He had still not completed his inquiry. But he did reveal to me that he had obtained evidence linking President Kagame with the assassination.

He did not elaborate. But I asked him to give my team access to the evidence, so the members could make a proper evaluation. Bruguière agreed. He also said his investigation had discovered credible witnesses whom he had placed under protection. There were difficulties, however, because France's foreign minister, Hubert Védrine, was not willing to continue providing protection. "I know Védrine," I said, "Better not to insist on anything with him." Both of our investigations had recruited witnesses in the Democratic Republic of Congo and in Uganda, and the Office of the Prosecutor attempted to arrange safe passage for other prospective witnesses who sought to leave Rwanda. Several did make it out of the country but chose to return home, and we eventually learned that they had revealed to the authorities in Kigali everything they had told our investigators.

I visited Rwanda for the annual commemoration of the genocide in the spring of 2002. The government had given us no help. And now, my team members and I sensed that we were no longer welcome. We drove three hours by car to the ceremony held at the site of an atrocity. President Kagame was there. Gahima, the prosecutor general, was there. Other officials with whom we had enjoyed frequent contact were there. Nobody looked at us. Nobody greeted us. I sat there in my assigned seat in the diplomatic section listening to speeches in the Kinyarwandan language, understanding nothing, feeling nothing but frustration, and constantly sipping water to keep from becoming dehydrated. The car ride back took another bladder-straining four hours. I knew something was amiss. I recognized the cold shoulder. I knew it was not an oversight.

CONFRONTING BELGRADE
2003 AND 2004

Dressed in black on a cool spring day, I made a private visit to the grave of Zoran Djindjić. I had asked the government not to allow a media circus to disrupt the tranquility of the Novo Groblje, Belgrade's New Cemetery. Foreign Minister Goran Svilanović, in this matter at least, honored his word. The authorities deployed police officers and positioned sharpshooters in the area. My aides and I carried bouquets to the grave. Sprays of carnations, pastel-colored Gerbera daisies, roses of red, yellow, and white, and greenery covered the marble slab. I lit a candle in the Orthodox Christian tradition, and lingered in silence for a quarter of an hour or so. Then I touched the cross, said my goodbye to another good, brave man, and turned away.

I had wanted to attend Djindjić's state funeral. I had wanted to pay my respects with the hundreds of thousands of other mourners who had stood in silence to bid him farewell and, in so doing, had made a tacit demonstration of their disgust with the criminal mafia corrupting their country, its economy, and its institutions of government, especially its security institutions. Svilanović was the first to advise me not to come for the funeral. He said my presence would be provocative and complicate future cooperation with the tribunal. He told Switzerland's chargé d'affaires in Belgrade, Jean-Daniel Ruch, that my desire to attend the funeral was a cynical attempt to grab media attention. This I found offensive. I called Dušan Mihajlović, the interior minister, and he invited me to attend. Then, suddenly, Belgrade informed me that the Djindjić family did not want me attending. This I could not believe. My aide, Anton Nikiforov, contacted Djindjić's wife, Ružica, and she sent word that the family would be grateful if I would attend. After this, Mihajlović informed us that the "entire government" had decided to bar me from attending. Svilanović told me I would be treated as a persona non grata if I arrived at any Serbian border crossing.

Svilanović and others in Belgrade seem to have concluded that they could exploit the Djindjić assassination to lighten the onus of Belgrade's failure to cooperate with the tribunal by maintaining that Djindjić had been killed because he had cooperated. This explanation for the murder is ludicrous. The assassins of Zoran Djindjić had clear motives. Foremost among them was preserving a privileged position that had allowed them to engage in criminal activities with impunity. The assassins belonged to the Red Berets, the elite military unit of Milošević's security service, whose members had taken part in ethnic cleansing in Croatia, participated in the genocide in Bosnia and Herzegovina, massacred Albanian civilians in Kosovo, paraded around Belgrade as if they were heroes, and moved into racketeering, prostitution, drug-trafficking, gunrunning, murder for hire, and other misdeeds from which organized thugs draw profit. The commander of this unit, Milorad Ulemek Luković, a deserter from the French Foreign Legion who called himself "Legija," "The Legionnaire," had engineered the hit on Djindjić. In the crucial years before Milošević's fall, Luković's direct superiors had been Frenki Simatović and Jovica Stanišić, men who operated at the core of the disastrous campaign of violence to create a Greater Serbian state.

I had no intention to ease the pressure upon Serbia to cooperate with the tribunal after Djindjić's assassination, for this would have been like rewarding an incorrigible child for bad behavior. My intention was to seize whatever opportunities might arise out of the Djindjić tragedy to secure the arrests of Mladić and Karadžić and the twenty or so other fugitives still at large in Serbia; to complete indictments against the likes of Stanišić, Simatović, and the Milošević regime's other high-end security and military leaders; and to obtain, as quickly as possible, documentary evidence linking their activities as leaders with the crime scenes in Croatia, Bosnia and Herzegovina, and Kosovo.

An opportunity soon presented itself. The Belgrade authorities mounted a massive nationwide crackdown on organized crime after the Djindjić killing. Code-named Operation Saber, this police sweep yielded hundreds of arrests and cast new light upon a spate of unsolved crimes, including political assassinations and gangland killings linked with Milošević, his wife, and members of his regime. I was disappointed to learn, however, that Operation Saber had somehow failed to net even one of the tribunal's fugitives. Djindjić had promised me a number of times that he would deliver Mladić. I was concerned that his successor as prime minister, Zoran Živković, would fail to live up to Djindjić's legacy.

On April 2, 2003, Svilanović and the interior minister, Dušan Mihajlović, a man whose claims I no longer trusted, traveled secretly to The Hague. We met late in the afternoon at the official residence of Belgrade's ambassador to the Netherlands. I was not surprised when the two ministers began serving up a message spiced with expressions like "mutual assistance," "common interest," and "cooperation." Svilanović said there was a need to identify the common interests of the Office of the Prosecutor and the Belgrade authorities. He wanted the tribunal's help and said the time had come to reach a mutual agreement on the high-ranking targets of our remaining investigations. As we spoke, the ambassador personally served us juice and water, apparently because she did not want her domestic staff to overhear the conversation.

After a few minutes of hesitation, I agreed to reveal the names of individuals for whom we were preparing indictments: General Pavković, General Djordjević, General Lazarević, and General Lukić for Kosovo; Jovica Stanišić, Frenki Simatović, and General Perišić for Croatia and Bosnia; and Goran Hadžić for Croatia. The investigation teams had also produced a list of second-tier targets.

Svilanović asked that we either strike Lukić, Pavković, Lazarević, and Perišić from our list or allow them to face trial in Serbia. I asked Svilanović to clarify whether he was requesting impunity for these men. "Yes," he answered. He said that Belgrade would not even discuss handing over Lukić and Lazarević and that preserving Pavković was important because it would help the government retain the army's support.

Interior Minister Mihajlović repeated the legal argument Djindjić had presented in February, insisting that the Serbian government would not, as a matter of policy, accept any tribunal indictments based upon "command responsibility." Any indictment based upon "direct responsibility," that is, based upon evidence of direct orders to commit war crimes, would be accepted, but if the tribunal issued indictments against people caught in the chain of command—men such as Lukić, Pavković, Lazarević, and Perišić—then the government would oppose. Such indictments against the likes of Sreten Lukić and General Lazarević would have tragic consequences for Serbia, Mihajlović asserted.

Thus, these ministers attempted to frame the discussion to preempt demands that the Office of the Prosecutor might make for the arrest and transfer of these high-ranking military and security-service officers, as if we were turning "the best" into the enemy of "the good," as if our determination of how far down the chain of command we were going to proceed in bringing indictments was a completely arbitrary decision. It was clear that political expediency was driving the efforts of these ministers to save Lukić, Lazarević, Pavković, and the others from arrest, probably because these officers or their friends had assisted the police crackdown that had followed the Djindjić assassination. When any government begins to fight corruption by arresting tainted members of the police, some of the tainted claim to undergo a miraculous conversion. Perhaps it is expedient politically to cut some of them a break. But who was going to speak for the thousands of victims of these generals who had, allegedly, carried out Milošević's will?

The ministers tried to tell me that the police and the army were just dupes during the Kosovo violence and that the real culprits were Milošević, Nikola Šainović, local leaders of Milošević's party, and true-believer nationalists among the rank and file. At the top was Milošević. Next came the interior minister, Vlajko Stojiljković, who had committed suicide on the steps of the parliament a year earlier. On the third level were the two assistant ministers: the state security chief, Rade Marković, who had a direct link with Milošević, and the chief of public safety, General Vlastimir Djordjević, who had reportedly fled to Russia. Mihajlović maintained that Sreten Lukić, whom we knew to be a commander of the police units on the ground in Kosovo, was "two or three levels" below Djordjević. Mihajlović vouched for Lukić's character. "We know full well," Mihajlović maintained, "that Lukić is an honest man who did not enrich himself during Milošević's rule." Lukić, he said, had not been in Milošević's inner circle. Milošević had not promoted Lukić. Milošević's party had accused Lukić of protecting Albanians. Lukić had issued no order that would show his responsibility for crimes. And Lukić had personally arrested the assassins of Zoran Djindjić. In no way, Mihajlović said, was Lukić connected with the Red Berets implicated in the Djindjić assassination and other political killings.

Foreign Minister Svilanović stepped in and diverted the conversation away from discussion of the generals. He said the government wanted as quickly as possible to transfer to the tribunal two of the Office of the Prosecutor's key targets, men who had for years handed down orders to Lukovic and the Red Berets. These targets were Jovica Stanišić and Frenki Simatović, who had been swept up by Operation Saber. "We can't hold them for long," Svilanović explained, urging us to indict them. "Speed it up, so we can send them to The Hague." Svilanović then explained that the parliament would soon amend the Law on Cooperation with the Tribunal and rescind the article forbidding the arrest and transfer of persons the tribunal had indicted after the law's passage. I agreed with no hesitation to accelerate completion of the indictments against Stanišić and Simatović. But I refused to refrain from submitting indictments against the generals and others.

Mihajlović next said that the police would use Operation Saber to locate Bosnian Serb fugitives who might be in Serbia. He stressed that the army was now fully engaged, including General Krga and the newly appointed chief of military intelligence, who had received unambiguous instructions to locate all fugitives who had links to the army, including two former Bosnian Serb Army officers who had allegedly acted as middle managers of the Srebrenica massacre: Ljubiša Beara and Vinko Pandurević.

Mihajlović told us that the army had cut off Mladić's support, that Mladić had joined Karadžić for a time in Bosnia before Karadžić sent him away, and that Mladić had returned to Serbia. Mihajlović refused to elaborate or to indicate where Mladić's trail had led, but this conversation marked the first time that he confirmed Mladić's presence in Serbia and Karadžić's presence in Bosnia and Herzegovina. We would later learn that, even as Mihajlović was telling us his story, the Yugoslav Army was providing Mladić housing, transportation, health care, and sustenance. Mihajlović then revealed that the Serbian police were ready to work with foreign intelligence services to locate and arrest Karadžić and Mladić, especially since Koštunica and his people were no longer occupying positions of power.

Promises about other fugitives continued to circle the room in the ambassador's residence before landing in my lap: Šljivančanin, the accused linked with the murders of prisoners at Vukovar, would be arrested and transferred to The Hague if he did not surrender voluntarily within a few weeks. The government would be overjoyed if the tribunal were to indict General Djordjević. The time had come to coordinate our investigative efforts and examine the war crimes in Kosovo. The government would seek to interview both Šešelj and Milošević at the tribunal's detention unit.

I used the opportunity to press again for Belgrade to allow prosecution investigators and lawyers access to prospective witnesses and the documents we had been demanding for over a year, including the minutes and verbatim transcripts of the Supreme Defense Council. This elicited the usual mumbling, and at the end of the discussion Mihajlović announced in *Mission: Impossible* fashion that, of course, our discussion had never taken place.

The parliament of the State Union of Serbia and Montenegro did amend the Law on Cooperation with the Tribunal, removing the troublesome Article 39. On May 19, I returned to Belgrade for discussions with the Serbs on securing more arrests and moving our investigative work ahead. Djindjić's successor, Serbia's Prime Minister Zoran Živković, said his government wanted, by the end of the year, to resolve the outstanding issues related to the tribunal, including the arrests and transfers of fugitives on the territory of the Republic of Serbia. He explained that the government was undertaking a radical reform of the country's army, which would require approximately six months and help overcome resistance to the inevitable arrest of Ratko Mladić. Živković provided written intelligence on the whereabouts of Mladić and Šljivančanin—who was now reported to be under surveillance and had threatened to blow himself up with dynamite—and said he would be ready to transfer Stanišić and Simatović in the near future.

Živković, too, asked me not to proceed with indictments against General Perišić, Sreten Lukić, General Pavković, and General Lazarević in order not to upset the stability of the country. "This," I answered, "is not possible." I could not and would not promise to abandon investigations against any of these four men, and if investigators discovered sufficient evidence, I would submit indictments to the Trial Chamber. I would, however, be flexible. I might not indict them for the time being and would notify Živković. "We might," I said, "speak about this after the arrests of Mladić, Šljivančanin, and other fugitives." And by this, I clearly meant that good intentions and attempts were not enough. I also complained that we had not yet received access to key documents, including Ratko Mladić's personnel file and transcripts of military and police intercepts of communications by the Albanian militia in Kosovo, the Kosovo Liberation Army.

Next came a luncheon with Foreign Minister Svilanović, Defense Minister Boris Tadić, and their deputies. Tadić opened the conversation by asserting that it was the responsibility of the police, and not the Defense Ministry or the army, to undertake arrests of tribunal fugitives. These remarks bore a familiar scent. I cautioned Tadić that General Krga had already tried to explain to me that locating and arresting fugitives was not the army's job, while the former interior minister, Dušan Mihajlović, had gone on and on explaining that the police were not authorized to arrest members of the army. Tadić responded only by asserting that cooperation between the army and police was very good, for the present, and that they were "investigating" the Mladić case.

After a discussion about securing waivers for prospective witnesses to testify against Milošević, Svilanović criticized me for having stated publicly in the United States that, when it came to discussing the arrest of fugitives, I did not know whom to trust in Belgrade. He called this a "challenge to the government's integrity." Then he assured me that "Belgrade's doors were always open" and that it was not necessary to go public with criticism. I was not going to accept this without comment, and I somehow succeeded in remaining diplomatic. "So many declarations, so many statements of political will, so many commitments, and so few results," I said. "The authorities must cooperate. . . . They must give something and not just ask."

I had already reminded Svilanović of our outstanding requests for the records of the Supreme Defense Council, including the minutes and transcripts of its meetings, records the prosecution team knew would be crucial to establishing beyond a reasonable doubt the links between Milošević and the rest of the political leadership in Belgrade with the war crimes committed in Croatia, Bosnia and Herzegovina, and Kosovo. I pushed Svilanović to hand over the documents. He refused, saying, as he had said so many times before in our private meetings and in the press, that these documents could not reach the eyes of the judges at the International Court of Justice who would decide the lawsuits that Croatia and Bosnia and Herzegovina had filed against the Federal Republic of Yugoslavia, the ancestor of the new State Union of Serbia and Montenegro. Svilanović said, however, that the government would provide these documents only if the Trial Chamber imposed "protective measures," so that they would be cited only in closed court before the tribunal's judges and not appear before the general public where they would find their way before the International Court of Justice. Svilanović proposed that the Office of the Prosecutor either present the Trial Chamber presiding over the Milošević case with a motion to provide these documents protective measures or submit to the Trial Chamber a written expression of support for a motion by the Belgrade government for such protective measures. I informed Svilanović that it was his government's responsibility, and not mine, to request protective measures.

On May 24, 2003, I did so in writing. I sent Svilanović a letter explaining that the prosecution in the Milošević case required the Supreme Defense Council documents. Zoran Lilić, who had been telling Geoffrey Nice about these documents for months, would be taking the stand in a matter of weeks. The Serbs were ready to provide records in a way that would help us sink Milošević with the millstone of genocide tied around his neck. If we did not seize this break in the political cloud cover, the Office of the Prosecutor might not acquire these documents for months or years. I was prepared to say I would not oppose if the protective measures were indeed *reasonable* under the applicable procedural rule, 54 bis, which expressly limits such protective measures to material that touches upon *national security interests*. I sent Svilanović a letter making exactly these points:

It was suggested by you, as the President of National Council for Co-operation (NCC) with the [Yugoslavia Tribunal], that in order to release the above mentioned documents for the purposes of trial a commitment is made by the Prosecutor to support the application of Serbia and Montenegro for protective measures in respect to those documents or parts of the documents, for which the Government believes such measures are required.

Having reviewed the proposal and acting in the spirit of co-operation and good will, and further to our discussions in Belgrade, I am prepared to confirm my commitment that the [Office of the Prosecutor] shall support in general terms the application of Serbia and Montenegro for protective measures in respect to those documents or parts of documents of the [Supreme Defense Council] records from the time of Z[oran] Lilić's Presidency (1993–1997), for which the Government believes such measures are required.

It is understood that the application for protective measures shall be reasonable and shall take into consideration the interest of transparency of the court proceedings. It is also understood that it shall be for Serbia and Montenegro to argue before the Trial Chamber in support of application for protection measures, and, therefore, it will be for the Trial Chamber to accept or reject the application. . . . In any event Rule 54 bis . . . provides good grounds for proper protection measures *when national security interests are involved.*

In regard to the [Supreme Defense Council] documentation sought by the prosecution, I understand that upon receipt of this letter immediate access will be granted to my staff to review the said documentation. The

[Office of the Prosecutor] staff after the review will compile a list of documents wanted for the trial, and then the NCC will review the list and determine for which documents, or parts of documents, the Government would like to file a request for protective measures. The rest of the documentation from the list shall be provided immediately.

I would also like you to consider, for purposes of expediency in preparation of the requested materials for the court proceedings, making all documentation selected by the [Office of the Prosecutor] staff and reviewed by the NCC available to the [Office of the Prosecutor] immediately (with identification of the documents, for which protective measures will be sought). The [Office of the Prosecutor] will then be able to work on and prepare all documents, including the sensitive ones, for trial. The [Office of the Prosecutor] staff would of course, handle the sensitive documents in the most confidential manner, *pending determination of the Trial Chamber as to whether their use in court will or will not be subject to protection measures.*[1] [Emphasis added.]

When Belgrade's lawyers met with the Trial Chamber's judges to request protective measures for the Supreme Defense Council documents, they produced this letter, which in no way constitutes any kind of agreement or deal.

Belgrade soon began arresting and transferring more of the tribunal's accused to The Hague: on May 17, the transfer of Miroslav Radić, who allegedly participated in the execution of prisoners removed from Vukovar's hospital; on May 30, the transfer of Frenki Simatović; on June 11, the transfer of Jovica Stanišić; on June 13, the capture of Šljivančanin, at home, in his underwear; on July 4, the surrender of the alleged former commander of the notorious Omarska concentration camp, Željko Mejakić; on August 15, the transfer of Mitar Rašević, allegedly a commander of the guards at an infamous prison in Foča; on September 25, the surrender of Vladimir Kovačević, who allegedly commanded an artillery attack on Dubrovnik.

By June 16, Zoran Lilić had also flown to The Hague, not to take up residence in the tribunal's detention unit beside Milošević and the others, but to become the highest-ranking Serb insider to testify in the Milošević trial. Lilić did not provide smoking-gun evidence of Slobodan Milošević's complicity in genocide. He even chummed around with Milošević during cross-examination. But Lilić's testimony, especially during direct examination, amounted to a quantum leap into the realm of crucial evidence. In the opinion of prosecution analysts, Lilić's testimony demonstrated that Milošević played the dominant role in the Supreme Defense Council and linked him with the establishment of the clandestine mechanism to pay the hundreds of Yugoslav Army officers, including Ratko Mladić, who had been directing the armed forces of the Serbs in Croatia and in Bosnia and Herzegovina. Lilić confirmed that the notorious Red Berets fit within the structure of the Ministry of Interior in Belgrade, that their political commander was Stanišić, and that Stanišić had reported directly to Milošević. Lilić's testimony showed that Belgrade and the Serbs in Croatia and in Bosnia and Herzegovina had established a special council to coordinate "state policy." Lilić's testimony showed that key Serbs from Bosnia and Croatia, including Ratko Mladić, met frequently with Milošević and that General Perišić met with Milošević on military issues outside of the Supreme Defense Council framework. But most importantly, and most damaging for Milošević, were those Supreme Defense Council records Lilić brought into evidence, which represented only a fraction of the Supreme Defense Council documents the Office of the Prosecutor was seeking from the Belgrade government.

The fight to obtain the complete set of these records from Belgrade continued behind closed doors. On June 5, 2003, the Trial Chamber granted protective measures and ordered the documents handed over. Unfortunately, the protective measures themselves as well as confidentiality requirements prevent me even now from revealing the details of even the legal arguments and rulings by the Trial Chamber and Appeals Chamber concerned with the granting the protective measures to these records. I can say, however, that neither Geoffrey Nice, nor I, nor any other members of the team believed that the protective measures that the Serbian government sought were reasonable, because the measures sought went beyond the "national security criteria" provided for in Rule 54 bis. In press statements, Svilanović's former legal adviser, Vladimir Djerić, revealed that the government sought the protective measures to safeguard the country's "national interest"—and by this, they meant the outcome of the case before the International Court of Justice. Rule 54 bis does not provide for such protection. The fact that the issue bounced back and forth between the Trial Chamber and Appeals Chamber clearly indicates that the prosecution found the requested protective measures to be unreasonable and appealed. Even after the Trial Court's ruling on June 5, 2003, the Office of the Prosecutor began receiving the documents only intermittently, and obtaining them required making relentless demands that Belgrade hand them over.

The names Mladić and Karadžić arose time and again during the summer of 2003. On June 25, I met with President Jacques Chirac at his office in the Élysée Palace in Paris. The monumental spaces, with their decorative marble, glistening chandeliers and gold leaf, and furnishings with vegetal flourishes, seem haunted by Louis XV, the Marquise de Pompadour, and legions of courtiers, revolutionaries, presidents, and ministers from centuries past. During an earlier meeting with Chirac, he mentioned President Boris Yeltsin of Russia. Yeltsin, he said, had informed him that Russia would not allow the tribunal to arrest Radovan Karadžić and that Yeltsin had advised Karadžić to leave Serbia and go into hiding in Belarus. "I am prepared to take him out of Bosnia by helicopter," Yeltsin had said. I was alone on this visit to the Élysée. I was carrying especially sensitive documents to present to President Chirac for comment, and I did not want to put him in the position of having to react in the presence of my aides. The set of documents I handed him were, until this moment, secret. But the prosecution was about to disclose them to Milošević, because the judges hearing the case might have considered the information they contained exculpatory. Milošević and his shadow defense team were surely going to enter the documents into testimony, making them a public record. I wanted to extend Chirac the courtesy of knowing in advance what was coming.

These documents were transcripts of intercepted telephone conversations between Serbian leaders, including Milošević. The conversations took place during December 1995, that is, during the period between the initialing and the final signing, in Paris, of the Dayton Peace Agreement. At that time, the Bosnian Serbs were holding, effectively as hostages, two French pilots and making demands of France to win their release. The pilots' plight went right to the offices of President Jacques Chirac.

I handed Chirac the transcript of a conversation between Zoran Lilić, the president of Serbia, and General Momčilo Perišić, the commander of the Yugoslav Army, that took place on December 10, 1995, just two days before the Serbs released the pilots. The dialog between Lilić and General Momčilo Perišić is intriguing. Perišić's words refer, from the first sentence, to the tribunal's indictment against Mladić:

Perišić: The important thing for [Mladić] is that the [tribunal] take this off his shoulders, you get what I mean?

Lilić: Fine, everyone has promised it to him, damn, [Momčilo] . . .

Perišić (later in the conversation): Look at what he says. If they drop the [tribunal's] charges against him, there is no problem. He is prepared to resolve the problem immediately. I said to him that . . .

Lilić: Are your word and mine not enough? And those of Chirac and Slobodan [Milošević], are they not enough?

Perišić: OK, I'll check it.[2]

I asked Chirac, "Is the suggestion in this document true, that you promised not to arrest Mladić if the pilots were freed?" Chirac has very sincere-looking eyes. Women love his eyes. And he looked at me and answered, "Absolutely not."

Chirac admitted that he had spoken with Milošević about the release of the pilots. But he denied having made any deal, and certainly not a deal that would have given Mladić, the man allegedly responsible for massacring eight thousand captive men and boys at Srebrenica, immunity from prosecution. "How could I have made a deal?" he asked rhetorically, explaining that France was in no position to offer Mladić immunity from arrest because it was NATO, not France, that was going into Bosnia as a peacekeeping force under the Dayton Peace Agreement.

The allusion to a deal in the conversation animated Chirac, however. It was as if he wanted to prove concretely to me that no deal existed. He immediately stood up, strode to his desk, picked up the telephone, and called the commander of the Army of the Republic of France.

"*Alors, Général,*" he said, "Mladić, he is still at large. This is unacceptable. He must be arrested immediately. France must do everything necessary to have him arrested."[3] Chirac ordered a search of a specific location.

I rushed back to The Hague, beaming with confidence based on the tone of Chirac's orders over the phone, the firmness of his conviction, and the clarity of his instructions. I was sure Mladić would be welcomed to the tribunal's detention unit and might even arrive before me. *Alors. Le mur du caoutchouc.* The *muro di gomma* in French.

A week or so later, a delegation from Serbia made its way to Washington, D.C. Prime Minister Živković of Serbia made the trip, along with Foreign Minister Svilanović. They met with Secretary of State Powell; the head of the National Security Council, Condoleezza Rice; Ambassador Pierre Prosper; and others. I was sure they were going with the same package of promises they had offered me, and with the same appeal for assistance. We soon heard that arresting Mladić had been the central theme of the meetings and that Washington pledged new support for the arrest effort while making it clear that other United States assistance for Serbia and Montenegro depended upon the resolution of this issue.

On September 4, I received a message from Zoran Živković assuring me that Mladić had now become Belgrade's top priority. The government had established a task force of thirty people whose sole aim was to arrest the fugitive general. This task force included members of the civilian intelligence service, the police, and the military, Živković said, and it had at its disposal all the necessary technical and operational means, including the capability to undertake simultaneous human and electronic surveillance of a number of individuals suspected of having ties to Mladić and his family, friends, and former comrades-in-arms. The task force also had the authority to conduct immediate operations anywhere within the country, including military facilities. Three weeks later, the Belgrade authorities told us that they had received a tip on Mladić's whereabouts from a friendly foreign intelligence service. Several hundred police officers and members of special security units had descended upon the location, but Mladić was nowhere to be found. I wondered why the tribunal had not been invited to participate. I wondered whether the story was any more credible than the stories about NATO operations we would read from time to time in the press or hear about during diplomatic discussions. I did not know whom to trust. I had begun to think that these operations amounted to little more than theatrical attempts to demonstrate to us that something was happening when, in fact, nothing of significance had happened. Results were certainly lacking.

I was skeptical about the reports of the big Mladić arrest operation. And on October 3, when I flew to Belgrade for what turned out to be the most unpleasant visit of my tenure as chief prosecutor, I was skeptical about almost everything emanating from Belgrade. By now, it was clear that the reformist zeal in Serbia had cooled. The army was unregenerate despite a purge of twenty or so generals. Still lurking inside the civilian intelligence service were persons with war crimes haunting their past and connections to organized crime haunting their present. Credible press reports and a paper by the International Crisis Group had named the newly appointed chief of military intelligence, Momir Stojanović, in connection with a massacre of 129 civilians during the violence in Kosovo in 1999.[4] Unrelenting pressure from the United States and the European Union was driving whatever real cooperation Belgrade was giving the tribunal.

The key topics on the day of my visit were Mladić and the case against Belgrade at the International Court of Justice. In fact, it soon became apparent that the Serbs' strategy was to apprehend Mladić, serve him up to answer before the tribunal for the genocide in Bosnia and Herzegovina, and work to convince the Bosnian government to drop its genocide lawsuit against Serbia before the International Court of Justice. My suspicions rose during my first meeting, with the president of the State Union of Serbia and Montenegro, Svetozar Marović, and Vladimir Djerić from the Union's Ministry of Foreign Affairs, the gatekeeper Svilanović made responsible for preventing damning evidence of Serbia's complicity in the genocide in Bosnia and the land-grab in Croatia from getting before the tribunal and, especially, the International Court of Justice.

Marović is a Montenegrin. At the time of my visit, Montenegro and Serbia were at loggerheads. Marović, therefore, was not at all concerned about Serbia's legal troubles. Nevertheless, he seemed to be flattering me excessively when he said that he understood my displeasure at aspects of Belgrade's lack of cooperation with the tribunal. He suggested that I place observers from the Office of the Prosecutor in his office to monitor the efforts of the State Union government to overcome internal obstacles to cooperation. I told Marović that I had noticed some improvement. I mentioned, however, that the Office of the Prosecutor still had no responses to requests for seventy-nine waivers for witnesses to testify, which was unacceptable. I also informed him that Belgrade was now demanding protective measures for certain documents and that it was taking an inordinate amount of time for these documents to pass through the government's gauntlet of clearances and authorizations. At this, Djerić leapt in, asserting that there were *only* seventy-two outstanding waivers, an admission that, I felt, proved my point. Djerić also said the Belgrade government had presented the Trial Chamber handling the Milošević case with a request for protective measures for only some of the Supreme

Defense Council documents. I suggested that his government give us those documents for which it had not requested protective measures, so attorneys and investigators might begin analyzing them. This suggestion led nowhere. I then complained about restrictions on the tribunal's access to other archives. But Djerić replied that, once again, the government's caution was driven by its sensitivities about the lawsuits before the International Court of Justice.

They left it to me to raise the embarrassing problem of fugitives roaming free across the territory of Serbia and Montenegro. Marović said the authorities were now concentrating all of their resources on Mladić and believed Mladić still enjoyed the protection of "dangerous men who were prepared to fight to the last." I could see the shadow of the army descend across his face. "What about Mladic's personnel file?" I asked. "The file isn't a fugitive." Marović blurted out something to seem helpful and made a call to someone to fetch the file, which, of course, never arrived. He mentioned the dismissals of twenty-two generals. He even suggested that I extend my stay in Belgrade, that my continuing presence in Belgrade might help push cooperation forward.

Svilanović's was the next name on my *scheda di ballo*, my dance card. Again, Djerić, his gatekeeper, was present. After complaining about waivers for witnesses, I told Svilanović that Belgrade's treatment of our request for access to archives was scandalous. It had not elicited a definitive response in seven months, I said, and the only positive answer we had received was approval to examine records from the period *after* the conflicts in Croatia and in Bosnia and Herzegovina had ended. I said it was fortunate that the judges in the Milošević trial were holding hearings only three days each week, because the extra time would make Belgrade's stalling tactics less effective.

Svilanović responded by again referring to Serbia's problem defending itself against the lawsuits before the International Court of Justice. He insisted that Belgrade had to "work on this issue." He then warned me not to file another motion for a binding order to provide access to the archives, advising me that the prosecution had little chance to prevail and that filing any such motion would "not help matters," meaning that Belgrade might cooperate even less. Perhaps Svilanović intended to irritate me as much as he did. The Belgrade government had only begun providing the tribunal with significant documents, and only in fits and starts, *after* Geoffrey Nice had gone to the Trial Chamber with the motion for a binding order for the Supreme Defense Council records almost a year earlier. Svilanović once again mentioned the genocide lawsuit against Serbia before the International Court of Justice, clearly implying that he knew the information the documents contained would be catastrophic for Serbia if the judges at the International Court of Justice ever obtained it.

"There is," Svilanović reminded me, "a count of genocide against Milošević." He said it was clear that, if the Yugoslavia tribunal found Milošević guilty of genocide, it would weaken Serbia's defense to the lawsuits before the International Court of Justice. "This," he said, "is why the authorities are adamant now to get Mladić arrested." He suggested that all the blame for the genocide at Srebrenica and the other outrages the Serbs had committed in Bosnia could be foisted upon Mladić, that Mladić could become a scapegoat, and Belgrade might be able to convince the government of Bosnia and Herzegovina to drop the case. He cited precedent: After the arrest of Šljivančanin, the Yugoslav National Army major who was in command when the combined Serb forces overran Vukovar, expelled its population, and summarily executed 260 unarmed prisoners, it had become easier for Belgrade to speak with Zagreb. By this, Svilanović clearly meant that it was easier to speak to Croatia about dropping its case before the International Court of Justice. "The most important point is to avoid responsibility of the state," Svilanović insisted. He said that the government wanted to resolve all difficult problems with the tribunal before the end of the year. "And this means Mladić," he exclaimed. I could think of little else to say except that I would deliver a report critical of the State Union of Serbia and Montenegro in my report to the United Nations Security Council a week later. Thus ended the high point of my day.

Next came the bad-news meeting: the face-to-face with Serbia's prime minister, Zoran Živković. I would be the one delivering the bad news. By now we knew that Belgrade's newfound obsession with Mladić was being fueled by energy radiating from the United States. This would have been a wonderful development if only we had known what the United States was doing and to what ends. Would Washington, if Mladić were captured, play Svilanović's scapegoat game and advise Bosnia to withdraw its lawsuit against Serbia and Montenegro? Was this the reason for Washington's obsession with Mladić and not, say, Karadžić? We had no idea. Washington kept us in the dark. As he sat across from me on a sofa in his office,

Živković toed the line already taken by Marović and Svilanović. He stressed the Serbian government's role in the effort to locate and arrest the fugitives residing in Serbia. He stressed that there were no political barriers to arresting indicted accused, including General Mladić. Živković said that during his last trip to the United States he had agreed to accept Washington's assistance for the effort to apprehend Mladić. He mentioned the massive arrest operation a week earlier. He promised that the campaign would continue unabated until the end of the year, until Mladić was arrested, or until I was convinced Mladić was no longer on Serbian soil. "Can a staff member of the Office of the Prosecutor take part in the task force to arrest Mladić?" I asked. Živković said it would be fine with him. But the United States would have to agree.

"The government," he added, "is ready to arrest any of the fugitives, so long as they were successfully located, apart from those whose cases the tribunal would agree to defer to Serbia's courts." The only issue that would bar the Belgrade government from making arrests, he said, was the technical issue of locating fugitives.

With this sentence, Živković let his words race out in front of his government's actual willingness to cooperate. And at this moment, I no longer had any will to listen to all the talk of pursuing Mladić and the other fugitives to the edge of the Serbian universe, all the talk of big operations that yielded no arrests, and all the talk of cooperation with the tribunal being dependent upon a genocide case in some other court. I was ready to assert my will to test Serbia's will to cooperate. I showed Živković several binders and presented him a document, a receipt for four new indictments charging General Lukić, General Djordjević, General Pavković, and General Lazarević with crimes that took place during the massive ethnic cleansing of Kosovo in 1999, the violent expulsion of hundreds of thousands of people from their homes that had taken place live on worldwide television. I asked Živković to sign the receipt and thereby acknowledge that he had accepted service of the indictments and attached warrants for the generals' arrests. Živković's sofa seemed to launch him into space.

"What is this?" he said, feigning surprise as he examined the receipt, the names of the generals, and the blank line for his signature. "After this we can hardly cooperate."

Živković seemed to struggle to utter the proper nouns "Sreten Lukić." Then he began to speak so rapidly in Serbian that my translator, my Russian aide, Nikoforov, started to sputter. Živković said the government would have to find another police department. He said Djindjić and Svilanović had already discussed with me the difficulty of indicting Lukić, the second-ranking person in Serbia's police, a man who had been involved in so many sensitive operations, including the arrests of Djindjić's assassins. "Indicting Lukić means that no one in the Serbian police will work on the tribunal's requests," Živković said.

He went through the names on the other three indictments: Djordjević, no problems at all. Pavković, to be prosecuted in a local court on other charges. Lazarević, still active in the military. "His arrest," Živković said, "will create chaos among the military at a time of reform. . . . To issue this indictment means spoiling all efforts to arrest Mladić. If Milošević himself wanted to think of something harmful to do to this government, he would think of this."

I expressed my surprise at Živković's hesitation, especially since I had informed the Belgrade authorities months earlier that these indictments would be forthcoming. I stressed that, since the evidence against these four accused was sufficient to support the indictments, I had no choice but to issue them, regardless of political considerations.

Živković was desperate to ward off the inevitable. He said the United Nations Security Council was interested only in Karadžić, Mladić, and Croatia's General Gotovina. He whined that the tribunal would not issue indictments against Kosovo Albanian leaders for crimes against Serbs. He said I was seeking to bring down the Serbian government. "Lukić can arrest me, and he can arrest you," Živković told me. "But I can't arrest him. . . . This indictment will explode like a bomb next week. . . . Don't touch Lukić."

I told him a judge had already confirmed the indictments, and they could not be undone.

"You are not simply some mail carrier," he fired back, adding that I would soon be speaking to a new prime minister, because he was "not crazy enough to arrest his own police" and put the lives of his people at risk.

I thought to myself, "If Lukić was so innocent, so upstanding, why was the prime minister so terrified?" I expressed my deep disappointment. It was a Friday, and I informed Živković that the indictments would be made public on the following Monday. I stressed that it would be impossible for the tribunal to accomplish anything if it allowed itself to work only within the bounds of political considerations in places like Serbia.

Živković said it would now be impossible for the government to continue its cooperation with the tribunal. He said this was my fault. He said that cooperating with the tribunal required the cooperation of the police, and that no one, not the police, not the army, would be willing to arrest Lukić or even Mladić.

In the end, Živković admitted that Svilanović had warned him about the indictments a day earlier, so all the shock he had expressed was just bad theater. But Živković refused to sign the receipt or accept the indictments and arrest warrants, saying he lacked the authority to communicate directly with the tribunal. He told me to go back to Svilanović.

After leaving the seat of Serbia's government, I was driven to the residence of the Swiss ambassador to Serbia and Montenegro in order to brief a group of diplomats accredited in Belgrade. Before the briefing, however, I met privately, at my request, with United States Ambassador William Montgomery. I told him about the four indictments. I asked him whether he felt the tribunal should keep them sealed or go public.

"Go public," he said, in no uncertain terms. He explained that it would be politically beneficial to do so, because the indictments would reveal to the Serbian people what the Serbian people needed to know about who was running their country. "The government is going to fall anyway," he said. "It may only precipitate the inevitable."

After the briefing at the Swiss residence, we traveled to a complex known in Belgrade as the parliamentary club, a cluster of houses for hosting foreign dignitaries just up Tolstoy Street from the former residence of Slobodan Milošević. During a brief conversation, Boris Tadić, then the minister of defense, looked petrified with fear as he spoke of reforming the army. He asserted that he had no information on Mladić's whereabouts and no information that anyone in the army was protecting Mladić. "You must believe me," he exclaimed, before mentioning rumors that Mladić had gone to Bosnia and Herzegovina or Russia. Looking lost and forlorn, he asked me to refrain from criticizing the army constantly.

Svilanović arrived with Tadić's departure, and the only topics of interest were the four indictments. Svilanović said the indictments would make cooperation with the tribunal difficult and derail the Kosovo negotiations about to begin in Vienna. He said Lukić had involved himself in all important arrests. He said Pavković and Lazarević were senior army generals and this would make reform of the military difficult. Svilanović then asked me "to postpone" the indictments while the government "would

Switzerland and the Swiss ambassador had no interest in making that information public. Ambassador Montgomery had no interest either; though later, displaying a lapse of memory, he told the press that I had shown insensitivity to the political realities in Serbia, and I was essentially doing what he had advised me to do. This leaves the Serbian side, and perhaps someone who was willing to compromise a listening device in the parlor of the Swiss residency. Whatever the fact, I concluded that there was no point in keeping the indictments and arrest warrants secret anymore.

Before I filed a motion to lift the seal, Ambassador Pierre Prosper of the State Department's office on war crimes called, apparently from Washington. He asked me not to do anything to make the indictments public. Prosper was trying to arrange some kind of deal with the Serbs: delivery of Mladić in exchange for allowing the four generals to be tried in Belgrade. We knew this, though Prosper had never notified the Office of the Prosecutor of any deal in the works, had never consulted us, and apparently had never considered that he might be trampling on the tribunal's independence. I was just hours away from leaving on a trip to the United States and would be visiting Ambassador Prosper at the State Department in just four days. I did not want to face pressure to hold back my motion to lift the seal on the indictments. So I had the motion filed before I departed from Amsterdam for New York.

On October 9, 2003, I told the Security Council exactly what I had told the authorities in Belgrade. "I was inclined to speak about some improvement in Belgrade's cooperation with the [Yugoslavia tribunal] before my visit to Belgrade last week," I said, "but I am not in a position to do it. There is no true commitment for cooperation or readiness to take difficult steps, badly needed not only from the point of view of the tribunal. The authorities are unanimous in stressing the necessity to cooperate with the tribunal; however, when it comes to tough decisions or need to provide sensitive documents, we face obstruction and negative attitude."

I also informed the Security Council on the position I had taken concerning the Supreme Defense Council records:

> I showed understanding for the Serbian concerns regarding protective measures for some materials, even providing the government with my written commitment in the Milošević case.

It is understood that protective measures ought to be reasonable and not contradict the public interest and principle of transparency of the trials. It is regrettable that the requested documents only started to arrive in my office in the recent months and only as a result of binding court orders issued by the Trial Chamber and not as a result of my Requests for Assistance or voluntary contribution. . . .

In the Milošević trial and other cases, I sense a willingness on the side of the authorities to retain crucial material that could prove the implication of the then Belgrade authorities [former regime] in the crimes committed in Bosnia and Herzegovina. Belgrade invokes national security concerns in regard to these materials, but in fact such approach is limiting or slowing down Tribunal's access to critical evidence. This contravenes the interest of justice and truth, and also does not help in terms of our completion strategy.[5]

The problem of fugitives was still unsolved, despite the surrenders of low-ranking accused. More than half of the seventeen fugitives at large, including Ratko Mladić, were residing in Serbia and Montenegro, and the authorities admitted that seven of them were living in Serbia. My office had transmitted precise information to the Serbian authorities to expedite their arrests. "Unfortunately," I said, "we received very limited feedback after such intelligence was passed, and it was not convincing." The authorities of the Republika Srpska still had not located and arrested a single indicted fugitive. Karadžić was moving between the Republika Srpska and Montenegro, and it appeared that there were still influential elements in the Republika Srpska's police and army structures who were actively protecting and supporting fugitives and war crimes suspects.

The next day my advisers and I visited Washington. Ambassador Prosper raised the issue of the indictments against the four Serbian generals. I told him the Serbs had enjoyed advance notice that the indictments were coming. I said Belgrade had even decorated these men whom the tribunal had indicted for massive ethnic cleansing that had gone under the nose of the United States during the 1999 NATO bombing campaign.

Prosper explained that Washington was pressing the Serbs on Mladić. "I want it solved by end of year," he said. As for Djordjević: no problem. Pavkovic: let Serbia try him first. Lukić and Lazarević: problems. These indictments were problematic because of the timing, he warned. "They should remain sealed."

"It is always these political issues," I complained. "They threatened no more attempts to arrest Mladić if these indictments remained."

"We would hate to see this matter disrupt our effort to get Mladić. Can you wait a few months? . . . What do you have to lose waiting two months to release the names on the indictments?"

This is no longer an issue for me, I said, explaining that I had already filed a motion to make the indictments public. "I cannot accept political reasons. The announcement was held back to facilitate arrests, and they simply do not want to make arrests and there was, of course, a government leak to the media. So the secret isn't a secret anymore."

"Our bottom line is to preserve the Mladić option," Prosper said. "They made a commitment to get Mladić before the end of the year."

Secretary of State Colin Powell also remembered that Živković and Svilanović had promised to arrest Mladić. He asked me to give thought to the political issues in Serbia. He asked me to keep the indictments quiet. But I never withdrew my motion. And before I left Washington, I told Ambassador Prosper that I hoped General Lukić had not been involved in the task force to arrest General Ratko Mladić. This would have been rich: one Serbian general indicted in connection with, among other things, a massive ethnic-cleansing operation, massacres, and concealing bodies of civilian victims hunting down another Serbian general indicted in connection with, among other things, a massive ethnic cleansing operation, massacres, and concealing the bodies of civilian victims, and no tribunal representative is allowed even to observe the operation.

On October 20, the Trial Chamber lifted the seal on the indictments against Lukić and the other three generals implicated in the Kosovo violence. It had to have been morning in Washington when Ambassador Prosper called me to express his displeasure at the announcement. Ambassador Montgomery soon started criticizing me for taking the position he had advised me to take. Then, on October 31, Prosper visited The Hague. He said that he and Washington were disappointed. It was regrettable and inappropriate that the tribunal had issued indictments against the four generals. He said the indictments had come as operations to arrest Mladić were ongoing. "You know you had an open door in Washington," he said. "Now you will have to knock."

This hand-wringing about timing and political sensitivity reminded me of the occasions when I had asked the United States to cooperate with the Office of the Prosecutor in mounting an effort to make arrests of the tribunal's accused. I recalled Washington telling me about the difficulty of such operations. I remembered how both George Tenet, the CIA director, and Colin Powell had described how complicated it had been to capture Manuel Noriega in Panama after the United States had invaded the country. I recalled Tenet and officials from the National Security Council explaining that the United States could not share intelligence with anyone, even the tribunal. And now we were in a classic snafu, a situation where one hand did not know what the other hand was doing. The United States had told us nothing of the Mladić effort or what kind of *quid pro quo* might be involved. (I can only assume they figured we would never have agreed to it.) The United States, which had no trouble sharing with the authorities in Serbia and Montenegro—whose intelligence agencies including people who had committed war crimes, were protecting war criminals, and were engaged in organized crime—left us to navigate by the stars we could see and weather the criticism that inevitably resulted whenever we collided with something in the dark.

There were, it seems, attempts to cut us in a little better. A few weeks later, Ambassador Montgomery informed the Office of the Prosecutor that another joint operation to apprehend Mladić was under way and that cooperation with the local authorities was excellent. He described attempts to correct the deficiencies of the arrest effort and to ensure real-time communications and operational coordination with the NATO forces in Bosnia and Herzegovina. Mladić, however, was not apprehended. And three months later, an opportunity to arrest Karadžić tested the capacity of the NATO force to react in real time. This time, near Zaovine, a Bosnian village near the border with Serbia, an informant told a member of the tribunal's tracking unit that he had spotted Karadžić. "Call NATO," the tracking unit member urged. "Call NATO." This was not just another hearsay report, he insisted. The informant had seen Karadžić, and had him located in a specific house.

The Office of the Prosecutor called NATO immediately. And NATO got back to us, not directly, but through an embassy in The Hague, to say it could do nothing. It did not have enough details on the house. Where was it situated? What were the circumstances of Karadžić's presence? How many windows? How many doors? They would send no reconnaissance helicopter due to overcast weather.

So nothing happened.

A few months later, NATO troops raided the home of an Orthodox priest, Father Jeremija Starovlah, in an effort to arrest Karadžić. NATO used explosives to blow the door down. Both Father Starovlah and his son, Aleksandar, were seriously injured and had to be kept on life support systems.

By late January 2004, the Milošević trial was grinding toward the end of the prosecution case. At one moment, Judge May, normally so lucid and articulate, uttered words that were strange and incoherent. The hearing proceeded to its close. But afterward, we discussed whether the judge might have suffered some mild stroke or was experiencing some more critical health problem. It was soon clear that the members of the Trial Chamber knew something was wrong. The judges announced a cancellation of the hearings scheduled for the next week and attributed it to Milošević's ill health. February 5, Judge Robinson signed an order scheduling the hearings that were to take place before the close of the prosecution case. At that time, as the order noted, the prosecution had seven more days to finish presenting evidence, about twenty-seven hours of court time. The order stated that, "in the interests of justice," the prosecution case was to be brought to a close by February 19, 2004. The remaining court time was to be compressed into five days of hearings, each running from nine in the morning to almost five in the afternoon. Other members of my staff and I interpreted this as an attempt by the Trial Chamber to allow the prosecution to finish presenting its case within the time allotted and to abide by the rules governing how long a Trial Chamber could sit while one of its judges was absent due to ill health.

Then we heard rumors that Judge May was suffering brain cancer. I requested a meeting with the tribunal's president, Judge Theodor Meron, to discuss the matter. In a brief conversation, Meron explained that he and the other judges knew of Judge May's illness and had taken measures to manage its consequences for the Milošević trial, which was the Trial Chamber's discretionary decision. On February 10, 2004, the hearings resumed. Judge Robinson made the first statement for the record referring to Judge May's illness: "Judge May being indisposed, Judge Kwon and myself are sitting pursuant to the provisions of Rule 15 bis." During a break between witnesses that day, Milošević complained that the Trial Chamber had decided to accommodate Judge May's ill health by ordering longer workdays and had increased the burden on Milošević without taking into consideration his heart condition:

Milošević: Well, I'm asking you, Mr. Robinson, you, and justifiably so, take note of the fact that Mr. May is ill and that he cannot attend, and at the same time in the previous paragraph you also take note of the fact that I'm ill, but you prescribe that we should work longer hours. So I'm not quite clear how you mean, why you think that the Registrar should help me under conditions of that kind to prepare myself and function properly. You recognise one man's right to be ill, which is quite logical, of course, however, you do not recognise the same right when it comes to me. Can you explain that, please?

Judge Robinson: The order speaks for itself. The Chamber was of the view that since you're ill, it would be appropriate for the Registrar to render whatever assistance he could to you, and I expect that he's doing that. The Chamber is of the view that it is important that this—the Prosecution case be completed within the next two weeks. That is as much as we'll discuss in relation to that matter.[6]

Milošević, as his own counsel, did not question the fact that only two judges were now in the courtroom. The trial went on that day as scheduled, and continued in fits and starts. On Sunday, February 22, 2004, Judge Meron issued a press release stating that he had received a letter of resignation from Judge May, to be effective on May 31, 2004.[7] Three days after Meron's press release, the prosecution rested its case.

The trial team worked night and day thereafter crafting a brief to counter a motion the *amici curiae* had filed on Milošević's behalf for the Trial Chamber to dismiss the charges against him for lack of sufficient proof. Documentary evidence, such as the Supreme Defense Council minutes and transcripts; a video of Milošević praising Jovica Stanišić, Frenki Simatović, Milorad Luković (later convicted as Djindjić's assassin), and the Red Berets for their exploits in Bosnia and Croatia; testimony from insider witnesses such as Zoran Lilić and Milan Babić; as well as testimony from diplomats and other officials who, like General Wesley Clark, had dealt with Milošević, had all bolstered the evidence against him, especially on the genocide count, which, toward the end of the trial, Dermot Groome, Geoffrey Nice, and the other attorneys on the case had worked to prove.

On June 16, 2004, the Trial Chamber, with Lord Iain Bonomy taking Judge May's place beside Judge O-Gon Kwon and the panel's new presiding member, Judge Patrick Robinson, handed down its decision on the motion to dismiss the case. Among other things, the judges ruled that there was sufficient evidence for a Trial Chamber to find, beyond a reasonable doubt, the following:

• Slobodan Milošević and the Bosnian Serb leadership belonged to a joint criminal enterprise whose aim and intention were to destroy a part of the Bosnian Muslims as a group.

• The aim of the joint criminal enterprise was to commit other crimes than genocide and it was reasonably foreseeable to Milošević that, as a consequence of the commission of those crimes, genocide of a part of the Bosnian Muslims as a group would be committed by other participants in the joint criminal enterprise, and it was committed.

• The participants in this joint criminal enterprise committed genocide in the municipalities of Brčko, Prijedor, Sanski Most, Srebrenica, Bijeljina, Ključ, and Bosanski Novi.

• Milošević aided and abetted or was complicit in the commission of the crime of genocide in that he had knowledge of the joint criminal enterprise and that he gave its participants substantial assistance, being aware that its aim and intention was the destruction of a part of the Bosnian Muslims as group.

• Milošević was a superior to certain persons who he knew, or had reason to know, were about to commit or had committed genocide of a part of the Bosnian Muslims as a group. Milošević failed to take the necessary measures to prevent the commission of genocide or punish the perpetrators.

• The scale and pattern of the Serb attacks, their intensity, the substantial number of Muslims killed in the seven municipalities, the detention of Muslims, their brutal treatment in detention centers and elsewhere, and the targeting of persons essential to the survival of the Muslims as a group were all factors that pointed to genocide.[8]

The Trial Chamber also rejected motions to dismiss the case based upon the components of the indictment for Kosovo and Croatia.

It was not without a sense of vindication that I recalled how Nice, Blewitt, and others in the office had sought, during the autumn of 2002, to abandon the genocide count, to decide at the level of the Office of the Prosecutor, rather than at the level of the Trial Chamber, to spare Milošević from answering for the full extent of the crimes perpetrated during the Bosnian war. In the end, the puzzle pieces showing his complicity were there to assemble. And what mockery would we have suffered from survivors of the genocide's victims, among them thousands of mothers who had lost their sons, thousands of wives who had lost their husbands, and thousands of children who had lost their fathers, had we not shown the will to put our prima facie evidence for genocide to the test of a trial? Two years would pass before we knew the full significance of passing this crucial test.

Sir Richard May passed away in Oxford on July 1. His funeral service honored his memory with the dignity and grace he had displayed in the courtroom, and we all had many reasons to be thankful for his contributions to the tribunal as well as his wit and his willpower. After the prayers and hymns and eulogies had ended, the mourners, his family members and men and women of the law, politics, and other areas of community life, found themselves outside on a lawn. I looked over and watched pallbearers place Judge May's coffin into a hearse. Then, alone, his widow, Lady Radmila, followed behind as the vehicle rolled slowly toward his place of repose. The other mourners remained behind, and then began filing away to a reception. I found it so strange, watching this lovely, dignified woman accompanying her beloved to his final rest. I found it so lonesome.

A few months earlier, my brothers and I had followed our mother's casket to the graveyard in Bignasco. Angela Del Ponte had suffered a massive stroke a few weeks earlier at the age of eighty-three. I went to visit her once in the hospital. I came away feeling that the person I had seen lying there was not the mother I had known, not the confident hand at the wheel of the MG, not the woman whose hair had blown in the turbulent air, not the mother who had scolded us for hunting snakes and who told me how to walk and curtsy in the hallway so long ago. She could not communicate. She was not there. I told my brother Flavio that I would only come back for the funeral. We kept her body in a casket in the library of the house for one day and one night, for that is our tradition. The mass was said at San Rocco's, and at the cemetery, each mourner tossed a flower into the grave.

I had visited her as often as possible over the years, and had called her on the phone practically every evening until the day she slipped out of consciousness. There was always my son Mario to discuss. There were the successes and failures in her garden. There were the repairs to her Golf. There was gossip from Bignasco and tales of Ticino. She rarely referred to my work, and I was reluctant to bring it up. Once, however, she asked me: "You are so hard. Why are you so hard on these people? Why are you so harsh?"

9

CONFRONTING KIGALI
2002 AND 2003

On April 2, 2002, six years after it had detained Théoneste Bagosora, the Rwanda tribunal opened his trial, the trial of accused *génocidaires* from the Rwandan military. This was the Rwanda tribunal's highest-profile media event, just as the Milošević trial was the Yugoslavia tribunal's. Colonel Bagosora had allegedly assumed de facto control of military and political decision making in Rwanda after surface-to-air missiles blew up the airplane carrying President Juvénal Habyarimana on the evening of April 6, 1994. The genocide began almost immediately. Unfortunately, on the day the trial opened, Bagosora and his three co-defendants refused to step outside their cells in protest, because their defense counsel had not received French translations of an expert report prepared for the prosecution and statements by prosecution witnesses. The judges allowed the prosecution to make its opening statement, but ruled out having the tribunal's security personnel bring Bagosora and the other three defendants to the dock.

"These four men are among the principal perpetrators of the genocide," I said in my prefatory remarks before the court. "Who is responsible for close to a million deaths in a few months? Who is responsible for all the other victims, mutilated, tortured, raped, left for dead?" The indictment alleged that Bagosora and the other commanders on trial were part of a group of senior Hutu officers who had, for several years, planned the systematic extermination of the Tutsis and moderate Hutus in order to secure the Hutu extremists' political dominance of the country. The indictment alleged that Bagosora was so opposed to peace talks with the Tutsi leadership in 1993 that he left one negotiating session saying he was returning to Rwanda to "prepare the apocalypse."

It would seem illogical that Rwanda's Tutsi leaders, the leaders of the community that had suffered the genocide, would want to stymie criminal proceedings against accused Hutu *génocidaires* like Bagosora. In early June 2002, however, Rwanda's Tutsi-dominated government introduced new travel regulations for the country's citizens, and these new rules were implemented for at least one reason that had nothing to do with regulating the movement of Rwandans in general. Kigali, of course, denied this, but it had imposed these regulations, at least in part, to restrict the movement of witnesses traveling from Rwanda to the tribunal in Arusha to testify. Despite repeated requests, the Rwandan government refused to authorize the temporary transfer of a number of detained witnesses whose testimony was crucial to prosecuting genocide cases. On June 26, the judges adjourned until August the trial of Rwanda's former information minister, Eliezer Niyitegeka, because no prosecution witnesses had turned up. After six aborted hearings in two weeks, on June 27, the judges adjourned until October the tribunal's largest trial, which involved six Hutu defendants facing charges related to massacres of Tutsis at Butare. Again, none of the prosecution witnesses had arrived from Rwanda. And soon, the "media" trial involving Jean-Bosco Barayagwiza, the defendant who had almost walked free on a procedural question in 1999, would be in jeopardy.

The Tutsi-dominated Rwandan government was effectively blackmailing the tribunal, sabotaging its trials of accused Hutu *génocidaires* in order to halt the Office of the Prosecutor's Special Investigation of crimes allegedly committed by the Tutsi-dominated Rwandan Patriotic Front (RPF) in 1994. By now, Rwanda's military prosecutor, having provided the prosecution nothing, seemed to be hiding from us. The authorities brought genocide survivors into Kigali's streets to protest that the tribunal's progress was too slow, that suspected *génocidaires* were working for the tribunal as defense investigators and in other capacities, and that judges had allowed defense counsel to demean witnesses, including Tutsi rape victims, in open court. Some of these complaints were not without merit, but halting the genocide trials was the Rwandan government's objective, so long as there was a possibility that the tribunal would indict Tutsi leaders and army officers. The motive, it seemed, was preserving the Tutsi regime's legitimacy and, by extension, the rule of President Paul Kagame.

On Friday June 28, 2002, my team members and I went to the presidential compound in Kigali in an attempt to resolve this problem with Kagame. He kept us waiting for twenty minutes, I'm sure to make a point, and on this occasion he made no attempt at false modesty. The venue was a spacious salon decorated in a rococo kitsch worthy of Louis XV. At one end of the room, Kagame had placed himself on a golden chair, like a throne, with a Rwandan flag draped behind. "Why this ostentation?" I thought. "Why this overcompensation, with all the misery in Rwanda?" To Kagame's side sat Gerard Gahima, Rwanda's prosecutor general; Martin Ngoga, Rwanda's eyes and ears in Arusha; and a number of Rwandan army officers. I took a seat, stage-left as I recall. After Kagame and I had exchanged compliments, the substantive discussion began. Once again, I informed Kagame that we needed the files of the military prosecutor's investigations of the killings of the archbishop and the other clergymen and other alleged atrocities committed by the RPF in 1994. I confess that I am sometimes too blunt. I admit that at times I can be gruff. But on this occasion, I was reserved to a fault, almost reticent. It was President Kagame who launched into a diatribe.

"No," he declared. "Absolutely not." He instructed me that the tribunal must not investigate the Tutsi militia, the militia he had commanded, the militia that had metamorphosed into Rwanda's army.

"You are destroying Rwanda," Kagame charged. "You must investigate and prosecute the genocide. You haven't gotten Kabuga, go and get him. Don't look into the military. We have done this, and we will do this."

By now, he was fuming: "You will disrupt the reconstruction of the nation. . . . I'm rebuilding this country. . . . I have to maintain internal order. . . . If you investigate, people will believe there were two genocides. . . . All we did was liberate Rwanda."

I tried to interrupt. I tried to explain to President Kagame that our initial request was relatively modest: the investigation of the murders, by members of the RPF, of an archbishop, two bishops, nine priests, and three girls. The RPF had even admitted to the killings. We needed only the facts, the names, the witnesses, the evidence. President Kagame interrupted me, just as Yugoslavia's President Koštunica had done during our first encounter. It was as if Kagame was dispatching orders: "You misunderstood what I told you before. Now I'm telling you what we are doing. Don't touch. . . . Stop the investigation. . . . We know what you are doing. . . . We will not allow you to do this. It is damaging our country. It is possible that soldiers have committed crimes. But we have punished these soldiers. And we will do it."

Then Kagame, clearly alluding to Bruguière's inquiry into the 1994 assassination of Rwanda's president, raised well-known allegations that the French army, whose personnel certainly did not perform admirably in Rwanda at all times during 1994, had intentionally abetted the slaughter. "France was involved in the genocide," Kagame insisted. "Go and investigate the French participation in the genocide."

"You give me the evidence," I replied, "and I'm ready to do it. But I'm not going to do anything based upon your baseless accusations. Give me evidence."

I was incensed. The heat of Kagame's accusations stunned aides on both sides of the room. Gerard Gahima was aghast. Laurent Walpen stared through the window. I notified Kagame that I would continue the Special Investigation. I told him I would report Rwanda's failure to cooperate to the United Nations Security Council. And, with that, the last conversation I ever had with Kagame came to an abrupt close. I refused even to consider answering questions from journalists. This was a mistake. I should have exploited the opportunity to explain to the world how Rwanda's government was obstructing justice in order to blackmail the tribunal to drop an investigation of these men who had become the country's political and military elite.

I departed Kigali pursued by a nagging realization that Rwanda's cycle of impunity, which had emerged from colonial times and produced numerous massacres and one certified instance of genocide, would continue to turn. The Rwanda tribunal, it seemed, was going to administer nothing more than victor's justice. Hundreds of thousands of armed exiled Hutus were clamoring for a return to their native land, just as Kagame's Tutsis had done before April 1994; it seemed inevitable that sooner or later the horrors would return. I was concerned that the United Nations Security Council would do nothing of any consequence in reaction to President Kagame's announced refusal to cooperate with the tribunal and Rwanda's campaign to frustrate the tribunal's work. Only Bruguière's investigation, I thought, could do something significant to break the pattern of impunity. I could only conclude either that Kagame feared he would be indicted or that Rwandan military officers, including men who felt vulnerable to the tribunal's Special Investigation and Bruguière's inquiry, had threatened to overthrow Kagame if he ordered the government to cooperate with these investigations. Rumors of a coup wafted through the capital. International pressure had forced Rwanda to sign a peace treaty and withdraw most of its troops from the neighboring Democratic Republic of Congo, so there were plenty of available men with guns, and over many of their heads hung the question of accountability for atrocities committed in Congo after the 1994 genocide.

On July 23, I went before the United Nations Security Council and reported that the Rwandan government was intentionally hindering the progress of the genocide trials in Arusha as a way of pressuring me to halt the investigations of crimes the Tutsi-dominated RPF had allegedly committed while Hutus were engaged in the genocide:

> Powerful elements within Rwanda strongly oppose the investigation of the Prosecutor, in the execution of the [Rwanda Tribunal's] mandate, of crimes allegedly committed by members of the Rwandan Patriotic [Front] in 1994. Despite assurances given by President Kagame to the Prosecutor in the past, no concrete assistance has been provided in response to repeated request[s] regarding these investigations. Currently, there is no genuine political will on the part of the Rwandan Authorities to provide assistance in an area of work that they interpret to be political in nature, when, obviously, the Prosecutor limits herself to the technical implementation of her judicial mandate.
>
> In these circumstances, the Prosecutor is effectively unable, at this stage, to achieve the investigation of crimes alleged to have been committed by the Rwandan Patriotic [Front] in 1994.

The tribunal's president, Judge Navanethem Pillay of South Africa, formally reported Rwanda's failure to fulfill its obligation to cooperate. The United States and other countries privately pressed Kigali to resume cooperation, which the tribunal appreciated greatly, because, even before the Rwandan genocide, even while they were refugees in Uganda, Kagame and the Tutsi leadership had looked to the United States and Great Britain as its main allies outside of Africa. The director of Human Rights Watch, Ken Roth, wrote the president of the Security Council, United States Ambassador John Negroponte, urging action to enable the tribunal to prosecute those persons on all sides of the Rwandan conflict who were accused of the gravest crimes committed in 1994. Roth explained why the Rwandan government in 2002 could not be trusted to investigate and prosecute persons who had been, in 1994, ranking members of the RPF:

The Rwandan government suggests that the tribunal should try only cases of genocide and leave prosecution of [RPF] crimes to Rwandan courts. It asserts that these courts have tried, convicted, and punished [RPF] members who committed abuses. But the trials have been few and the penalties of those convicted have been light. Only one senior officer, a major, has been tried for massacres committed in 1994. Convicted by court martial in January 1998 after confessing to having ordered the slaughter of more than thirty civilians, he was sentenced to life in prison, but he successfully appealed his sentence and was freed soon after. By June 1998 five others had been convicted of capital offenses committed in 1994, but four were privates and one a corporal, and all received light sentences. The corporal, convicted of having killed fifteen civilians, was punished by only two years in prison.

Most Rwandans know nothing of these [RPF] trials or discount their importance because of the small number and light penalties involved. Victims of [RPF] abuses in 1994, their families, and many other Rwandans continue to demand justice for these crimes.

The Rwandan government has just launched an innovative popular justice program called [*gacaca*] courts, with the stated purpose of delivering justice and contributing to reconciliation. Although the law establishing these new jurisdictions mandates them to try crimes against humanity and war crimes, Rwandan government authorities have made it clear from the start that these popular courts are to deal only with accusations of genocide. Despite such clear orders, Rwandans continue asking [*gacaca*] courts to list those killed by [RPF] soldiers among the victims of 1994 and they ask that these local courts bring implicated [RPF] soldiers to justice. So far their requests have been in vain.

Rwandan authorities have told Rwandans, as they have told the Security Council, that Rwandan courts will deal with [RPF] crimes. Had Rwandan prosecutors wanted to try these crimes, they have had ample time to act. . . . *Victims of* [RPF] *crimes have virtually no chance of obtaining justice in any Rwandan court, whether military court or* [gacaca] *court.* Failing to provide them justice at the international tribunal as well will feed resentment and desire for revenge, explosive sentiments in a region where armed groups continue to operate in opposition to recognized governments. [Emphasis added.]

The United Nations Security Council waited months to respond to the reports Judge Pillay and I made on Rwanda's failure to cooperate, and the response the council managed to muster was only a mild reprimand. I pulled the prosecution's investigators from Kigali. Staying there would produce nothing without the government's cooperation. We had received no documents from Rwanda on the reported RPF atrocities. The investigators had interviewed the few witnesses willing to talk. And operations outside of Rwanda, after numerous trips throughout Africa and Europe, had passed the point of diminishing returns. I sent the investigators to Geneva to draft a status report on the evidence at hand. From it, I concluded that the quality of the evidence was still insufficient to submit an indictment and always would be, unless the team was able to obtain the evidence held in Kigali. The witness crisis waned in September 2002. The Rwandan government, clearly trying to save face after Judge Pillay and I had voiced our complaints before the Security Council, started spreading stories that, by withdrawing my investigators, I had suspended the Special Investigation. Then, the Rwandan authorities allowed the flow of prosecution witnesses to Arusha to resume. The genocide trials delayed in the spring, including the trial of Bagosora and the other accused military *génocidaires*, began anew in the autumn.

I did not drop the Special Investigation. I was still determined to fulfill my mandate by seeing to it that justice was done on all sides of the Rwanda conflict. On November 18, I said as much to representatives of the Alliance for the Liberation of Rwanda, a Hutu opposition group operating in exile within the Democratic Republic of Congo. The Rwandan government wasted no time issuing a press release criticizing me for consorting with "terrorists":

> Carla Del Ponte's meeting with a known Rwandan terrorist and genocidal organization . . . comes as a culmination of her deliberate policy of dangerously veering from the issues of justice, to a point where she is now wining and dining people whose confessed ideology and practice is genocide. Today, the people of Rwanda have lost faith in Del Ponte's objectivity and capacity to deliver justice. . . . It is in light of these shocking revelations, therefore, that the Government of Rwanda calls upon the international community and the United Nations Security Council in particular to hold her accountable for her deliberate conduct.

A response was clearly in order. During a speech in London on November 25, 2002, I tried to clarify:

For me, a victim is a victim, a crime falling within my mandate as the [Rwanda tribunal's] prosecutor is a crime, irrespective of the identity or ethnicity or the political ideas of the person who committed the said crimes. The political and military leadership of Rwanda has to accept to respond to the allegations of crimes that may have been committed by their own side. If they are genuinely interested to foster true peace and reconciliation in their country and in the [region], they should fully and unconditionally cooperate.

At the end of 2002, my dream job, the job I had described to the *Time* reporter four years earlier, was available. The International Criminal Court was finally opening its doors. A two-day conference in The Hague marked the occasion. During the receptions and breaks in the formal discussions, I received encouragement from representatives of several governments and nongovernmental organizations to seek appointment as the new court's chief prosecutor. My diplomatic adviser, Jean-Jacques Joris, warned me that I would not get the job for a variety of reasons: the Swiss government was apparently promoting a candidate for one of the judicial positions on the new court; the Milošević and Bagosora trials would last for several more years; and the tribunals for Yugoslavia and Rwanda had not finished their other work. Still, I wanted the job, and I knew this opportunity might never again present itself, this opportunity to continue working in international prosecution, to meet fantastic challenges and, yes, enjoy perquisites. I was confident I had the experience, energy, and judgment to launch the International Criminal Court's prosecution effort. I informed Secretary-General Annan of my interest in the position, and he phoned me late one night while I was having dinner with some Dutch friends. "Listen Carla," he said, "if they make the offer, say you are at their disposal." I later met with Prince Abdulluh of Jordan, who was chairing the selection committee. He seemed to imply that my chances were good. But the inference I drew from his words was mistaken.

At the end of his presidency, Bill Clinton had signed the Rome Statute, the treaty that established the International Criminal Court. The Bush administration, however, opposed the new court's existence, arguing, I think solely to gather political points from a largely uninformed electorate, that the court might mount politically motivated prosecutions of United States political and military leaders. President Bush, in an unprecedented act, effectively erased Clinton's signature from the Rome Statute. And the State Department began forging bilateral agreements with a number of countries—most of them weak and dependent upon United States largesse—to exempt each other's citizens from prosecution before the new court. The Department of State announced on March 3, 2003, that the United States and Rwanda had signed such a bilateral agreement. President Paul Kagame was visiting Washington at the time. He held discussions with President Bush at the White House a day after this bilateral agreement was announced. My advisers and I suspected that, in return for Rwanda's signature on the agreement, President Kagame had sought United States support in the campaign to prevent the Rwanda tribunal from completing its Special Investigation and bringing indictments against senior Rwandan military officers, and perhaps Kagame himself, in connection with massacres Tutsis had allegedly committed in 1994.

A sign that this was indeed the case emerged during the next trip I took to Washington, D.C., in May 2003. The United States ambassador-at-large for war crimes, Pierre Prosper, called me to meet with Rwanda's prosecutor general, Gerard Gahima; Rwanda's ambassador to Washington, Richard Sezibera; and the Rwandan diplomat monitoring the tribunal in Arusha, Martin Ngoga. On May 15, 2003, an elevator lifted my team members and me to an upper floor of the State Department's headquarters. We were surprised to enter a well-appointed, formal reception room. My earlier meetings in Foggy Bottom had usually taken place in the matchbox of an office Prosper was now inhabiting, and when I entered the spacious reception room I mistakenly assumed for a minute that the State Department was feting me for some reason. The honor actually belonged entirely to the Rwandans. Prosper's people had billed this meeting, at least to me, as a general conversation about cooperation between the Office of the Prosecutor and Rwanda's government. After a few minutes of amorphous discussion, we hit upon the real topic of the day: the Special Investigation. Prosper yielded the floor to the Rwandans. They wanted their local judicial authorities, the Tutsi-dominated authorities and not the international tribunal, to conduct the investigations into alleged wrongdoing by members of the RPF. The Rwandans' demands did not surprise me. Prosper surprised me, because he backed the Rwandans. He suggested that I surrender responsibility for investigating and prosecuting the alleged crimes of the RPF, along with all the highly sensitive evidence we had collected against individual Tutsi suspects, to the same Tutsi-dominated Rwandan government that had for nine years failed to undertake this investigative effort, the same government that had, according to Human Rights Watch, given the victims of the RPF's crimes "virtually no chance of obtaining justice in any Rwandan court."

I did not want to seem obstructive, because we had a problem that desperately needed a solution. I agreed that handing over the investigations to the Rwandan authorities was theoretically possible. After all, the Rwandan authorities and the international tribunal on Rwanda were supposed to have concurrent jurisdiction of the crimes committed in 1994. But, I continued, there were sound reasons to presume that Rwanda would not undertake this work in good faith. My proposal was that, if Rwanda concretely demonstrated to me that it was willing and capable of undertaking such investigations and prosecutions, I might, in principle, support an arrangement under which the international tribunal would impose its primacy only if the Rwandan authorities failed to undertake these investigations and prosecutions properly.

The United States apparently wanted my agreement so badly that nobody objected when I lit up a Marlboro in an antechamber during a break that followed an especially intense exchange. The Rwandans were sure that Prosper had prepared the groundwork with me for an agreement on handing over the Special Investigation. He had not. He simply pressed the issue, as if it were a foregone conclusion that I would sign away the investigations of allegations against the RPF before the Tutsi-dominated Rwanda government had done anything to demonstrate that it was willing to investigate and prosecute its own officers. At one moment, Prosper produced a piece of paper, a draft "agreement," that he wanted me to sign. I politely refused. I kept insisting that Rwanda first demonstrate its good will and capability. Without this, I would continue to presume that Rwanda was incapable of carrying out investigations and prosecutions of RPF members. Without this, I would not hand over evidence that would have compromised our witnesses and other sources. The meeting adjourned with no signature on the paper.

Prosper increased the pressure later in the day. An hour or so after the meeting with the Rwandans, I arrived for a luncheon at the residence of the Swiss ambassador to Washington. Prosper had been invited to attend. But he stayed only briefly and used the time to find me in the garden and take me aside. Prosper and I are about the same height. And we were look-ing each other straight in the eye. No white wine. No canapés.

"I wanted to inform you," Prosper said, "some states think that the [international tribunal for Rwanda] should have its own prosecutor. You will not be reappointed. And for the [Yugoslavia tribunal] you will be reappointed only for two years." My mandate at the tribunals was due to expire in September 2003, just four months away. I was expecting to be reappointed to another four-year term. Prosper mentioned Great Brit-ain, and was careful not to mention that the United States was among the "states" to which he referred, but it was patently clear that its ambassador-at-large for war crimes agreed with whatever it was the British were say-ing. So now, it was not just the Rwandans who were involving themselves in blackmail. Prime Minister Zoran Djindjić had just been assassinated in Belgrade, and I had just refused to refrain from bringing indictments against a number of Serb generals. And here I was refusing to cede the tribunal's authority to investigate the Tutsi-dominated RPF. These prose-cutions, in one way or another, involved disturbing a developing po-litical status quo that people in the diplomatic community wanted to develop further.

I barely maintained my composure after Prosper tried to tell me that appointing a new prosecutor would improve the Rwanda tribunal's "effi-ciency," because I had been the one who had charged headlong into the United Nations bureaucracy in the campaign to cut away the dead weight from the Office of the Prosecutor and brought in Laurent Walpen, who sharpened its investigation operations "How is this possible?" I said. "I cannot believe this. This is impossible." After a few minutes, Prosper scur-ried off to some more pressing engagement.

On May 20, an unclassified fax arrived on State Department letterhead. Prosper had attached another version of the draft agreement ready for my signature. This version said the government of Rwanda would share in-formation on the Rwandan army's prosecutions of military personnel for violations of international humanitarian law in 1994; it said that the Office of the Prosecutor would share with the government of Rwanda a list of sites where massacres may have been committed in 1994 by members of the RPF as well as any evidence related to these alleged massacres; it said that the government of Rwanda would have the first opportunity to prosecute such cases; it said that the Office of the Prosecutor would have an opportunity to review the trials once they were concluded by the government of Rwanda, and if the government of Rwanda concluded that no prosecution was warranted, the Office of the Prosecutor would have an opportunity to review the investigation. The key sentence, however, was this: "The [Office of the Prosecutor] will not seek an indictment or otherwise bring a case before the [tribunal] unless it is determined that the [government of Rwanda] investigation or prosecution was not genuine." This sentence is vague, unskillfully vague. Who is to make this determination? Upon what criteria? What is the definition of genuine? In my opinion, this sentence would have presented Rwanda with an opening to kill the Special Investigation and every other effort the tribunal might take to exercise its primacy and independence.

I flew to Arusha to discuss Prosper's plan with the prosecution team and, by telephone, with the Office of Legal Affairs in New York, which informed Secretary-General Kofi Annan of the situation. New York backed our assessment. And, from the Rwanda tribunal's offices in Arusha, I sent Prosper a reply by fax, saying that I regretted to inform him that the new draft of the plan did not accurately reflect the essence of our discussions in Washington or take into consideration what my deputy and I had expressed there. I refused to soften my position. I saw no grounds to believe that Rwanda could or would conduct a credible investigation or prosecution. I informed Ambassador Prosper that I would continue to assert the tribunal's primacy, which was my discretion.

This decision angered Prosper. He telephoned my political adviser for Rwanda, Cécile Aptel, and expressed his views in an ear-piercing voice. He brought his decibel level down to within the diplomatic, "full-and-frank" range when I came on the line, but the sentiments were the same. Thereafter, we heard from French diplomats that the United States had begun to lobby against my reappointment and that my remaining at the Yugoslavia tribunal was not assured beyond a one- or two-year, renewable appointment, something no self-respecting prosecutor would accept, because so brief a mandate affords a prosecutor less independence than a dog with a choker chain clipped to a short leash.

I was in Paris during the last week of June 2003, and, after a conversation with President Chirac, I met with Jean-Luis Bruguière in the same office where he had delivered me Carlos the Jackal half a decade earlier. Bruguière showed me into a side room of his office. There, occupying shelf after shelf, were hundreds of files and binders. "*Voila*," he said, "The investigation." Gazing at the rows of paper and cardboard, I recalled that

Bruguière had once sent the Rwandan government a request for assistance and that, of course, Kigali had sent nothing in response. I had even asked President Kagame why Rwanda refused to cooperate. Looking stiff and uncomfortable, Kagame had answered, "Tell Judge Bruguière to come to Kigali for cooperation." I passed Kagame's invitation to Bruguière, and, before I realized what I was saying, recommended that flying to Kigali might further his investigation of the downing of the French airplane.

"*Merci, non,*" he laughed.

Now, Bruguière informed me that he was ready to issue an indictment and several arrest warrants. He explained, however, that France could not seek the arrest of Paul Kagame because, as Rwanda's president, Kagame enjoyed immunity under French law as a head of state. Bruguière and I then made an informal agreement. He would issue an indictment against Tutsis allegedly implicated in the plane downing—some of them now senior officers in Rwanda's army—and pass to me the evidence collected against Kagame. Later, if and when I found it appropriate, I would submit an indictment against Kagame. It was clear that if we kept investigating the RPF's alleged misdeeds, we might develop enough evidence to indict Kagame, because he was the man who had command responsibility for the entire RPF in 1994. The early summer of 2003 was certainly an inappropriate time to issue an indictment, however. If the Rwanda tribunal were to announce the opening of an investigation of Kagame, he clearly would have shut down crucial genocide trials that still had years to run. If Bruguière provided sufficient evidence to indict Kagame, I thought, we would do so only as the Rwanda tribunal approached the end of its lifetime, when the genocide trials were almost concluded and the tribunal was less vulnerable to Kigali's blackmail. Bruguière and I decided to arrange a meeting with Kofi Annan in September to discuss the next move. It was not to be.

Within a few days, I heard that Jack Straw, head of the United Kingdom's Foreign Office, had approached Secretary-General Annan and proposed appointing a new prosecutor exclusively for the Rwanda tribunal. "Improving efficiency" was Straw's rationale. On Wednesday morning, July 2, 2003, the United Kingdom's envoy to The Hague, Ambassador Colin Budd, paid me a visit. I told him I had learned that the government of the United Kingdom had sent Annan a letter regarding the appointment of a separate chief prosecutor for the Rwanda tribunal. I expressed my surprise, and said that Annan had just told me that he saw no reason for such a structural change. "This is the wrong time," I told Ambassador Budd. "We have achieved a functioning Office of the Prosecutor for Rwanda." Once we had resolved the personnel problems and reorganized investigative operations, the deficiencies of the Rwanda tribunal were no longer in the Office of the Prosecutor. The Security Council was about to pass a resolution mandating a completion strategy for the Yugoslavia tribunal as well as the Rwanda tribunal. The Office of the Prosecutor was already implementing this strategy.

Budd detailed the United Kingdom's position. He said that Straw strongly favored the proposed change and that it had something to do with cutting costs. I replied that the only cost-savings would be for my airplane tickets and a few *per diems*, which the salary, living expenses, airplane tickets, and *per diems* of a new prosecutor would outstrip several times each year. Then Budd said the United Kingdom wanted maximum effort to be invested in the Yugoslavia tribunal, which was, he asserted, not running at full speed whenever I was in Arusha. Budd subsequently mentioned that Straw had spoken with Annan about the matter and that Annan had agreed.

"If there are complaints about the work, they should be expressed," I said. "And if the real motives are political, they should be aired as well." Budd said nothing about what I thought was the real reason for the proposed changes: the Rwandan government's opposition to the Special Investigation of alleged atrocities by members of the RPF. I asked him to arrange a meeting for me with Straw in London. Regrettably, he said, Straw was facing intense time constraints. At that time, the insurgency in Iraq was just gathering pace. And there were, I suppose, weapons of mass destruction to find . . . somewhere.

Word had already begun spreading up and down the halls of the Yugoslavia tribunal that senior staff members in its Office of the Prosecutor had joined the fray, seeking to unseat me from the Yugoslavia tribunal as well. I know that the British embassy in The Hague called in members of my staff for "consultations." I was informed that one senior staff member, an American, had asked the United States embassy in The Hague to get involved but that the diplomats there had refused.

During the last week of July 2003, Marlise Simons of the *New York Times* reported that the Rwandan government had been campaigning to have me replaced as chief prosecutor of the Rwanda tribunal. The

Times, citing anonymous Western diplomats and tribunal officials, said Rwanda was furious that the Office of the Prosecutor had been investigating senior civilian and military figures in Rwanda's Tutsi-led government for reported atrocities in 1994 and that Rwanda had apparently won support from the United States and United Kingdom. "We and others have been heavily lobbied by the Rwandan government complaining about Del Ponte, saying her work has lagged behind because she is too busy in The Hague," said one quotation attributed to a diplomat of a Security Council member state. The newspaper reported that British diplomats had said the change would entail dropping investigations of allegations about members of the RPF.

I flew to New York to seek Annan's backing. I wanted to explain to him that this was anything but the right moment to split the two positions. Despite every indication, I was still sure Annan would back my position.

Unfortunately, by the time I walked into the United Nations Secretariat on Monday, July 28, everything had already been decided and, it seemed to me, in the wrong way for the wrong reasons. The countries on the Security Council were finalizing a draft resolution requiring the Yugoslavia tribunal and the Rwanda tribunal to complete their investigations by the end of 2004, their trials by the end of 2008, and their appeals processes by the end of 2010. Great Britain had been successful in marketing its proposal to name a separate chief prosecutor for the Rwanda tribunal as an efficiency-enhancing and cost-saving move that would further the completion strategy.

Ralph Zacklin, an English member of the United Nations Office of Legal Affairs, told me that Annan had asked him to consult with the Security Council's fifteen member-states on the proposal to appoint a new person to the position of chief prosecutor of the Rwanda tribunal. Zacklin elaborated the scenario that would follow: Annan would propose the appointment of a new Rwanda tribunal prosecutor and my reappointment for another four-year mandate at the Yugoslavia tribunal. "The completion strategy is at risk," Zacklin explained. I tried to describe the real reasons why Rwanda, the United Kingdom, and, apparently to a lesser degree, the United States were pushing for this change. Even Zacklin agreed with my assessment, but, he said, the Security Council is a political institution that makes political decisions. "You are right," he quipped, "but you lose." He insisted that two or three of the five permanent members favored the proposal and that the secretary-general would likely concur.

Only one member of Annan's closest staff lamented that the decision to appoint a new prosecutor for the Rwanda tribunal was political, but he was so afraid to discuss the matter that he asked me at least twice not to mention his opinion to anyone.

"This will be the end of the Special Investigation," I told him.

"Yes," he said. "I know."

I met Annan next. "It is nothing personal," Annan consoled me. "They said you're a very good prosecutor and have done a good job." But Annan said that he could not even stand aside and take no position on appointing a new prosecutor to the Rwandan tribunal. "It will be too messy," he explained, saying it was his position to have different chief prosecutors for each tribunal.

I tried to provoke Annan. I asked him if I could remain at the Rwanda tribunal instead of staying at the Yugoslavia tribunal in The Hague. I would move to Arusha. I would live there and continue to do the job as I saw fit, and by this I made it clear that I intended to keep the Special Investigation open.

"No, Carla. You stay at the ICTY," Annan answered, referring to the International Criminal Tribunal for the former Yugoslavia. "The trial against Milošević is too important to be left in someone else's hands."

With this admission, it was clear to me that the problem was the Special Investigation and not the inefficiencies of having a single chief prosecutor juggle one position in northern Europe and another in eastern Africa.

Before the meeting's end, Annan agreed to delay sending a letter to the Security Council recommending this change until I had a chance to state my case to the council's member states. Annan allowed me twenty-four hours, and I appreciated this gesture. Our conversation ended in fifteen minutes. Before they were up, however, I handed Annan my talking points and told him: "You will not have a Special Investigation. You'll see. Keep these for history."

My aides and I used the next twenty-four hours to warn the Security Council's member states that, by appointing a separate prosecutor for the Rwanda tribunal, the council would effectively be undermining the Rwanda tribunal's independence and sacrifice breaking the cycle of impunity for short-term political expediency.

"I do not see any serious reasons for separation of the positions except for political ones," I said time and again that day. "I know very well why the government of Rwanda and others support separation. It is all about my Special Investigation. Who else but the United Nations Security Council will support the prosecutor in this respect?"

We found that most member states had simply accepted uncritically the British government's "efficiency" argument. (I wondered whether anyone had bothered to perform a cost-benefit analysis.) France supported us. Mexico and Spain supported us. Even Angola and Cameroon supported us, despite the fact that the Africans had longed for an African prosecutor. The United States said it had no strong opinion, but would go along with the majority. Four international human rights organizations agreed with my assessment that appointing someone to the Office of the Prosecutor for the Rwanda tribunal would be a blow to the tribunal's independence and impartiality. Human Rights Watch and the Lawyers Committee for Human Rights suggested in a letter that the proposed changes before the Security Council might make it more difficult to prosecute accused officers of the RPF.

On August 28, the decision came. Everything went according to the script Ralph Zacklin had elaborated during the first few minutes I spent with him in the Secretariat Building a month earlier. The Security Council passed Resolution 1503. I was no longer the chief prosecutor of the Rwanda tribunal. But I did receive a four-year mandate to continue at the Yugoslavia tribunal. Five days later, the Security Council named an African, an able justice of the Gambian Supreme Court, Hassan Bubacar Jallow, to be the Rwanda tribunal's chief prosecutor.

The only concession I could draw from this defeat was a paragraph my aides and I succeeded in having inserted into Resolution 1503 in an effort to prevent the new chief prosecutor from closing the Special Investigation. In this paragraph, the Security Council called upon "all States, especially *Rwanda*, Kenya, the Democratic Republic of the Congo, and the Republic of the Congo, to intensify cooperation with and render all necessary assistance to the [tribunal], *including on investigations of the Rwandan Patriotic* [Front]" [emphasis added]. We even tossed a sop to the Rwandan government, by calling for the named states to hand over Félicien Kabuga, the Hutu financier who was still living *la dolce vita* in Kenya and other countries willing to accept his phony passports.[1]

I later had a pleasant conversation with Hassan Jallow, and used the opportunity to recommend that he keep the Special Investigation open even after 2004, the deadline set in the completion strategy for all indictments to be completed. Surely, I urged him, the Rwanda tribunal's duty to interrupt the cycle of impunity and prosecute the most responsible persons on all sides for alleged war crimes should take precedence over an arbitrary time constraint. I asked Jallow to contact Bruguière. But I do not know whether they ever spoke or whether tribunal investigators ever examined the evidence Bruguière had collected on the shelves of his office. I also do not know what the Rwanda tribunal did with the Special Investigation. I have not heard any clamor about the murders of the archbishop, the two bishops, the nine priests, and the three girls, or any other atrocities allegedly committed by members of the RPF. I have noticed no complaints from the direction of Kigali. And Rwanda's passport controllers seemed to be allowing witnesses to board the Beechcraft for the flight to Arusha.

By November 17, 2006, the Rwanda tribunal had convicted twenty-six people and acquitted five. None were Tutsis. On that day, Jean-Louis Bruguière of France issued an indictment alleging that Paul Kagame and other top commanders of the Tutsi-dominated militia were responsible for deliberately downing President Juvénal Habyarimana's plane in April 1994. The Rwandan military's two top generals, Charles Kayonga and Jackson Nkurunziza, were among nine individuals against whom international arrest warrants were issued; no warrant was issued naming Paul Kagame, because he enjoyed immunity under French law. Bruguière said, however, that it was the responsibility of the Rwanda tribunal to issue an indictment against Kagame, because, he asserted, there was a link between the assassination and the genocide.

I have no inside knowledge of the evidence upon which Bruguière constructed his indictment. I do not know whether I would ever have presented an indictment of Kagame to the Rwanda tribunal's Trial Chamber for certification. I wondered about the amount of care that had gone into the document, because misspellings should not mar any indictment this sensitive. Predictably, the authorities in Rwanda exploded in rage after Bruguière announced the indictment, but I am sure most of the invective pouring forth from Kigali was intended to impress the Tutsi audience in Rwanda. The government sang a familiar refrain. It alleged that France was trying to destroy Rwanda. The foreign minister, the same Charles Murigande who once gave public assurances that Rwanda would cooperate with the tribunal's Special Investigation, seemed to protest too much when he asserted that Bruguière's indictment was an attempt by France to conceal its complicity in the killings of 800,000 Tutsis. Murigande now asserted: "The French are trying to appease their conscience for their role in the genocide and are now trying to find someone else to hold responsible for their acts." A week after Bruguière issued the arrest warrants, Rwanda severed relations with France and notified its ambassador in Kigali that he had twenty-four hours to leave the country. I assume he flew safely from the capital's airport.

10

CONFRONTING ZAGREB
1999 TO 2007

Many Serb officials I encountered over the years have openly denounced the Yugoslavia tribunal. Their approach to the tribunal involved confrontation, open defiance, and unflinching denial. No matter how compelling the countervailing facts or logic, these Serbs preferred relentless frontal assault to stealth and backstabbing. And in a way, I had a strange respect for their warped concept of candor. Many Croat officials, however, chose to express their defiance and denial in a different manner. The Republic of Croatia's first president, Franjo Tudjman, and his protégés in Croatia and in the Bosnian Croat–controlled areas of Bosnia and Herzegovina had for years pledged to cooperate with the Yugoslavia tribunal. They would smile at me. They would shake my hand, make promises, construct a magnificent *muro di gomma*, and then resort to stealth and deception and attack from behind. One of the tribunal's lawyers, a Canadian famous up and down the halls for sharing quips and tales, had a down-home aphorism that captured the difference between the Serbs and Croats who were attempting to frustrate the tribunal's work: "The Serbs are bastards," he would say. "But the Croats are sneaky bastards."

The tribunal's prosecutions of Croat accused were based upon crimes that took place during two military campaigns: The first was the open campaign the Republic of Croatia undertook to win back control of its own territory that rebel Serbs, with the Yugoslav National Army, had seized in 1991. The second was the campaign that the Republic of Croatia, working through a proxy Bosnian Croat militia, known as the Croatian Defense Council, undertook from 1992 to 1994 to wrest territory from Bosnia and Herzegovina and join it with the Republic of Croatia; Tudjman and the other leaders in Zagreb tried to keep the Republic of Croatia's military and financial support for this campaign a secret, but they fooled no one. It took most of a decade, two cancer deaths, and a political up-heaval in the Republic of Croatia before the Office of the Prosecutor's analytical staff was able to gather sufficient documentation to report to me in detail what Tudjman and his protégés had been doing for years to thwart the tribunal's efforts and to secure impunity for themselves and Croat military leaders.

Many Croats consider General Ante Gotovina a war hero. Sharp-eyed, square-jawed, and devastatingly handsome in his Croatian Army dress uniform, Gotovina was born in Croatia but he left home and served in the French Foreign Legion from 1973 to 1978. I signed the indictment against him. It says Gotovina had returned to his homeland by June 1991, at about the time the Republic of Croatia declared its independence from the former Yugoslavia. Violent clashes between Croatia's police and armed members of Croatia's Serb minority, who were receiving guns, money, and other support from the Yugoslav National Army and Milošević's government in Belgrade, had been marring the peace in Croatia for a year as the rebel Serbs overran police stations and the Croatian government made feckless attempts to reestablish its control. War erupted in the autumn of 1991. By the year's end, the Yugoslav National Army had seized about a third of the Republic of Croatia's territory, and Serb leaders had declared this territory to be the Republic of the Serbian Krajina, or simply "Krajina." Outmatched militarily, the government of Croatia agreed in December 1991 to a United Nations–mediated peace plan that provided for the establishment of four United Nations Protected Areas whose territory almost exactly corresponded with the Serb-held territory in Croatia. Everyone except the Serbs, however, recognized the Republic of Croatia's sovereignty over this land. In early 1992, the United Nations deployed a peacekeeping force, UNPROFOR, in these Protected Areas.

Ante Gotovina rose through the ranks of the armed forces of the Republic of Croatia after the 1991 conflict in Croatia. By 1995, the Foreign Legion corporal had become a Croatian Army general in command of a military district headquartered in Split, a city on the Adriatic Sea. The indictment against Gotovina would allege that, by early August 1995, Croatian political and military leaders had begun implementing a military operation, code-named "Storm," which was designed, among other things, to bring Serb-controlled, and United Nations–protected, swaths of the Republic of Croatia's territory back under the Croatian government's authority and drive out their Serb populations. Psychological warfare began before the decisive military strike commenced. The Croatian authorities spread warnings of an imminent attack. Radio and television bulletins announced that the Serbs were "free to leave" the Krajina and that large convoys of Serbs were already departing the area. Maps depicting "exclusively Croat" territory were shown to Serb civilians, and "exit routes" from this territory were publicized. Fear infected the Serb population.

The indictment would allege that a massive exodus began even before military forces under General Gotovina's command launched the attack on the Krajina on August 4, 1995. Croatian artillery shelled civilian areas. Croatian troops allegedly entered civilian Serb settlements at night and, using gunfire and other forms of intimidation, threatened those Serb civilians who had not fled. Soldiers rounded up some Serbs, loaded them into vehicles, and transported them to detention facilities and collection centers. Soldiers allegedly opened fire on groups of fleeing Serb civilians. People were forced to watch as family members were executed. Corpses littered the roads. Some victims were allegedly burned alive, some died from multiple stab wounds, some were dumped into wells, some simply disappeared, never to be seen again.

The Gotovina indictment would allege that, after the Croatian forces had overcome Serb military resistance, which was minimal in most places and nonexistent in others, acts were undertaken to ensure that displacement of the Serbs from the Krajina would be permanent. Croatian forces and civilians looted Serb homes and businesses. Croatian arson squads left towns and numerous villages in ruins. In places where Serb and Croat homes stood side by side, Croat homes were spared and the Serb homes put to the torch. Livestock was shot or burned alive in barns and stables. Wells and water supplies were intentionally fouled with carcasses. By November 15, 1995, when mopping-up operations effectively ended, the Serb community in the southern Krajina was practically destroyed. Croatian troops and civilians were moved into many abandoned Serb homes. While Serb refugees were granted the right to return to reclaim their homes, the destruction of both their property and the deeds to their property made such relief effectively unavailable. All of this, the indictment would allege, was by design.

The Office of the Prosecutor was still working on drafts of the Gotovina indictment when I made my first visit to Zagreb in November 1999. I was using the trip to demand that the Croatian authorities cooperate with the Office of the Prosecutor's investigation of the crimes committed during Operation Storm and the military campaign Tudjman had led from 1992 to 1994 to take territory from Bosnia and Herzegovina. Instead of attempting to uncover the crimes and bring the perpetrators to justice, as they had promised to do, Tudjman and other Croatian leaders had, for more than three years before my visit, mounted an organized, covert effort to obstruct the tribunal's work. Members of Croatia's civilian- and military-intelligence services had taken steps to prevent the Office of the Prosecutor from obtaining documents providing details about crimes committed in Croatia and in Bosnia and Herzegovina. They had worked to identify prosecution witnesses who had received promises of protection from the tribunal and had agreed to testify during closed-door hearings; the tribunal would eventually receive a secret transcript capturing Tudjman himself organizing a leak to the press of the identity of at least one highly sensitive and protected witness, Stipe Mesić, a former Tudjman confidant who had broken politically with the Croatian president over his campaign to partition Bosnia and Herzegovina. Tudjman's protégés had worked to keep the tribunal from apprehending Croats named in indictments. For example, Ivica Rajić, the commander of Bosnian Croat militia units that had killed dozens of Muslims, including women and children, in October 1993 at a village named Stupni Do, received a promotion, a new identity, and fake papers and went into hiding; his family was resettled in Croatia, and his fingerprints disappeared from police files. The Republic of Croatia's intelligence services had also assisted efforts to mount a defense of Bosnian Croats brought to trial before the tribunal on charges stemming from the massacre of Muslim civilians, including women and children, at Ahmići in April 1993, providing defense attorneys with documents, conducting interviews of witnesses, gathering information on prosecution witnesses, and preparing defense attorneys for hearings.[1] Croatia's military-intelligence service had even reported to Tudjman that there was a real danger the tribunal would indict the Republic of Croatia's leadership.[2] And, clearly, the Croatian authorities had undertaken their obstruction and legal-defense efforts primarily to stymie the tribunal's investigation of Tudjman and other Croatian political and military officials and thwart any effort to bring charges against them.

I cannot forget the defiant statement Tudjman issued from his deathbed on the eve of my arrival in Zagreb. He declared that Croatia should never allow the arrest and transfer to The Hague of Croatian military officers who had taken part in the military effort to restore Croatian territory to the Croatian government's control. In a terse apology for impunity, Tudjman said, "Croatian men, who were liberating the country from evil, cannot be held accountable." In a statement of my own, I said that the Republic of Croatia had to acknowledge the tribunal's authority to proceed with all investigations of the armed conflict on its territory, including Operation Storm, and that, if Croatia did not comply with its obligations, I would have no choice but to report this to the United Nations Security Council: "Even in a just war, or in a fully justified military operation, the laws of war must be respected. Brutal abuse of civilians, for instance, is not permissible in any military context. I am required to investigate whether crimes were committed during Operation Storm."

Tudjman's statement turned out to be his swan song. His closest adviser, Defense Minister Gojko Šušak, had died of cancer in May 1998. An hour before midnight on December 10, 1999, the disease also claimed Tudjman's life. Ironically, the same cancer cells that had until now deprived the Office of the Prosecutor of the opportunity to present indictments against Tudjman and Šušak had also altered the political realities in Croatia, which eventually enabled the office to obtain the evidence to prosecute other political and military figures and shed light upon the military effort Tudjman and Šušak led to partition Bosnia and Herzegovina.

Within weeks of Tudjman's death, Croatian voters ousted his nationalist party, the Croatian Democratic Union, from power. I sent one of my assistants, Anton Nikiforov, to Zagreb for discussions with men and women who would play roles in the first post-Tudjman government. Our main messages were three: cooperation was in the strategic interests of Croatia and its people and would promote law and order; the new government would have to be prepared to comply with some unpleasant requests for assistance; and Croatia would have to meet its obligation to cooperate even if its nemesis, the Federal Republic of Yugoslavia, that is, Serbia and Montenegro, had not.

A few weeks later, Croatia's voters elected Stipe Mesić, who had become one of Tudjman's most vocal opponents, to be the country's second president. Now, there was a government in Zagreb run by leaders who had opposed Tudjman's military adventure in Bosnia and Herzegovina and who appeared to be willing to meet one of the prerequisites for the Republic of Croatia's entry into the European Union: cooperation with the tribunal. During a meeting with officials from the Office of the Prosecutor a few weeks after Mesić's inauguration, Croatian officials revealed that the government was in possession of crucial evidence about Croatia's complicity in the war in Bosnia and Herzegovina as well as the Croatian military operations against the Serbs in Croatia itself. This evidence included Croatia's equivalent of Nixon's White House tapes: transcripts of scores of meetings Tudjman had chaired in his office from 1991 until the cancer incapacitated him. Within a few weeks, the Tribunal staff would learn that the government had discovered, stashed on military bases in Zagreb and Split, the entire military archive of the Bosnian Croat militia. This archive, which Tudjman's protégés had secretly transferred from Bosnia and Herzegovina in order to prevent the documents from falling into the tribunal's hands, was the mother lode of records the Office of the Prosecutor had been seeking for years. It contained background and detail on crimes the Bosnian Croat militia had committed in Central Bosnia, including the massacres at Ahmići and Stupni Do and the ethnic cleansing of Mostar and other areas. Records in this archive, along with other documents the Croatian government would soon release, also described how Croatia's intelligence organizations had worked to thwart the tribunal's investigative efforts.

This evidence, so long held back by Tudjman's regime, would arrive in The Hague too late for consideration by the Trial Chamber presiding over the case against a Bosnian Croat commander, Tihomir Blaškić. We did not feel until years later the full impact that Tudjman's campaign of obstruction would have upon the Blaškić's case's ultimate outcome, which would mark a low point of my years as chief prosecutor.

On March 3, 2000, after presiding over a trial that lasted more than two years, after weighing the credibility and the accounts of 158 witnesses, and after considering more than 1,300 pieces of evidence, the Trial Chamber announced its judgment in the Blaškić case. The three judges found that units of the Bosnian Croat militia under Blaškić's command had attacked the Muslim hamlet of Ahmići, a place of little, if any, military significance, while its inhabitants were asleep or at morning prayers. The judges found that the villagers had mounted no significant effort to defend themselves and had either attempted to flee or had taken refuge inside their houses and cellars. Groups of five to ten Bosnian Croat soldiers then passed from

Muslim house to Muslim house, shouting insults, executing military-age Muslim men on sight, and setting fire to the village using incendiary bullets, grenades, and gasoline. British peacekeepers who investigated the scene found the remains of scores of Muslims, a third of them women and children. On a stairway inside the front door of one house, peacekeepers found two burned corpses, one apparently a man's, the other apparently that of a teenaged boy whose arm was lifted skyward and whose hand, in the words of the British commander, Lieutenant Colonel Bob Stewart, "resembled a balled claw." In a cellar behind the house, was a blackened, reddish mass of burned human flesh. Two small bodies appeared to be lying on the floor stomach down, but the heads were twisted backward, over their arched backs; the flames had not completely consumed the eyeballs of one.[3]

The Trial Chamber found that the attack on Ahmići was planned at a high level of the Bosnian Croat militia's hierarchy in Central Bosnia. The judges found that the attack involved the Bosnian Croat militia's military police, among them a paramilitary group known as the *Džokeri*, or Jokers, as well as regular units of the Bosnian Croat militia, including its Vitez Brigade; that, on the day before the attack, Blaškić had issued three written attack orders, couching them in terms to make the operation seem defensive in nature when it was, in fact, offensive; and that, at the very least, Blaškić knew there was a risk of crimes being committed and had accepted such a risk. In the end, the Trial Chamber found Blaškić guilty of having ordered a crime against humanity and of failing to take reasonable measures that would have prevented these crimes or reasonable measures to punish their perpetrators.

I was delighted, not only by the verdict, but because the sentence Blaškić received, forty-five years, fit the crime better than many of the sentences I have seen the Trial Chamber hand down. In the corridor after the Trial Chamber had read out its judgment, I congratulated Mark Harmon, the senior trial attorney who prosecuted the case. He cautioned me to hold my tongue until after the Appeals Chamber had ruled, for everyone expected Blaškić to appeal. I saw no reason to be anything but optimistic. I assumed that if the prosecution team's evidence and arguments had resonated so strongly with the Trial Chamber, there would be no radical change in the outcome at the appeal level. How wrong I turned out to be.

The Office of the Prosecutor was determined to obtain from Croatia the transcripts of Tudjman's conversations, the Bosnian Croat militia's archive, and other documents from the Republic of Croatia's Ministry of Defense and armed forces in order to bolster the evidence in the other cases against Bosnian Croat defendants, including Dario Kordić, a political leader in Central Bosnia, who was also facing charges related to Ahmići; to reduce the possibility that the Appeals Chamber would overturn the Trial Chamber's conviction of Tihomir Blaškić; and to support indictments against other leadership figures, including General Gotovina. We informed Washington, Paris, Berlin, and other world capitals as well as the United Nations Security Council that the Republic of Croatia's new government had taken a constructive approach toward cooperation with the tribunal. On April 4, 2000, I arrived in Zagreb for a series of meetings with Croatian officials. As I recall, it was the late afternoon when my meeting with Stipe Mesić took place in the Presidential Palace on the hillside above Zagreb. I told Mesić that we had been excited to hear about the discovery of Tudjman's presidential transcripts and the Bosnian Croat militia's archive. Now that the existence and custody of this documentation had been established, the question was access for the tribunal.

Mesić interrupted me: "Madame Prosecutor, I must advise you that President Tudjman recorded much of what was said in this room. There may be other listening devices concealed here. We are searching for them. But I am not sure we have found them all. So be careful with what you say." He was laughing, and I appreciated his quirky sense of humor as well as his message. Although I trusted Mesić implicitly, I did not trust the people around him, and I was not sure he did either. I spoke carefully. Mesić then said that the Yugoslavia tribunal would play a significant role in developing the history of the Yugoslav conflicts and that reconciliation would be difficult without punishment of those persons who committed crimes. He described the transcripts and tapes of Tudjman's conversations and confirmed that the Republic of Croatia's intelligence agency had possession of the Bosnian Croat militia's archive spirited out of Bosnia and Herzegovina by Tudjman's people. I told Mesić that we would request access to these documents in writing and asked him for help with leads on Serbian perpetrators, including information on Slobodan Milošević and other accused, because, during Tudjman's rule, Croatian officials had been hesitant even to cooperate in these investigations.

I subsequently met with Croatia's new prime minister, Ivica Račan, in a conference room jammed with officials and clerks. Račan, with his gray, neatly trimmed beard and the demeanor of a university professor, was a genuine politician. On the one hand, he knew Croatia could not avoid cooperating with the tribunal, and, personally, he was willing to cooperate because he knew cooperation would, among many other benefits, ease Croatia's entry into the European Union; on the other hand, Račan felt the constraints of domestic political realities. He tried repeatedly to convince us to soften our demands. "Our first two and a half months in office," he said, "have seemed like an entire year. It is an extremely difficult situation, and we have the need to find radical answers. . . . We will probably lose power at the end, but Croatia will be better off." Račan then informed us that the government would, based upon our written requests, provide copies of any documents we wanted from the Bosnian Croat militia's archive.

"Fine," I answered. "We will wait for seven days." And to help him understand that the tribunal was not biased, I told him that we had reorganized our investigation teams to put more focus on crimes committed against mostly Croats in the towns of Vukovar and Dubrovnik. I then requested information on Tudjman's foreign bank accounts.

After four or five hours of group discussion, Račan and I met one-on-one so I could share with him a piece of particularly sensitive information. I told Račan that I would soon present an indictment against Tudjman's favorite military commander, General Janko Bobetko, whom many Croats regarded as a hero of their "Homeland War" against the Serbs and Yugoslav National Army. Bobetko, an obese veteran of the Communist underground during the 1930s and Tito's Partizans during World War II, was the commander of the Army of the Republic of Croatia when its units mounted an attack on the Serbs in the southern part of the Krajina in September 1993. We knew from the beginning that General Bobetko was an old man, but age is not a crucial factor when determining criminal responsibility. The indictment against him alleged that the attack on the Krajina had involved serious violations of international humanitarian law and crimes against humanity, including the killing of Serb civilians and Serb soldiers who had surrendered as well as the plunder and destruction of buildings and property. The indictment also alleged that Bobetko knew Croatian forces under his command had committed crimes and that he had failed to take necessary and reasonable measures to prevent such acts or to punish their perpetrators.

At the instant I mentioned the name Bobetko, Račan placed his hands on his head and exhaled two words: "Oh, no." I explained that it was now

Račan's obligation to place Bobetko under police surveillance: "It is your responsibility to make sure Bobetko does not disappear. And you must keep this a secret."

During the years after the "Homeland War," Bobetko had written a book in which he practically implicated himself in war crimes. Bobetko bragged in writing about how he, as commander of the Croatian Army, was also in command of the Bosnian Croat militia, and this angered Franjo Tudjman, who had desperately denied and tried to conceal the symbiotic connection between the Republic of Croatia's army and the Bosnian Croat militia. Now, Račan acknowledged that Bobetko's memoir was practically an admission of his command responsibility for the crimes outlined in the indictment. Still, Račan was hesitant to proceed against the aging general: "If I cooperate in this, my government will fall. Do you want Croatia's government to fall?" Račan warned me at least ten times about the potential political consequences of the Bobetko indictment. Each time he did, I answered that I would not alter my position: "If I start taking into account your political situation, I will never complete my work." Račan later declared that he would never go into another private meeting with me.

On April 14, 2000, I wrote to President Mesić and requested, as soon as possible, the audio tapes and transcripts of meetings in Tudjman's office. On April 25, tribunal officials, including Ken Scott, a senior trial attorney, and Patrick Treanor, the head of the research team for leadership cases, met with one of Mesić's advisers, who provided them with a register of meetings and conversations recorded on tape in the office of the former Croatian president. Two days later, staff members from the Office of the Prosecutor received the first set of transcripts.

The archive of the Bosnian Croat militia proved to be technically more difficult to obtain, because this archive was now in the custody of Croatia's civilian intelligence service. The service's new director, a former university professor, did not object to giving the Office of the Prosecutor access to the archive. But some members of the intelligence service, most of them holdovers who still felt an allegiance to the late President Tudjman and his son, Miroslav, the head of the intelligence agency until just after his father's death, were loath to see the archive handed over. On May 2, analysts for the prosecutor's office traveled from central Zagreb by van to a Croatian government safe house in Samobor, a town west of the capital, to begin secretly poring over documents from the Bosnian Croat militia's archive. Each morning, intelligence-agency staff members loyal to the post-Tudjman government quietly removed batches of documents from the agency's headquarters and transported them to the safe house for examination. For several days, the Croats cautioned the prosecution's team of analysts not to leave the safe house even to buy sandwiches, because they feared that pro-Tudjman agents would spot them and expose the operation.

By May 23, the cover was blown. A Zagreb newspaper ran a story about the document-collection operation beside a photograph of the Samobor safe house. Within hours of the newspaper's appearance, special police units surrounded the intelligence agency's headquarters and barred access to the building. The government was apparently concerned that disloyal subordinates might destroy the Bosnian Croat militia's archive in order to prevent the most compelling evidence of Croatia's involvement in the war in Bosnia and Herzegovina from ever reaching the tribunal or the Croatian public.

These events were unfolding while I was in Sicily attending the annual service commemorating the death of my friend Giovanni Falcone. On the morning of May 24, an urgent message from Zagreb arrived. The document harvest had stopped. The Croatian government was refusing to hand over papers on the Ahmići massacre that my staff members had reviewed a week earlier. The Zagreb press was screaming about the tribunal and about how some of our fugitive accused were hiding in Croatia.

I flew to Zagreb immediately, arriving in the mid-afternoon, and joined Graham Blewitt and Ken Scott in meetings with Prime Minister Račan and other government officials. I was blunt. I told Račan I was not at all pleased with these developments: "We had everything arranged. Everything. It was a regular lovefest, and now, after only a few weeks, this happens. The situation is unacceptable. Your government has an international obligation. Why are you breaking our agreement? How am I supposed to trust you?"

Račan and the other Croatian government officials admitted they had grave problems with the government's intelligence service and would dissolve the agency on that same day. "I am going to dismiss two hundred police officers," Račan said. Then he announced that the government would transfer the Bosnian Croat militia's entire archive, including documents that had been secretly stored in Split and in Croatia's Ministry of Defense in Zagreb, to the custody of the Republic of Croatia's state archive and ensure that the tribunal's investigators and analysts would have access to the documents. He honored his word. For the next several years, analysts from the Office of the Prosecutor would review hundreds of thousands of records from this archive and pick tens of thousands of them to add to the tribunal's evidence base. These documents contained information that had significant evidentiary value for both the prosecution and the defense in the Blaškić case.

A month later, in June, I gave the Croatian government advance notice that the tribunal would hand down a sealed indictment against General Ante Gotovina, alleging that he was criminally responsible for crimes committed as part of a joint criminal enterprise whose goal, during Operation Storm, included removing the Serb population from the southern Krajina. The charges included persecution on political, racial, and religious grounds; deportation; forcible transfer; plunder of public and private property; wanton destruction of towns and villages not justified by military necessity; murder; and inhumane acts and cruel treatment. The indictment also alleges that General Gotovina knew or had reason to know that one or more of his subordinates was about to commit or had committed such crimes and that he had failed to take necessary or reasonable measures to prevent such crimes or punish the perpetrators. My trust in the Croatian authorities was misplaced. Gotovina escaped, or was allowed to escape. Soon, reliable informants began telling the Office of the Prosecutor that Gotovina was living under an alias and enjoying *la dolce vita* in Croatia.

For the next year, Croatia's government sent the tribunal mixed signals. Senior figures like Mesić and Račan made favorable private and public pledges of cooperation. Their reasons were obvious. Self-preservation was no longer hampering cooperation, because the tribunal was not targeting any more members of the Croatian government. Croatia's economy was suffering. Croatia had already felt the warm embrace of the European Union, the Council of Europe, and NATO and wanted to keep its record clean in order to gain a lifetime membership in all the right clubs of the developed Western world. To this end, local courts in the Republic of Croatia launched trials of Croats accused of committing crimes against the Serbs at the towns of Gospić and Bjelovar, a military prison in Split, and other sites.

I again traveled to Croatia on May 6, 2002. Early in the morning, outside Tudjman's former presidential palace, several Croatian officials, my aides, and I boarded a Croatian-government helicopter and set off for the war-scarred agricultural districts along the banks of the Danube River. The interior of the helicopter was luxuriously appointed, and someone mentioned that it had been for Tudjman's personal use.

At the town of Erdut, one of the Tribunal's investigators, Vladimir Djuro, a tall, unflappable, Czech police detective who spoke Serbo-Croatian and instinctively understood the mentality of the Balkan Slavs, gave me a tour. We visited the former headquarters of the notorious Serb paramilitary group run by Željko Ražnatović Arkan, a secret police assassin who was murdered by someone in the Belgrade underworld before the tribunal had had a chance to arrest and try him on charges connected with acts of violence perpetrated against Croats and Muslims in Croatia and in Bosnia and Herzegovina. At Dalj, Djuro showed me a police station where Serbs executed Croat police officers. We stopped at Borovo Selo, a bedroom community for a shoe factory, and examined a mass grave. A mile or two further down river, I saw the shrapnel-pocked stucco and brick of Vukovar and its hospital, the last building to fall when the town surrendered to the Serbian forces. From there, we followed a narrow asphalt road to a farm at a village named Ovčara, where Serb executioners had shot at least 264 prisoners taken from the hospital. Finally, we went to Lovas, where members of a Serb paramilitary unit had allegedly forced about fifty civilians to clear a mine field by joining arms and walking across; more than twenty had died.

Later in the day, we had dinner at Vukovar's Franciscan Monastery. I was exhausted until some local aperitif miraculously restored my energy and enthusiasm. The abbot began speaking about his hilltop monastery, its rich library, and the fighting that had reduced Vukovar to a wasteland so filled with broken brick, shattered roof tiles, and other rubble that its streets were practically impassible. Some kind of speech impediment seemed to slur the abbot's words. My translator grimaced, struggling to decipher his sentences. Later, another friar told us that the abbot was having trouble speaking because a dentist had just pulled his teeth and his set of false teeth had still not arrived. The abbot, embarrassed about hosting a dinner in a toothless state, had done us the honor of jamming someone else's set over his gums.

My official meetings did not cut such a deep impression. I raised the Gotovina problem with Prime Minister Račan, who said he believed the fugitive general was in Croatia and assured me that the government was doing all it could to arrest him. Croatia's authorities, Račan said, would appreciate any assistance from foreign intelligence services, because the government still could not rely upon its own secret police.

I returned to Račan's office on October 23, 2002, in an attempt to resolve the problem of Janko Bobetko. Račan began the meeting with a positive diversion. He said the government had obtained information on the whereabouts of Ivica Rajić, whom the tribunal wanted on charges connected with the massacre of Muslims at Stupni Do. This information had arrived just a few days earlier, Račan said, and, if it proved to be correct, Croatia would arrest Rajić. Prime Minister Račan then stressed that Croatia was going to cooperate in the Gotovina case. Several tips about Gotovina's whereabouts had led to dead ends, he said, but a special unit was on standby to arrest Gotovina once he was located. I told Račan that Gotovina was still in Croatia or the Croat-controlled cantons of Bosnia and Herzegovina. He had even been spotted in Zagreb. A Canadian in the NATO peacekeeping force in Bosnia and Herzegovina had recognized him in August, crossing the border from Croatia. "It seems Croatia's intelligence service must have known this," I said.

Finally, the conversation turned to Bobetko. Račan conceded that there was a clear and open disagreement between Croatia and the tribunal on the Bobetko case. Bobetko, Račan said, enjoyed a huge reputation, partly undeserved, partly tragic-comic, thanks to Bobetko's own bumbling efforts to nurture a myth about his military prowess. Bobetko was now frail, Račan continued, and radical nationalists would be happy to exploit his death by blaming it upon the government. Račan said he had tried personally to persuade Bobetko to accept the indictment, but the old general's family and supporters had intervened. During these months, Bobetko's backers sometimes linked arms in a human chain around his residence to prevent service of the indictment and arrest warrant, and the extreme end of Croatia's right wing was making noises in the country's national assembly. The government, Račan maintained, could not risk coercive action that might result in the injury or even death of the aged war hero.

I answered Račan that I was aware of the political situation in Croatia, but was also restricted by the law. I reminded Račan that I had given him advance notice of the indictment against Bobetko, not to excite Račan's curiosity, but to enable him to make the necessary preparations to arrest Bobetko once the tribunal had handed down the indictment. Instead, I said, information about the indictment had been leaked to the Croatian press, and not by the Office of the Prosecutor. All reactions to the indictment coming from within the government had been negative. Only then had Bobetko's health become an issue. I told Račan that attempts by Croatia to argue against the legality of the arrest warrant were a transparent attempt to buy time.

"It is natural for an accused to oppose an indictment," I said. "It is not natural for a government to enter as a state into the litigation." No one from the government had come forward to serve the tribunal's documents on Bobetko. The proper course of action, I said, would be for Croatia to fulfill its obligation, serve the indictment and arrest warrant, and report to the tribunal's Registry that the arrest warrant could not be executed because the accused was infirm. Then the Trial Chamber might order a medical examination and other measures.

"What does the government want, to avoid a transfer?" I asked.

"I can't accept the indictment, because I'm not a mail carrier," Račan answered.

"Sometimes I have to be a mail carrier," I said.

In the end, the Croatian authorities followed our advice. They served the indictment and arrest warrant through Bobetko's defense attorney, and raised the issue of Bobetko's health to justify not executing the arrest. The Trial Chamber ordered Croatia to submit regular reports on Bobetko's health to the tribunal's registrar. On April 29, 2003, about two months after Croatia submitted its official application for accession to the European Union, General Janko Bobetko died a free man.

The Croatian authorities arrested Ivica Rajić on April 5, 2003. Eleven days later, I went to Zagreb in response to an invitation from the government. After we had doled out congratulations for apprehending Rajić, I spoiled the party by telling Prime Minister Račan that Croatia, so far as we knew, was still not doing enough to apprehend Gotovina. Račan assured me that the state would prosecute the Croats who had hidden Rajić for so many years and that these were not the same men who were still hiding Gotovina. Račan explained that some of the government's efforts to apprehend Gotovina were so secret that even the tribunal could not know of them, and he repeated his public rhetoric that Croatia should not be held hostage to Gotovina and that he would not allow me the chance to block Croatia from entering the European Union. I heard that the rapid-reaction unit of the Croatian police was prepared to arrest Gotovina upon thirty minutes' notice. I heard that Gotovina might be living on a yacht owned by an Austrian. I was told about some Italian connection. I was told that Gotovina might be getting support from other former members of the French Foreign Legion, and this intelligence sounded true; I recall one French intelligence official telling me that he felt such loyalty toward Gotovina as a former Legionnaire that he, personally, would take no action to expedite Gotovina's arrest unless Gotovina were located in France itself.

We were all back in Zagreb six months later, and again we were talking about Ante Gotovina. Račan asked me not to hold Croatia's ambitions hostage to Gotovina, because the government had nothing to do with his flight from justice. "I can't sleep because of Gotovina and the constant media attention," Račan lamented. "Croatia's future should not depend upon one man." Later in the day, however, President Mesić revealed that the government had neither cut off financial support to Gotovina nor frozen his assets. Gotovina's wife, a Croatian Army colonel, was still receiving her salary despite the fact that she was not appearing at work. She was also drawing Gotovina's pension.

A new, center-right government assumed power in Croatia on December 22, 2003, following the victory of Franjo Tudjman's former party, the Croatian Democratic Union. Stipe Mesić remained Croatia's president. But we feared the new government might revive Tudjman's nationalist and isolationist policies. After all, the new prime minister was the same Ivo Sanader who had told me during my first trip to Zagreb that Croatia would not cooperate with the investigation of Operation Storm, the investigation that had produced the indictment against Gotovina. One of the Sanader government's first actions, however, was to initiate a dialogue with political representatives of the country's Serb minority and undertake a number of measures aimed at facilitating the return of Serb refugees to their homes. In March 2004, the Sanader government played a key role in securing the voluntary transfer to The Hague of two retired Croatian Army generals, Mladen Markač and Ivan Čermak, whom the tribunal wanted on charges linked with Operation Storm in 1995. On April 5, the Croatian government facilitated the transfer to the tribunal of six top Bosnian Croat political and military leaders: Jadranko Prlić, the former prime minister of the "republic" the Bosnian Croats had proclaimed on Bosnian territory; Bruno Stojić, this "republic's" former defense minister; Slobodan Praljak and Milivoj Petković, the former top commanders of the Bosnian Croat militia; Valentin Ćorić, the former head of its military police; and Berislav Pušić, who was allegedly responsible for exchanging prisoners and providing Muslims documents to leave for third countries. The indictment alleges that these men—together with four deceased individuals, President Franjo Tudjman; Gojko Šušak, Croatia's former defense minister; General Janko Bobetko; and Mate Boban, who had been the dominant Bosnian Croat political leader during the war— had established and participated in a joint criminal enterprise whose purpose was to subjugate and permanently remove Bosnian Muslims and other non-Croats who were living in areas on the territory of the self-declared Croat "republic" in Bosnia. Anyone who reads this indictment cannot help but see that it would have named Tudjman, Šušak, Bobetko, and Boban as co-accused if they had still been among the living.

In a report to the European Commission, I congratulated the Croatian government for demonstrating its cooperation with the tribunal, and this removed an obstacle that helped enable the commission to conclude, on April 20, that Croatia had fulfilled the political and economic criteria required for initiating negotiations on accession to the European Union. The commission stressed, however, that Croatia still had to take "all necessary steps" to ensure that Ante Gotovina was located and transferred to the tribunal's custody. In June 2004, the Republic of Croatia was recognized as a candidate for accession to the European Union, allowing Croatia to gain financial assistance for building institutions, and for improving economic and social cohesion, the environment, transport, and rural development. Gotovina, needless to say, was still at large.

The Blaškić case had taken on new life by the autumn of 2003. After the Trial Chamber had sentenced Blaškić to forty-five years in prison, his defense had presented the Appeals Chamber with hundreds of pages of new evidence. On its own initiative, the Appeals Chamber had called for a hearing to determine whether or not to retry the case. The Office of the Prosecutor, represented by Norman Farrell, had argued against a retrial, saying the Appeals Chamber had an obligation to assess the evidence and consider additional evidence but not to allow the defense to benefit because the Croatian government, which had been providing assistance to the defendant, had intentionally withheld documents.

On October 31, 2003, two weeks after my meetings in Zagreb, the Appeals Chamber ruled against ordering a retrial of the Blaškić case. The Security Council had just decided to adopt the tribunal's completion strategy and ordered it to close its doors in 2010. Perhaps the Security Council's decision had something to do with the Appeals Chamber's decision not to retry the entire case but to admit additional evidence and rebuttal material, call several witnesses, and listen to oral final arguments before deciding Tihomir Blaškić's guilt or innocence. In hindsight, a retrial would have been the better option for the prosecution. We had by now received the bulk of the new documentation from the archives of the Bosnian Croat militia, and the Office of the Prosecutor's analysts were continuing to sift through stacks of records. One document, received by the prosecution only on July 23, 2004, was a report prepared by the military police of the Bosnian Croat militia in Central Bosnia in November 1993; the report stated that military police units had been under General Blaškić's control when they took part in the attack on Ahmići in April.

This document was potentially smoking-gun evidence. In presenting their case before the Appeals Chamber, Blaškić's attorneys had argued, among other things, that new evidence supported the contention that members of the Bosnian Croat militia's military police along with the "The Jokers" had committed the crimes in Ahmići, but that these units had *not* been under Blaškić's command. In addition, Blaškić's attorneys submitted a document the prosecution found unusual, a twenty-page report that Croatia's Ministry of Interior had prepared *after* the Trial Chamber had found Blaškić guilty; this report asserted, without any substantiation, that on the day before the Ahmići attack the local political boss, Dario Kordić, and other Bosnian Croats had met to plan the operation and that Blaškić had not been present. The prosecution team found this document unusual, because the report's conclusions about the Ahmići massacre were identical to the arguments of Blaškić's defense attorney, Ante Nobilo.

On July 29, 2004, a few weeks after I had visited Zagreb yet again to demand the arrest of General Gotovina, the Appeals Chamber essentially threw out the Trial Chamber's judgment against Blaškić. The appeals judges ruled that the military-police units of the Bosnian Croat militia that had carried out the Ahmići massacre had not been under Blaškić's command and that the written orders Blaškić had issued on the eve of the massacre foresaw a "preventive" and not an "offensive" strike. The Appeals Chamber also found that Blaškić had taken steps to denounce and investigate the crimes. Based upon these findings, the Appeals Chamber, by a vote of four judges to one, concluded that the prosecution had not demonstrated Blaškić's guilt beyond a reasonable doubt for anything except abuse of prisoners in a detention facility. A day earlier, the head of the Appeals Chamber, Judge Fausto Pocar, had signed a decision rejecting the prosecution's motion to admit the November 1993 report by the Bosnian Croat militia's military police, the report that General Blaškić had, in fact, been in command of the military police units at Ahmići; the decision called this report "vague, unspecific and merely the expression of an isolated opinion." There was no explanation. And perhaps this is because such a determination is inexplicable. The prosecution had the opportunity to review the 1993 report, which revealed that the very same commander whom the Appeals Chamber had found to be responsible for the crimes had actually been under Blaškić's command. It upset us even more to discover that the evidence cited by the Appeals Chamber included the twenty-page report the Croatian Ministry of the Interior had prepared *after* the Trial Chamber had sentenced Blaškić to forty-five years, the report whose thesis strangely mirrored the defense's argument, the report that had cited no sources to support its assertions.

Zagreb and Vitez celebrated on the night of Blaškić's release. Ivo Sanader, perhaps seeing an opportunity to woo a few nationalists, personally welcomed Blaškić home. In our offices, shock and gloom fell over the Blaškić trial team. This Appeals Chamber decision was scandalous. The appeal process had effectively turned into a second trial, but one in which the judges assessed the credibility and reliability of the evidence without ever having seen or heard the witnesses who had appeared at trial.

The lone dissenting member of the Appeals Chamber was Judge Inés Weinberg de Roca of Argentina, whose opinion was for me the only redeeming aspect of the entire appeals process in the Blaškić case. Judge Weinberg de Roca wrote that it was inappropriate for the Appeals Chamber to have retried the facts: "[T]he Appeals Chamber is only able to reach this conclusion by disregarding the deference normally accorded to the trier of fact." Judge Weinberg de Roca subsequently commented on the Appeals Chamber's evaluation of the evidence:

> Providing only bare descriptions of the additional evidence, the Appeals Chamber has not made any findings of credibility or reliability in relation

to this new evidence, instead seeming to accept each document or testimony as the truth. Where there is a contradiction between the additional evidence and the trial evidence, the Appeals Chamber has not articulated any reasons why it has preferred the additional evidence over that adduced at trial.

Judge Weinberg de Roca also mentioned the Appeals Chamber's reliance upon the twenty-page report by the Republic of Croatia's Ministry of Interior on the massacre at Ahmići and observed that the credibility and reliability of this document were questionable. Events would soon prove her assessment of this unusual report to be correct.

Prosecution analysts continued to pore over stacks of the documents that Tudjman and intelligence agencies had withheld from the Tribunal for so many years. Before the Appeals Chamber handed down its judgment, one analyst in Zagreb discovered a document indicating that, at 10 p.m. on the eve of the Ahmići massacre, a meeting had taken place. At this meeting, Bosnian Croat political leaders in the area of Ahmići received an oral order to prepare the Croats living in the vicinity to deal with the effects of an attack by the Bosnian Croat militia on the Muslims that would take place early the next morning. A few weeks after the Appeals Chamber's judgment, prosecution analysts discovered a second copy of this same document with a handwritten notation mentioning a potential witness, the director of an explosives factory in Central Bosnia who had attended the meeting. A witness statement subsequently given by the factory director offered proof that the commander of the Bosnian Croat militia's Central Bosnia Operative Zone—the same Tihomir Blaškić—had issued the oral order on the night before the Ahmići attack and that this oral order was for an offensive and not "preventive" operation. The statement showed that the local Bosnian Croat political leaders had found the oral order to be so unacceptable that they had attempted to convince Blaškić to reissue it in writing. When this effort failed, they attempted to delay the attack Blaškić had ordered because they were concerned it would have "catastrophic consequences." The statement also indicates that members of the municipal government also approached both Dario Kordić, the local Bosnian Croat political boss, and General Slobodan Praljak, a Croatian army general who was managing, on Tudjman's behalf, the Republic of Croatia's military adventure in Bosnia and Herzegovina, in an effort to have them override Blaškić's attack order at the last minute. Both Kordić and Praljak refused to intervene.

As the Office of the Prosecutor gathered more evidence pointing to Blaškić's complicity in the Ahmići attack, my appeals staff and I began discussing whether to file a request for review of the Appeals Chamber's decision. I was sure that, from a legal perspective, the Appeals Chamber would grant a request for a review of its judgment. The new facts we had discovered were stronger than the new facts we had presented in the Barayagwiza appeal in 2000. I did not think we should have proceeded recklessly, but I was ready to go forward immediately. Mark Harmon, Norman Farrell, and other members of the prosecution team advised me that the tribunal's rules gave us an entire year to file the request and that we needed this time to analyze all new evidence we might acquire from the ongoing search of the Bosnian Croat militia's archive.

Patience yielded dividends. On a trip to Zagreb in early 2005, a team of analysts discovered another relevant document: a forty-page report by Croatia's Ministry of Interior on the Ahmići massacre. Upon closer examination, it appeared to the analysts that the forty-page report was a complete version of the twenty-page report that the Appeals Chamber had relied upon in making its ruling in favor of Blaškić. Moreover, the forty-page document contained crucial information that the twenty-page version was lacking: the sources of the information.

On July 29, 2005, the Office of the Prosecutor's team submitted its request for review of the Appeals Chamber's decision, arguing that new facts, that is, facts unknown to the prosecution or the court at the time of the proceedings, had come to light. The prosecution team argued that these new facts provided evidence that Blaškić had been involved in ordering the Ahmići attack and that the operation would involve criminal acts. The prosecution team argued that these new facts demonstrated that Blaškić was operating in conjunction with and pursuant to orders from Kordić, the local Bosnian Croat political boss, and that Kordić's acts during this miserable episode should be seen as implicating Blaškić in the criminal acts and not distancing him from them. This was not some eccentric position. The Trial Chamber in the tribunal's case against Dario Kordić had already found that Kordić had, together with Blaškić, taken part in a meeting concerning Ahmići on the night before the attack, and the Appeals Chamber itself had upheld this finding when it affirmed Kordić's conviction and twenty-five-year jail sentence, saying that Kordić and "the commander of the Central Bosnia Operative Zone," the same Tihomir

Blaškić, had been involved in planning the Ahmići attack on the evening before it was launched.

Aside from the new facts connected with the oral order and other evidence, the prosecution argued that the twenty-page Croatian Ministry of Interior report filed by the defense and relied upon by the Appeals Chamber in its judgment had been altered from its original form and that, if the Appeals Chamber had known the twenty-page report was effectively a deceptively bowdlerized version of the forty-page report, it would not have relied upon the report and its judgment would have been different. The stunning revelation in the forty-page report was that it attributed many of its most significant assertions solely to Blaškić's defense counsel, Ante Nobilo. For example, one passage of the twenty-page Ministry of Interior report cited by the appeals chamber in footnote 705 of its judgment read:

> [O]n the night of 15/16 April 1993 a meeting of an informal group, composed of Ignac KOŠTROMAN, Dario KORDIĆ, Ante SLIŠKOVIĆ, Tomo VLAJIĆ, SLIŠKOVIĆ's deputy Paško LJUBIČIĆ, Vlado ĆOSIĆ and Anto FURUNDŽIJA, who wanted conflict with the Muslims at any price, was held at Dario KORDIĆ's house. At this meeting it was agreed that an order would be issued to kill the entire male population in Ahmici and to torch the village.[4]

The newly discovered forty-page Ministry of Interior report stated:

> *According to NOBILO* . . . on the night of 15/16 April 1993 a meeting of an informal group, composed of Ignac KOŠTROMAN, Dario KORDIĆ, Ante SLIŠKOVIĆ, Tomo VLAJIĆ, SLIŠKOVIĆ's deputy Paško LJUBIČIĆ, Vlado ĆOSIĆ and Anto FURUNDŽIJA, who wanted conflict with the Muslims at any price, was held at Dario KORDIĆ's house. At this meeting it was agreed that an order would be issued to kill the entire male population in Ahmici and to torch the village. [Emphasis added.][5]

Other paragraphs of the forty-page report also carried the "according-to-Nobilo" attribution. So it was no wonder that the twenty-page report the Appeals Chamber cited had followed the same arguments Nobilo had presented, in this regard, on behalf of Blaškić. The Office of the Prosecutor's request for review argued that someone had abridged the original forty-page report and hidden the source. The request continued:

It is submitted that no Chamber would rely on factual assertions from defence counsel, without substantiation, as the basis for acquitting an accused. It is hard to imagine that the accurate passage above including the words *"According to Nobilo"* would have been placed in footnote 705 as the basis for the Appeals Chamber's findings had the Appeals Chamber been fully apprised of this.

The review application then asked: "How can the Appeals Chamber rely on an assertion by Defence Counsel when there has been no evidence admitted on behalf of the Defence which substantiates such a claim?"

For its part, the defense argued that, in ten years, the prosecution had been unable to produce any credible evidence linking Tihomir Blaškić with the Ahmići massacre. The defense contested the "newness" of the new facts the prosecution team had submitted. And the defense argued that the prosecution had not proven that the twenty-page Ministry of Interior report on the Ahmići massacre was a forgery of the forty-page version, that these two documents actually were not the same report, and that "the Appeals Chamber admitted the 20-page Report, with full knowledge that Nobilo was a source . . ."

On November 23, 2006, the Appeals Chamber delivered its final decision in the Blaškić case. The judges somehow found that the prosecution had failed to introduce any new facts and had failed to show that Blaškić had issued an oral order to conduct preparations for the attack on April 16. The judges also found, among other things, that the forty-page Ministry of Interior report failed to constitute a new fact under the tribunal's rules and that, even if this had constituted a new fact, the prosecution had failed to demonstrate that it could have affected the verdict reached in the appeals judgment that the evidence submitted at trial and on appeal did not support a finding that Blaškić was responsible either individually or as a superior for crimes committed at Ahmići on April 16, 1993.

A sense of disillusionment now weighed upon me and the members of my staff. I felt that the judges were seizing upon legal technicalities and engaging in sophistry rather than making a reasoned effort to reach the truth of the matter and administer the justice those victims burned up in the houses of Ahmići deserved. I believe that the Blaškić case showed in boldface the damaging effects upon justice inflicted by the quintessentially political pressure to close the tribunal by 2010.

In the end, Tihomir Blaškić served nine years, not for complicity in the massacre at Ahmići and crimes at other nearby villages in central Bosnia, but for the mistreatment of Muslim prisoners, including use of Muslim prisoners as human shields. The Tudjman regime—now five years dead—had succeeded in its efforts to frustrate the tribunal's work.

The Ivica Rajić prosecution had also by now come to an end. On October 25, 2005, Rajić pleaded guilty to four of the ten charges he was facing. This plea agreement contained a statement of facts that would make most normal minds shiver in terror. Rajić stated that, on October 23, 1993, the head of the Bosnian Croat militia's high command, Slobodan Praljak, had ordered Rajić and others to "sort out the situation in Vareš showing no mercy toward anyone." Rajić stated in writing that, in Stupni Do, Bosnian Croat militia commanders and soldiers under his command forced Bosnian Muslim civilians out of their homes and hiding places, robbed them of their valuables, willfully killed Muslim men, women, and children, and sexually assaulted Muslim women. The attack resulted in the deaths of at least thirty-seven Muslim children, elderly persons, women, and men, about six of whom were combatants. In separate episodes of the Stupni Do massacre, three Muslim men and one woman were executed by being shot or having their throats cut; one woman was taken into a house by a Bosnian Croat militia soldier where she was executed; two elderly women, one of whom was an invalid, were immolated inside a house; one Muslim man was shot several times at close range after he refused to give a Bosnian Croat militia soldier his money; a Muslim man, nine women, and three children were killed attempting to flee; three young Muslim women who escaped an initial encounter with the Bosnian Croat militia soldiers were found hiding in a small cellar and killed; seven members of a Muslim family, including two children ages two and three, were found burned inside their shelter; one Muslim man, who had been severely wounded in both legs, was carried into a house which was later set ablaze by Bosnian Croat militia soldiers; one Muslim woman was taken into a room and shot, and her house was set afire.

For commanding an operation that produced this mayhem, the Trial Chamber sentenced Ivica Rajić to twelve years in prison. Just twelve years for thirty-seven dead, many of them executed. The prosecutors, based upon the light sentences the tribunal's judges had handed down after the original Blaškić decision in 2000, had asked for only a fifteen-year jail term. But reducing it was ludicrous.

I do not know why the tribunal's judges are so reluctant to hand down sentences that match the crimes. It is better, I suppose, to be the banker who robs the bank because you have fine suits and belong to the right clubs and to be a commander who commits the war crime because you don't have blood splattered on your uniform. Perhaps the judges are unsure of themselves, because there is so little precedent for sentencing political leaders and military commanders in war-crimes cases. Perhaps too many of the tribunal's judges, many of them legal scholars and law professors, lack experience as judges. But this is no excuse for handing down ridiculously short sentences. I think it reveals weakness and a lack of courage to look real evil in the face. A man who murders his wife and two children almost routinely receives a life sentence. And here we have persons found guilty of participating in the deaths of dozens, or hundreds, and even thousands of dead. How can it be, that if you command soldiers who kill dozens of people, you get only a dozen years? It is as if some of the judges have grown numb and consider the victims to be less human than the killers. No, these killers deserve life sentences. And this means that they die in jail, that they don't go free after several dozen years, or get to go home on sick leave.

Croatia seemed ready to clear another hurdle in December 2004. The European Union announced that it would open accession talks with the Croatian government, if Zagreb demonstrated its full cooperation with the tribunal. In March, however, the launch of talks was postponed, because Zagreb had not met the prerequisites. These months were punctuated by meetings in Geneva and Paris and reports and rumors of Gotovina sightings and rendezvous between him and members of the French intelligence service and former Legionnaires. At a meeting on April 19, 2005, Sanader was adamant that his government was doing all it could to arrest Gotovina, not because of the European Union, but because it was a national and an international obligation. "How can we proceed?" he asked. "I want to resolve the case. I want Gotovina to be in The Hague and you to give a positive assessment. I am ready to develop an action plan to do the maximum. . . . I have invested all my political capital for normalization of life in Croatia. This includes the rule of law. . . . If I knew where he is, I would deliver him immediately."

"I am not so sure," I told Sanader. "I am starting to doubt your political will. Since March, what have you done?" I went on to describe how the man responsible for informing the tribunal about Croatia's efforts to cooperate did not know what was going on.

"You are correct," Sanader agreed. "I am ready to change."

"I have been expecting a report since March 10," I said, before discussing the French and the former Legionnaires and asking what the Croatian authorities were doing to disrupt Gotovina's protection network. I told him the French intelligence agent involved was protecting Gotovina. "I spoke to Chirac," I said, "and I told him he is close to Gotovina."

I also brought up a lead indicating that Gotovina was hiding out in Franciscan monasteries.

"What can be done on the Catholic Church, the monasteries, and the Franciscans?"

Sanader said he had spoken with the Church authorities in Croatia.

We went on to discuss many specifics involving operations to locate and apprehend Gotovina, and near the end Sanader asked me what I would be telling the European Council in Luxembourg a month later. Croatia's aspirations to enter Europe depended upon it.

In my remarks to the European Union on April 26, 2005, I said there had been no change in my team's evaluation of Croatia's failure to apprehend Ante Gotovina, who was still in Croatia and moving from time to time to Bosnia and Herzegovina. In a press statement, I said I had given Croatia details of the networks protecting Gotovina and had told the Croat leaders that I would say Croatia was fully cooperating with the tribunal only after Croatia brought Gotovina to The Hague or revealed to the tribunal his whereabouts." I thought the Croatian government was stalling and trying to convince Gotovina to surrender, and spare Sanader political fallout. I was wrong.

I met Sanader again in early June, before submitting another key report to the United Nations Security Council. He was even more desperate to resolve the Gotovina problem and once again pledged to do his utmost. Sanader had taken a political risk and was giving interviews to Croatian newspapers and pledging publicly to arrest Gotovina. He assured me the government wanted to work together with the tribunal to apprehend Gotovina. He would see to it that all leads and information were checked immediately. The government would investigate the financial dealings of members of Gotovina's protection network.

I thanked Sanader for the efforts, and asked him whether the Croatian authorities were willing to undertake searches of the country's Franciscan monasteries. He answered yes. With this agreement, and a lead from a friendly intelligence service that Gotovina was hiding in a monastery, I traveled to Rome to speak with Monsignor Giovanni Lajolo, the Vatican Secretary for Relations with States, the pope's foreign minister. It was July. I wanted to know from Monsignor Lajolo what the Church could do to support the effort to find Gotovina. (There are dozens of monasteries in Croatia; we actually made a list of them.)

I remember being driven with my Swiss aide, Jean-Daniel Ruch, through the Vatican's gates, protected by the long swords and halberds of the famous Swiss Guards. I joked to myself that I hoped my Swiss background and my years in Catholic convents might give my arguments some traction. The car came to a halt deep inside the walls. From there, several priests led us on foot through a maze of foyers and corridors. Finally, from an open-air walkway, a door opened to a hushed, austere antechamber. Such was the solemnity that I thought I was back in church. Monsignor Lajolo emerged from inside his office, greeted us, and showed us inside.

He was raised in the Piedmont region of Italy, just below the Swiss Alps where I had grown up. Our conversation had begun in a subdued Italian. The monsignor told me that the Vatican is not a state, so it could do nothing.

I interrupted him.

"*Scusi, monsignore,*" I said. "What you're saying is a revelation to me. Don't we always speak of the Vatican as a state? Didn't we once speak of the Papal State?" I remembered seeing the Papal State on the maps of the Italian peninsula in my history textbooks. I always assumed that the Vatican, however minuscule, enjoyed sovereignty. I assumed it could make its own diplomatic decisions. And I still think it can, when it so desires.

I then asked the Monsignor Lajolo whether the Vatican would be so kind as to ask the Croatian Catholic Bishops' Conference to intercede and stop its members from voicing defiant expressions of support for Gotovina. The monsignor now explained that the Pope of Rome has no authority over the Bishops' Conference. I replied that I thought Catholic bishops were supposed to obey the pope, and I thought there had been some kind of schism over just this question. "No, no," was the response.

In the end, I requested an audience with Pope Benedict XVI himself. Without a pause, Monsignor Lajolo responded by saying that the pope only receives presidents and government ministers. I answered that I had read in *Corriere della Sera* that Benedict had just received the head of an Italian political party who was neither a president nor a minister: "I think it would be appropriate for him to receive the prosecutor of an international war crimes tribunal who is working to protect human rights."

Monsignor Lajolo leveled a gaze at me and said, "If you wish to meet the pope, you can come to the Saint Peter's Square on Saturday." By this, he meant I could stand before the gathered masses with all the other people pre-selected to shake Pope Benedict's hand and kiss the ring of the fisherman and, in the middle of the wide-eyed believers, ask the Pontiff to help me find Gotovina.

"*Grazie*," I said, "I am not here as a pilgrim, I'm a prosecutor. I have heard that our fugitive is hiding in a Roman Catholic monastery. I have heard that the Vatican has the best intelligence service in the world. So I think it would be easy for you to find out whether he really is in one of the monasteries in Croatia." Somewhere along the way, I had slipped into diplomatic English. I never asked Monsignor Lajolo to undertake a search. All I wanted was a discreet inquiry to see if any friars were aiding and abetting a fugitive wanted on war crimes charges.

The monsignor glowered at me. He had brought me a kind of official gift, a set of Vatican commemorative coins. He tossed it over with a flick of his wrist, then he bid us farewell and left the chamber. Ruch, the Swiss Protestant, and I, the lapsed Roman Catholic, the graduate of two convent schools, sat there, deep within the Vatican labyrinth, surrounded by crucifixes and relics and statues and all of those Raphaels and Michelangelo's ceiling fresco of Judith and Holofernes, the library, the gardens, the center of the Catholic universe. When I had reached for my handbag and no other mortal could overhear us, Ruch leaned to my ear and whispered: "He is going to excommunicate you."

On Friday morning, September 30, 2005, I was stuck at Schipol airport. The airplane had developed some mechanical problem, and the Swiss government had sent us another aircraft to arrive and fly us to Zagreb. My mobile telephone rang. It was Croatia's prime minister, Ivo Sanader. He had good news. Come.

A few hours later, my team members and I were seated in a room with Prime Minister Sanader, President Mesić, and other Croatian officials. Sanader announced that Croatia's security people had located Gotovina.

Only a day or two earlier, he said, Gotovina had spoken with his wife on one of her eighteen or so mobile phones.

"Is this true or not?" I asked Sanader, skeptical. I was in no mood to accept a claim like this at face value, walk out of the room, and hit my excommunicated nose on another *muro di gomma*. Sanader and Croatia had so much to gain. I was scheduled to appear before a European Union task force in just three days to provide an assessment of the degree of the Republic of Croatia's cooperation with the tribunal. A positive assessment would help Croatia draw closer to the European Union. Everything now depended upon the authenticity of this telephone intercept. If I accepted it as genuine, I would have to report that Croatia was fully cooperating with the tribunal. It would be a huge risk, because Gotovina was still at large.

Croatia's chief state prosecutor, Mladen Bajić, led me and my aide, Anton Nikiforov, upstairs into a room with audio equipment and played the tape of Gotovina's telephone conversation. The voice matched Gotovina's. He even referred to my visit to Zagreb. He boasted something like, "She'll never get me."

The Croats explained that Gotovina's wife had failed to change the phone's SIM card after using it once before. Perhaps the wife had simply made an oversight, I thought; but perhaps, after so many years with her husband on the run, she had done it purposely. Whatever the reason, the police intercepted the transmission. They had traced the call to somewhere in the Canary Islands. But exactly where in the Canary Islands remained a mystery.

Distinguished members of the press were gathered outside, waiting to hear my reaction to the meeting with Sanader, Mesić, and the other Croatian government officials. Of course, I had agreed with the Croats not to mention the Gotovina intercept. I walked out, trying to make myself look grim and dissatisfied. I stressed my disappointment that General Ante Gotovina, whom we had been seeking for over half a decade, was still not in The Hague. This was my own *muro di gomma*. I purposely never gave any assessment of the Croatian government's cooperation. If someone had asked that specific question, I don't know how I would have answered. Fortunately, no one asked. And the journalists heard in my answer exactly what they wanted to hear. They reported that I was dissatisfied with Zagreb's cooperation and that, once again, one man, Ante Gotovina, and one woman, Carla Del Ponte, would frustrate Croatia's efforts to join the European Union. As they were submitting these accounts, the tribunal's chief of investigations, Patrick Lopez-Terres, was flying toward Madrid with the Croatian prosecutor, Bajić, to assist the Spanish authorities in the search for Gotovina.

Three days later in Luxembourg, I shocked everyone, except, of course, Sanader, Mesić, and the other Croats, by giving the European Union a glowing report on Croatia's cooperation with the tribunal. Now the journalists ran off speculating that I had come under massive political pressure from within the European Union and had been forced to alter my assessment. I was unable to explain publicly why I was so satisfied, because this would have tipped off Gotovina. In a way, the misinformation about political pressure had helped. Without this, Gotovina might have suspected something was amiss and run off in some unknown direction, and I would have lost my gamble.

The Croatian police failed to detect any more phone calls from Gotovina. The police and intelligence services in Spain were monitoring the airports all over the Canary Islands. We had heard stories that Gotovina was traveling aboard a yacht, and were concerned that he might depart the Canary Islands by sea. Then we caught a break. My spokeswoman, Florence Hartmann, happened to pick up a book Gotovina had authored. In it, he mentioned having visited the Canary Islands, and he described a specific location where he had acquaintances. We alerted Madrid, and the Spanish authorities arrested him on December 7 in a restaurant on Tenerife. He was in the company of a beautiful woman. And I thought that, perhaps, Gotovina's wife had become just another jilted spouse, like so many of those divorcing women whose stories I had suffered through so many years earlier in Lugano.

In mid-December 2005, during an address to the Security Council, I expressed the tribunal's gratitude toward the European Union and its member states for having provided the Yugoslavia tribunal with political support that had contributed so much to Gotovina's capture. "This can serve us as a model to overcome the difficulties we meet in Bosnia and Herzegovina and in Serbia and Montenegro," I said. "The key to success was a combination of international incentives, provided mainly by the European Union's consistent policy of conditioning [European Union] accession to the full cooperation with the [Yugoslavia tribunal], and an effective joint operational plan between Croatia and the [tribunal]. The United States have also provided valuable support by insisting that Croatia could not join NATO before Gotovina [was delivered to] The Hague. . . . This mix of political will and operational effectiveness leads to results."

During our first meeting in early 2000, Stipe Mesić told me that Franjo Tudjman, like Milošević, had failed to understand the trend toward European unification and the removal of the borders between European states. He said Serbia and Croatia had launched the war in Bosnia and Herzegovina because Milošević and Tudjman had sought to take Bosnia's territory. Now, Croatia was on its way toward Europe. But how many lost years had Tudjman and his men cost Croatia with their futile efforts to defy the international community, to conceal evidence, and to hide fugitives indicted for war crimes and facing international arrest warrants? Today, Slovenia, Romania, and Bulgaria are all under the European Union's umbrella. Croatia, despite all its aspirations, despite the fact that Zagreb lies north of Rome and west of Vienna, is not. And time may have run out while Tudjman, so blind to the trend in Europe after the fall of the Berlin Wall, wove empty nationalist myths and brought grief to so many hundreds of thousands of people.

In April 2006, the tribunal commenced the trial of the six Bosnian Croats accused of playing key political and military roles in the campaign of violence Tudjman had waged in his effort to partition Bosnia and Herzegovina. I had met one of the accused, Jadranko Prlić, years earlier, in late 2000, at a five-year commemoration of the peace agreement at Dayton. Taut but seemingly sophisticated, Prlić was Bosnia and Herzegovina's foreign minister at the time. He spoke to me in Italian. He presented me with a copy of his book on the war. I gave him no hint that he was under investigation. But he surely had to have known it, just as he surely had to have known that any indictment against him and the other highest-ranking Bosnian Croats would inevitably be an indictment by proxy of the deceased Tudjman, Šušak, Bobetko, and Boban. The documents that Tudjman and his intelligence chiefs had tried their best to conceal—the Bosnian Croat militia's archives and the transcripts of the meetings Tudjman had recorded in his office—yielded much of the evidence presented during the trial. The hearings would continue for months after I departed the tribunal. I was confident that this case, unlike the Blaškić case, would deliver justice for the victims of Ahmići, Stupni Do, Mostar, and the other towns and villages who had suffered during Croatia's campaign, with Serbia, to wrest territory from Bosnia and Herzegovina. I was confident that the evidence capturing the realities of this campaign would stand forever in defiant contrast to the legacy of denial and deceit Tudjman and his protégés had bequeathed.

CONFRONTING KOSOVO
1999 TO 2007

Violence, fear, and poverty silence witnesses. And in the first years of the new millennium, Kosovo, the province of Serbia that was the former Yugoslavia's least developed region, was suffering violence, fear, and poverty. How do you find witnesses and prosecute war crimes in a land with traumatized, enraged populations that have not had time to find and bury their dead; in a land with no institutions and little concept of the rule of law except the *lex talionis*, the ancient code of vengeance described by Homer and the ancient Greek tragedians; in a land where the United Nations and other international organizations are struggling with limited resources to establish law and order and where local militia leaders, many of them thugs promoting themselves as heroic defenders of a victimized people, are seeking political power and using violence to eradicate their enemies and rivals? Kosovo presented the Office of the Prosecutor all of these challenges.

During the spring and early summer of 1999, Serbian soldiers and police officers undertook the wholesale ethnic cleansing of Kosovo's majority Albanian population. Serbian fighting units went village by village, town by town, killing and burning. From their homes streamed Albanian peasants and shopkeepers, university professors and doctors, fathers and mothers, grandfathers in makeshift wheelchairs, grandmothers loaded into the backs of horsecarts, children in their parents' arms, teenagers moving on foot and carrying what belongings they could in backpacks and suitcases. They filed up to border crossings where Serbian policemen confiscated identification cards, robbed their valuables, and cast everyone into neighboring Albania or Macedonia. This displacement of hundreds of thousands of Albanians was the culmination of decades of ethnic strife whose antecedents lie deeper in the past than I need to delve, because these distant antecedents become something worse than irrelevant—they become pathetic alibis for the crimes at hand. Many, but certainly not all, Serbs claim to regard Kosovo as a kind of *Terra Santa*, a Holy Land, because it is home to an array of medieval Serbian Orthodox monasteries and was the seat of a fourteenth-century Serbian emperor; present-day Serb leaders also value Kosovo, as their medieval counterparts once did, for its mineral wealth.

A communist elite composed of local Albanians governed Kosovo from the early 1970s. In 1981, a year after Marshal Tito's death, Albanian separatists took to the streets of Kosovo's capital, Priština, demanding that the province become the old Yugoslavia's seventh republic, independent of Serbia. Yugoslavia's post-Tito presidency, a committee of eight, sent in troops who violently suppressed the demonstrations. By the mid-1980s, members of Kosovo's Serb minority were complaining about mistreatment at the hands of Albanians, who by now accounted for about 90 percent of the province's population. Slobodan Milošević rose to power championing the Kosovo Serbs' cause. Under his guidance, Belgrade quashed Kosovo's autonomy in 1990 and imposed direct rule, the rule of *force majeure* that carried the assumption of impunity. Serbian police officers drove the Albanians from the halls of government, from their jobs, from schools, from even hospitals. The Albanians responded by developing parallel governmental, educational, health, and security structures and, following the advice of Western embassies in Belgrade, refrained from taking up arms during the wars in Croatia and Bosnia and Herzegovina, when Serbia was most vulnerable.

In the spring of 1993, however, a small group of Kosovo Albanians who favored armed resistance to Belgrade's rule established a clandestine militia, the Kosovo Liberation Army (KLA). Its professed aims were to mobilize Kosovo's Albanians for a war of liberation and to answer with violence the acts of violence the Serbian authorities were committing. In the early years of the KLA's existence, only a small number of its members were based in Kosovo; most of them operated from the United States and countries in Western Europe, including Switzerland.

In late 1995, it became clear to politically aware Albanians everywhere that the international peace processes for Croatia and for Bosnia and Herzegovina had bypassed Kosovo. Two years later, an armed clash between Serbian forces and the KLA claimed the life of a local teacher; thousands of Albanian mourners attended his funeral, and among them were three men wearing black balaklavas and military uniforms with KLA patches. The KLA had now emerged from underground. On February 28 and March 1, 1998, Serbian police units equipped with helicopters, armored vehicles, mortars, and machine guns launched surprise attacks on the KLA in a number of villages in an effort to obliterate its leadership and use terror to subdue the civilian population. During these attacks, the Serbian forces fired indiscriminately at civilians. On March 5, 1998, Serbian security forces attacked the family compound of the KLA's leader, Adem Jashari. The gun battles continued for about thirty-six hours. Eighty-three Albanians reportedly died, including at least twenty-four women and children. Jashari and every member of his family except an eleven-year-old girl were counted among the dead. One pregnant woman was shot in the face. Serbian police reportedly executed some of the men in front of their homes.

The Serbian forces' terror tactics backfired. Tens of thousands of mourners attended the funerals of the Jasharis and the other dead. A member of the KLA's command delivered a patriotic eulogy. The KLA's popular support increased. Young men filled the militia's ranks. Its local commanders regrouped their forces and struck back. The Serbian police continued to draw civilian blood. By 1998, the United States and other Western countries were applying massive pressure upon Belgrade to halt the violence against Albanian civilians in Kosovo. By October of that year, the NATO countries were threatening to launch air strikes if Belgrade did not stop its attacks.

In the early spring of 1999, after renewed Serbian and KLA violence in Kosovo and a failed peace conference in France, NATO launched air attacks in an effort to force Belgrade to withdraw its police and military forces from the troubled region. The massive Serbian ethnic-cleansing operation began under the cover of the NATO air strikes. The exodus and the bombing continued simultaneously until June 1999, when Milošević agreed to withdraw Serbia's troops from most of Kosovo. NATO troops raced Russian forces to occupy the vacuum. The United Nations Mission in Kosovo (UNMIK) was set up to help Kosovo construct a political and, more urgently, a security framework. KLA commanders emerged as a political force. In many corners of Kosovo, these commanders were the only law. And the Office of the Prosecutor began receiving information that some of them had participated in war crimes against Serbs, Roma, Muslim Slavs, and members of other ethnic groups, as well as against Albanians whom KLA members accused of disloyalty. The Office of the

Prosecutor's mandate, which had been designed to attack the culture of impunity, required investigation of allegations against the highest-ranking leaders *on all sides* of the conflicts in the former Yugoslavia. This meant investigating and, if appropriate, prosecuting those leaders of the KLA most responsible for the crimes the militia had committed. It was left to UNMIK and the local authorities to prosecute lower-ranking accused.

There were numerous reports of alleged KLA crimes to investigate. The Office of the Prosecutor received reports that, in 1998 and 1999, KLA soldiers had abducted hundreds of Serbs, Roma, Albanians, and members of other ethnic groups; some of these captives were detained in makeshift camps, some were locked in a basement flooded with a foot of standing water, some were confined in a cattle stall, some were beaten, some were raped, some were tortured, some were executed, some simply disappeared. The Office of the Prosecutor received reports that KLA soldiers had used violence and intimidation to force Serbs and Roma families from their ancestral villages and had killed people who remained behind. It received reports that KLA soldiers had used prisoners as human shields. It received reports about a KLA execution ground near a lake. It received reports that the bodies of victims and even prisoners had been transported into Albania.

Nataša Kandić had sent the Office of the Prosecutor a published report indicating that 593 persons—Serbs, Montenegrins, Roma, and Slavic Muslims—had either disappeared or were abducted after June 12, 1999, the day the NATO-led international peacekeeping force, KFOR, deployed in Kosovo, and were still missing on December 31, 2000. Several aspects of these disappearances were strange, and suggested that they were not simply acts of post-conflict vengeance. Most of the disappearances had taken place in districts where there had been no large-scale violence by Serbian forces against Kosovo Albanians during the NATO air campaign. Dozens of Yugoslav Army soldiers had also disappeared during the bombing and contemporaneous fighting against the KLA. Additionally, more than 1,500 Albanians disappeared after the KLA had taken them into custody during the bombing; and more than three hundred Albanians had disappeared in the second half of 1999 and in 2000.[1]

On January 25, 2001, during my first visit to Belgrade, I had met with family members of missing persons from Kosovo who had gathered inside the foreign ministry building. In the streets outside, a few hundred demonstrators were filling the air with noise. The chairman of the Kosovo group, Ranko Djinović, briefed me and my delegation about the persons who had disappeared in Kosovo between 1998 and 2001. The association had in its possession evidence of criminal activities by KLA members. This evidence, he said, included witness accounts of abductions of men, women, and children, three quarters of whom were taken captive *after* the arrival of KFOR and UNMIK. Djinović accused the KLA's top leaders, Hashim Thaçi, its political director, and Agim Çeku, its commander, of responsibility for abductions and killings in Kosovo; Djinović said the association had collected the names of two hundred kidnappers, all of them KLA members. Djinović asked me to investigate crimes committed after KFOR's arrival in Kosovo in June 1999. I said I would try. But I asked him to urge Yugoslavia's government to support extending the tribunal's mandate to cover these alleged crimes. At this time, many family members of the disappeared Serbs believed their relatives were still alive and had been transported across the border into Albania, but, strangely, there had been few if any credible requests for ransom payments. Back outside after the meeting, I saw the demonstrators waving placards and heard them shouting, "Carla is a whore." Some of them used slingshots to pelt my car with marbles as it pulled away.

The Office of the Prosecutor would eventually receive information, which UNMIK investigators and officials had acquired from a team of credible journalists, about how, during the summer months of 1999, Kosovo Albanians had trucked one hundred to three hundred abducted persons across the border from Kosovo into northern Albania. These captives were initially locked inside warehouses and other facilities, including locations in the towns of Kukës and Tropoje. According to the journalists' sources, whom they identified only as Kosovo Albanians, some of the younger, fitter captives, who were kept well fed, examined by doctors and never beaten, were transferred to other holding facilities in and around Burrel, including a shack behind a yellow house about twenty kilometers south of the town. A room inside this yellow house, the journalists reported, had been set up as a makeshift surgical clinic; and there, doctors extracted the captives' internal organs. These organs were then smuggled through Rinas airport near Tirana for transplant into paying patients in surgical wards abroad, according to the sources, including one who described delivering such a shipment to the airport. Victims deprived of only their first kidney were sewn up and confined again inside the shack until they were killed for their other vital organs; in this way, the other captives in the shack learned of their approaching fate, and they reportedly pleaded in terror to be killed immediately. Among the captives reportedly taken to this shack were women from Kosovo, Albania, Russia, and other Slavic countries, and two of the sources said they helped bury the bodies of the dead around the yellow house and at a nearby graveyard. According to the sources, the smuggling operation occurred with the knowledge and active involvement of mid- and senior-level KLA officers. Tribunal investigators found that, while the information from the journalists and UNMIK officials was sketchy, the details were internally consistent and corroborated information the tribunal had developed in-house. "The [Office of the Prosecutor's] in-house material does not . . . contain material about Albania as such; however, the few witness statements and some other material that we have do corroborate to a certain extent the information above," I read in a memo on this activity. "All the individuals that the sources have mentioned to be in the camp/s in Albania in late summer 1999 have gone missing in summer 1999 and have not been seen since."

The recommendations were obvious: "Bearing in mind the extremely serious nature of these cases, the fact that practically none of the bodies of the victims of the KLA have been found in exhumations in Kosovo and the fact that these atrocities were allegedly committed under the supervision or command of the KLA mid- or high-level leadership, they should definitely be investigated as properly as possible by professional and experienced investigators." The known victims in these cases had probably been abducted after the NATO air campaign had ended—at a time when Kosovo was crawling with foreign peacekeepers and legions of human-rights investigators and aid workers—so it was unclear whether or not the crimes committed during this period fell under the Yugoslavia tribunal's mandate. The Office of the Prosecutor wanted the journalists and UNMIK to provide the sources' names and other personal details and all other information they had about these allegations. The office had to compile and analyze all in-house material related to the case. If the journalists and UNMIK were uncooperative, the office had somehow to identify, locate, and interview the journalists' sources, without knowing their identities or whereabouts; undertake a mission with the sources to the locations in Albania; and, if necessary, conduct a crime scene investigation and exhumations.

The KLA investigations proved to be the most frustrating the Yugoslavia tribunal would undertake. Kosovo had no police in June 1999, and NATO and UNMIK took up the job of policing the region with little enthusiasm. The Albanian community had political leaders, including Ibrahim Rugova and other moderates who had strived against all odds to apply nonviolent methods to resist Serbian oppression during the late 1980s and the 1990s. But these political leaders found themselves with no functioning institutions of government. For these reasons, investigators from the Office of the Prosecutor could not amass evidence by relying upon the local Kosovo authorities. The few Albanians in Kosovo willing to provide information and bear witness in court against KLA suspects had to be protected, and this meant, in some cases, resettling entire families in third countries at a time when most states were reluctant to accept such people. Police detectives from Berne and Brussels to The Bronx know how frustrating it is to investigate Albanians involved in organized criminal activity. The Albanian language, one of Europe's oldest, poses problems, because there are so few speakers who are not Albanian; and recruiting native Albanian translators, like recruiting Albanian informants and witnesses, is difficult because Albanian society is so tightly knit and many Albanian clans recognize only their traditional law of vendetta, which exposes family members to retaliation. Serb witnesses had fled across Kosovo's borders into Serbia and Montenegro; and Milošević and the Serb nationalist political leaders, in an effort to shield themselves and members of the military and police from prosecution, had refused to allow tribunal investigators access to Serb victims of alleged KLA crimes.

During my initial visit to Kosovo, the head of UNMIK, Bernard Kouchner, agreed that pursuing KLA targets was politically crucial. Members of his staff said they were interested in the crimes perpetrated after the end of the NATO air campaign, and we informed Kouchner that these crimes, including systematic killings and abductions, were a part of the tribunal's mandate. The high-level support for prosecutions seemed to continue for a time. But we eventually collided with the *muro di gomma.*

I am sure some UNMIK and even KFOR officials feared for their lives and the lives of members of their missions. I think some judges at the Yugoslavia tribunal feared the Albanians' reach. Swiss compatriots warned me to be careful of retaliation. (Some Swiss officials even cautioned against discussing certain Albanian-related issues in this memoir, and I am discussing them here only with extreme care.) But the impunity that shrouds powerful political and military figures feeds upon fear-driven reluctance to apply the law. Impunity also thrives when perceived political imperatives obstruct the administration of justice. I think UNMIK officials would eventually deceive themselves into believing that they could rely upon former KLA leaders with dubious backgrounds to help develop functioning institutions and the rule of law. This is obviously like squaring a circle. But drawing order out of anarchy was not my problem. My mission was to prosecute persons against whom the Yugoslavia tribunal's investigators had obtained sufficient evidence of war crimes.

On October 6, 2000, I met again with the head of UNMIK, Bernard Kouchner. We had heard that UNMIK and KFOR were alarmed by speculation in the local press that the tribunal had issued secret indictments against Hashim Thaçi, Agim Çeku, and a number of other KLA leaders. UNMIK and KFOR considered Thaçi and Çeku to be more than just security threats to their personnel and their missions; they considered Thaçi and Çeku to be threats to the entire peace effort in the Balkans. Theoretically, Thaçi and Çeku could ignite violence in Macedonia and Southern Serbia and other areas by inciting their restive Albanian minorities. I informed Kouchner that these stories about secret indictments against Çeku and Thaçi had no substance. I told him that tribunal investigators were probing allegations of KLA war crimes against Serbs, Roma, and others. But we were not ready to draft an indictment against any Albanians.

A few weeks later, I was in Dayton, Ohio, for a conference commemorating the fifth anniversary of the Dayton Peace Agreement, which had ended the violence in Bosnia and Herzegovina. Unlike the hosts of the 1995 Dayton peace talks, the people who organized the anniversary conference had invited representatives of Kosovo's Albanians. I found myself sitting at the speakers' table next to Hashim Thaçi for a panel discussion. We began conversing. Thaçi admitted that Albanians had committed crimes during the Kosovo violence. But he asserted that they had been civilians in KLA uniforms. Then he made some inappropriate comment that provoked me. I looked him in the eyes and said I had opened an investigation of crimes committed in Kosovo by Albanians. I never referred to an indictment against Thaçi, but he certainly inferred that I had, because his face turned to marble.

By 2002, it was clear that the Office of the Prosecutor's investigations of the violence in Kosovo had encountered snags as frustrating as those UNMIK was suffering in its attempts to put on trial hundreds of lower-ranking KLA members accused of war crimes. We needed evidence of the KLA's chain of command, we needed to know which KLA officers were in charge of units fighting in particular areas and when these officers had taken command. During my visit to Washington, D.C., on March 18, 2002, I reminded American officials that the Office of the Prosecutor had submitted a number of requests for assistance of critical importance for the KLA investigations and had, despite several reminders, received nothing in response. "If the process of justice is to gain some acceptance in Serbia, and thus open the way to some degree of reconciliation, KLA crimes must be exposed," I said. "Injustice is the seed of future wars." The United States, through NATO's air power, had provided decisive military support to the KLA. I was concerned that, despite its rhetorical backing for the tribunal, Washington would not welcome indictments against KLA leaders, because these indictments would complicate the international effort to build new institutions in Kosovo and delay the day the Pentagon could redeploy its troops in Kosovo to Afghanistan and other fronts in the war against al Qaeda. Other NATO countries were no better. In October 2003, I was in London and met with the head of the Foreign Office, Jack Straw. He was apparently in pain, having just had his wisdom teeth removed. We complained about lack of cooperation by the United Kingdom. The Office of the Prosecutor had requested information about the KLA's structure, and we emerged from the meeting sure that the British government was only pretending it had nothing.

A month after the trip to Washington, I was back in Belgrade. Even Nataša Kandić told me she could not help the tribunal's investigators find Albanians willing to testify against KLA perpetrators like Thaçi, Çeku, and a third commander, Ramush Haradinaj, who had emerged as the KLA's leader in areas of western Kosovo adjacent to the Albanian border. Kandić said Albanian witnesses were even refusing to speak with Albanian human rights investigators about these incidents. Later in the day, we told Serbia's deputy prime minister, Nebojša Čović, that the Office of the Prosecutor was planning, with UNMIK and other organizations, to carry out a forensic examination of two locations, including a reported execution site near Radonjić Lake in western Kosovo. Čović said that his team would provide the tribunal with a list of 196 possible execution sites and that he had given this same information to UNMIK a year earlier but had received no results. Ćović asked us to push UNMIK and KFOR to provide the Serbian government with more information on missing persons. Ćović was pessimistic about UNMIK's new head, Michael Steiner, a German diplomat who had participated in the international effort in postwar Bosnia and Herzegovina. Ćović warned me that Steiner might advise us to avoid indicting Albanians and that the Albanians would present all kinds of excuses. "They will tell you what you want to hear," Ćović said.

After our conversation, Ćović and I had another tense meeting with representatives of the families of missing and abducted persons from Kosovo. They posed legitimate questions: Why had the tribunal provided no information about their missing relatives? Why had the tribunal failed to find mass graves? Why were no suspected places of detention found or searched? Why were no Albanian kidnappers indicted after the association had provided the Office of the Prosecutor lists of suspects? These family members trusted no one, not even Serbia's government; in fact, they once told me they had received better cooperation from Kosovo Albanians whose relatives had disappeared. "We are doing our best," I said. I told them the Office of the Prosecutor was insisting that KFOR and UNMIK provide full cooperation but that we could not investigate all the crimes that had taken place. I knew I had failed to satisfy them.

The next day, April 19, 2002, we were in Priština for meetings with KFOR's commander, General Marcel Valentin of France, and UNMIK's Michael Steiner, whom I had not seen since we toured the roof of the Reichstag in Berlin almost a year earlier. I asked Valentin to supply the Office of the Prosecutor with information on the KLA's command structure and zones of operation. I was sure the KFOR contingents that first arrived in Kosovo in June 1999 had to have compiled intelligence reports and charts showing this information. How else would KFOR's commanders, intelligence officers, and political and civil-affairs advisers have known with whom they were dealing? It would have been negligent not to compile such information. Valentin responded that KFOR had already begun providing the Office of the Prosecutor with information. But, he said, documents from KFOR's first contingents were by then stored at NATO's headquarters in Belgium or at the facilities of individual NATO nations. I informed Valentin and Steiner that I wanted to have the first KLA indictment ready by June, that the indictment and arrest warrants would be served on KFOR directly, and that it would be impossible to give prior notice because a judge had to confirm any indictment. I asked Valentin to have KFOR prepared to arrest the accused as soon as possible, and I asked if KFOR preferred sealed or public indictments. Valentin's political adviser, an American, said the time was right to come forth with indictments against Albanian perpetrators. He recommended issuing public indictments against some of our targets, because these people would have nowhere to run and no way of avoiding surrender to The Hague. I was encouraged by these words. But I also knew about the legendary mountains of northern Albania, and I wondered whether KFOR would be any more adept at capturing Albanian fugitives than the NATO force in Bosnia had been at capturing Karadžić.

My advisers and I later met with Kosovo's prime minister, Bajram Rexhepi. Here the goal was to secure the cooperation of the local authorities for the day the tribunal would issue indictments against Albanian accused. I told Rexhepi that the role of Kosovo's Albanian political leaders would be to explain to the Albanian people that crimes on all sides had to be punished. Rexhepi understood that flattery is the mortar of the *muro di gomma*. He praised the tribunal's work. He praised me. He praised our achievements. He declared that no one is above the law. He said it would be an easy task to explain this to Kosovo's people. But, he asserted, most Albanians in the KLA had fought for the idea of an independent Kosovo and not to kill people. He maintained that the crimes committed by Albanians in Kosovo were the misdeeds of individuals and were, therefore, on a different plane than the crimes committed by Serbs. "I was a surgeon with the KLA," he said. "I did not notice KLA violations of customs of war, because it was the KLA's motto to fight only people in uniform—the police and the army." Thus, according to Rexhepi's logic, no commander could be held accountable for killings and abductions carried out by his subordinates. I told Rexhepi that the Office of the Prosecutor's investigators were having difficulty. Witnesses, I said, were suffering intimidation and were so terrified to speak about the KLA that they would not even discuss its presence in specific areas. Rexhepi said he understood this reticence. Kosovo's local police were still ineffective, he said, and the conflict had removed all taboos.

During the summer of 2002, the Office of the Prosecutor continued to have trouble amassing evidence of sufficient quality to submit indictments. The investigators continued to have trouble finding evidence linking ranking officers with episodes of criminal behavior. Trial attorneys discussed jurisdictional problems in presenting charges based upon incidents that had occurred after the Serbian authorities had departed Kosovo. Many of our victims were elderly men and women who had remained in their villages alone after all the younger people had fled, so we had dead or missing victims and few, if any, witnesses. We still lacked documents outlining the KLA's structure and witnesses prepared to speak about this structure. Teams of forensic anthropologists developed information on about thirty bodies found near Lake Radonjić, but, by the autumn, the investigators, using DNA testing, had positively identified only eight.

On October 22, 2002, I was back in Priština. KFOR's new commander, Fabio Mini, an Italian general, assured me that his forces would be ready to arrest any of the tribunal's accused at any time and that the appropriate threat assessments of fourteen potential KLA targets had been completed. I told General Mini that one or two indictments might be confirmed by the end of the year. Mini said KFOR would plan first to persuade the accused to surrender voluntarily, but would also have an arrest operation ready to proceed immediately. He, like Valentin before him, expressed concern about UNMIK's trustworthiness. "It will be necessary to cooperate with UNMIK at the last minute," General Mini said. Then he joked about the close relationship between some UNMIK personnel and former KLA leaders. When the first arrests happen, Mini said, "we will see many local leaders going on vacation with a U.S. escort." We also spoke of missing persons, indications that there were mass graves in three areas of northern Albania, and the possible involvement of Albania's secret service. Mini instructed his people to make immediate arrangements for air reconnaisance, including infrared scanning of possible mass grave locations before the winter snows arrived. At UNMIK we learned that one source had demanded 50,000 euros to identify each of two graves in northern Albania.

Only months later did tribunal and UNMIK investigators travel to central Albania and visit the yellow house the journalists' sources had identified as the place where captives had been killed for their organs. The journalists led the investigators and an Albanian prosecutor to the site. The house was now white; the owner denied that it had ever been repainted even though the investigators saw obvious blotches of yellow along the base of its walls. On the ground, investigators discovered pieces of gauze. Nearby lay a used syringe, two empty plastic drip bags crusted with dirt, and spent medicine vials, some of them for a muscle-relaxer routinely used during surgery. A forensic chemical spray revealed blood splatters along the walls and floor of a room inside the house, except for a clear area of the floor about six feet in length and two feet wide. The owner offered up a variety of explanations for the blood stains during the two days the investigators spent in the village. Initially he said that his wife had given birth to their children in this room years earlier. Later, after his wife had revealed that her children had actually been born elsewhere, he asserted that the family had used the room to slaughter animals for a Muslim holiday.

The investigators' findings, combined with the anecdotal information the journalists had provided, were tantalizing. Stories of prisoners being killed by organ smugglers arise from many conflict areas, but rarely is there hard evidence to lift these accounts out of the realm of urban myth. The syringes, the drip bags, and the other medical paraphernalia were clearly corroborative evidence, but this evidence was, unfortunately, insufficient. The investigators could not determine whether the blood traces had been human. The sources had not pinpointed the locations of the alleged victims' graves, so we found no bodies. The mission did not convince any of the people in and around the yellow house to come forward with truthful information. The journalists had all along refused to reveal their sources, and the tribunal's investigators were unable to identify or locate them. There were also jurisdictional obstacles, given the dates of the reported abductions, the transport of the victims across the border into Albania, the criminal activity in Albania, and the crime scene there. The local Albanian prosecutor revealed another dimension of the "cooperation" problem; he boasted that his relatives had fought in the KLA and he told the tribunal's investigator: "No Serbs are buried here. But if they did bring Serbs over the border from Kosovo and killed them, they did a good thing." So, in the end, the attorneys and investigators on the KLA cases decided that there was insufficient evidence to proceed. Without the sources or a way to identify and find them, without bodies, and without other evidence linking high-level accused to these acts, all avenues of investigation were barred. It would be up to UNMIK or the local Kosovo and Albanian authorities, perhaps in conjunction with the Serbian law enforcement agencies, to investigate these accounts further and, if necessary, prosecute them.

On January 27, 2003, thanks to investigative support from UNMIK, the tribunal issued its first KLA-related indictment, alleging that four Albanian accused had, from May to late July 1998, abducted at least thirty-five Serb and Kosovo Albanian civilians in central Kosovo and detained them under inhumane conditions in a cowshed and the basement of a house within a walled compound in a village that had been a base of KLA operations. In its final form, the indictment alleged that the accused, Fatmir Limaj, who had become a member of Kosovo's parliament, and two other KLA members, Haradin Bala and Isak Musliu, subjected their captives to assaults, beatings, and torture; the indictment against the fourth defendant, Agim Murtezi, was withdrawn. Fourteen prisoners were allegedly killed in the makeshift prison; another ten were allegedly executed in nearby mountains when the KLA abandoned the area as it came under attack from advancing Serbian forces.

KFOR's arrests of two of the accused went smoothly. The third was a different matter. Three weeks after the tribunal had issued its indictment, I received a call from a senior KFOR commander who said Fatmir Limaj had been allowed to board a regularly scheduled airline flight to Slovenia for skiing with his business partner, Hashim Thaçi. I was outraged. The tribunal had alerted the law-enforcement agencies in Kosovo about the indictment and arrest warrant against Limaj and his co-accused. Limaj had not assumed a false identity when he drove to the Priština airport. He had not been hiding out in some safe house. He had walked up to a counter, obtained his boarding pass, made his way through passport and, presumably, security checks, and flew away, supposedly without anybody noticing. On February 18, our office had information that Limaj had already left Slovenia. I issued a statement urging the international community to face up to its responsibilities before Fatmir Limaj took his place beside Ratko Mladić, Radovan Karadžić, and the tribunal's other famous fugitives. Within a few days, the Slovenian authorities arrested Limaj in a ski resort, and he surrendered to the tribunal's custody, shaking his head and smiling and claiming it was all a misunderstanding. The defendants pleaded not guilty.

Violence against witnesses in local criminal cases involving members of the KLA had already begun by the time the tribunal issued the Limaj indictment. In December 2002, a bomb exploded in Priština; the press reported that the intended victim was a prospective witness in a local criminal trial of five former KLA members charged with running a detention center and torturing their captives. In late 2002, several Albanians testified in a second local trial of five former KLA members, including Daut Haradinaj, a brother of Ramush Haradinaj, a former KLA commander; Ramush Haradinaj had, by 2003, become both a political leader and one of the Albanians the tribunal was investigating. The UNMIK court convicted Daut Haradinaj and his four co-defendants of having detained and killed four Kosovo Albanians in 1999.[2] On January 4, 2003, one of the prosecution's witnesses in this case, a former KLA officer, Tahir Zemaj, was killed in a drive-by shooting with his son and nephew in western Kosovo's largest town, known to Albanians as Pejë and to Serbs as Peč. At least forty persons reportedly witnessed the shooting. Two other prosecution witnesses in the same trial—Sadik Musaj and Ilir Selimaj—were also killed.[3] Eight days after the UNMIK-supported local police made an appeal for witnesses to the Zemaj killing, someone fired an anti-tank rocket into the UNMIK regional police building in Pejë.[4] Later, two police officers investigating Zemaj's death were gunned down. Several other witnesses survived attempts on their lives, including Ramiz Muriqi, who told journalists that the convicted defendants were taking vengeance upon the witnesses.[5] The Office of the Prosecutor unofficially obtained an UNMIK report on the Zemaj killing; in response to a request for an official copy, UNMIK sent the document with all relevant passages but one blacked out. The legible passage stated that, before his violent death, Zemaj had said, apparently to UNMIK personnel, that if he were killed, the likely suspects would include one of our targets, Ramush Haradinaj, and another man. Ramush Haradinaj told journalists that neither he nor his brother were involved in the Zemaj killing.

The Limaj trial team had already begun reporting to me that they were encountering witnesses who were refusing to speak, as well as witnesses who had previously spoken with attorneys and investigators but were now refusing to testify. The rampant violence against witnesses in criminal cases, whether this violence was related to the testimony these persons had given or whether the violence was connected with unrelated criminal activity or vendettas, clearly created an atmosphere of fear that struck dumb other Albanians who might have been willing to provide information and testify. The absence of credible law-enforcement agencies and witness-protection programs was only part of the problem.

Beginning in June 2004, one man and his son attempted to interfere with two witnesses who had agreed to testify, with protective measures, for the prosecution in the upcoming trial against Limaj and his co-defendants. Bashkim Beqaj, the son, approached one of the protected witnesses, designated later as B2, while he was walking along a road in Shtime, a village in

Kosovo. Bashkim Beqaj accosted B2 outside a restaurant and accused B2 of having sent his uncle, Isak Musliu, to prison in The Hague. Passersby stopped the bullying. B2 went to the Beqaj house, and the father, Beqa Beqaj, apologized for his son's behavior and told B2 that Musliu had called him six times from The Hague and told him to go and see B2.

In early September 2004, two months before Limaj and his co-defendants went on trial, Beqa Beqaj approached the relative of another protected witness, B1, who had allegedly been tortured and survived two assassination attempts and a massacre during which one of his parents had been killed. Beqaj told B1's relative to pass along a message that Isak Musliu would give B1 land if he withdrew the sworn statement he had given to the prosecution. On September 27, 2004, Beqa Beqaj twice asked B1's relative to relay a message that Beqaj was speaking on behalf of Fatmir Limaj and Isak Musliu and that they wanted B1 to withdraw his sworn statement and return to Kosovo urgently to speak with Limaj case lawyers. On October 6, 2004, the police intercepted a telephone conversation during which Beqaj told B1 to "come and just give us one statement . . . come and say that you have nothing to do with Fatmir Limaj and Isak [Musliu]." In this conversation, Beqaj admitted that he had spoken with Fatmir Limaj's brother Demir Limaj. Beqaj asked B1 to meet the lawyers of Limaj and Musliu in Priština and assured B1 that nothing would happend to him. In another telephone conversation intercepted on October 13, 2004, Beqaj again asked B1 to return urgently to Kosovo to meet Limaj's lawyers and Limaj's brother and make a statement repudiating his earlier statement to the prosecution.[6]

Proving witness tampering is extremely difficult, especially in a lawless region. The Trial Chamber eventually found Beqaj in contempt, but only on those charges backed up by telephone intercepts. His sentence: four months in jail. This was no deterrent in a land where the Serbs once locked up Albanians arbitrarily for months at a time and where witnesses in criminal trials were being gunned down. During the Limaj trial, more witnesses told prosecution attorneys that they had received threats. Some received notes. Some received phone calls. Some heard automatic weapons fire into the air outside their houses. Some reported that local police officers had searched their houses and followed their children. One man noticed the red dot of a laser target spotter painting his wife's face. Attorneys from the Office of the Prosecutor traveled repeatedly to Kosovo under armed guard and visited the houses of prospective witnesses to convince them to testify. They tried to convince community leaders, telling them that if they had the courage to step forward, others would follow, and the rule of law would grow stronger in their homeland. After one of them gave evidence, gunmen fired several dozen rounds from an automatic weapon into his car, miraculously missing him and his fourteen-year-old son. Another had his car blown up and lost his leg before the tribunal moved him to a third country.

On November 13, 2005, the Trial Chamber acquitted Fatmir Limaj and Isak Musliu, but found the third defendant, Haradin Bala, guilty on charges of torture, cruel treatment, and murder. In explaining the acquittal of Limaj, the judges observed that the courtroom testimony of a number of former KLA members subpoenaed to testify as prosecution witnesses was materially different from the accounts they provided in their previous sworn statements to the prosecution. The judges reasoned that seven years had passed since the incidents described in the indictment, and this might have weakened the witnesses' recollections. The judges reasoned that the witnesses might have offered different responses because they faced questions during the trial that differed from those posed during the pretrial interview. The judges noted that some witnesses explained discrepancies while on the stand. And the judges said that they were willing to accept the possibility some discrepancies remained unexplained:

> At times it became apparent to the Chamber, in particular taking into account the demeanour of the witness and the explanation offered for the differences, that the oral evidence of some of these witnesses was deliberately contrived to render it much less favourable to the Prosecution than the prior statement. The evidence of some of these former KLA members left the Chamber with a distinct impression that it was materially influenced by a strong sense of association with the KLA in general. . . . It appeared that overriding loyalties had a bearing upon the willingness of some witnesses to speak the truth in court about some issues. It is not disputed that notions of honour and other group values have a particular relevance to the cultural background of witnesses with Albanian roots in Kosovo.

The judges even pulled a quotation from an expert report as authority for their assessment:

> [The] Albanian concept of honour governs all relations that extend beyond blood kinship. . . . Solidarity with those individuals that share the

same "blood" is taken for granted, but faithfulness to a group or cause that reaches beyond the family needs to be ritually invoked. Honour can also be explained in terms of an ideal-type of model of conduct, and a man's perceived potential of protecting the integrity of the family or any wider reference group (such as the clan or a political party) against outside attacks. . . . [The pledge of allegiance or *besa*] requests absolute loyalty, and it requires the individual's compliance with family and group values in general. At the same time it justifies the killing of those within the group who break this code. . . . However . . . the members of a group can chose [sic] to avoid violence. The reaction to conflict, insult, treason, or other transgressions to group norms, depends on the members' interpretations of the facts and these may vary greatly.

The judges observed that a significant number of witnesses requested protective measures at trial and expressed concerns for their lives and the lives of their family members. Nevertheless, the Trial Chamber effectively threw out the prior statements of two witnesses, two former KLA members, Shukri Buja and Ramadan Behluli, that contained evidence that Fatmir Limaj was a commander when the alleged crimes occurred. Each of these two witnesses, however, testified during the trial that, upon reflection, what they had said earlier in their respective interviews with the prosecution was mistaken. Each of these witnesses placed events relevant to the command of Fatmir Limaj at points later in time than the apparent effect of their earlier statements, in each case later than the time material to the indictment. The circumstances and the nature of their evidence suggested the possibility that this partial disavowal was the result of what could be perceived as a sense of loyalty toward the KLA in general, and Fatmir Limaj in particular, on the part of Shukri Buja and Ramadan Behluli. The effect was to remove the foundation of the prosecution case in this respect. The prosecution in essence was forced to submit that the chamber should disbelieve the evidence given in court by these two witnesses and, instead, accept the truth of and make factual findings on the basis of the earlier interviews with the Office of the Prosecutor, despite their express disavowal. The chamber said it was not able to be so convinced of the truth and reliability of the earlier statements as to make findings contrary to the oral evidence of each of the two witnesses. At least on this issue, the evidence of Shukri Buja and Ramadan Behluli about Limaj's command role was effectively neutralized.

I considered this decision to be an example of the triumph of the lack of will. The impunity that feeds upon fear was allowed to prevail. We appealed.

Thousands of Albanians rioted across Kosovo for two days in March 2004, after the local Albanian media spread a false accusation that a group of Serbs were responsible for the drownings of three Albanian children in a river. According to an investigative report by Human Rights Watch, the institutions responsible for security in Kosovo—KFOR, UNMIK and its international police force, and the nascent local police force—failed to protect the province's minority Serbs and Roma. Nineteen persons, eight Serbs and eleven Albanians, died. The wounded numbered more than one thousand, and they included more than 120 KFOR soldiers and UNMIK police officers and fifty-eight local police officers. Gangs of Albanians burned entire Serb villages and destroyed or damaged more than five hundred Serb houses as well as thirty Serbian Orthodox Churches and monasteries. When the violence ended, no Serbs were left in Priština and other towns.

The tribunal was not responsible for prosecuting crimes committed during these riots. But the unrest affected the cooperation that the tribunal would receive in Kosovo, especially from leaders of international institutions working in the province. On June 16, 2004, Søren Jessen-Petersen of Denmark, who had extensive experience with the United Nations and other international organizations, became UNMIK's new head. He and the other foreigners trying to manage the Kosovo problem were clearly interested in forging ties with local Albanian leaders upon whom they could rely to improve security in the violence-ridden region, strengthen its institutions of government, and prepare Kosovo for the ultimate decision about its future status.

In December 3, 2004, Kosovo's assembly elected Ramush Haradinaj, the head of a party known as the Alliance for the Future of Kosovo, to be the region's prime minister. Right at the completion strategy's deadline for new indictments, the Office of the Prosecutor filed with the Trial Chamber an indictment against Haradinaj. A judge took weeks to pore over the evidence and the charges, and, on March 4, 2005, confirmed it. Rumors had been rampant in Kosovo since November 2004 that the tribunal woud indict Haradinaj, and he enjoyed a significant amount of support within the international missions working in Kosovo. Even a month before the Office of the Prosecutor submitted the indictment, senior diplomats from the United Kingdom informed my advisers that London would not support the tribunal unless the indictment was robust. I thought it was. So, apparently, did Lord Iain Bonomy of the United Kingdom, who had been the confirming judge.

The indictment, in its final amended form, alleges that Haradinaj had been the KLA's commander in most of western Kosovo, an area designated by the KLA as the "Dukagjin Operational Zone," and that he had command authority over the co-accused, Idriz Balaj and Lahi Brahimaj, as well as other KLA personnel. The indictment alleges that the accused formed a joint criminal enterprise whose purpose was to consolidate the KLA control over the Dukagjin Operational Zone by the unlawful removal and mistreatment of Serbian civilians and by the mistreatment of Albanians, Roma, and other civilians who were perceived as collaborators with the Serbian forces or did not support the KLA. The indictment charges Haradinaj with seventeen counts of crimes against humanity and twenty counts of violations of the laws or customs of war.

When it comes to crimes of war, the devil really is in the details. The indictment alleges that, during March and April 1998, KLA forces resorted to harassment and beatings to drive Serb and Roma civilians out of villages in the Dukagjin Operational Zone and killed Serb and Roma civilians who remained behind in their homes. By mid-April 1998, following acts of violence against Serb civilians by KLA forces, much of the Serb population had fled. In the course of several days after April 19, 1998, KLA attacks allegedly forced out or killed almost every Serb civilian remaining in KLA-controlled parts of this area. Between March and September 1998, in the municipalities of the Dukagjin Operational Zone, the KLA allegedly abducted more than sixty civilians and subsequently killed many of them. KLA soldiers allegedly executed people in the area of Lake Radonjić/Radoniq[7] and a concrete canal leading into a river that drains into the lake. Reportedly, the KLA required a pass to travel in this area, and local residents, fearing KLA reprisals, avoided going into this area. During late August and early September 1998, Serbian forces reportedly mounted a counteroffensive and temporarily retook the area around Lake Radonjić/Radoniq and the drainage canal. A Serbian forensic team reportedly conducted an investigation near the lake and canal and, in mid-September, recovered human remains from thirty-two bodies that were identified; the team also recovered remains from about ten unidentified individuals. All of the remains reportedly showed evidence of a violent death, all were subsequently released to family members and buried in an Orthodox cemetery in Djakovica.

I am providing details in the following summary not only to show the unheroic nature of the allegations that arose out of the KLA's execution ground beside Radonjić Lake, but also to show that the alleged victims, people for whom too few have raised their voices, people who had first names and last names and parents and sons and daughters and hopes and fears, were not just Serbs, they were Albanians, Roma, and Slavic Muslims, they were Roman Catholic, Eastern Orthodox, and followers of Islam:

- Between April 21 and September 12, 1998, the co-accused, Idriz Balaj, and KLA soldiers allegedly abducted two Serb sisters, Vukosava Marković and Darinka Kovač, from their home. Forensic examination reportedly revealed gunshot wounds on both bodies and multiple bone fractures to Vukosava Marković's body.

- On or about April 21, 1998, KLA soldiers allegedly abducted a Serb married couple, Milovan Vlahović and Milka Vlahović. The KLA soldiers allegedly threatened to kill local Albanians who tried to prevent the abduction.

- On or about July 20, 1998, the co-accused Ramush Haradinaj and KLA soldiers allegedly abducted Hajrullah Gashi and Isuf Hoxha, both Kosovo Albanians, from a bus. A forensic examination of the body of Hajrullah Gashi allegedly revealed wounds consistent with blunt trauma. Forensic examination of the body of Isuf Hoxha allegedly revealed multiple bone fractures and several missing skull bones.

- In August 1998, Ilira Frrokaj and her husband, Tush Frrokaj, both Catholic Kosovo Albanians, were allegedly traveling in a car when KLA soldiers abducted them at a checkpoint. The body of Ilira Frrokaj, reportedly recovered adjacent to her bullet-riddled vehicle, revealed the presence of a projectile in one leg, multiple bone fractures, including skull fractures, and evidence that the body had been burned. The body of Tush Frrokaj was reportedly not recovered.

- In August 1998, Idriz Balaj detained Zenun Gashi, a Roma who was a former policeman; Misin Berisha; and his son, Sali Berisha, at a KLA headquarters.

Sali Berisha's nose was allegedly cut off in the presence of Idriz Balaj. Idriz Balaj allegedly wrapped the three men in barbed wire, driving the barbs of the wire into their flesh. Idriz Balaj allegedly stabbed Zenun Gashi in the eye. The three men were allegedly tied behind Idriz Balaj's vehicle and dragged in the direction of Lake Radonjić/Radoniq. Their bodies were subsequently identified by DNA analysis.

• Afrim Sylejmani, a Kosovo Albanian, allegedly disappeared in April 1998. Members of the KLA allegedly abducted Rade Popadić, a Serbian police inspector, while he was traveling with a fellow police officer in a van on or about May 24, 1998. Ilija Antić, a Serb, was allegedly last seen alive on May 27 or 28, 1998, when he visited the home of his brother; Antić's body allegedly revealed multiple bone fractures, including skull injuries. Idriz Hoti, a Kosovo Albanian, allegedly disappeared in June or July 1998. On July 4, 1998, KLA soldiers allegedly abducted Kujtim Imeraj, a Kosovo Roma. On July 12, 1998, KLA soldiers allegedly abducted Nurije Krasniqi and Istref Krasniqi, both Kosovo Albanians, from their family home.

• On July 18, 1998, Zdravko Radunović, a Serb, allegedly disappeared after leaving his home; KLA soldiers allegedly abducted him and handed him over to a local KLA commander; allegedly, while in KLA custody, Radunović was shot in the head and killed. Velizar Stošić, a Serb, allegedly disappeared on July 19, 1998; examination of his remains reportedly revealed gunshot wounds to the head and legs and a rope ligature around his neck.

• On or about July 27, 1998, a Kosovo Albanian named Malush Shefki Meha disappeared. In August 1998, a Roma named Xhevat Berisha disappeared. The son of Kemajl Gashi, a Kosovo Albanian, last saw his father at a KLA barracks, whose commander told the son that his father had been arrested as a Serbian spy; the son allegedly heard KLA soldiers beating his father. On or about July 10, 1998, a Catholic Kosovo Albanian named Pal Krasniqi allegedly went to a KLA headquarters to enlist; Krasniqi allegedly remained at the headquarters for a few days before being arrested as a spy; subsequently, Krasniqi was allegedly beaten severely until he made a false confession; he was allegedly last seen alive on or about July 26, 1998, at the KLA headquarters.

The tribunal had been relying upon KFOR and UNMIK to secure the arrest and transfer of Haradinaj to The Hague. In the course of November 2004, the Office of the Prosecutor had been in touch with KFOR's French commander, Lieutenant General Yves De Kermabon, who asked for only ten days' to two weeks' notice to prepare contingency plans to deal with Haradinaj's arrest and any social unrest that might result in reaction to it. Haradinaj learned of the indictment on March 8, 2005, made a patriotic speech in which he denied all wrongdoing, and, to his credit, resigned immediately from his office and announced that he would surrender the next day. Thanks in large part to United States and European Union pressure, no demonstrations or violence took place. The head of UNMIK, Søren Jessen-Petersen, seemed to be even less welcoming of the indictment than Haradinaj himself. Jessen-Petersen had befriended Haradinaj, and made no secret of this fact in a statement he issued the following day:

> I cannot hide the fact that his departure will leave a big gap. Thanks to Ramush Haradinaj's dynamic leadership, strong commitment and vision, Kosovo is today closer than ever before to achieving its aspirations in settling its future status. Personally, I am saddened to no longer be working with a close partner and friend.
>
> In his decision today, Mr. Haradinaj has once again put the interests of Kosovo above his own personal interests. It is important that the people of Kosovo respond with the same dignity and maturity as shown by Ramush Haradinaj.
>
> I understand the sense of shock and anger over this development. I appeal, however, to the people of Kosovo to express your feelings through peaceful means. A violent response will not help Kosovo. It will only serve the interests of those determined to block Kosovo's way forward. It will be a major setback to everything Kosovo has achieved recently and it will defeat all the recent achievement, notably those reached during Mr. Haradinaj's leadership.
>
> The decision announced by Mr. Haradinaj to co-operate with the Tribunal, despite his firm conviction of innocence, and although painful for him, his family, Kosovo, and for his many friends and partners, including UNMIK, is at the same time an example of Kosovo's growing political maturity as a responsible member of the international community. I trust that Mr. Haradinaj will again be able to serve Kosovo to whose better future he has sacrificed and contributed so much.
>
> It is important that we all remain calm and dignified during these difficult days.[8]

Jessen-Petersen's laudatory words seemed to imply that UNMIK was not only weak and at the mercy of the Albanians who had practically emasculated the United Nations mission during the riots of 2004, but that the head of the United Nations mission in Kosovo, a special representative of the secretary-general, had publicly taken the side of Ramush Haradinaj in a case before the United Nations tribunal. Read the last sentence again: "It is important that *we* all remain calm and dignified during these difficult days." To what *we* was Jessen-Petersen referring? On the day Jessen-Petersen wrote his farewell to Haradinaj, the accused flew to the Netherlands aboard a German private airplane. During a stopover in Germany, an honor guard wearing white helmets and gloves turned out to greet him.

Haradinaj and the other accused pleaded not guilty in mid-March. A month later, Haradinaj's defense counsel filed a motion for his provisional release. Haradinaj submitted a written statement pledging that he would not in any way interfere with any victims or witnesses. The defense argued that Haradinaj enjoyed an "exceptional personal and political reputation," and it submitted statements vouching for Haradinaj's character by a number of high-ranking international politicians, military officials, and diplomats. General Klaus Reinhardt, who had commanded KFOR from October 1999 to the spring of 2000, stated that Haradanaj "is a man in whom I trust wholeheartedly and whose advice I sought actively" and that Haradinaj is a "politician with outstanding features who will be a key factor for the reconciliation of the different ethnic groups in Kosovo." For his part, Jessen-Petersen wrote that Haradinaj is a man of "dynamic leadership, strong commitment and vision" and that Haradinaj had shown "dignity and maturity" in his decision to surrender himself. UNMIK, predictably, agreed to provide the necessary guarantees to ensure Haradinaj's compliance with any conditions the Trial Chamber might impose. It had taken exactly the opposite stance when Fatmir Limaj had requested provisional release in 2003; on that occasion, UNMIK asserted that it had limited resources available and that, given Kosovo's geographical position, it would be relatively easy for an accused to flee into neighboring territories—meaning across the frontier into the lawless mountains of high Albania. For Haradinaj, the same UNMIK that had practically melted down during the riots of 2004 now submitted a confidential written declaration that it had "full authority and control over law enforcement in Kosovo" and was in a position to provide specific guarantees regarding Haradinaj. UNMIK's second-ranking official, Larry Rossin, came to the provisional-release hearing and assured the Trial Chamber that UNMIK was under an obligation to cooperate fully with the tribunal.

The prosecution opposed Haradinaj's request for release. The attorneys argued that Haradinaj was a flight risk because, if he were found guilty of the charges against him, he would likely receive a significant prison sentence. The danger that Haradinaj would flee, however, was not the prosecution's only concern. The prosecution, as its filings make clear, was concerned that Haradinaj would pose a danger to witnesses and victims and that his mere presence in Kosovo would deter prosecution witnesses from testifying. The prosecution had already requested protective measures for a third of the witnesses it proposed to call to testify in the Haradinaj case. The prosecution did not possess information that witnesses had been intimidated, much less intimidated by Haradinaj, something that is extremely difficult to show. But the prosecution did cite numerous incidents illustrating that Kosovo remained an exceptionally dangerous place for witnesses testifying in criminal proceedings. A protected witness in another case had been the target of an assassination attempt even as the Trial Chamber was deciding whether to allow Haradinaj to await trial at home. The prosecution argued that Haradinaj's provisional release would substantially undermine the confidence witnesses had in the tribunal.

In the end, the Trial Chamber ruled that "there is no doubt that UNMIK, being the interim civilian administration in Kosovo and with full authority over law enforcement, will fully cooperate and assist in any matter connected to proceedings before the tribunal." The Trial Chamber decided there was no evidence that, if released, Haradinaj would pose a danger to any victim witness or other person. For a period of ninety days, it barred Haradinaj from any public appearance and any public political acitivity, but it did permit Haradinaj to participate in his political party's administrative or organizational activities. After the ninety-day period had elapsed, the Trial Chamber effectively lifted the ban, citing a report by UNMIK saying that it anticipated positive effects from Haradinaj's involvement in public political activities and the upcoming negotiations for the final status of Kosovo.

In 1996, Radovan Karadžić had been banned from taking part in political activity. What kind of message did UNMIK and the Trial Chamber now send? Imagine a person in Kosovo deciding whether to risk testifying before the tribunal against a KLA defendant. Kosovo was suffering widespread and systematic witness intimidation that was having a significant impact upon court proceedings both locally and before the tribunal. I told the United Nations Security Council that witness tampering may have influenced the judgment in the Limaj case. I knew that Haradinaj's every public appearance was effectively a message to anyone who was considering testifying against him, and we brought this to the Trial Chamber's attention. I wondered why the international administrators in Kosovo, and, it seems, the governments of the United States and the United Kingdom, were investing so much in Haradinaj. At a meeting in Washington in December 2005, I asked how important Haradinaj was to the United States. I explained that UNMIK had managed to convince the judges of the Trial Chamber that he was key to Kosovo's stability. I was told the United States would not work with him.

On December 15, 2005, during an address to the United Nations Security Council, I described the problems we were having with UNMIK. "My office encounters difficulties in accessing documents from UNMIK. They are at times redacted or delivered in such a way that they cannot be used in court. The cooperation provided by UNMIK in the protection of witnesses has also been sometimes less than optimal. Furthermore, my office is not convinced that UNMIK is properly exerting its control over the conditions set . . . for Haradinaj's provisional release."

The next day I met with Secretry-General Kofi Annan to discuss the UNMIK situation. Our witnesses had lost confidence in UNMIK. In that same month, UNMIK had provided a delayed and improper response to an incident involving a threat to a witness. UNMIK was handing over the police effort in Kosovo to locals who were former KLA soldiers and, instead of protecting our witnesses, were threatening them. I informed Annan about a billboard in central Priština with a picture of Haradinaj and a quotation from Jessen-Petersen supporting him.

"I agree," Annan responded.

We complained that during the autumn of 2005, UNMIK's number two had participated in a wedding of a close relative of Haradinaj.

"Bad political judgment," Annan responded.

The secretary-general eventually advised us to engage in dialogue with UNMIK, just as he had to engage in dialogue with member states. Haradinaj, said Annan, is seen as "a reasonable man in this cast of strange characters," but it is not UNMIK's business to decide who should be Kosovo's leader. Annan promised to try to have the poster removed and to look into our other problems. He asked me to stay in touch with Nicolas Michel, the United Nations undersecretary-general for legal affairs.

This I did. On March 15, 2006, I wrote Michel, describing in detail UNMIK's lack of cooperation with the tribunal since my meeting with the secretary-general on December 15, 2005. I informed Michel that I had corresponded on a number of occasions with Jessen-Petersen and that serious matters raised in this correspondence remained unaddressed. I told Michel that UNMIK's handling of witness-protection issues in Kosovo continued to pose serious problems, despite the fact that I had drawn Jessen-Petersen's attention to them at least six times. UNMIK was taking no steps to address these issues. For example, the tribunal and UNMIK had established a system to protect the most sensitive witnesses by rapidly moving them from their homes to places of safety. This system relied upon files containing critical information about protected witnesses and their families. UNMIK held these files until October 2005, when it was agreed that they be transferred to the tribunal. Tribunal staff members met with UNMIK for the agreed transfer, but UNMIK said that all the files had been destroyed. After the tribunal's staff requested that UNMIK provide a written statement that the files had been destroyed, UNMIK's position changed. Now the tribunal staff was told the files did still exist and would be handed over. When the files were actually delivered, however, half of them were missing. The tribunal then had to search out another UNMIK officer who handed over the remainder of the files.

"It is simply incomprehensible to me," I wrote Michel, "how such important and sensitive files could be handled in such a careless and negligent manner. Despite my bringing this matter to the special representative of the secretary-general, our legitimate concerns appear to have been totally disregarded."

I also raised another witness-protection problem: a serious conflict of interest involving a key UNMIK police official whose spouse had been hired as an investigator for the Haradinaj defense team. UNMIK acknowledged that, in the course of his duties, the police official had acquired knowledge of sensitive issues related to the Haradinaj case and had had direct possession of critical files related to witnesses. I wrote:

Jessen-Petersen proposed that [this UNMIK police official] simply recuse himself from any activities related to the *Haradinaj* case and that his immediate subordinate take over his duties. This is clearly unacceptable. [The police official] had access to extremely sensitive information relating to witnesses and continues to supervise the person who is responsible for witness protection matters in the *Haradinaj* case. The conflict of interest is patent and the chilling impact on witnesses is abundantly clear; moreover, such an arrangement clearly undermines the public's confidence in police functions. Nonetheless, UNMIK appears to be oblivious to these real concerns and allows the situation to continue. I dare say that such a situation would not be allowable in any properly functioning national system.

UNMIK was creating obstacles when it came to documentary evidence as well. Despite the fact that UNMIK's second in command, Larry Rossin, had so unequivocably assured the Trial Chamber that it would fully cooperate with the tribunal, UNMIK was persistently providing prosecutors key documents under a rule that barred them from being submitted as evidence in court. The tribunal's rule was intended primarily to protect intelligence information received from sovereign states, and not to allow a United Nations organization to prevent a United Nations tribunal from obtaining evidence that could be used in court proceedings. "We have pointed out this improper use . . . repeatedly," I wrote Michel, "but UNMIK has refused to change its practice."

[W]hen we requested information relating to the investigation of the . . . murder of Tahir Zemaj in 2003, we received a redacted version of the document with the most important information redacted. Put simply, this is not a proper way for a UN body to treat a UN court and undermines both our credibility and the rule of law more generally. You may be interested to know that we have reliable information that Tahir Zemaj was killed because he was collecting material for the [Yugoslavia tribunal], in anticipation of his testimony in the *Haradinaj et al.* case. This makes it all the more unacceptable that this information was withheld from the [tribunal] and sends a terrible message to insiders who desire to cooperate with my office.

I pointed out that Haradinaj was meeting frequently with high-level officials from KFOR, and UNMIK, including Jessen-Petersen. "[This] undermines the [Yugoslavia tribunal's] credibility in Kosovo, sends a chilling message to witnesses, e.g., Haradinaj is supported by the most senior UN officials in Kosovo, and is simply inappropriate. How can the rule of law be upheld when senior UNMIK officials give such open support and succor to someone indicted for the most serious crimes under international law? . . . [I]t sends signals that the ICTY's indictments are meaningless, that an indicted person is welcome and even supported by UNMIK at the highest level. These are very troubling developments and are seriously undermining our efforts in the Haradinaj case."

Nothing significant changed. The poster of Haradinaj remained in place. Jessen-Petersen and Haradinaj appeared together, walking side by side, at the funeral of Kosovo's first president, Ibrahim Rugova. In late March, Jessen-Petersen announced that he and Haradinaj intended to organize a Denmark-Kosovo soccer match. Press reports spoke of how Haradinaj was allowed to take part in a Kosovo Protection Corps ceremony and sit beside the British and American ambassadors.[9] And the prosecution's witnesses continued to complain of threats. Criminal justice in Kosovo was so riddled by fear that, in late August 2006, Kosovo prosecutors and judges were balking at UNMIK's efforts to set up a special unit that would have had to deal with war crimes.[10]

On March 5, 2007, the trial of Ramush Haradinaj and his co-defendants began. I made an opening statement that focused on the victims, on the bodies dumped in the killing field around Radonjić Lake, and on the fears of the prosecution's witnesses:

> The three men come before you accused of crimes—ugly, cruel, and violent crimes; crimes of murder, deportation, torture, rape, abduction, forced imprisonment, and the most brutal assault; crimes that took place out of sight, away from the eyes of international observers or monitors. Be in no doubt, as the Prosecution will prove, that these men—this warlord with his lieutenant and his jailer—have blood on their hands.
>
> And it is the blood of innocent civilians, victims who did not support the accused or the cause of the KLA; victims who were very often alone and vulnerable, and who were systematically targeted, abducted, murdered and made to vanish. If these accused had had their way, their victims would never have been seen again. They would have been simply swallowed up among the other horrors of this conflict and would quite literally have sunk without a trace in the silent waters of Lake Radonjić, in the inner reaches of the Dukagjin Zone.
>
> But the murdered victims in this case did not disappear. Their bodies and their stories have been uncovered, and in the weeks that follow, as the evidence emerges, they will speak to you in their own way from their graves.

The voices of those who were last seen in KLA hands, whose bodies remain undiscovered or unidentified, will be heard through the anguished voices of their grieving loved ones. The voices of some of those who were tortured and brutalised by the KLA will be heard directly in the courtroom. There may not be many such voices, for this is not a case, like others, that deal with mass exterminations and thousands of deaths.

We will not be able to bring before this Court evidence of all the crimes that were committed in this part of Kosovo. That would be impossible. But as each day of this trial passes, as each witness is examined and each document produced, I am sure the Chamber will begin to penetrate the closed world of the Dukagjin Zone, which was the heartland of the Haradinaj clan, in the centre of Ramush Haradinaj's power base. Perhaps also, as in no other case, geography will be the key to understanding the facts. Geography itself is another of the silent witnesses in this case, and I would urge the Trial Chamber to pay particular attention to the locations, the distances, the scale of the activities, and the accessibility of the places that will feature in the events. I would even encourage the Trial Chamber, at a suitable point in the trial, to make a site visit to crime scenes so that you can see these places for yourselves.

I make no apology; this will not be an easy prosecution. It is a prosecution, frankly, that some did not want to see brought, and that few supported by their cooperation at both international and local level. But I insisted on this prosecution, and I bring it with the confidence that the Trial Chamber will find the Prosecution evidence compelling and convincing.

The protection of witnesses who have had the courage to come forward has been, and will continue to be, of critical importance. You know that many witnesses are reluctant to testify. Some are even terrified. The intimidation and threats suffered by witnesses in this case has been a serious ongoing problem for the individuals concerned and for this Prosecution. This problem has not gone away. Witnesses continue to receive threats, both veiled and direct. Just this weekend, our first direct victim witness—

The defense counsel objected, as I expected he would:

MR. GUY-SMITH: Your Honor, if I might.
JUDGE ORIE: Mr. Guy-Smith.

MR. GUY-SMITH: I believe that the statements now are not only highly prejudicial but go well outside the purpose of any opening statement.

JUDGE ORIE: Madam Del Ponte, it is mainly understood that—just to give an example, that where the witnesses are well—are going to tell the truth or not, that's an evaluation already of—what will happen is not appropriate during an opening statement. I wonder whether—of course, this Chamber will have to decide on—it has not decided yet, as I mentioned before, on matters of witness protection, and of course we'll hear, I take it, from the Prosecution the need for such protection. If no further detail would be needed in relation to the reluctance of witnesses to testify, and that's one of the problems you encountered in preparing this—preparing this case, then I would suggest that we proceed with hearing from you what the evidence will bring us, unless you would disagree with me and then I'd like to hear you.

MS. DEL PONTE: Mr. President, I'm just informing the Court that this weekend—that this weekend—I received an information about threats that a witness have received now.

JUDGE ORIE: I do understand that that's—

MS. DEL PONTE: So I wonder why I could not inform the Court about an event, about the facts that occurred during the weekend and it's directly related with this trial. Because, Mr. President, if I have no witnesses appearing in court, I will be obliged to withdraw this indictment.

JUDGE ORIE: Madam Prosecutor, I think there's nothing inappropriate informing the Court about threats. But whether, at the opening statement, where in general terms you have set out that this is of major concern to the Prosecution, whether to go into any further details, where we'll not be able to further inquire into the matter, whether that would be the best course is subject to doubt. One second.

[*Trial Chamber confers*]

JUDGE ORIE: The Chamber invites you to proceed.

MS. DEL PONTE: The Chamber has already granted protective measures to more than a third of our witnesses. I know that you understand and appreciate the difficulties that witnesses face in testifying against these accused. But what I want to say, Mr. President, is that I have full confidence that you will take every possible measure to allow the witnesses to travel to The Hague to testify safely and to allow the truth to be heard. Your Honours, there was nothing noble or heroic about the crimes in this case. There was nothing patriotic or virtuous about them. They were brutal and bloody murders. The three accused were gangsters in uniform and in control, and as the Trial Chamber will see, that proved to be a sinister and deadly combination for the victims in this case.

Thus the trial began. My years at the tribunal would come to an end before the Trial Chamber decided the case.

12

CONFRONTING BELGRADE
2004 TO 2006

The death of Judge Richard May darkened the shadow that the assassination of Zoran Djindjić had cast over the Milošević trial. During the summer days before the opening of Milošević's defense case, the prosecution team prepared to cross-examine the witnesses Milošević had proposed to call. (The initial list numbered about 1,400 and included scholars and politicians, military officers, and diplomats from the major Western countries.) Other investigative teams in the Office of the Prosecutor were working to submit the last of the tribunal's indictments to the Trial Chamber before the end of 2004, as the completion strategy adopted by the Security Council required. It was still too early to gauge the extent of the damage the completion strategy would inflict upon our efforts to see justice done. But from early on, it was clear that the Security Council's deadlines were having detrimental effects. I also took little comfort in the news that the Serbs had formed a new, minority government that was subject to the whims of Milosevic's Socialist Party for survival. Vojislav Koštunica was now back, as Serbia's prime minister; Boris Tadić had escaped the Ministry of Defense and won election as Serbia's president; and the militant ultranationalists, Šešelj's Radicals, controled a third of the parliament and shouted down anything that smacked of a concession to the West. I recall lamenting that Serbia's voting-age population—so diminished by the emigration of the republic's brightest and most motivated young people since the early 1990s, and so browbeaten, as Djindjić had told me, by communists and nationalists—seemed incapable of delivering a fresh face. There was little reason to believe Belgrade's cooperation with the tribunal would improve. How could anyone ever trust Serbia to be a stabilizing force in the Balkans?

On June 29, 2004, I again went before the United Nations Security Council. There was nothing positive to report since my last appearance in December. The authorities of the State Union of Serbia and Montenegro had shown almost no cooperation. The country of two names was a safe haven for at least fifteen fugitives, including General Ratko Mladić. I had by now become so suspicious of the Belgrade authorities that I was hesitant to share information with them. The last time I had provided the whereabouts of a high-level fugitive, a man charged in connection with the Srebrenica massacre, Belgrade deemed the political climate inappropriate for undertaking an arrest; then, as if by mere happenstance, the fugitive vanished. My report concluded: "I trust the Council realizes that, should this pattern of non-cooperation continue, not only will the objectives set in the completion strategy become endangered, but also the whole positive *acquis* of the Tribunal may be put at risk."

It took only a few weeks for the president of the Security Council to issue an official statement that did nothing more than demand, once again, that Serbia and Montenegro cooperate with the tribunal and arrest Mladić and Karadžić. This presidential statement appeared all the more toothless because, a few days after I delivered my report in New York, someone inside the foreign ministry in Belgrade had added insult to our injury. At 9:30 a.m. on Tuesday, July 13, tribunal officials served a warrant upon the competent authorities in Belgrade for the arrest of Goran Hadžić, the one-time president of the self-proclaimed republic Milošević and the Yugoslav National Army had carved out of Croatia in 1991. The tribunal wanted Hadžić on charges of aiding and abetting the persecution of Croat and other non-Serb civilians in the rebel-Serb republic in Croatia; Serb soldiers and members of paramilitary groups had killed hundreds of these civilians, including women and elderly persons, and expelled tens of thousands of people from their homes. A certain friend of the tribunal had Hadžić under surveillance at the time the indictment was issued. He was living in Novi Sad, a city straddling the Danube to the northwest of Belgrade. He was dressed in shorts and working in his garden when his mobile phone rang a few hours after the warrant was served in Belgrade. The conversation, the tip off from an individual in the foreign ministry, lasted only a few seconds. Hadžić scurried into the house and reappeared a few minutes later wearing long pants and carrying a suitcase. Then he got into a car and sped away. The observer snapped photographs of him receiving the call and fleeing. We released these photographs to the public to shame the Belgrade authorities. We also received information that on the same day General Ratko Mladić was residing near the Serbian town of Zaječar, close to the Bulgarian border.

Pressure from the United States and the European Union, my report to the Security Council on Belgrade's flagrant refusal to cooperate, international news coverage of the ninth anniversary of the Srebrenica massacre, and the scandalous images of Hadžić's escape clearly helped goad Prime Minister Koštunica to take a different tack toward the tribunal. Hadžić's trail had not even gone cold before Koštunica appointed a special envoy, Nebojša Vujović, to oversee relations with the tribunal; then Koštunica sent Vujović to inform us that Belgrade was now serious about meeting its obligations. Vujović refused to enter the tribunal's headquarters through the front door. Once we had gotten him, unnoticed, into my office and seated at the conference table, he professed that the tribunal had become Belgrade's most pressing foreign policy issue. Serbia's future, he said, depended upon cooperation with the tribunal. It would determine whether Serbia would join the European Union's accession process. It would determine whether Serbia's military had any chance to associate itself with NATO. For this reason, Vujović said, Serbia wanted to resolve, in a rapid and rational manner, all outstanding issues involving the tribunal. We had heard all of this fourteen months earlier.

Vujović then began a presentation that my aides and I would hereafter refer to as the "bear-in-the-woods" speech, because Vujović used this analogy to describe how Serbia intended to hunt down all of its lesser fugitives, press them to surrender voluntarily, and thereby isolate and capture Mladić, apparently the bear in the woods, and hand him over within two or three months. Belgrade's civilian and military security services, Vujović assured us, were now cooperating with foreign intelligence agencies to locate Mladić. But, he cautioned, other accused, including Goran Hadžić and four of the police and military generals the tribunal had indicted in connection with the ethnic cleansing of Kosovo—Sreten Lukić, Vladimir Lazarević, Vlastimir Djordjević, and Nebojša Pavković—would have to go on trial in Serbia as a preliminary step before their transfer to The Hague. Vujović said that influential figures in Serbian society, including His Holiness Patriarch Pavle, the head of the Serbian Orthodox Church, would send Mladić "a clear message." Vujović announced that a publicity campaign, including television broadcasts, had begun a week earlier to make it plain to the Serbian people that their country needed a new approach to the tribunal. Then he added: "We are aware of what happened in Srebrenica, and we need to put an end to the embarrassment. . . . We see converging interests between the Office of the Prosecutor and our state. We want to integrate into the European Union, and you want to finish the Tribunal's work. . . . We will do our best to help you, if you help us." A representative of the United States was present and taking note of everything Vujović was promising.

So, I thought, either the message the Serbs had been hearing for almost ten years was finally beginning to resonate with Koštunica, or Koštunica had somehow brought in the Americans to help him construct a grand *muro di gomma.* I raised the embarrassing fact of Goran Hadžić's escape. "We knew where he was," I said. "The indictment was sealed. But it was leaked to the media anyway." Vujović said Koštunica had nothing to do with Hadžić's flight from justice or the leak, and he asserted that the indictment had arrived at the worst possible time, the exact moment Belgrade was starting to implement its new strategy.

I was skeptical, to say the least, of Belgrade's capacity for conducting legitimate war crimes trials. Serbia's justice system existed at that time in a kind of virtual reality where Milošević appointees and loyalists were still holding key positions. But I knew the United States was providing the Serbian government significant technical assistance to establish a local war crimes chamber, and it would soon offer Belgrade financial help to protect sensitive witnesses. So I offered to begin testing the integrity of this nascent judicial system by filing a motion requesting the Trial Chamber to transfer to Belgrade's jurisdiction one relatively straightforward case. This, however, would certainly not be the Hadžić case or any of the cases against the four generals indicted in connection with the ethnic cleansing of Kosovo. "You must give me Hadžić and Mladić," I said. "The generals we can talk about later. . . . You must arrest Hadžić this week, and Mladić next week."

Mladić, I cautioned, "has protective networks connected to the military, and they may prefer to kill him." Then I took a swipe at General Krga, the chief of staff of the Yugoslav Army, apparently renamed the Army of Serbia and Montenegro, who, together with Koštunica's confidant and Mladić's guardian angel, General Aco Tomić, had lied to my face months earlier about how the army was not protecting Mladić. "Krga can help you," I told Vujović with as much sarcasm as I could muster. "In May 2003, I passed information on Mladić's location . . . and I know that Mladić received this information soon afterward." After our discussions,

Vujović and the American stole away through the Tribunal's back door, apparently unrecognized.

We waited. The telephones rang, but the calls brought us no news of any arrest of Mladić, Hadžić, or any other Serbian fugitive. Then, nine days into our vigil, the Trial Chamber announced its decision on a motion to release from pretrial detention two of the accused who had, according to the indictments against them, operated at the epicenter of Milošević's violent campaign to seize territory in Croatia and in Bosnia and Herzegovina. These two accused were Jovica Stanišić and Frenki Simatović, the overseers of the Red Berets, the paramilitary unit of Serbia's security services whose members were implicated in war crimes as well as the assassination of Zoran Djindjić in 2003. Within days of the Djindjić murder, Stanišić and Simatović had found themselves in local police custody, but the Belgrade authorities had been so afraid of these two police operatives that Minister of Interior Dušan Mihajlović and Foreign Minister Goran Svilanović had practically begged me to finish the indictments against the two men so Belgrade could transfer them to The Hague. Now, as the Office of the Prosecutor did what it could to fight to keep Stanišić and Simatović behind bars, the new Belgrade government, the same government that had just wooed us with words of love, told us stories about bears in woods, and failed to undertake any arrests, stepped forward and offered a written guarantee that it would, if called upon, rearrest Stanišić and Simatović and send them back.

The Office of the Prosecutor's policy is to support provisional release only for those accused who have surrendered voluntarily and have agreed to be interviewed by our investigators and attorneys and cooperate with the prosecution. Stanišić and Simatović, in our estimation, had not surrendered voluntarily; they had agreed to come to The Hague, but only to extract themselves from some miserable Serbian jail so they could check into the facility in Scheveningen, which is Club Med–North Sea by comparison. They could have contributed useful testimony for almost every case brought before the Yugoslavia tribunal, but they chose instead to give our investigators nothing. The prosecution argued that, since Stanišić and Simatović were facing the possibility of life imprisonment, they were likely to flee, as Hadžić had, rather than surrender to the tribunal's custody at the end of their provisional release. The prosecution argued that, once free, there was a significant risk that Stanišić and Simatović would ply their influence with the police and underworld in order to intimidate witnesses and their families. In a statement submitted for the Trial Chamber's consideration, one prosecution investigator said that a significant number of potential witnesses, for the cases against Stanišić and Simatović and the case against Milošević, had already refused to be interviewed for fear of their safety. According to the investigator, "They made it clear that as long as these men were at liberty they would not feel safe speaking to me." One of the prosecution's potential witnesses informed the investigator that he had been a member of the Red Berets and that he considered Stanišić and Simatović to be "the most powerful persons in the country and . . . did not want to annoy them as that could have dangerous consequences for him."

Confidentiality requirements preclude me from revealing anything I know of recommendations the Trial Chamber received in support of the request by Stanišić and Simatović for provisional release; confidentiality requirements also preclude me from revealing anything about those organizations that may or may not have provided such recommendations, which, of course, may or may not have existed. In the end, the Trial Chamber said it was satisfied that, if released from custody, these two accused would not pose a danger to any victims or witnesses. In their decision, the judges based their reasoning upon, among other things, "personal guarantees" by Stanišić and Simatović and the fact the judges had instructed both of them not to interfere with any victims or witnesses.

Stanišić and Simatović immediately made their way to Belgrade. Suffice it to say that our office had no police powers, and proving witness intimidation is a challenge even if a prosecutor has an entire police force to investigate allegations. Unfortunately, I am also not at liberty to discuss direct complaints we may or may not have received from prospective witnesses who may or may not have felt the presence of two more bears in the Serbian woods. But I can say that, months after the Trial Chamber's decision granting provisional release, a Western diplomat who closely followed political developments in Serbia and its relations with the tribunal told me he was concerned that Stanišić had become involved in Mladić's efforts to remain at large and that even Koštunica's government had come to regret the decision to free them.

On August 31, 2004, Courtroom 1 sprang to life once again as Milošević began presenting his defense case. True to form, he mounted no legal defense in the conventional sense. Rather, he chose to dabble in politics and to make speeches to his true believers in Serbia and elsewhere about his interpretation of Yugoslavia's break demise:

> There is a fundamental historical fact that one should proceed from when seeking to understand what happened and which led to everything that happened in the territory of Yugoslavia from 1991 until the present day, and that is: the violent destruction of a European state, Yugoslavia, which was derived from the statehood of Serbia, the only ally of the democratic world in that part of the world over the past two centuries.

Milošević then characterized Serbia as a victim and nothing else. He contended that the Vatican, the United States, and European Union nations, especially Germany, had conspired to destroy Yugoslavia. He maintained that the Serbs in Croatia were facing the imminent threat of genocide in 1991. Milošević described a military parade in Zagreb on May 28, 1991, during which Franjo Tudjman appeared in a military dress uniform worthy of Tito and showed off ranks of soldiers toting automatic rifles, allegedly supplied by Germany. Milošević, needless to say, did not mention that he had met twice with Tudjman during the preceding weeks to negotiate the partition of Bosnia and Herzegovina.

Next, Milošević characterized the war in Bosnia and Herzegovina as a religious struggle pitting Christianity against militant Islam. He once again proclaimed the Yugoslavia tribunal to be an illegal entity. This kind of defense would continue for most of the next two years. And for much of this period, Milošević concentrated his rhetoric upon historical topics linked with Kosovo and not with Bosnia and Herzegovina or Croatia. To its credit, just two days after Milošević had begun his opening statement, the Trial Chamber tried to impose a kind of defense counsel. But this attempt sputtered after Milošević and many of his witnesses refused to cooperate with the attorneys the trial chamber had named, Steven Kay and Gillian Higgins, the British *amici curiae* who had followed the trial from its earliest days. The attempt collapsed when Milošević won an appeal challenging the Trial Chamber's action. Now, as the months wore on, the judges found themselves facing a terrible quandary: the time allotted for the defense case was running out, and Milošević was neglecting to present any discernible defense for the two components of the prosecution's case that were arguably its strongest: the indictments derived from crimes committed in Bosnia and Herzegovina and in Croatia. This incredible situation, I thought, would never have arisen if the Trial Chamber had forced Milošević to accept appointed defense counsel from the beginning.

By early October, it was time for me to return to Belgrade in preparation for another report to the United Nations Security Council on Serbia and Montenegro's cooperation with the tribunal's efforts. We had ended our Mladić vigil without fanfare, even though, a few weeks earlier, Belgrade had informed us that its civilian and military intelligence agencies, together with representatives of friendly governments, had established a special investigatory cell whose sole purpose was to arrest Mladić. We heard that Mladić's wife and his son, Darko, were under surveillance. We heard that searches conducted on Mladić's home in Belgrade and on a house in a village on Mount Zlatibor, a rural area adjacent to Serbia's border with Bosnia, had yielded nothing. (As I recall, this was about the time we heard tales that Mladić was tending bees and living near Valjevo in a vacation cottage belonging to the army. So it appeared that the bear really was in the woods.)

At the beginning of my conversation with Koštunica on October 1, he admitted the obvious: that even if Serbia somehow managed to apprehend the twenty or so accused still at large in Serbia and the Serb entity in Bosnia and Herzegovina, the Belgrade government's cooperation would be judged only by whether it managed to apprehend Ratko Mladić. (Karadžić, the other high-profile fugitive, was considered the Republika Srpska's and NATO's problem.) Koštunica assured me, just as Vujović had done five months earlier, that Serbia and friendly countries were doing their utmost to find Mladić and locate all other fugitives, except for the four generals indicted in connection with Kosovo. Arresting the generals would be very difficult politically, due to the question of Kosovo's future status, he explained. "There is a court in Serbia capable of doing the job," he insisted. "The government is fully aware of the necessity to cooperate, but it has also a responsibility for the political situation in the country."

I thanked Koštunica. He had finally, after all, acknowledged to me that Serbia had to cooperate. I reminded him, however, that months had passed with no arrests, even after the tribunal and other parties had provided Belgrade with timely information disclosing the whereabouts of accused fugitives. "I understand the country's difficulties," I said. "But I need to see results in order to go before the United Nations Security Council and say that Serbia is providing full cooperation." I informed Koštunica that we had just received information from intelligence sources that Mladić had decamped from Oplenac, a town south of Belgrade, and was now under surveillance in a military complex in the capital city itself. I also said our information included a disturbing detail: the Serbian authorities were refraining from placing Mladić under arrest because Belgrade was going to demand, in exchange for his handover, guarantees from the international community that Kosovo would remain a part of Serbia.

Koštunica chuckled.

Then I asked him to freeze Mladić's military pension. Koštunica conferred with his advisors, who immediately answered that local laws made it impossible to suspend Mladić's pension benefits. This I found utterly preposterous. (Imagine an indicted mass murderer roaming free in a country and able to draw on his pension to support himself. Now imagine a government that says it cannot freeze the fugitive's bank account or even divert his pension benefits into an escrow account until his surrender. And now imagine a government that will not place the fugitive mass murderer under arrest, but will only politely request that he surrender voluntarily. This warped world is what Koštunica was asking us to accept.) I then asked Koštunica what would happen once the government's policy to convince the accused fugitives to surrender voluntarily had run its course. When this produced no satisfactory answer, I told him I wanted the accused arrested and transferred. I said I could not wait forever for the Serbian authorities to convince him to surrender voluntarily.

I flicked Koštunica a crumb when I said the Office of the Prosecutor was prepared to cooperate with local prosecutors in Serbia and transfer some cases back to Belgrade. Koštunica then commented that, despite rumors and promises, the tribunal had indicted no leaders of the Albanian militia that had caused Serbs such grief in Kosovo. I responded that the Office of the Prosecutor would present one indictment by the end of the year against a high-level commander of the Kosovo Albanians' militia, the Kosovo Liberation Army, despite the fact that neither Serbia nor the international organizations on the ground in Kosovo had given us meaningful cooperation. I informed Koštunica that his justice minister, Vladan Batić, had also been crowing about providing the Office of the Prosecutor with piles of documents for its investigation of the Kosovo Liberation Army but that these documents turned out to be unhelpful.

On October 10, the tribunal got lucky. The Office of the Prosecutor's tracking team received a tip on the whereabouts of Ljubiša Beara, a former subordinate to Ratko Mladić in the Bosnian Serb Army who had been indicted on charges of genocide, murder, and other crimes in connection with the takeover and ethnic cleansing of the Srebrenica safe area and the subsequent massacre of the eight thousand or so Muslim boys and men. Beara had been living within shouting distance of Belgrade. We immediately informed the Serbian authorities that, if, after the embarrassment of the Hadžić escape, they really wanted to demonstrate their willingness to cooperate with the tribunal, they should surround Beara's house, take him into custody, and transfer him immediately to The Hague. We also passed along this information to the United States. Beara had no choice but to surrender, but the Belgrade government maintained the fiction that he gave himself up voluntarily. He was airlifted from Belgrade to Rotterdam in a private plane, accompanied by the justice minister who called me to meet him at the airport. I was waiting there at about eleven o'clock at night, when the plane pulled to the terminal. I was expecting to hear something significant, some confidential message, some news of pending arrests. It seems, however, that the only reason the minister had summoned me was to witness how he and Beara, the alleged middle manager of the Srebrenica massacre, embraced and did their *bacini bacetti*, their ritual Balkan cheek-kissy-kissy, a moment before the security people slapped handcuffs on Beara and packed him off to Scheveningen Prison. It was clear that Beara had received some kind of tangible reward for surrendering himself. I never learned what incentives package the Serbian authorities gave him. We caught rumors that Belgrade was dangling cash payments and even new automobiles before the eyes of the tribunal's other accused. Now more than ever, the tribunal needed this strategy to work. The trials were dragging on for years, and the end of 2008 was rapidly approaching.

A month after Beara's arrest, I thought the "voluntary surrender" strategy might have bagged us the bear himself. Dušan Mihajlović and Nataša Kandić met me in the VIP lounge at the airport terminal in Zurich. Mihajlović said he had received a message from members of Mladić's security entourage, whose identities Mihajlović refused to reveal. The message said Mladić was willing to surrender to the authorities in Bosnia, Serbia, or Greece, but only if his family received financial support and only if he could serve his sentence in Russia. I could not take this offer at face value. "I want proof that this is really from Mladić," I insisted. "I need a recent photo and a sample of his handwriting." The funds, I continued, would be no problem. The United States or another country might help us come up with the money. As for serving the sentence in Russia, I would speak with the tribunal's president and see whether Moscow, which had no bilateral agreement with the tribunal, and, together with the Vatican, only grudgingly answered our mail or acknowledged receiving our requests for assistance, would give the necessary provisos. The Zurich meeting, however, came to naught. More weeks passed. I assumed that the new attitude Koštunica had displayed, both through his special envoy, Vujović, in July, and in person during our meeting in October, was actually just another *muro di gomma.*

I flew from Zurich to the United States after the meeting with Mihajlović and once again addressed the United Nations Security Council on Serbia's lack of cooperation. Twenty or so fugitives were at large in Serb-controlled areas, including Karadžić, Mladić, the four generals wanted in connection with the events in Kosovo in 1999, and a number of accused indicted for crimes stemming from the Srebrenica massacre. I stressed that the tribunal would not meet the objectives the Security Council had established unless these accused were tried in The Hague. It was of critical importance that arrests be effected as soon as possible in order to hold joint trials of all of the accused indicted in connection with the same criminal acts—for example, all of the accused indicted in connection with the Srebrenica massacre—in order to avoid duplicating trials and wasting precious time and resources. "Prime Minister Koštunica has made it clear that he is not willing to arrest fugitives, but only to try to convince them to surrender voluntarily," I said. "The Serbian government has deliberately chosen to ignore its legal obligations. . . . All in all, the lack of cooperation of Belgrade remains the single most important obstacle faced by the tribunal in the implementation of the completion strategy."

A few weeks later, we received information that Ratko Mladić was in Bosnia and Herzegovina, which put him within range of NATO's peacekeepers. Our source said that Mladić was near his home village in Kalinovik, a municipality enclosed by mountains, and that he would be attending services in a local church. We notified NATO immediately and waited to see what would happen next. NATO responded that it could take no action. The notice received was too short. The location was too difficult to approach by road. Helicopters would be ineffective.

I do not know what it was, exactly, that produced Belgrade's efforts during late 2004 and early 2005 to pressure the tribunal's accused to surrender voluntarily. Perhaps the rush to cooperate began because prominent Serbian Orthodox Church clerics had started complaining that their countrymen were sliding into penury because a few obdurate individuals were refusing to surrender themselves. Perhaps word had spread through the halls of government that the United States really was prepared to pay cash rewards for information leading to the arrest of the tribunal's fugitives just as that medical lab in Locarno was willing to pay my brothers and me a bounty for venomous snakes. Perhaps a significant number of wealthy Serb expatriates were moving home from abroad, repatriating their assets, and demanding, behind closed doors, that Serbia's government normalize the country's relations with Europe and the United States. Perhaps some foreign donor stepped up and enabled the government to sweeten the incentives package the government could offer the fugitives to surrender. (A minister in Belgrade subsequently told us that the government drew no money from the state budget for this purpose, even though a law already on the books provided for such expenditures and a budget line did exist. This made me wonder: Where did the payoff money come from?) Perhaps Koštunica admitted to himself that his policies were leading Serbia into diplomatic isolation. He had been hearing harsh words from the United States and the European Union from at least the latter part of 2004. This was evident to the entire world on January 13, 2005, the day Serbs were celebrating their New Year's Eve, when the State Department announced, almost two months before its deadline, that it would be unable to certify Serbia's compliance with the conditions the Congress had established for foreign assistance. On January 14, the American ambassador to Serbia and Montenegro, Michael Polt, announced that Washington had cut substantial portions of aid and would withdraw technical advisers. On January 25, the European Commissioner for Enlargement, Olli Rehn, said Belgrade's failure to cooperate with the tribunal was stalling progress on Serbia's integration into the European Union.

Whatever the reason, from early December 2004 to the late spring of 2005, the tribunal witnessed a rapid, almost phantasmagoric, series of voluntary surrenders. All at once, fugitives poured forth from Serbia and the Republika Srpska:

- A former commander of the Bosnian Serb Army's forces besieging Sarajevo who had been indicted for using artillery and snipers to terrorize Sarajevo's populace from 1994 to the end of the siege in 1995: Dragomir Milošević, surrendered December 3, 2004.

- A commander of a prison near the Bosnian town of Foča, indicted for persecuting, enslaving, torturing, beating, and killing Muslim and other non-Serb prisoners: Savo Todović, surrendered January 15, 2005. (The Republika Srpska ministry of interior sent a representative to ask Todović's mother to convince her son to surrender. A pathetic scene unfolded. Todović entered the room and announced that he could no longer stand living in a garage. We heard that he had been reduced to such penury that the police had to contribute money to buy him a decent pair of trousers.)

- The first of the four generals indicted for complicity in the massive Kosovo ethnic-cleansing operation of 1999: Vladimir Lazarević, surrendered February 3. (His hero's send-off from Belgrade included an audience with Prime Minister Koštunica and His Holiness Patriarch Pavle, who praised Lazarević for his sacrifices on behalf of the homeland. A government jet whisked Lazarević to The Netherlands. The Belgrade press later reported that Lazarević's son had received a new car from a governmnent minister.)

- General Ratko Mladić's assistant commander for "morale, legal, and religious affairs," who allegedly passed down the order to attack the Srebrenica safe area, including observation posts manned by Dutch peacekeepers: General Milan Gvero, surrendered February 24.

- The chief of operations of the Bosnian Serb Army, indicted in connection with the forcible transfer and deportation of the Muslim populations of the Srebrenica and Žepa safe areas and allegedly the author of a document known as "Directive 7," which was signed by Radovan Karadžić on March 21, 1995, and called for the Bosnian Serb Army to "create an unbearable situation of total insecurity with no hope of further survival or life for the inhabitants of Srebrenica and Žepa": Radivoje Miletić, surrendered February 28.

- General Momčilo Perišić, chief of the Yugoslav Army's general staff from August 1993 until November 1998, indicted for using his authority to provide to the Bosnian Serb Army substantial military assistance, which he allegedly knew would be used, in significant part, in the commission of the crimes, including the siege and shelling of Sarajevo and the massacre at Srebrenica. Despite being aware of allegations of serious crimes being committed by members of the Bosnian Serb Army and the Serb army in Croatia, Perišić allegedly failed in his duty to apply any disciplinary or preventative mechanisms: surrendered, March 7.

- The minister responsible for police and state security in the Republika Srpska, indicted, among other things, for torture, cruel treatment, and deportation of Bosnian Muslims and Bosnian Croats: Mičo Stanišić, surrendered March 11.

• A paramilitary leader in Foča, indicted for involvement in the sexual abuse and rape, including gang rape, of women detainees at the Foča High School: Gojko Janković, surrendered, March 14. (Janković was hiding in Russia, and his wife convinced him to surrender for his family's well-being.)

Despite these surprising surrenders, on March 16, the European Union sent Belgrade an unambiguous signal that it would continue to make cooperation with the tribunal a condition for closer relations: Brussels announced that it would delay membership talks with Croatia because Ante Gotovina was still at large and Croatia's efforts to arrest him had been inadequate. According to the International Crisis Group's political analysis of the situation in Serbia at the time, it was at this point that the Serbian government began to threaten the accused that they would stop receiving their pensions, that their bank accounts would be frozen, and that local arrest warrants would be issued against them. Now the phantasmagoria intensified with the arrival of new fugitives:

• The commander of security for a brigade of the Bosnian Serb Army, indicted in connection with the forcible transfer and deportation of the populations of Srebrenica and Žepa and allegedly assisted in planning, organizing, and supervising the transportation of Muslim prisoners to execution grounds: Drago Nikolić, surrendered March 17.

• A brigade commander in the Bosnian Serb Army, indicted in connection with the forcible transfer and deportation of the populations of Srebrenica and Žepa, allegedly commanded units involved in the attacks on the Srebrenica and Žepa enclaves and the movement of people out of the enclaves, including Muslim men transported to the killing fields: Vinko Pandurević, surrendered March 23.

• A deputy commander of a military brigade within the Republika Srpska police ministry, indicted in connection with the forcible transfer and deportation of the populations of Srebrenica and Žepa, allegedly helped disable the United Nations forces around Srebrenica and had responsibility for the handling of all Bosnian Muslim prisoners and commanded troops who assisted in detaining and transporting Muslim men from the Srebrenica enclave to the detention centers from which they were taken to the execution grounds: Ljubomir Borovčanin, surrendered April 1.

- General Sreten Lukić, the second of Koštunica's four generals, indicted in connection with the ethnic cleansing of Kosovo: surrendered April 4. (Lukić voluntarily surrendered clad in bathrobe and slippers at a hospital where he was receiving medical treatment. We heard that, at the last minute, Lukić tried to arrange for himself to be tried in Serbia by offering to capture Karadžić.)

- The assistant commander for security of the Bosnian Serb Army's Drina Corps, indicted in connection with the forcible transfer and deportation of the populations of Srebrenica and Žepa, allegedly helped control the movement of Muslims from the enclaves, supervising and overseeing the transportation of Muslims from Potočari to areas outside the Republika Srpska and allegedly assisted in the transportation and organization of Muslim men from Bratunac to detention centers from which they were taken to execution grounds: Vujadin Popović, surrendered April 14. (Popović had been hiding in Russia.)

- The commander of the Yugoslav Army, Nebojša Pavković, the third of Koštunica's generals, indicted in connection with the massive ethnic cleansing of Kosovo in 1999: surrendered April 25.

Serbia did not have to wait long to reap benefits for this concrete proof of its government's new attitude toward the tribunal. On April 12, a European Union feasibility study gave Serbia and Montenegro a positive assessment, and on April 25, it won approval to negotiate a stabilization and association agreement. Against the backdrop of the Serb surrenders came the arrival in The Hague of the highest-ranking Albanian indicted by the tribunal, the commander of the Kosovo Liberation Army, Ramush Haradinaj, along with two other accused Kosovo Liberation Army commanders. The Trial Chamber also agreed to the provisional release of former Milošević associates: Milan Milutinović, a former president of Serbia; General Dragoljub Ojdanić, a former Yugoslav Army chief of staff; Nikola Šainović, Yugoslavia's former deputy prime minister; and General Vladimir Lazarević, who might have been able to enjoy the automobile his son had reportedly received in exchange for his surrender only three months earlier. In sum, the spate of surrenders proved that Serbia would cooperate with the tribunal, but only if the European Union and United States insisted strongly enough that cooperation with the tribunal remained a precondition for Serbia to enjoy a closer relationship with them. Conversely, the surrenders demonstrated that, when the United States and the

European Union were not firm in demanding conditionality, Serbia would do nothing. I recalled Kofi Annan's letter of 2001, taking exception to our efforts to convince the United States and the European Union to maintain their conditionality policy. Where would we be now, I thought, if we had not insisted on this link being maintained? The answer was obvious. Our investigators would have been piling up stacks of meaningless documents. Our attorneys would have been cobbling together fact-starved indictments and writing scholarly articles for law journals. And the tribunal's judges would have been trying no one except low-ranking Serbs captured abroad, a few Croats handed over after Tudjman's death, and Muslims from Bosnia and Herzegovina who had surrendered without complaint.

Following this flourish of Serb surrenders, however, Koštunica's voluntary-surrender model failed. His willingness to use police powers to arrest our remaining fugitive accused proved to be inadequate. On May 8, 2005, I reached out to President George W. Bush for assistance, and for about ten seconds I had him. It was the sixtieth anniversary of the end of World War II in Europe. Bush came to the Netherlands to pay homage to the Americans, Canadians, and Europeans whose mortal remains lie at rest in the Margraten Cemetery near Maastricht, men and women who had given their lives to help deliver millions of Europeans from Nazi tyranny.

The United States Ambassador to the Netherlands, Clifford M. Sobel, invited me to attend the commemoration and agreed to help me meet President Bush. Ambassador Sobel positioned me in the front row of VIPs chosen to shake hands with President Bush. Her Royal Highness Queen Beatrix was there. The prime minister of the Netherlands, Jan Pieter Balkenende, was there. And even I failed to understand how I, a prosecutor of a United Nations tribunal for a defunct Balkan state, had found my way into such company. Bush eventually made his way down the line and spoke with each person one at a time. Like a true Texan, he shook my hand and looked me straight in the eye, as if he had been my friend for years. I delivered the one sentence I had rehearsed.

"Karadžić," he responded, pronouncing the name no better than I do. "We'll get him." Then he moved on.

It was Holland in May, so the day was gray and cold. And as the commemoration was ending, I spotted Condoleezza Rice, by now the secretary of state, scurrying toward the parked motorcade ahead of the crowd in order to warm up inside her limousine. I set off in pursuit, my heels sinking into the moist earth. Just beyond the cemetery's entrance, I asked Ambassador Sobel where Secretary Rice had gone.

"Third car," he answered.

I approached. Her security detail had the vehicle surrounded. But at the critical moment, my blonde hair paid off.

"Madame Prosecutor," one of the bodyguards spoke up, smiling, "I remember you! I guarded you in San Diego!" I smiled as if he were a long-lost brother and told him I urgently needed to speak with the secretary of state.

"Why sure!"

He opened the door to her limousine, said a few words, and signaled for me to climb in. In an instant, I found myself sitting face to face with Secretary of State Rice. She was surprised, I'm sure, but probably not pleasantly. I told her I had just spoken with President Bush about Karadžić. "I must have Karadžić," I insisted. Then I said something like: "Look, working with your CIA is impossible. You're not doing it, not making the arrest. It is impossible that the most powerful nation in the world can't get him."

"We're looking for bin Laden," she answered.

I replied with a smile: "Bin Laden is your problem, Karadžić is mine."

She chuckled, or maybe she shivered. The guard opened the door. I hopped out as the motorcade began to move, got into my car, and had the driver tag along behind President Bush and the others. Sirens wailed. Blue lights flashed. Motorcycle police stopped the cross-traffic. We raced through Dutch towns and villages like the old days at Hockenheim. And all along the road, people applauded and waved.

In the late morning of June 1, 2005, Geoffrey Nice was conducting a cross-examination of one of Milošević's defense witnesses, General Obrad Stevanović, a former assistant minister of the interior of Serbia. Stevanović had just finished explaining that he did not know whether any paramilitary units had ever crossed the border between Serbia and Republika Srpska and perpetrated crimes during the Bosnian war. "I would not have tolerated any such thing," Stevanović crowed. "I would not have turned a blind eye to it."

"No," I thought, "never." I knew what was coming next.

Nice announced that he would now present a video. The lights in the courtroom dimmed. Someone pushed the "play" button. The monitors flashed to life. On the screens appeared a Serbian Orthodox priest blessing members of a paramilitary unit known as the Scorpions, which was affiliated with the Serbian Ministry of the Interior and wore its requisite red berets and blue police uniforms. Stevanović commented that the image was just too fuzzy to recognize the faces of the unit's members, but that the sound was sufficiently clear to make out a name or two. Nice proceeded to play more segments of the videotape, pausing the action from time to time. "This video," Nice said, "reveals that men were brought from Srebrenica in batches to this group of Scorpions to be executed and they were executed, and what you see here is a lorry load of six young men. . . . And you can see the red berets." The monitors showed the six young prisoners led up a hill and into a clearing with tall grass. Two by two, they were shot from behind. Crumpled bodies appeared lying among grass and weeds. The living prisoners moved the dead until the Scorpions, these Serbian heroes, shot the last two.

Stevanović was asked to comment:

> As I am upset, I have to say that this is one of the most monstrous images I have ever seen on a screen. Of course I have never seen anything like this in—live. I am astonished that you have played this video in connection with my testimony because you know full well that this has nothing to do with me or the units I commanded. I attempted to explain this yesterday, and I have also attempted to explain it today. I'm not saying that you do not have the right to do this, but I have to say that I am really upset.

And this was the point. Satellites beamed the images of these "Scorpions" killing Muslim young men in cold blood all over the world. The victims were just six of the eight thousand or so Muslim men and boys executed after the fall of the United Nations safe area at Srebrenica. Slobodan Milošević sat stone faced in the dock. I have no idea whether he heard the voice of the cameraman telling the killers to finish the job in a hurry because his battery was dying. If I had been Milošević at that moment, however, despair would have paralyzed my soul. During the first half of 2005, Milošević had seen his cellblock filling up with familiar faces from Belgrade, Bosnia and Herzegovina, and Croatia; in fact, almost the entire Serb leadership was now behind bars or free only on provisional release, so it must have seemed his declarations that the tribunal was illegal had resonated with no one of any circumstance. The motion by the *amici curiae* to dismiss the prosecution's case had failed a year earlier. Milošević's political defense was failing to chip away at mountain of fact looming before him, and more facts were going to come to light during the upcoming trials of his accomplices. Everyone except a few diehards was ignoring his political diatribes. Only a handful of apologists in Serbia and abroad could any longer deny that the Srebrenica massacre had happened and that Serbs from Serbia had participated as killers. The Internet would make the Scorpion video available to anyone at any time with a left-click on a computer mouse, and this would grind Milošević's legacy into the dust of the Bosnian roadside where these Scorpions had killed their victims, so sure of their own impunity that they had taken pains to videotape the act and show their faces and their victims' to the camera, as if they were dancing at some wedding reception. Consciously and, perhaps more significantly, subconsciously, Milošević had to know that he would never be a free man again.

Serbian television broadcasted the Scorpion video in its entirety that evening. And the next day, I was in Koštunica's office as part of a previously scheduled trip to the former Yugoslavia to prepare a progress report for the United Nations Security Council. He looked as he always did, weary and bedraggled, as if he wanted it to seem that the weight of his entire country was resting upon only his shoulders. Koštunica started the meeting by stressing, naturally enough, the progress Serbia had made since my last visit. He mentioned that the strategy of voluntary surrenders had worked well and said he appreciated the understanding I had shown. He said the Trial Chamber's decisions to grant provisional release had been an important contribution, as were the tribunal's indictments against high-ranking members of "other" nationalities, and by this he meant the Albanians. He said he was "working" on the Mladić case with a complete understanding of its importance, and he commented that, when it came, Mladić's arrest would be a huge relief for all. Only then did Koštunica mention the Scorpion video: "I want to tell you that we were shocked by what we saw yesterday on television, and we immediately conducted an operation and arrested six of the Scorpion members." He called the execution of civilians brutal and shameful. He said the government was determined to find all the perpetrators and punish them. And that was that. Objective. Bereft of emotion. No mention of anyone further up the chain of command. As if the arrests of these grunt executioners would be enough to satisfy the world.

Sometime during Koštunica's monologue, Rade Bulatović, the head of Belgrade's government intelligence agency, walked into the meeting in blue jeans and a T-shirt, apologized for his appearance, and said he had worked through the night to identify and apprehend members of the Scorpions who were living in Belgrade and other parts of Serbia. After the video had aired on television, one of the gunmen was so cocksure he would never be arrested for killing Muslims that he had even approached the Serbian police seeking protection, presumably against Muslims or human-rights activists. My sense was that Koštunica had felt obliged to take action before my arrival and was resentful that the international furor over the Scorpion video had forced him to carry out arrests instead of waiting for the gunmen to surrender voluntarily. The arrests of the Scorpions had demonstrated what the Serbian police could do when they received orders from on high.

I mentioned that the tribunal still had seven fugitive Serbs at large, including two reportedly in Russia, and that we needed the Serbian government to take them into custody within two months. I demanded Mladić's arrest before the tenth anniversary of the Srebrenica massacre on July 11. Koštunica, for all his talk about the purgative benefits Mladić's arrest would have on the Serbian body politic, avoided making any promises about arresting him before the anniversary; Koštunica did say, however, that Mladić would be arrested before a European Union deadline set for October 5.

A day later, I was in Sarajevo, meeting with representatives of the widows and mothers of the men and boys killed at Srebrenica. I told them the Office of the Prosecutor was doing all it could to apprehend Karadžić and Mladić before July 11. I told them that Mladić was in Serbia and that we had received credible reports that Serbian Orthodox monks were harboring Karadžić. I said it appeared that Koštunica was finally willing to cooperate. Then I announced that I would boycott the tenth anniversary of the Srebrenica massacre unless Mladić had been taken into custody. I had had enough public displays of mourning by powerful people. This year's commemoration would be special. The president of Serbia, Boris Tadić, would be present. The head of the World Bank, Paul Wolfowitz, would be there. Javier Solana, who had called Srebrenica "a colossal, collective, and shameful failure," would be there. The tribunal's president

Theodor Meron, would represent our institution. Shaikh Saleh Al-AsShaikh would lead a Saudi delegation. Ambassador Richard Holbrooke, the architect of the Dayton Peace Agreement, would be there, as would Ambassador Pierre Prosper. Refusing to take my place among them would be my protest against the lack of effective action by the Serbian authorities and the international community, my absence would be a reminder that Mladić and Karadžić were not where they belonged either.

On June 13, I went before the Security Council. I told the members that there had been an apparent change in the attitude of the authorities in Belgrade and that, since late December 2004, fourteen of our accused, six of them wanted in connection with the Srebrenica massacre and seven of them long-term futigives, had surrendered. Access to witnesses had improved. Access to documents, including military files, had become easier. These were all positive developments. But I could not in good conscience ignore the continuing failure of the authorities in Belgrade and Zagreb to arrest the remaining fugitives, including Radovan Karadžić and Ratko Mladić. Seven of the accused were within the reach of the Serbian authorities.

On August 8, 2005, we celebrated another arrest. Milan Lukić, one of the Bosnian war's most notorious killers, an accused whose dossier my office had, appropriately, code-named "Lucifer," had been taken into custody. The authorities in Argentina had tracked his cell phone and followed his wife as she traveled from Bosnia to join him with their daughter. Lukić, a relative of General Sreten Lukić, commanded a militia that terrorized Muslims living in and around the Bosnian town of Višegrad. According to eyewitnesses who had known Lukić since childhood, he had also taken part in the killings at Srebrenica. I met several of Lukić's victims. One was a mother who said she would never forgive me if Milan Lukić did not get his just desserts in The Hague. She described in detail how Lukić had invaded her home and raped her in front of her two children, who were nine and twelve years old; she described how Lukić took her into the kitchen and told her to choose a sharp knife; and then she described how, before her eyes, this Lukić used it to slit her children's throats. My skin twitched. And I recall now how Lukić, after his transfer to The Hague, had come into my office, dressed in a suit like a business man, and bragged that it was all a mistake and that he would, of course, prove it. I stood up to show him out at the end of our meeting. And again my skin twitched as he bent and kissed my hand.

Milan Lukić's cousin and alleged accomplice, Sredoje Lukić, was taken into custody on September 16 upon his arrival at Belgrade's airport on a flight from Russia. Two weeks later came the arrest of Dragan Zelenović, who was taken into custody, we believed mistakenly, by a Russian police chief in Khanty-Mansiysk, an oil-rich region east of the Urals. Zelenović eventually received a fifteen-year prison sentence after pleading guilty to charges of torture and rape in connection with assaults on Muslim women, including one fifteen-year-old girl, whom he and other Serb soldiers had taken prisoner in Foča during the summer of 1992.

I was back in Belgrade on September 29, 2005. This time, the question was how best to press for greater cooperation by using the European Union's deadline for arresting Mladić, the deadline Koštunica had pledged to meet back in June. I again acknowledged the progress Serbia and Montenegro had made during the year. The list of the tribunal's fugitives had shrunk to these six: Mladić, Karadžić, Hadžić, and General Vlastimir Djordjević; General Zdravko Tolimir, Ratko Mladić's top deputy, who was wanted in connection with, among other things, the ethnic cleansing of Srebrenica and Žepa and the massacre of Muslim prisoners after the fall of the enclaves; and Stojan Župljanin, the top Serb security commander in western Bosnia, who was wanted on charges of, among other things, genocide and persecution connected with the ethnic cleansing of Muslims, including the mistreatment of Muslims held in a number of detention camps. There was no point in dwelling upon the October deadline set by the European Union, so I suggested that the Serbs apprehend Mladić by the end of the year. I mentioned disturbing reports about the lack of coordination between Serbia's civilian and military intelligence services. Koštunica replied by saying that rivalries between military and civil services exist everywhere in the world. He said voluntary surrender was no longer the only option available for dealing with the fugitives, suggesting that arrests might be in order. Mladić's whereabouts, however, were unknown. He said it was important for Serbia to reach the end of this road and that Belgrade would soon be facing specific European Union deadlines.

Three weeks later, Rade Bulatović and Nebojša Vujović briefed me in greater detail on the effort to apprehend the remaining six fugitives. Vujović began the substantive part of the meeting by explaining Serbia's position on Kosovo: any solution short of independence and violating Serbia and Montenegro's sovereignty was acceptable. "The moment independence is mentioned," he said, "there will be 100,000 Serbs from

Kosovo on the tractors in Belgrade in front of the government building, and any government will be gone." I asked specifically whether there was any linkage in Belgrade's eyes between the Kosovo talks and resolution of the Mladić case. Vujović assured me that, of course, no connection existed and that the government had the political will to resolve the Mladić case. "Delivering Karadžić and Mladić to The Hague would only strengthen Belgrade's position in the Kosovo negotiations," he said. Then, he repeated, the thing that was important for the Serbian government was the "perception of the province being within Serbia."

Bulatović, whose credibility in my eyes had practically run out, said that the last confirmed appearance of Ratko Mladić in Serbia dated back to 2002. Since then, there had been only rumors that he had been in Belgrade, Valjevo, Novi Sad, Macedonia, and even Moldova and other places. Next, Bulatović said Serbia's civilian intelligence service had begun trying to reconstruct Mladić's support network from 2002. They had identified eighty or so people around Mladić and learned that they were all from the army. Either the civilian or the military intelligence agency had twenty-six of these persons under surveillance. The authorities were seeking any trace of contacts between Mladić and his family, because family contacts had led the authorities to the fugitives captured earlier in the year. The homes and telephones of Mladić's family members were being monitored. For the first time an officer of the civilian intelligence agency had established contact with Mladić's wife and son, Darko. (He apparently asked: "Where have you been all these years?") Bulatović said that, if Mladić was still in Serbia, he was somewhere near the towns of Gornji Milanovac or Valjevo or in the border area with Bosnia and Herzegovina. Bulatović's prognosis was that the intelligence service might have him in custody by the end of the year, 2005.

Bulatović said there was no information on Karadžić and no apparent connection between the persons hiding Karadžić and Mladić. Bulatović had no news on Hadžić, but mentioned that all his friends and family connections were under surveillance. Tolimir had almost been captured five or six months earlier, after his wife was spotted apparently attempting to bring him medicine. She had been fired from her job with the army, and military intelligence was tailing her. Tolimir was probably close to Mladić, Bulatović concluded, because their families were close.

By now, the government of Croatia had begun cooperating with the tribunal, providing key information that led to the arrest in Spain of

General Ante Gotovina on December 7. This success increased the pressure upon Belgrade to cooperate with the tribunal. I know Koštunica was explicitly informed that Serbia had "no chance" of establishing normal relations with the United States until Mladić was arrested.

By mid-December, there was, again, nothing new to tell to the United Nations Security Council about Belgrade. I decided to use my progress report to make two points clear to the council members. First, the tribunal was now solely dependent upon Serbia and Montenegro to arrest the six remaining fugitives, including Radovan Karadžić and Ratko Mladić. Despite Belgrade's assurances that the issue of fugitives could be resolved within a few months, I still saw no credible attempt to locate and apprehend them. Second, there was no mechanism for coordinating the various activities of the tribunal itself with the individual former Yugoslav states and the European Union military contingent in Bosnia and Herzegovina. These entities were displaying no will to share even the most mundane intelligence, and, when it came to operations, they were at cross-purposes. In Bosnia and Herzegovina, for instance, the tribunal managed to learn who was doing what to track Karadžić and Mladić—or rather who was not doing what. So we had asked the Republika Srpska authorities to have their police monitor the movements of Karadžić's family members, including his daughter Sonja. At one point, without prior warning, Montenegro's police notified us that Sonja had crossed the border from Bosnia into Montenegro. We were upset. The Republika Srpska police had given us no alert of her movements, so we demanded an explanation. The police informed us that someone from NATO had told them to desist. We tried to identify who, exactly, gave the Republika Srpska authorities these instructions. We went to NATO, and they replied, "Not us." We later discovered that someone from the CIA told the Republika Srpska police that the Office of the Prosecutor had agreed to call off surveillance measures. We had agreed to no such thing. My efforts to learn why this had happened produced only an unsatisfactory, two-word answer: "Communication gap."

I told the council members that our intelligence assets and the intelligence of major countries indicated that Mladić was still in Serbia, still under the protection of the Army of Serbia and Montenegro, still refusing to surrender voluntarily, and still enjoying his freedom because Koštunica's government, which could arrest him at any time, lacked the will to do so. Karadžić, whose protectors were taking advantage of the disorganized way the international community was proceeding against him, was still meandering back and forth between Serbia and Montenegro and the Serb-controlled area of Bosnia and Herzegovina, probably with the help of clerics within the Serbian Orthodox Church. Goran Hadžić, Zdravko Tolimir, and Stojan Župljanin were also within reach of the authorities of Serbia and Montenegro. Twice in two years, the Office of the Prosecutor had informed the Russian authorities of Djordjević's whereabouts in Moscow and Rostov-on-Don, but the authorities there responded by saying they had gone looking and found no Djordjević. We know now that they were probably right, for, it seems, Djorjdević left Russia sometime in 2003.

Based upon this assessment, I wanted the international community, and especially the European Union and the United States, to insist that cooperation with the tribunal remained a prerequisite for Serbia and Montenegro to receive financial and technical assistance and develop closer relations with NATO and the European Union. I wanted improved coordination of the fugitive-hunting efforts of the tribunal, the individual states, the European Union, NATO, and the United Nations missions in the various parts of the former Yugoslavia. I wanted to have representatives from NATO and the new European Union force in Bosnia and Herzegovina sitting in meetings with the local officials involved in the pursuit. I wanted real intelligence sharing. I wanted to see a new coordination mechanism created for meaningful planning and exchanges of information between those agencies involved in intelligence-gathering activities.

Serbia and Montenegro still had no serious, well-articulated plan to locate and arrest the fugitives on their territory midst. There was a lack of coordination between the central government in Belgrade and the republican authorities of Serbia and Montenegro individually. The rivalries between their agencies had become palpable. The Army of Serbia and Montenegro was continuing to hamper Belgrade's cooperation with the tribunal. The army, despite assurances by the government, continued to refuse to provide the tribunal with Mladić's military and medical records and documents related to the Kosovo campaign.

For ten years, the international community has been playing cat-and-mouse with Karadžić and Mladić. And for much of this time, the cats chose to wear blindfolds, to claw at each other, and to allow the mice to run from one hole to another. It is time now for the cats to remove their blindfolds.

It is time for the international community and the local governments, especially in Serbia and Montenegro and the Republika Srpska, to take concerted action to find the places where these fugitives are hiding and to arrest them and turn them over to the [Yugoslavia tribunal], so it can administer the justice the Security Council promised the people of the former Yugoslavia in 1993. It is time now for the cats to stop suffering the ridicule of the mice.

I was concerned. I had begun to hear that members of the NATO alliance—Italy, Greece, Spain, and several other countries—were prepared to accept Serbia and Montenegro into the Partnership for Peace, which was essentially NATO's get-acquainted program for prospective new members. I was also concerned that, despite assurances from the United States and other countries, the international community might be prepared to negotiate away conditionality in exchange for a softening of Serbia's position on Kosovo. A meeting with Koštunica and Bulatović in Belgrade in early February produced nothing new. Koštunica, yet again, stressed the ability of the domestic system to process the war crimes, but assured me we were "on the same side."

A month later, troubles began that gave the Belgrade authorities an excuse to slow whatever arrest efforts they had been making. On Sunday, March 5, 2006, Milan Babić, Goran Hadžić's predecessor as president of the rebel-Serb republic in Croatia, committed suicide in his jail cell at Scheveningen prison.

Here was an accused who had attempted to do the honorable thing. Despite threats to his well-being and the well-being of his family, he had surrendered. Instead of remaining silent and partaking of the incentive package Serbia was offering fugitives who had been on the run for years, Babić had confessed and pleaded guilty to one count involving a crime against humanity. In great part thanks to the relentless efforts of Hildegard Uertz-Retzlaff, the German prosecutor who was in charge of investigating links between Milošević and crimes committed during the conflict in Croatia in 1991, Babić had expressed remorse for his actions and asked his "Croatian brothers to forgive their Serb brothers." In testimony before the tribunal, he had gravely damaged Milošević's claims that the outside world was responsible for the violence that had erupted in the former Yugoslavia. Babić told the Trial Chamber that the short-lived Serb state he had helped Milošević create on Croatia's territory could not have survived in any way without an umbilical cord that stretched to Belgrade. The Serb rebels in Croatia had received weapons from Serbia, including tanks and rockets, he testified, and their "national bank" had effectively been a branch of the National Bank of Yugoslavia in Belgrade. Babić was serving a thirteen-year prison sentence, and was staying temporarily in the detention unit at Scheveningen. He had begun to complain that other inmates in the detention unit were threatening him. He requested a transfer to the Dutch wing of the jail, away from his fellow Serbs, Croats, and Muslims. He complained that his wife and sons could not return to Belgrade, because he had testified against Milošević and the Greater Serbia project. He begged that his sons be allowed to enroll in a university in Holland and pay local tuition. Babić's defense counsel approached me seeking support in solving his family problem. I spoke with the tribunal's registrar about the situation and urged him to resolve it. No viable solution was found before Babić found one himself, in the most tragic way on that first Sunday in March. I felt the institution, the Yugoslavia tribunal, had let Babić sink into despair. I felt I had done what I could. And, paradoxically, I felt that I should have done more.

I was away from The Hague on a vacation at that moment on the next Saturday morning, when Slobodan Milošević died. As I recall, the prison authorities discovered his body sometime before ten in the morning. My mobile phone rang within the hour. Milošević's fellow detainees, I am sure, spread the news to the world that he was dead. My first concern was to return to The Hague and issue a statement to counter any notion that the death of Milošević had in any way diminished the tribunal's significance, an interpretation of this awful event the institution's opponents were sure to market.

In our first press conference, we made it clear that the Yugoslavia tribunal was something more than just the Milošević tribunal and that its success or failure did not depend solely upon the case against Milošević. We had to try other senior Serb leaders indicted in connection with the same crimes for which Slobodan Milošević had been called to answer. These defendants included six former Serbian leaders and military officers indicted in connection with crimes committed in Kosovo. The trial of eight officers on charges connected with the Srebrenica genocide was soon to begin. Now more than ever, I expected Serbia to arrest and transfer Ratko Mladić and Radovan Karadžić to The Hague.

In many ways, on a deeper level, Milošević's death angered me. After four years of hearings, only forty hours remained for the defense to present its case. The proceedings were likely to end in a matter of weeks. We had complained for months that Milošević had not been using his prescribed blood-pressure medicine; we did not know that he had been taking non-prescribed drugs that had dampened the beneficial effects of his medicine. He had asked the Trial Chamber to allow him provisional release so he could travel to Russia for "medical treatment." We saw this for what it was: a desperate attempt to avoid a guilty verdict by trying to make his physicial infirmity seem worse so he could join his wife and son, who were fugitives from the Serbian authorities, and go on the lam. No one can do more than speculate that Milošević's death was suicide by recklessness. But Milošević knew of his medical condition, and, by tampering with his medication, he should have known that he was toying with his life.

Slobodan Milošević had nothing to gain by living longer, and he had everything to lose. In death, Milošević had escaped. He had deprived his hundreds of thousands of victims of the full degree of justice they deserved. The best result the Milošević trial provided them was the Trial Chamber's decision to reject the motion, presented on Milošević's behalf, to dismiss the charges for lack of evidence. He went to his grave knowing that the Trial Chamber had allowed the genocide charge to remain.

I made a point of concluding the statement I issued after Milošević's death with a tribute to Zoran Djindjić, his wife, Ružica, and their family. It was Djindjić who had, more than anyone else, shown the courage to do what was needed to bring Slobodan Milošević to The Hague so that he could face justice, so that the tribunal could demonstrate that no head of state could any longer assume that he or she would enjoy immunity from prosecution for daring to commit massive crimes. In this way, the will of Zoran Djindjić had made possible a trial that punctuated the end of a long and miserable era. It encouraged me to learn that more Serbs turned out to commemorate the anniversary of Djindjić's death than turned out to pay their respects at Milošević's funeral.

13

CONFRONTING BELGRADE AND MONTENEGRO
2006 AND 2007

The death of Slobodan Milošević portended a collapse of the political support the tribunal was relying upon to complete its mission. Milošević had become the Yugoslavia tribunal's marquee defendant, the tribunal's Hermann Göring, Hitler's second-favorite Nazi, who was tried at Nuremberg before he committed suicide, and the tribunal's General Hideki Tojo, the Japanese prime minister who was condemned at Tokyo. Too many journalists, propagandists, and political leaders had come to equate the tribunal and its work with the Milošević trial and ignored the tribunal's other cases. The prosecution of the Bosnian Croat leadership, which was effectively the case against Franjo Tudjman's legacy and presented perhaps the clearest historical record ever to demonstrate how the boardroom decisions of political leaders produce war crimes in the field, would garner little attention beyond doses of disinformation administered through Croatia's press. The trial of Ramush Haradinaj would attract attention because he had ensconced himself in Kosovo's political establishment and endeared himself to diplomats and international administrators. Now that Milošević was savoring his cigarillos and cognac with Tudjman in the afterlife, it was obvious that the Office of the Prosecutor would have to redouble its efforts to convince the European Union to maintain the pressure it was applying upon Serbia. This was the last significant leverage we had upon Koštunica and the authorities in Belgrade as well as the leaders in Montenegro and the Serb entity in Bosnia and Herzegovina to arrest the last six of the 161 persons the tribunal had indicted. I opposed any relaxation of the European Union's stance. Perhaps my position was too rigid.

On March 15, 2006, I met with Hans Winkler, deputy minister of foreign affairs of Austria, the member state of the European Union occupying the organization's presidency. My message was consistent: the authorities in Belgrade knew where Ratko Mladić was hiding in Serbia; instead of arresting and transferring him to The Hague, Koštunica and the other Serbian leaders were killing time and squandering resources in vain attempts to convince him to surrender voluntarily and then trying to convince us all that this fecklessness amounted to cooperation for which Belgrade should be rewarded. Winkler explained that the European Union was continuing to demand Mladić's arrest and had decided that, if Serbia did not demonstrate full cooperation and transfer Mladić by the end of March, the European Union would "disrupt" the negotiations with Belgrade on a stabilization and association agreement. Belgrade was desperate to conclude this agreement. It represented the only hope Serbia and Montenegro had of someday working their way into the new Europe. So, according to Winkler, cooperation with the tribunal remained a key prerequisite barring entry to Europe.

"For now," I thought.

As the weeks passed, the Belgrade government continued to promise stepped-up efforts to arrest Mladić. But the army was still contributing nothing of significance, and there was good reason to believe that active and retired officers were doing exactly the opposite. Rivalries between the country's civilian and military intelligence agencies were hindering investigations, or so we were told. Inconsistencies in the various progress reports Belgrade provided the tribunal led me to suspect that some of the contents had been doctored. The failure to arrest Radovan Karadžić, a shared responsibility of Serbia, the Republika Srpska, NATO, and the new European military force in Bosnia, EUFOR, had become a mockery. The planned downsizing of EUFOR would further aggravate the situation. In the early spring of 2006, we received an alert from the Montenegrin authorities that they had intercepted a message from Karadžić's niece to a man in Switzerland, requesting the delivery of certain medicines Karadžić himself apparently needed. The Montenegrins tracked the man from Switzerland to Montenegro, where he passed the medicine to a bus driver. The bus driver then traveled to Belgrade. The Montenegrins informed the tribunal that they could not continue tracking him, because Belgrade was in Serbia, a different jurisdiction. The driver was now the responsibility of the Serbian authorities. The Office of the Prosecutor alerted the authorities in Belgrade. We received word that the driver's trail had gone cold; no explanation was offered. Out of sheer desperation, I asked the United Nations Security Council to grant the Office of the Prosecutor special powers and adequate resources to act alone to arrest the tribunal's fugitive accused wherever they were hiding; this, I knew, would be a nonstarter.

I packed the assurances I had received from Winkler into my handbag and made a tour of Banja Luka, Belgrade, and Podgorica to concentrate as much pressure as I could upon the Serbs of Republika Srpska, Serbia, and Montenegro, for whom Belgrade's efforts to grow closer to Europe were crucial. I had heard that the official overseeing the processes of the European Union's expansion, Olli Rehn of Finland, was preparing to announce the cancellation of the next round of stabilization and association talks with the Union of Serbia and Montenegro, which were set to begin on April 5. I knew that Montenegro had scheduled, for May 21, a referendum on independence. If the talks with the European Union collapsed, the pro-independence Montenegrins might, to Koštunica's greater chagrin, garner the votes they needed to break away from Serbia.

In Banja Luka, I found myself sitting across from Milorad Dodik, who was again prime minister of the Republika Srpska, Bosnia's Serb entity. I reminded Dodik about all the promises that he had made six years earlier and that had come to nothing. Dodik responded by blaming Serbia, asserting that he had suspended all financial assistance to the families of the tribunal's fugitive accused, and making a series of new promises. I had little reason to trust any of it. In the eleven years since it was recognized in the Dayton Peace Agreement, the Republika Srpska had arrested none of the tribunal's fugitives, and the authorities there had sapped the term "criminal justice" of all its meaning. We had to inform Dodik and his interior minister that the interior minister's new adviser for issues related to the tribunal was suspected of having committed war crimes and was a cousin of one of our fugitive accused; the interior minister was in the room; he, of course, asserted that he had not known; and I supposed nobody had bothered to check even though the adviser and the fugitive had the same last name: Župljanin.

My conversations in Serbia also rang with familiar promises and assurances. We heard that, even after Milan Babić's suicide and Milošević's death, Belgrade's desire to deliver Mladić was genuine, because handing the fugitive general over would open the door to the European Union. We heard ministers say they would resign if no success was achieved soon. We heard that Belgrade's military and civilian intelligence services were now singing in two-part harmony. We heard that Mladić was no longer hiding in the army's facilities. We heard that some individual military officers might have been involved in protecting Mladić, but, of course, no commanding officers and certainly not the country's army as an institution. We heard that Serbia's military intelligence service was monitoring forty-two persons believed to be assisting Mladić and that there had been confirmed contacts between Mladić and certain beekeepers near Valjevo and other Serbian towns. We heard that the authorities had identified 518 apartments in Belgrade alone as possible hideouts, and that 192 apartments belonging to the military had been searched. We heard that, in January 2006, Mladić had stayed for about twelve days with a certain military officer named Stanko Ristić in a cottage Ristić owned near Serbia's border with Croatia. We heard that Mladić had, during early February 2006, moved to the apartment of Ristić's mother in the town of Sremska Mitrovica. We heard that the intelligence agency would now pressure this Ristić to provide information on Mladić's present whereabouts. We heard that Mladić was isolated, baking his own bread, using drugs, and communicating with his family by mobile telephones and letters. We heard that Mladić's family had been providing him money through another military officer, a certain Jovan Djogo. We heard that all members of the Mladić family were under surveillance. We were told that General Aco Tomić, now retired, was "a very dangerous man" whom the police had not even bothered to interview.

Late in the afternoon of March 29, 2006, I met Koštunica at the seat of the Serbian government in central Belgrade. Koštunica, usually so wooden, so obdurate, seemed uncharacteristically bubbly. He said he had spoken to Olli Rehn and knew that I would be meeting with him in Brussels. He said apprehending Mladić was in the interests of Serbia and the tribunal. He admitted that Mladić was in Serbia. He confirmed that the police had tracked Mladić's movements to mid-February, but had since lost his trail. Then Koštunica let it slip that if negotiations with the European Union were halted, it would "make it more difficult to locate and arrest Mladić."

I was skeptical of everything I had heard. My team members and I wondered why the Serbian authorities had provided this flood of information only as I was making a visit to Belgrade, and just before a crucial European Union decision, rather than on an ongoing basis. I wanted proof that Belgrade was actually doing something. I told Koštunica that I believed he was still only attempting to force Mladić to surrender voluntarily. Koštunica denied it immediately. He said both options, arrest and voluntary surrender, were still open, but Mladić first had to be located.

"How long?" I asked.

Rade Bulatović, head of Serbia's government intelligence agency, the BIA, said, "Soon . . . several more weeks."

Then, without prompting, Koštunica produced something I should have expected: a promise that Mladić would be in custody by the end of April. He asked me to give Olli Rehn a positive, or at least encouraging, assessment of Serbia's cooperation, because this would be good for Serbia. "Serbia's success will be the tribunal's success," he said. This *coup de théâtre* seemed too good to be true. But I had little choice but to tell Koštunica that I would give him until the end of April.

I assumed the trying circumstances Serbia and Montenegro were facing would force Koštunica to comply. How could he and his supporters squander so much of the future prosperity and security of their children for the sake of a bull-headed refusal to hand over a few aging men, not to face persecution, but to answer legitimate charges, including genocide charges, stemming from acts of mass killing that had made the entire country a pariah? During the flight back to The Hague, I confided in my advisers: This time—again—I was sure Mladić would soon be in our custody.

On March 31, I traveled down the expressway from The Hague to Brussels. Olli Rehn informed me that he had just telephoned Prime Minister Koštunica and President Boris Tadić and told them that, based upon the assessment I would provide on Belgrade's cooperation with the tribunal, Rehn would inform the European Parliament whether talks with the State Union of Serbia and Montenegro would continue.

I told Rehn, "They could have arrested Mladić three times in the past month, but instead they sent him messages." I explained that at the end of January, a Serb, this Stanko Ristić who was supposed to have been under around-the-clock police surveillance, had chauffeured Mladić from Belgrade to some safe house near Serbia's border with Croatia. Now, the leadership was unwilling to reveal Mladić's whereabouts. But, I explained, Koštunica was under significant pressure; he told me they had lost a few weeks because of Milošević's death; he appealed for a few more weeks to bring Mladić to justice.

"End of April," I told Rehn.

"Are they seriously trying?" Rehn asked.

"I suppose yes, they are trying this time. . . . Ristić is supposed to be arrested. . . . And I told Koštunica I would take a risk and ask for continuation of the talks, and, if he didn't deliver Mladić, there would be hell to pay." Rehn agreed that this was a risk worth taking. I advised him to have sanctions ready if Koštunica did not deliver.

Rehn turned toward his staff: "Do we have any good deadline in May?"

Heads shook. The staff members decided to create one. They split the agenda of a meeting set for April 5 and delayed undertaking the second part until a new meeting scheduled for the first half of May, which was, coincidentally, just before Montenegro's referendum on independence. Rehn then called Koštunica and, according to Rehn, Koštunica said he would resign if Mladić were not taken into custody.

We waited, and soon realized Koštunica's promises had been nothing but a *muro di gomma*. In March, Patrick Lopez-Terres, the chief of investigations, returned to The Hague from a trip to Belgrade with a dismal assessment: The Serbs, despite Koštunica's pledge, were still only attempting to convince Mladić to surrender voluntarily. They had apparently assumed that if they were able to delay the European Union's early March deadline, they would buy themselves several more months.

April came. April went. The spring rains watered Holland's blooming tulips. The North Sea winds blew hard against the dunes and the fairways and the walls of the Scheveningen prison. Vojislav Koštunica did not deliver, and did not resign. On May 3, I told Olli Rehn that the Office of the Prosecutor had received a complete report on the Belgrade government's efforts to apprehend Mladić. Instead of arresting the fugitive, the Serbian authorities had arrested people suspected of harboring him. Moreover, the Belgrade press had published leaked information about the so-called pursuit.

Rehn replied that he would inform the president of the European Union that Belgrade had failed to honor its commitments. "This," he said, "is now about the credibility of European Union policy." Rehn immediately canceled the round of talks with Belgrade set for early May, and he won the support of the European Union foreign ministers, who met a few days later. On May 21, Montenegro held its referendum and, by a thin margin, the pro-independence vote won out. The subsequent Montenegrin and Serbian declarations of independence during the first week of June extinguished the State Union of Serbia and Montenegro, submerged the last vestige of lost Yugoslavia, the state that had sprung from the ashes of World War I, the state that Slobodan Milošević had once dreamed of dominating in its entirety. Koštunica and other Serb leaders, who never miss an opportunity to point a finger at someone else for their problems, blamed the tribunal.

In mid-June, Belgrade came to The Hague. Rade Bulatović, head of Serbia's government intelligence agency, the BIA, told us that our report to the European Union had been "inaccurate, malicious, and politicized." He summoned the gall to say that there was no obstacle to Mladić's arrest and that Belgrade was not working exclusively to convince Mladić to surrender voluntarily. He explained that his operatives had tried to pass messages to Mladić through his son, Darko, because they believed Darko was supporting the father and ready to discuss surrender. Milošević's death had disrupted everything, Bulatović said, and the suspension of negotiations with the European Union and the Montenegrin vote for independence had made it appear that the Yugoslavia tribunal was a political body manipulated only to put pressure on Serbia.

Bulatović now revealed to us a new set of measures Belgrade was taking to bring Mladić into custody. The government intelligence service, he said, was reappraising all of Mladić's links with the army and the political leadership. He told us that hardly anyone in Serbia was willing to shelter Mladić and that certain people who had given him refuge were under arrest. He mentioned that Djogo had been taken into custody and, in a revealing admission about the integrity of Serbia's judiciary, would be sentenced to four years in prison, which would send a stern message to anyone else who might be contemplating assisting Mladić. Bulatović said investigators were studying Mladić's medical records to see whether they could locate him through contacts with doctors who had been treating him. He complained about a lack of cooperation from the military. He told us that secret police officers were tailing the wife of another fugitive wanted on charges linked to the Srebrenica massacre, General Zdravko Tolimir, Mladić's assistant commander of intelligence and security, because Mladić and Tolimir might be in hiding together. He said Belgrade was also trying to locate Goran Hadžić, the former political leader of the Serbs in Croatia whose flight from the justice, after a tip from inside the Belgrade government on the day his indictment was delivered, had been caught on film by a friendly intelligence service.

"*Basta*," I thought when I had heard enough of Bulatović's exposé. It seemed that whenever we met with him, we needed to bring along a polygraph machine. Then I spoke up: "Mladić was supposed to have been handed over eight weeks ago. We are monitoring in the press everything the BIA is supposedly doing in secret. This is all so unprofessional. . . . My guess is that you are doing this intentionally simply to garner political support.

"We see nothing emerging from your investigative efforts," I continued, pointing out a few of the numerous inconsistencies in Bulatović's version of events, which, of course, meant that I was calling him a liar to his face. Then, I explained that, if Belgrade were really interested in capturing Mladić, it would have been more effective to have kept monitoring his support network than to arrest its members.

Bulatović tried to defend himself by blaming someone else. "Pressure from the political leadership forced us to use radical methods," he said. "We had to show we were doing something!" Bulatović protested even more when we told him that, in contrast to Serbia, Montenegro had undertaken significant efforts to track Karadžić. "We know at what time every member of the Karadžić family in Montenegro is going to bed and waking up in the morning," I said. "We know every word they utter in their house."

"You don't trust us?" Bulatović concluded.

"We have no idea what the people you interview are saying. We receive no information from you," I answered.

Bulatović seemed incredulous. "We know we have one or two months to capture him. We are having a serious conflict with the army, and all the people in the network protecting Mladić are from the military." He told us that Karadžić and Župljanin were, to a 90 percent degree of certainty, in Montenegro and that Tolimir needed frequent medical care.

Shortly after Bulatović's visit, the Belgrade authorities made another attempt to buy time, coming up with something they were calling their "action plan" to apprehend Mladić, Karadžić, and the other fugitives. Drafts of this plan transited the cyberspace between Belgrade and The Hague. We even had to protest that, in early versions, the verb "to arrest" had somehow gone missing from the Serbian government's list of objectives. Finally, on July 15, 2006, the action plan was finalized, on paper. Its purpose was to locate, arrest, and transfer Ratko Mladić and the remaining accused by means of a "synchronized action of competent state authorities." The state leadership was supposed to establish an "operative security structure"—a cell—to achieve these goals. The leadership was also required to make a continuous public display of a clear and determined stand to arrest Ratko Mladić and transfer him to The Hague and explain that his arrest, like the arrests of the other accused, was in Serbia's interests. Finally, a detailed operative plan was to be established in coordination with the Office of the Prosecutor, which was to be apprised of developments on a daily basis. In announcing the action plan to the Serbian public, Koštunica asserted that it was difficult to envisage the European Union without Serbia helping to provide stability in the Balkans.

For him, maybe.

Two chairs were missing from the dock inside Courtroom 1 on the morning of Monday, August 21, 2006, when the case styled *The Prosecutor v. Popović, et al.*, went to trial. The judges and clerks were there. The translators were seated in their booths. Behind the security glass in the gallery, security guards were showing onlookers and members of the press how to use the translation devices. There was an entire prosecution team, led by Peter McCloskey, a Californian who had presented the first Srebrenica cases. And there were seven defendants too little known even in Bosnia and Serbia. The two chairs missing from the dock were the ones that should have been set for Ratko Mladić and his accomplice, Zdravko Tolimir. This should have been the tribunal's final Srebrenica trial. McCloskey should have been outlining the Srebrenica case in a detailed opening statement for the final time. Now, at least one more trial would be necessary.

I used the opportunity to address the court and recall the victims of the Srebrenica massacre, an event, I fear, too many diplomats and political leaders dealing with Serbia would like to pretend never happened:

> It is beyond reasonable dispute that genocide and other crimes against humanity were committed. . . . An entire population erased, women, children and the elderly forced from their homes; defenseless men and boys executed by firing squads, buried in mass graves, and then dug up and buried once again in an effort to conceal the truth from the world.
>
> But the lasting tragedy of Srebrenica, the leading legacy of this atrocity is with the families left behind. The women and children forced to live their lives deprived of their fathers, without their husbands, their brothers, their sons, their neighbours, their community. . . .
>
> These seven accused, Your Honours, officers, serving below Ratko Mladić and Zdravko Tolimir, are among those most responsible, most

responsible for the terrible crimes committed in Srebrenica as set forth in the indictment. . . .

[T]he effort to bring to justice the most responsible for the terrible crimes in the former Yugoslavia, including the darkest chapter, the genocide in Srebrenica, is incomplete. Unfortunately, two men who should be sitting as accused before Your Honours right now in this courtroom are still at large. I refer, of course, to Ratko Mladić and Zdravko Tolimir.

It is absolutely scandalous that these men, along with Radovan Karadžić, have not been arrested and delivered to the Tribunal to face the charges brought against them. The government of the Republic of Serbia is fully capable of arresting these men. It has simply until now refused to do so. . . . [T]he inexcusable refusal to arrest and transfer Mladić means that another Srebrenica trial must be held in the future, when Mladić and Tolimir will be in custody. And make no mistake: He, Mladić, and Tolimir, Karadžić, and all the remaining fugitives will be arrested. They will be brought to The Hague and they will be tried for their crimes. This is our pledge to the international community, to the women who mourn for their loss in [Srebrenica], and to all victims of the conflict in the former Yugoslavia.

McCloskey and his team then set out on the marathon of presenting evidence and arguments. And I went back to the frustrating effort of forcing Serbia to comply with its international obligations. The action plan, needless to say, had produced no action.

The status quo—no arrests and otherwise dismal cooperation from Belgrade, but consistent European Union refusal to entertain stabilization talks with Belgrade—carried into the second half of 2006. Then, the question of sovereignty over Kosovo, Serbia's troubled, overwhelmingly ethnic-Albanian-populated province, rose to the top of the United States, European Union, and United Nations agenda regarding Serbia.

A United Nations effort to work out the future status of Kosovo was approaching a watershed moment. The secretary-general had engaged the former president of Finland, Martti Ahtisaari, as a special representative to propose a plan to settle the province's future. In an attempt to soften Belgrade's expected opposition to the Kosovo plan, some European Union member states began to advocate softening the European Union's opposition to stabilization and association talks. In so doing, it seemed to me, they were effectively rewarding Serbia's failure to comply with its obligation to cooperate.

United States policy also shifted. During the autumn of 2006, we received indications that the Bush administration was engaged in an internal debate about whether to allow Serbia to join NATO's Partnership for Peace, the orientation program it uses to ease the entry of Eastern European and former Soviet countries into the alliance. Some segments of the Serbian ruling elite sought entry into the Partnership for Peace, which brought with it financial assistance for upgrading the armed forces. The United States had had a long-standing policy that the Partnership for Peace was open only to those countries whose governments were fully cooperating with the Yugoslavia tribunal; Belgrade had been informed that it could join only after Mladić had been delivered to The Hague. The question now became whether Washington was going to drop this precondition. We heard that the National Security Council now supported lifting this conditionality requirement, arguing that bringing Serbia into the Partnership for Peace would prevent Belgrade from cozying up to Russia and require the Serbian military to undertake reforms that would make it easier to obtain the arrests of Mladić, Karadžić, and other fugitives. In the late autumn, not long before a key NATO summit in Riga that was to begin on November 28, we received word that the debate had ended and that Washington would stick to its conditions. We were confident that pressure on Belgrade would continue unabated.

On November 28, however, I received a phone call from the State Department informing us that, during the flight on Air Force One from Washington to Riga, President George Bush had decided to reverse United States policy. We heard that the Bush administration had received a letter from Serbia's president, Boris Tadić, appealing for entry into the Partnership for Peace because it would enhance the chances of pro-Western Serbian political leaders in upcoming elections. Despite last-minute resistance from a small number of member states, including the Netherlands, NATO decided to open its doors to Serbia, stating that the alliance had reaffirmed the "values and principles" set out in the Partnership for Peace documents, fully expected cooperation, and would closely monitor Serbia's cooperation.

I was not happy. I announced that that neither NATO nor the United States had consulted the tribunal in advance to assess the nature and degree of Belgrade's cooperation and that NATO's decision had taken us by surprise. I also said the decision appeared to be a reward for Serbia's refusal to cooperate. The Bush administration had, in effect, decided that it was within NATO's "values and principles" to allow into the NATO family the same military that was protecting Mladić, the fugitive indicted for the murders of 7,500 captive Muslim men and boys, not to mention other charges.

Deputy Prosecutor David Tolbert and my political adviser, Jean-Daniel Ruch, visited Washington a few weeks later and asked a staff member of the National Security Council why the United States had agreed to abandon the leverage it had upon the Serbs. "We still have leverage," he asserted. "We can influence the Europeans. We can tell Europe to remain firm and keep cooperation with the tribunal on all talking points." The policy reversal, he confirmed, was undertaken to improve Tadić's election prospects. We thought this assessment and approach were misguided. The new United States policy, we thought, would only strengthen Tadić's opponents: Koštunica and the rest of Serbia's right wing, who were consistent advocates for doing nothing, for waiting until the resolve of the international community had flagged and the memory of Srebrenica had faded to black. Events proved us right. The political leader who rose in the polls after the Washington's policy reversal was Koštunica, not Tadić, and the reversal had left the United States with no leverage on Serbia. Koštunica was clearly ready to accept manna from heaven. He announced that it was "a good thing" to be a member of the Partnership for Peace, because it strengthened Serbia's connections with the West and might help Serbia regain control of Kosovo, something Washington clearly did not want to hear, because it was anxious to have Kosovo's status resolved in the Albanians' favor so the Pentagon could redeploy its troops to more critical conflict areas like Iraq and Afghanistan. With the Americans now pulling strings connected to nothing, Koštunica was free to play the Russia card on Kosovo, and play it he did.

Washington's reversal on Partnership for Peace was only a few hours old before we noted a push within the European Union to soften its demands that Serbia cooperate with the tribunal. On November 28, 2006, the same day as George Bush's in-flight policy shift, the political director of the British Foreign Office, John Sawers, visited The Hague. Sawers began our meeting by assuring me that the British were, of course, the tribunal's staunchest supporters in the European Union and that the only differences between my office and the British government arose over tactics and not goals. "Let's talk about Serbia," Sawers said. "I agree that this is frustrating. At the political level, they have done nothing. But the two intelligence services are coordinating better, which we see as a small bit of progress."

"It is movement, not progress," I interjected.

Sawers asked how the European Union could maintain conditionality, that is, continue to require, as a prerequisite for stabilization and association talks, Serbia's cooperation with the tribunal: "The United States has decided to give them Partnership for Peace. It will be very difficult for Prime Minister Blair to stand up alone."

I wondered why Blair would have to stand up alone inside the European Union when the Netherlands, whose peacekeepers had witnessed the fall of Srebrenica, adamantly supported the tribunal. "So," I asked myself, "the Dutch can stand up alone. And the French and Belgians support us. But Blair cannot stand with them?"

Sawers said we could expect a push by Italy, Spain, Hungary, Austria, and Greece, Serbia's most ardent advocate in the European Union, to restart stabilization and association talks. "We will have to box clever," Sawers said, but then he gave an indication that Great Britain might be willing to throw the fight: "What we would like is to get the Serbs into a 'cycle of cooperation.' As a consequence, if there is a political commitment and positive signs of progress, *short of transferring Mladić to The Hague*, we could tell Olli Rehn to restart the negotiations." This was the key sentence. And Sawers had delivered it without even uttering the word *Kosovo*.

On January 21, 2007, Serbian voters cast their ballots. The result was a resounding victory for the right wing, though their seats in parliament were split between the Radicals and Koštunica's allies and no party had emerged with an absolute majority. Once again, the diplomatic community chose to see Koštunica not as the obdurate nationalist he is, but as a "moderate" keeping at bay the Radical Party—an ultranationalist, violence-inciting organization led by Vojislav Šešelj, who was enjoying room and board in the prison ward at Schevinengen while he awaited trial on charges connected with war crimes allegedly committed by his party's militia in Croatia and Bosnia. Announcement of the election results heralded months of negotiations to form a new government.

It did not take long for the British to return to The Hague. Geoffrey Hoon, the minister for European Union affairs, came to my office for a discussion on January 29. This time I spoke up. "The Serbs continue to say they want Mladić to surrender voluntarily. They could have given up Mladić long ago if they had wanted. . . . So I am afraid that a decision by the European Union to resume talks with Belgrade will send a bad, bad message."

"Where is Mladić?" Hoon asked.

"Probably in an apartment in Belgrade. . . . The heads of both intelligence services must know exactly where he is, but there has been no green light given by Koštunica to arrest him." Boris Tadić, Serbia's president, would certainly allow for Mladić's arrest, I continued, but, as president, Tadić has no power.

Hoon then trawled for any ideas we might have on actions Belgrade could take, short of Mladić's arrest and transfer, that would prompt me to declare that Belgrade was cooperating with the tribunal. I called the action plan a "smoke screen," but said, "If there were people I could trust in key positions who were providing us information, we might call that cooperation. . . . But I cannot trust Bulatović, because he is always lying."

Hoon said he would go to Belgrade before the next meeting of European Union foreign ministers, scheduled for February, and try to bring the Serbs under political pressure: "It is entirely in their interests to cooperate. I will make no further concession, otherwise we get nowhere."

"What about Kosovo?" I asked, referring to the possibility that Mladić would be dealt away in exchange for Serbia's agreement to let Kosovo go.

"There is no need for a tradeoff at this stage," Hoon said. "On the other hand . . . I'm not sure we can wait until Mladić is here before we restart the talks. . . . It is important that there be an objective test of progress. Then we can see if it is filled with substance." He asked about Karadžić, and I told Hoon we had indications that Karadžić was in Serbia but frequently crossing back into the Republika Srpska, helped by the Serbian Orthodox Church as he moved between monasteries and from village to village. "Karadžić depends on drug trafficking," I said, adding that we were seeking help from Bosnian Serb businessmen fed up with paying him protection money.

But the Republika Srpska authorities were doing nothing on fugitives. I complained that I did not know what the international community was doing anymore to apprehend tribunal fugitives in Bosnia. So, I concluded my comments with an offer to capitulate, to withdraw from the playing field:

If the international community is no longer interested in apprehending our fugitives, please tell us. We'll conclude our trials. We'll stop putting resources into pursuing fugitives. This would be a political decision. The resumption of the stabilization and association talks will be a sign. If you resume the talks, it means you are not interested in Karadžić and Mladić any more.

Hoon replied clearly: "This is not our position."

I hoped not.

On January 31, I traveled to Brussels and met with Javier Solana, instead of Olli Rehn, who had gone to Helsinki for family reasons.

"Ninety percent of our accused are in custody thanks to the European Union," I told Solana. "Now is the crucial moment to get Mladić. But Spain, Italy, Slovenia, Austria, Hungary, and others want to resume the stabilization and association talks because of Kosovo. . . . This will have the worst possible effect, because Koštunica received admission into the Partnership for Peace for doing nothing. Even he was surprised by it. And now he hopes the European Union will also lift conditionality. . . . If this is the case, then I will stop pursuing. But tell me."

"Oh, no, Carla," Solana replied in a way that seemed to cast a spotlight on the *muro di gomma.* "You have to continue. But you know the situation in the Balkans must be stabilized. We will continue to say the same things."

"We have to separate Kosovo from Mladić," I told him.

"Yes," he said, "but it is the same government, and the Russians will complicate things to buy them time." Solana then gave me a preview of Ahtisaari's proposed solution to the issue of Kosovo's sovereignty. The Albanians would gain independence, but under supervision. The final plan would come out later in the month. But the Mladić issue would remain unchanged.

"If the negotiations restart on February 12, you can forget Mladić and Karadžić," I told him, referring to the stabilization and association talks.

"Negotiations will not start unless there is cooperation," Solana answered, "but Mladić is not the condition." We noted that his words echoed the British position: *cooperation short of arresting Mladić,* lowering the standard.

"First, there has to be a change in the heads of the intelligence services," I said. "If I know what they're doing, I'm ready to confirm that there is full cooperation even though Mladić is not in The Hague. . . . But Kostunica can give Mladić to me now. Bulatović can give him to me.

Put pressure on Koštunica. I am not insisting on Karadžić for now. But I want Mladić."

I phoned Serbia's president, Boris Tadić, on an open line the next day, February 1, to follow up on a secret meeting we had had two months earlier in Berlin. One of the topics we had discussed was a report Tadić was seeking on Mladić from both of Serbia's intelligence services. Soon after the meeting, two of Tadić's advisers had come to The Hague and presented a schematic diagram showing the organizational structure of yet another new effort to arrest Mladić. This effort would report to Tadić, not Koštunica. During the telephone conversation, I asked Tadić about the report about Mladić from the security services. Here, two months later, he was still waiting.

"What about the new organization?" I asked. "If you implement this new structure, it could be very positive. And you should make decisions on the persons you want to have in this organization, a small group of people."

"I agree," he said, "changes are necessary."

"It would be good to restart the work now."

"Unfortunately," Tadić replied, "there is the problem of Kosovo." A year earlier, it had been Milošević's death. From the autumn, it had been the elections. Now it was Kosovo. "Without Kosovo," Tadić said, "things would be much easier."

I spoke with Olli Rehn on Monday, February 5 by telephone. "I'm going to Belgrade on Wednesday and want to hear your input," he said. "My idea is that, this week, we will not go into specifics in public as to what is expected of Serbia. But in private, we will go into details in order to make serious progress. In any case, the European Union will not make any decision on the talks before a new government is appointed. We need concrete benchmarks, overarching criteria."

Rehn asked me to have my office provide him with an assessment of Belgrade's cooperation and to send a list of steps Serbia might take both before and after the formation of its new government. "Fine," I answered, "this effectively means Belgrade has a month to prove it really wants to arrest Mladić. What they need to do is put the right people in the right positions. . . . But Koštunica must be persuaded to arrest Mladić, because he can deliver right away. Tadić will need a month. Tadić will need new structures, new people, and new ways to work. . . . So, please, what you should do is press the present government. This is about the credibility of the European Union. Cooperation is worse now than before. Koštunica got into the Partnership for Peace and received messages that the negotiations would soon resume. So why would he make a move?"

We immediately sent Rehn an assessment of Belgrade's failure to cooperate along with the requested list of things Belgrade could do to improve the situation. Since October 2006, we reported, Belgrade's cooperation had deteriorated both in terms of the search for fugitives and access to documents and witnesses. The last information we had received from the Belgrade authorities on the manhunts had come on October 13. The action plan was a nonstarter. An increasing number of requests for assistance, including a long-standing request for Ratko Mladić's personal military file, had gone unanswered. The Office of the Prosecutor had good reasons to believe that the Belgrade authorities could arrest Mladić and other fugitives, but were not willing to do so. Since March 2006, Belgrade had not provided any meaningful information on Mladić or his supporters, and potentially valuable leads were allowed to go cold. Likewise, Belgrade had shown no willingness to cooperate in apprehending Radovan Karadžić.

To demonstrate cooperation with the tribunal's efforts, a new government would have to undertake significant structural and personnel changes. In particular, Koštunica, still the acting prime minister, as well as the minister of interior, the minister of justice, the minister of defense, and the heads of the intelligence services could not be regarded as trustworthy partners. President Tadić must personally take responsibility for the arrest of fugitives, make a strong public commitment in this regard, and be given the authority and resources required to complete this task. At the operational level of the effort to arrest Mladić, a new structure had to be established and involve both the best civilian and military personnel under a unified command reporting directly to President Tadić and an operational coordination mechanism with the Office of the Prosecutor.

On February 6, we met with Foreign Minister Ben Bot of The Netherlands, who confirmed that the Dutch government, too, had received information indicating that the authorities in Belgrade could arrest Mladić but lacked the will to do it. Bot warned us to expect more pressure for resumption of the stabilization and association talks between Serbia and the European Union. He warned that some members considered it unthinkable that Serbia be left out of Europe and that isolation, which would push Belgrade closer to Moscow's sphere of influence, would be more problematic than a failure to apprehend a few war criminals. The policy of Belgrade and its supporters, he said, is that they would be off the hook if they managed to hold out for another year and a half.

A day later, on February 7, I began an effort to confront Serbia's supporters within the European Union. My first stop was Madrid. A few weeks earlier, I had told a Spanish newspaper that I was disappointed that Spain was supporting, without conditions, a resumption of European Union negotiations with Serbia; after this interview, Spain's ambassador to the Netherlands informed me that his foreign minister, Miguel Ángel Moratinos, was displeased with my comments and considered canceling our meeting in Madrid. The ambassador advised me to speak no more to the media before the meeting.

The atmosphere in the chambers of the Spanish Foreign Ministry was tense when I showed up for my conversation with Moratinos, and my aide, Jean-Daniel Ruch, told me later he was perched on the edge of his seat wondering who would act first to end the meeting, me, by reaching for my Louis Vuitton, or Moratinos, by showing us the door. I could not help but wonder that Madrid's anxiety about Serbia had much to do with the similarities between Serbia's problem with Kosovo and Spain's problem with the Basque region.

I briefly thanked Spain for the support it had provided the tribunal, especially in the effort to apprehend the Croatian fugitive, Ante Gotovina. "But," I began, "I am surprised that Spain, Italy, Hungary, and the others want to resume talks with Serbia even without its cooperation with the tribunal. I am also surprised that you were angry that I spoke to the media about these concerns. . . . I am a prosecutor, and I enjoy independence. And I did not appreciate the fact that the Spanish ambassador came to me and informed me that there was a risk I would not be welcomed here. This was blackmail, and I did not appreciate it."

"Madame," Moratinos replied, "an ambassador of Spain need not resort to blackmail. And I am myself surprised that you, Madame Del Ponte, prejudiced the Spanish position before you came to the country and heard directly the position of the government. . . . You have never heard our position from me. . . . So far as I know, you were not present at the council meeting where I expressed this position. If you have already formed a judgment, then maybe it was not necessary for us to meet. . . .

"We want to help you as we helped you on Croatia, which was a candidate country [for membership in the European Union] even before there was full cooperation. Why can't we have the same approach on Serbia?"

Moratinos assured me that welcoming Serbia back into the stabilization and association talks did not mean the European Union would stop pressing Serbia to cooperate fully with the tribunal. "We do not have to finalize the agreement if there is no full cooperation," he said. "We are telling the Serbs that they lost Montenegro, that they are losing Kosovo, and they have to deliver Mladić. But I'm concerned about stability in the region. We are going to encourage the Serbs, so we can have results on the ground."

Moratinos was by now red and loud and making gyrations in our Latin way. He said Spain and the other countries did want to resume negotiations with Serbia. "Not without conditions," he assured me, "but Mladić's arrest cannot be a condition."

"I am sorry I made you angry," I apologized. Then, to be clear, I related the entire story of why the negotiations had been "disrupted" in the spring of 2006. I told him about Koštunica's repeated empty promises. I told Moratinos that Koštunica's word was worth nothing. I told him we had had no cooperation from Belgrade since just before NATO decided to invite Serbia into the Partnership for Peace.

Moratinos admitted that Spain had supported breaking off the negotiations with Belgrade in the spring of 2006.

"Nothing has changed since then," I said.

Moratinos shot back that Karadžić is the responsibility of Bosnia and Herzegovina, as if the Sarajevo government were responsible for the utter lack of cooperation of the Bosnian Serbs in the Republika Srpska's government. "Why don't you say there is no full cooperation with regard to Bosnia," Moratinos said. "This approach has not worked. We need to find an approach that gives results. It is a question of life or death for many people."

By now the conversation was extremely tense. I turned to my aide, Ruch, who could see I was angry. "Say something," I told him. And Ruch injected some argument I can't even recall just to calm things down.

Moratinos toed the Koštunica line about the suspension of Serbia's talks with the European Union, as if they had been intended to prejudice the outcome of Montenegro's independence referendum. Then Moratinos repeated his pledge: "We'll do everything we can so Serbia cooperates. We want effective cooperation. If we come to the end of talks and there is no Mladić, then we do not sign."

"Give me two months," I said, meaning two months after the formation of a new Serbian government.

"I give you three months," Moratinos said. "In three months, you'll come back to me and beg for my support."

By this time both of us were standing.

On the next day, February 14, we I received a phone call from Brussels with an invitation to a luncheon at the Palais D'Egmont with Belgium's foreign minister, Karel De Gucht. After a mix-up at the airport, the minister's car arrived and whisked us to an encounter with delicious shrimp, tournedos, and glasses of Chablis Premier Cru and a ten-year-old Bordeaux. The minister reported that Belgium and the Netherlands had fought hard at the European Union foreign ministers meeting to keep Spain, Italy, Austria, Hungary, and Slovenia—he referred to these countries as the "Habsburgs"—from convincing the others to issue a statement that stabilization and association negotiations would be resumed with Serbia without meaningful conditions. Instead, thanks to Belgium, the Netherlands, and others, the statement read that talks would be resumed only after Serbia had formed a new government and demonstrated a clear commitment to cooperate with the tribunal and to take concrete and effective action. This was a softening of the earlier position—no talks without complete cooperation, including apprehension of the fugitives—but it was not unconditional. "It was the best we could get," De Gucht said. "They were willing to let Serbia off with only a vague commitment. . . . If we abandon Mladić, it will have an impact on the entire region." Then De Gucht said that Belgium would remain firm about cooperation even if it stood alone and that he would send a letter to the German foreign minister, who was presiding over the ministerial meetings, to request that I be heard at the next foreign ministers meeting.

From Brussels we flew to Rome for a face-to-face on February 15 with Italy's foreign minister, Massimo D'Alema, another proponent of lifting the conditionality of resumption of the stabilization and association negotiation talks with Serbia. The reception was much friendlier in the homeland of the *muro di gomma* than it had been in Spain. I began by telling D'Alema that I was thankful he had received me, because it was becoming so difficult to find ministers who had time for me anymore: "I am afraid the European Union will make a decision to resume negotiations with Serbia without any conditions, because we enjoy no more cooperation on fugitives or on documents.

"I need a full month after the government is formed to get Mladić. What we need now is to reestablish contacts. Moratinos agreed to give me three months after the new government is formed."

"But," D'Alema said, "you know that everyone except Belgium and the Netherlands agrees with me that the talks should resume if there is progress. It is not about abandoning the tribunal. We want results. Suspension has failed. Everything is linked. Kosovo is linked. . . . Don't forget, Tadić thinks our formula is the best one, and don't forget that Djindjić paid the ultimate price for his collaboration with the tribunal. . . . A hostile attitude will not encourage cooperation. A hostile attitude will whip up nationalism. This might destabilize the entire region. . . .

"So we are in a very delicate phase, but in substance we are firm. Nothing will happen before the formation of a new government. Then we have to see the credibility of the new government and review the position of the European Union. We don't need public polemics. This will make the message more confused. . . . So we have to make an assessment together, because, if the Serbs have the impression that the prosecutor is isolated, then they will stop cooperating with you entirely. Nobody in Europe believes the Serbs should not cooperate. We have to create a climate of confidence. I might be wrong. But I am of good faith."

It was not clear to me just how it would be possible for the Belgrade authorities to cooperate less. "The status of Kosovo has nothing to do with the tribunal," I said. "I am concerned that we will never get Karadžić and Mladić. The tribunal is scheduled to close in 2010. They are playing for time. They were given a gift with the Partnership for Peace, and you are offering them another gift."

I was becoming incensed again. "My office should be the one to determine whether the new government is really cooperating," I said. "I must make the assessment. Maybe Tadić has the will to work with me. But you must give me the necessary time to make an assessment. . . . If you resume talks and Mladić is still at large, it will even make the work of the prosecution in Croatia and in Bosnia much more difficult."

"Of course," D'Alema said, "the tribunal must determine whether the actions are concrete."

"So," I asked, "you agree that I make an assessment before you decide, whether to reopen negotiations."

"Well, I agree only that you are consulted as to whether the actions of the Belgrade government are effective."

"I am expecting the new government to contact me," I said. "I am ready to say there is full cooperation if they involve me in the work."

In conclusion, D'Alema said it was a problem of political will. "If you are afraid they are going to wait out the tribunal, we'll be ready to extend the mandate beyond 2010." At this point, I knew there was no point in continuing. Only the United Nations Security Council could extend the tribunal's mandate beyond 2010. Italy was not a member. And Italy was certainly not going to provide the funds to prolong the tribunal's life by even a single day.

The Srebrenica trial was just over two months old by the autumn of 2006, when the United States had dropped conditionality for Serbia's entry into the Partnership for Peace and the European Union countries had begun to waffle about the conditionality for restarting negotiations on stabilization and association. By the last week of February 2007, the prosecution was still months away from finishing the presentation of its case against Popović and the other defendants, absent the fugitive Mladić and his assistant for intelligence and security, Tolimir. Thanks to two of the prosecution's witnesses, I received one more reminder of why, despite the apparently eroding support for the tribunal from the Western powers, I had to persevere to bring the remaining fugitives to justice.

Just a few yards from my office, a prosecution witness, a man whose name and identity were withheld to protect him from retaliation, was sitting in the stand behind a screen that hid his features from the spectators in the gallery. The witness had been a supply driver for the Bosnian Serb Army. He had delivered food and drink to units of soldiers at the time of the Srebrenica massacre. In the crucial portion of his testimony, he described witnessing an execution of Muslim boys and men trucked to a killing field already littered with the dead. Then a life-altering event occurred:

> In that heap, in that pile of dead bodies [that] did not resemble people any longer . . . just a pile of flesh in bits . . . a human being emerged. I say

a human being, but it was actually a boy of some five to six years. It is unbelievable. Unbelievable.

A human being came out and started moving towards the path, the path where men with automatic rifles stood doing their job. And this child was walking towards them. All of those soldiers and policemen there, these people who had [had] no trouble shooting . . . all of a sudden . . . lowered their rifles and all of them, to the last one, just froze. And it was just a child there . . . an innocent, sweet child . . . covered in bits of bowel tissue of other people. . . .

This officer . . . I'm sure he was lieutenant-colonel or colonel . . . And he was . . . the most arrogant person . . . turned to the men, the soldiers, and said, "What are you waiting for? Just finish him off." And then these very men who had no trouble killing people earlier, said to him, "Sir, you have a pistol yourself, so why don't you finish him off? Go ahead, because we can't do that." All of them . . . were simply speechless; then the officer said, "Take the child, put him on the truck, and take him down there; and then bring him here with the next batch and then he'll be finished off."

I was there. I was completely powerless. I was an outsider . . . a logistics person. . . . I had nothing to do with what was happening there. They were executing people, and my job was just to bring in supplies; and then they took the child, not the men who were finishing off the people, no. The others took the child by the hand. . . . [H]e was saying, "Bab[o]," this is how they call father. He was saying, "Bab[o], where are you?" The child was in shock. They took him to the truck. The child, knowing that he had been on that truck earlier, started convulsing. He was shaking and saying, "No, no. I'm not going to do it."

Then I intervened. . . . I told them, "Listen, I'll turn the lights on in my van, and I will put the music on so that I can divert his attention from all of this that's happening. I'll turn the radio on," because I wanted the child to come to his senses. He was completely lost, he didn't know what was happening and who he was. I said, "I will try to take him wherever you want me to take him." So I came into the van and I put the light on . . . and it helped the child because to him everything was just pure darkness. . . .

I said to him, "Come here, come here, come to me." I said, "Look. I have light on, music on." All of a sudden he took me by the hand and came to me. . . . I don't want any one of you to experience that.

I used to be a strong man. I used to be a firm man. That was my reputation. But I wouldn't wish this upon anyone to experience this—the grip, the grip of him on my hand, and I was amazed at his strength. The strength of this child. And then I—I got into the car, I—I left him alone for a second, just because I had to turn the car on, and I put the music on, and then we went back with the rest—you know who the rest were—so that the next batch could be finished off.

Just four days later, on February 26, 2007, the closed-circuit video monitor in my office was again beaming the proceedings in Courtroom 1. A young man was giving testimony in closed session: the young man who, as a seven-year-old boy, bloody, dusty, and covered with shit, had crawled up out of the pile of dead bodies and approached the executioners who had killed his father.

Sadly, as I sat in my office listening to his words, I could almost hear a collective sigh of relief and a burst of malicious laughter from the direction of Serbia. On that same morning, in their grand chambers in the Peace Palace just a kilometer from the Yugoslavia tribunal, the judges of the International Court of Justice, the United Nations' most powerful judicial body, had issued a decision in a lawsuit the Republic of Bosnia and Herzegovina had filed alleging that Serbia was complicit in the genocide in Bosnia and Herzegovina from 1992 to 1995 because, among other things, Slobodan Milošević had armed, financed, and encouraged Bosnian Serbs to conduct the ethnic cleansing campaign that had cost tens of thousands of lives and driven hundreds of thousands of people from their homes. The International Court of Justice announced that its judges had voted thirteen-to-two to clear Serbia of complicity in the genocide in Bosnia and Herzegovina, including the mass killings at Srebrenica. The majority had ruled that Serbia had "not committed genocide, through its organs or persons whose acts engage its responsibility under customary international law." In the decision, the court's president, Judge Rosalyn Higgins of the United Kingdom, wrote: "The court finds that the acts of genocide at Srebrenica cannot be attributed to [Serbia's] state organs." This ruling was binding and final. No appeal was possible.

I was dumbfounded. The truth, I knew, had not been served. From the spring of 2003 onward, the Office of the Prosecutor had obtained hundreds of secret documents, including minutes of wartime meetings of Yugoslavia's political and military leaders, that provided clear evidence of Serbia's role in the Bosnian war. Serbia had obtained the Yugoslavia tribunal's approval to keep sections of these records out of the public eye, and, more importantly, out of sight of the judges of the International

Court of Justice. These judges might have made a different decision had they pressed for access to the full Supreme Defense Council records. The court, however, did not subpoena the documents directly from Serbia. The lawyers presenting Bosnia's case had asked the court to request that Serbia provide an uncensored version of the documents; but the court had refused, saying that "extensive evidence" was available at the war crimes tribunal. The court's ruling acknowledged that the judges had not seen the protected portions of the Supreme Defense Council minutes. Two judges of the International Court of Justice wrote dissenting opinions criticizing this failure. The court's vice president, Awn Shawkat al-Khasawneh of Jordan, wrote in his opinion that "regrettably the court failed to act" and added: "It is a reasonable expectation that those documents would have shed light on the central questions." The other dissenting judge, Ahmed Mahiou of Algeria, wrote that the judges had several reasons, "none of them sufficiently convincing" for failing to request the documents; these reasons included a fear of creating the impression that the court was taking sides and fear that it might intrude on the sovereignty of a state or be embarrassed if Serbia refused. This situation, I thought, would be laughable, if it were not so tragic.

The Supreme Defense Council's minutes and other secret personnel files provide compelling evidence of Serbia's control and direction of the Serb war effort in Bosnia and Herzegovina. They detail how Belgrade financed and supplied the Serbs' war effort. They show how the Bosnian Serb army, though formally separate from the Yugoslav Army after 1992, was an appendage of the Yugoslav Army. The records show that Serbian forces, including secret police, played a role in the takeover of Srebrenica and in the preparation of the massacre there. I might be held in contempt for saying this. But the matter is so important to clarify.

In a second part of its ruling, the International Court of Justice found, by twelve votes to three, that Serbia had "violated the obligation to prevent genocide," which was linked with the Srebrenica massacre in 1995. Judge Higgins said it was clear to the authorities in Belgrade that there was a serious risk of a massive slaughter in Srebrenica. However, Serbia had not "shown that it took any initiative to prevent what happened or any action on its part to avert the atrocities which were being committed." The ruling said that Serbia's claim that it was powerless to prevent the massacres "hardly tallies with their known influence" over the Bosnian Serb army.

The court found that financial compensation for the failure to prevent genocide at Srebrenica was not the appropriate remedy. The court said the most appropriate form of satisfaction would be a declaration that Serbia had failed to comply with the obligation to prevent the crime of genocide.

My legal team and I sat down that afternoon to see whether there was anything in the decision of the International Court of Justice we could apply to our diplomatic effort to put more pressure on Belgrade to hand over our fugitive accused. The court had declared that Serbia was in violation of the Genocide Convention, making it the first state ever tarred by this brush, because it had failed to arrest and transfer Mladić and Karadžić to the Yugoslavia tribunal. This ruling provided us with powerful arguments to bring before the European Union countries: Do you really want to integrate a state that is in violation of the Genocide Convention? What about your values and principles? What about "never again"?

On February 27, 2007, I wrote Angela Merkel, chancellor of the Federal Republic of Germany, which was now occupying the European Union's presidency. My letter pointed out that the International Court of Justice had found that Serbia had failed to prevent the commission of genocide in Srebrenica and failed to punish the perpetrators, including Ratko Mladić. "As past experience has shown, only the steady pressure and clarity of the message of the European Union will make Serbia cooperate. For the sake of justice and the rule of law, it is of the utmost importance that the EU maintain the principled position it has taken and that the negotiations on a Stabilization and Association Agreement restart only after Serbia has arrested and transferred Ratko Mladić."

A polite reply arrived a week later.

During the last week of May 2007, months after its parliamentary elections, Serbia's political leaders finally managed to form a new government. At about this time, the Office of the Prosecutor sent two experienced human-rights and war-crimes investigators, Stefanie Frease and Vlatka Mihelić, to Belgrade to monitor this new government's efforts to bring the last of the fugitive accused into custody. The situation began to evolve.

On May 31, 2007, the number of the remaining fugitives dropped from six to five, when the authorities in the Republika Srpska finally made their first arrest. It did not require much effort on their part. It was Bulatović's team in Belgrade, and not the Bosnian Serbs, who had discovered the whereabouts of Zdravko Tolimir, the former number two to Ratko Mladić, in an apartment apparently next to the residence of one of Mladić's relatives. Tolimir had been the only person in the Bosnian Serb army who could dare to disagree openly with Mladić. He was apparently not corrupt and lived with the austere simplicity of an Orthodox monk. Mladić trusted him completely, and he had been the key to Mladić's protection network.

The Serbs have never provided me a reliable account of this arrest effort, mostly because Koštunica, despite all of his promises, remained averse to arresting war criminals and, for some reason I have never been able to fathom, wanted to maintain a fiction that Serbia had nothing to do with Tolimir's apprehension. We were aware that Tolimir was in ill health and that Bulatović's personnel were monitoring Tolimir's doctors and his wife. Perhaps this effort led to the discovery of his whereabouts. A Serbian special unit took Tolimir into custody after he had refused to surrender voluntarily. Bulatović apparently called the Republika Srpska's police and alerted them that Mladić or somebody close to him would be crossing the border from Serbia into Bosnia and Herzegovina. Bosnian Serb police units descended upon Bratunac, which sits beside the Drina River, the natural border between the two countries. The Serbian authorities then, apparently, transported Tolimir across the river, because Republika Srpska police encountered Tolimir walking alone down a road on the Bosnian side, near a village named Sopotnik. Tolimir refused to answer any questions as he was transported to the Republika Srpska's capital, Banja Luka, where the Bosnian Serb authorities handed him over to the European military force. Following a prearranged procedure, NATO flew him to The Hague. Tolimir did not complain while he was in the custody of the international military contingent in Bosnia; on the contrary, its commanders later told me that Tolimir was calm and discussed his philosophy of life and mind control. The Bosnian Serb authorities later told me they would never again participate in such a charade just so Koštunica could say that none of the tribunal's accused had been arrested on Serbian soil. (One Republika Srpska police official joked that the Serbian authorities were looking to the Republika Srpska as a place for dumping "nuclear waste.")

Tolimir's arrest caught me by surprise. It was a significant boost to morale at the tribunal and seemed to presage the capture of Mladić himself. Tolimir was irate during his first hearings before the Trial Chamber.

He ignored the judge's instructions. He did not stand. He removed the headset transmitting the simultaneous Serbo-Croatian translation of the proceedings so he would not have to listen to the court clerk read aloud the eight counts in the indictment charging him with genocide and other crimes stemming from the massacre at Srebrenica. Tolimir refused to enter a plea and demanded that the tribunal investigate his "unlawful arrest and kidnapping" by a "criminal group." In Tolimir's mind, I am sure, he felt he had been betrayed by fellow Serbs. I did not understand why Bulatović did not hold Tolimir in custody longer in order to interrogate him about Mladić's whereabouts.

I had for months been planning a long trip to Belgrade to coincide with the naming of a new government. I wanted to camp in the Hyatt, meet as many officials as possible, fill my schedule with interviews to demand the arrest of the tribunal's last fugitives, and, in this way, bring as much pressure as possible to bear on the Serbian government to honor its international obligations. The arrest of Tolimir, just days before my visit began on June 4, deprived me of much of the heat I had wanted to bring. The halls of government in Belgrade reverberated with the familiar refrain—"Serbia must fulfill all obligations towards the Yugoslavia tribunal as soon as possible"—but this time, the lips uttering the words belong to Serbian ministers, police chiefs, and secret service chiefs.

My first meeting in Belgrade on that Monday was with Koštunica. Despite some pleasing rhetoric, it was not a pleasant encounter. Koštunica assured me that Serbia's cooperation with the tribunal had entered a new phase. "This last leg of the process will now will be easier," he said, assuring me that the coordinators of Serbia's relations with the tribunal, Vladimir Vukčević and Rasim Ljajić, had done a splendid job effecting Tolimir's arrest. "Everything was sorted out in cooperation with the Republika Srpska," he bubbled. Then he said the arrest of Mladić and the other accused would have been accomplished a year earlier, if only I had given Olli Rehn a glowing recommendation of Serbia's cooperation with the tribunal and if the European Union had not cut off stabilization and association talks with Belgrade. "Everything," Koštunica said, "would have been resolved by now."

I thanked Koštunica for the arrest of Tolimir. I agreed with his assessment that the prospects were now good for more arrests and for Serbia to restart the talks with the European Union. But I still sensed that something was amiss. Koštunica continued to insist that Tolimir had been apprehended in the Republika Srpska, as if he did not know what I knew, or did know and assumed I would not care. I asked Koštunica why he had neglected to comment publicly on Tolimir's arrest, to let the Serbian public know how crucial it was for the accused to be brought to justice.

"It wasn't necessary," he said. "It was enough that it was done." He then launched into criticism of the tribunal, and even voiced support for Šešelj, the radical Serb nationalist, saying there had been tampering with witnesses against him. The witness-tampering complaints Koštunica was referring to were ridiculous, and nobody was taking them seriously, except, it seemed, the judge presiding over the Šešelj case, Jean Claude Antonetti of Corsica, whose monologues from the bench had already prompted the other two judges on the Šešelj case to distance themselves from him publicly.

"I must continue to insist on full cooperation," I said.

Koštunica then asserted that arresting Mladić would be more difficult for Serbia than arresting Gotovina had been for Croatia, because, Koštunica explained: "Mladić is not known to us. We've never met him. He is from Bosnia. His whereabouts are unknown."

"Mladić was here in Serbia and Belgrade with the full knowledge of the authorities," I replied. "Can we be sure you have the political will to resolve this issue?"

"On Mladić," Koštunica answered, "yes."

I was not at all sure. I had little reason for trust. The Serbian prime minister had just, after all, managed this gem: "Mladić is not known to us." And only a few hours later we learned more of the truth about the Tolimir arrest. It turned out that Vladimir Vukčević, Serbia's chief war crimes prosecutor, and Rasim Ljajić, Serbia's official responsible for relations with the tribunal, had known nothing about the Tolimir arrest operation, and Vukčević had even pondered resigning because he had been kept out of the decision-making loop. "We all sit together in the meetings, and Bulatović lies to us," Vukčević told me. "Why wasn't Tolimir properly arrested in Serbia to show full cooperation?" In the end, Vukčević resigned himself to the fact that, as he put it, "the color of the cat matters less than whether the cat catches mice." After Tolimir's arrest, I had no choice but to do the same.

I remained in Serbia for another four days, holding discussions with officials, trying to make sure Tolimir's arrest would not be the last. At the beginning of my talks with President Boris Tadić, I said I would deliver to the United Nations and the European Union a positive assessment of Serbia's cooperation, and told him Olli Rehn had already mentioned that Serbia would receive considerable European Union financial support. I also told Tadić that, whatever our opinion of Bulatović might have been, he had been the main figure behind Tolimir's arrest. Bulatović had produced results. We needed him to succeed again. "Bulatović can deliver Mladić," I told Tadić, "so let him do it. Let's think how to finish all this." Tadić sounded off, because, for many good reasons I appreciated, he did not trust Bulatović and, in the reshuffling of the government, was trying to replace him.

"You of all people are asking Bulatović to stay?" he said, asking me whether I had joined Koštunica's party.

I had little faith in Bulatović. I had made this plain to everyone, including Bulatović, a year before Tolimir's arrest. But the clock was ticking down. Bulatović's team had been responsible for apprehending Tolimir. The support from other Serbian ministries was improving. Even the famous personnel file of Ratko Mladić had been delivered, with the exception of one document, an assessment of his performance during the year of the Srebrenica massacre, 1995. The next task was to arrest Mladić and the others. There was no point in substituting the players on the field now, especially when everyone involved in the European Union's expansion process was watching Belgrade's every move. "The ball is in the hands of the services. We will assist them as much as we can."

"I want Mladić," I said. "Now."

Police in Republika Srpska soon raided the homes of two relatives of Stojan Župljanin. On June 15, Serbian police helicopters searched for Mladić near two Orthodox monasteries in a highland area west of Belgrade. And on the same day, the Serbian intelligence agency received information from the Office of the Prosecutor about one of Vlastimir Djordjević's mistresses. She had apparently been arrested for some minor customs violation and, during questioning, revealed Djordjević's whereabouts—not in Russia, as we had all supposed, but in a resort town on the Montenegrin seacoast. Djordjević had returned from Russia no later than 2003, as his passport was about to expire. He had obtained bogus documents in Serbia and lived at least part of the time under a provocative alias: Novica Karadžić. He subsequently had traveled back and forth to Belgrade and even stayed in the city's landmark Hotel Moskva. Familiar waiters did not know him. His wife did not recognize him on the street. He had been working in construction in Budva, a resort town on the Adriatic where my team and I had once spent a wonderful evening drinking wine and walking the stone streets. It has enjoyed a construction boom employing thousands of unregistered laborers, and Djordjević had been able to blend in among them.

The Montenegrin authorities, apparently, had no idea Djordjević was in their country, and did not believe Bulatović when he called to tell them. Sometime after midnight on June 16, a plane landed in Montenegro with a group of Serbian police and intelligence officers and tribunal investigators. After a day of stakeouts and planning, police units descended upon one apartment in Budva. Djordjević was not there. They proceeded to another location, in which Djordjević was living as a kind of caretaker. He was in the garden.

I had embarrassing questions for the Montenegrin authorities when I visited them three weeks later. "Karadžić," I told President Filip Vujanović. "Karadžić. . . . Djordjević was living under the alias Karadžić!" This was a slap in the face. "How did Djordjević manage to live in Montenegro unnoticed?"

Vujanović and the others explained that nobody had been searching for Djordjević seriously in Montenegro, because everyone assumed he had been hiding in Russia. Montenegro had not received any request for information about him, while there were requests and tips for almost all of the other fugitives. They explained that Djordjević had hidden in places where he had developed connections during his years in the police. He had resided only in Serb-owned apartments and houses. He had dealt only with the Serbian citizens.

"But the name: Karadžić? How is it possible to reside in Montenegro under this name for more than a year and not be registered? How many people with the name Karadžić live here?"

I asked Vujanović to see to it that cooperation between the Montenegrin and Serbian police was strengthened. He assured me that the authorities would cooperate and follow any leads.

"It would have been better if the real Karadžić had been arrested," Vujanović said. He stressed that the real Karadžić and Mladić had been the priority. He reminded me of how the Montenegrins had planted a trusted agent inside one Orthodox monastery to watch for Karadžić and how they had people watching for Karadžić during the funeral of his mother. Vujanović said the Montenegrin authorities would continue to apply as much pressure as possible upon members of Karadžić's family. They had imposed a travel ban on forty-six persons suspected of being involved in the support network for fugitives; these included members of the Karadžić family and Bishop Filaret of the Serbian Orthodox monastery at Mileševa. In the end, the Montenegrins invited me to take a vacation at the Tara National Park.

"Afterward," I thought. "Afterward."

The first time I ever encountered any of the thousands of women who had lost their husbands, fathers, and sons at Srebrenica was during one of my initial visits to Bosnia and Herzegovina, sometime before the fall of Slobodan Milošević. The leaders of the group Mothers of Srebrenica had sought me out. They demanded a meeting. A sizable crowd of them, several hundred at least, gathered before the entrance to the United Nations building in Sarajevo. The security guards were refusing to let them inside and informed me that I would only be allowed to meet two or three representatives. This would have been a disaster. I told the guards that if they did not let all of the women inside, then I would go outside myself, alone. Only then did they organize a conference room. I made a point of shaking hands with each of the women on their way into the room. I was able to feel their calloused hands. I could see their threadbare clothes. I could smell the miserable conditions in which they were living. I fully expected them to complain about material things, about squalid housing, lack of food, inability to find work. Many of them spoke, and I did not want to stop them from speaking, and the only thing they spoke about was justice: "You represent justice," one of them said. "You must bring Milošević to The Hague." You cannot imagine how shrunken I felt, a symbol of the international community's failure to deliver justice.

The next time I met the women of Srebrenica was during the anniversary memorial on July 11, 2001. The Krstić trial was going on. Many of the women had shown up to bury loved ones whose remains were among the six hundred or so identified during the past year. When I entered the cemetery, a raucous chorus of female voices spoke up loudly in Serbo-Croatian. I understood not a word. But I recognized the guttural sound of frustration when I heard it. By then, Milošević had been arrested. But now the women were angry that the tribunal had not apprehended Karadžić and

Mladić. I could do nothing except speak up. "Why are you so loud?" I said. "We are gathered in a cemetery. Let us pray." I placed my palms together like a good Catholic girl at prayer. "Let us pray for those buried here and for the missing." The women went silent. They opened their arms in the Muslim way and prayed, and I spread my arms, too. Together, we stood there. One would pray aloud, then another, and another, and another.

After boycotting the tenth anniversary in 2005, I had returned to Srebrenica on July 11, 2006. I was practically alone with the Muslim clerics. The women were on bended knee. But they had given me a chair, and I remained there, the only one sitting, while the throng of kneeling Muslims bent forward, touched their foreheads to the ground, and rose up. It was not particularly comfortable, being the only one there not kneeling and bowing in Muslim prayer, but I felt honored. Then, before my final visit to Srebrenica, on July 11, 2007, the Mothers of Srebrenica announced publicly that I would not be welcome at the annual memorial ceremony because Karadžić and Mladić had not been arrested. I told them I would attend anyway, and my aides and I made a two-hour drive from Sarajevo on that rainy, overcast morning. The road into Srebrenica is narrow, and it was crowded with thousands of people who had lost many reasons for living and still wore on their shoulders the signs of the poverty in which the war had left them. My team and I walked uneasily behind our security guards and eventually made our way through the crowd and into a VIP reception room. I exchanged greetings with the ambassador of Germany. Then the spiritual head of Bosnia's Muslim community, Reis-ul-Ulema Mustafa Cerić, approached. He took my hand. He welcomed me warmly, clearly knowing that the Mothers of Srebrenica had not wanted me to be there. "I am happy to see you," he said. Cerić was very warm. He has always been a supporter of the tribunal, regardless of how the popular winds blow in Bosnia. He has always spoken up for holding leaders accountable. I felt more relaxed. Then he smiled. "Rasim Delić," he said, naming one of our accused, the former commander of Bosnia's army. "He is innocent." He was still grinning, and I smiled back.

"No," I said, "he is not."

He held my hand a few minutes more. He shared a few more pleasantries. Then he told me again: "Delić . . . he is innocent."

"No," I said, "he is not." It was almost tragicomic, but the Reis's welcome was important to me, and much appreciated, because he had made sure everyone had seen it.

The Muslims were burying the remains of 435 more Srebrenica victims that day, and they gave me a white headscarf to wear during their prayers. It was heartbreaking to see the long rows of coffins covered in green shrouds and to watch as members of the families approach loved ones they had waited twelve years to bury. After the prayers, I returned to the reception area. The leaders of the Mothers of Srebrenica were there, along with representatives of other groups of Srebrenica women, and members of the press. "I have come to speak with you as a private person, and not as the prosecutor," said Munira Šubašić, the chairwoman of Mothers of Srebrenica. The conversation soon became heated. "You told us they were going to be arrested last year, and you lied," she said.

"No, I did not lie," I said. "I told you I had been informed in Belgrade that they were going to be handed over."

"Then you are naive."

It was an absurd situation, and a sad illustration of how frustration, pain, and despair grind down the soul. I do not enjoy being called a liar; I am anything but naive; and I did not appreciate the fact that I had become a kind of scapegoat for these angry victims. But I understand the pain, and feel something of their frustration. Within a few minutes, the Bosnians were arguing with each other. Some believed I had made a deal with Zoran Djindjić not to arrest Mladić. Some believed that there was a secret agreement to allow the government in Belgrade not to disclose the Supreme Defense Council minutes. My aides and I tried to explain to them that there had been no deals. Perhaps some of them still trusted us. The group was quarreling among themselves when I left to catch the airplane.

The last four of the 161 persons the tribunal had indicted—Mladić, Karadžić, Župljanin, and Hadžić—remained at large into the fading days of my eight years in The Hague. A sense of failure loomed larger as the end of my mandate, December 2007, approached.

In the late summer of 2007, there were encouraging signs that Mladić's arrest was close. Bulatović told us the Serbian authorities were tracking eleven doctors, including a certain Doder, and monitoring cell phone traffic. Searches were conducted on locations in and around Belgrade, and as these operations were taking place, agents were keeping watch on Mladić's relatives and known supporters to see whether they would stir. There was no discernible reaction. The support network had apparently shrunk as the authorities offered its known members incentives and brandished before them threats of legal action. It would have been difficult to imagine that Djogo, Ristić, the doctors, and the others contacted by the intelligence services and the police would be reckless enough to approach Mladić.

Karadžić had disappeared, apparently somewhere in his ancestral highlands along the border between Bosnia and Montenegro. Nothing had come from the arrest of his son, Saša, which had even prompted a public plea from Karadžić's wife, Ljilja, for her Radovan to surrender. The family's bank accounts were frozen, but the Karadžić clan clearly had plenty of money; one search of the family home in Pale turned up 20,000 euros, which apparently represented part of the royalties from Karadžić's published books. We continued to receive reports that he was moving in and out of Montenegro. We heard about a hideout in a town named Priboj, just downriver from Mileševa, the home monastery of Bishop Filaret. I recalled that, three years earlier, there had been an offer to deliver Karadžić dead, not alive, for $5 million, something sought by no one except, perhaps, the local police who felt they were carrying him like a five-million-pound yoke around their necks.

Župljanin left a broad track that led nowhere. We received tips that he had shown up in Herceg Novi, on the Montenegrin coast. His wife and son were taken into custody. Pressure was being placed upon his sister-in-law and a lover, one of eight mistresses we had heard of, to convince him to surrender. Then we heard he might be in Moscow.

Hadžić, we were assured time and again, was soon to surrender, because he was almost out of money. But there were indications that he had fled from Serbia into Romania and talk that he might be hiding in Belarus. How much money does someone need to survive with delusions of grandeur in Belarus?

My wait would continue, until it ended, and passed to my successor. There is a strange vacuum that descends over the soul with such a failure after eight years of struggle and wildly oscillating expectations. The northern sun leaves the same emptiness when it sets so quickly on afternoons in late December. The winter winds blow across the dark, vacant fairways of the Netherlands and against the bare prison walls in Scheveningen and draw a cover of gray between the sodden dunes and the stars. For me, there is no way to ply wise words to cushion the disappointment and sense of anticlimax, because the simple fact of failure is the simple fact of failure, and because, at least for these four fugitives, two of them accused of genocide, my nemesis, impunity, seemed to have defeated my efforts to defeat it. I could almost hear the laughter coming from a Serbia that might, even after all the lies of its leaders, even after troops acting in its name left the thousands of rotting corpses at Srebrenica, be welcomed into the European Union, as if the sound did not bounce with a hollow thud from the *muro di gomma* stretching from Brussels to London to Paris to Rome to Washington and on to New York, as if all the rest of us had forgotten.

I have heard respected legal scholars argue that peace must take hold in war-torn lands before justice can be dispensed, that international justice cannot function while bullets and shrapnel are flying, while refugees are on the move, while prisoners are being seized, ligatures tightened, orders to fire shouted, and mounds of dirt piled atop twisted corpses. I have also heard diplomats argue that peace takes priority over justice, that no peace deal can be engineered without leaders from at least one side obtaining assurances that they will not be prosecuted.

I disagree.

International justice institutions can, I believe, begin to function and even begin to make a constructive impact before peace is achieved. The Yugoslavia tribunal demonstrated this. The United Nations Security Council established the Yugoslavia tribunal while war crimes were still being committed in Bosnia and Herzegovina. I am confident that with a more robust assertion of its authority during its tenuous early years, the tribunal would have had a greater deterrent effect and dampened violence against civilians. President Tudjman, in his presidential transcripts, insisted time and again that Croatia's backing for the Bosnian Croat militia and the Croatian army's military intervention in Bosnia and Herzegovina had to be kept secret, in part because he feared Croatia would, like Serbia and Montenegro, suffer economic sanctions and, I am sure, in part because he did not want to be held accountable for war crimes. In the autumn of 1993, the commander of a Bosnian Croat detention camp took time to write a report expressing concern that the prisoners' wretched living conditions were making him and others liable to prosecution. Ratko Mladić, in June 1995, a month before the Srebrenica massacre, expressed concern to United Nations officials that he not be considered a war criminal; so he recognized the tribunal as a threat, but the deterrent was insufficient. In 1999, Milošević understood the legal risks he was assuming when he had the Serbian police and Yugoslav Army drive the Albanians from Kosovo; why else would he have had his police exhume the bodies of Albanian victims, pack them into refrigerator trucks, and rebury them in unmarked mass graves inside the perimeter of an airbase near Belgrade? And how many more NATO bombs would have gone awry if Louise Arbour had not issued an explicit warning and the alliance's leaders had not had to worry about being hauled before the tribunal for failing to take adequate precautionary measures to protect civilians and to identify legitimate military targets? Imagine how much deeper the Yugoslavia tribunal's deterrent impact would have been if it had not come first, if international tribunals had already demonstrated that political and military leaders could be held accountable.

No, justice does not always have to wait for peace, and justice should not always wait for peace. The signatory nations of the Rome Statute knew this. They created the International Criminal Court to act as a deterrent to future war crimes. With a more robust assertion of will, it can sway political and military figures in the future from making the kinds of decisions that Pol Pot made in Cambodia, the *génocidaires'* leaders made in Rwanda, the militia commanders made in Sierra Leone, and Saddam Hussein and others made in Iraq—all believing they enjoyed impunity.

In every conflict area, political leaders, diplomats, military commanders, intelligence chiefs, and pundits will come up with compelling reasons to sidetrack the work of institutions of international justice. There will always be some initiative that, the diplomats will argue, must come first. There will always be pragmatic arguments to rationalize the failure, and sometimes the explicit refusal, of a country or its leaders to cooperate with a prosecutorial and judicial effort to end the culture of impunity. Pressing for cooperation with an international criminal tribunal or court will always seem to threaten some reconstruction program, some approaching election, some debate on a new constitution, some crucial economic or foreign policy decision. But peacemaking and nation-building efforts will neither make peace nor build nations unless they include, from their inception, a justice component to prosecute the worst violators of international humanitarian law on all sides, to end the culture of impunity, to make it clear to everyone that no one is above the law. Peacemaking with no justice component practically ensures future conflict. It allows diplomats to negotiate peace agreements at the cost of leaving in place powerful political leaders and military men to further poison societal relations. This almost happened with Milošević during the NATO bombing of 1999. This almost happened, with United Nations backing, in Kosovo. This has happened in Rwanda.

As time passes and weaponry becomes more lethal and less expensive, allowing impunity to win out and allowing bitter living memories of injustices to infect entire societies and entire cultural and religious groups will jeopardize the well-being of almost everyone everywhere. We must proceed on the assumption that there is no inopportune time to begin to amass evidence and recruit witnesses, to bring indictments, to make arrests, and, if cases are sustained, to issue judgments against perpetrators *on all sides* of a given conflict.

The International Criminal Tribunal for the former Yugoslavia and the International Criminal Tribunal for Rwanda were flawed from the moment they sprang from the collective will of the United Nations Security Council's members. Flaws were unavoidable in these justice institutions that had no precedent, that gathered staff from diverse cultures, combined sometimes incompatible legal traditions, and lacked so many of the basic powers national criminal justice systems normally possess. But, despite these flaws, and despite some failures, the two tribunals produced significant successes.

From its founding until the day of my departure at the end of 2007, the Yugoslavia tribunal indicted 161 individuals from all sides of the conflicts that marred the lands of the former Yugoslavia during the 1990s. I signed sixty-two war crimes indictments and, from the beginning of my mandate until mid-August 2007, ninety-one accused had been taken into custody.

The Yugoslavia tribunal inspired the establishment of the Rwanda tribunal, the special war crimes tribunals or chambers for Sierra Leone, East Timor, Cambodia, and Lebanon, and the permanent International Criminal Court. It also fostered the development of domestic war crimes courts in Bosnia, Croatia, Serbia, and Kosovo to try mid- and lower-level accused. As a result of its efforts to acquire evidence to underpin sound indictments, proceedings, and judgments, the Yugoslavia tribunal collected millions of pieces of evidence, including hundreds of thousands of documents submitted as exhibits; this record, if historians, writers, and journalists do their jobs effectively, will make it difficult for future demagogues in Croatia, Serbia, Bosnia and Herzegovina, Macedonia, and Kosovo to foment interethnic hysteria. Thanks to the tribunal's work, no one group in the lands of the former Yugoslavia can proclaim itself a victim and nothing else. No one group can point to their onetime leaders and claim they were faultless. Without the tribunal, it is hard to believe that Serbia's public would have ever viewed the Scorpions video or learned the details of the Srebrenica massacre and the names of its perpetrators, it is hard to believe that the Croatian public would ever have been able to read transcripts of their president and the high-ranking members of their government making the decisions to partake in the dismemberment of Bosnia and Herzegovina along with the transfers of populations. The Serbian authorities should summon the courage to release to the public the Supreme Defense Council minutes so Serbs everywhere can see once and for all exactly how Milošević and members of the Belgrade government and military participated in the war in Bosnia and Herzegovina and see for themselves whether this amounted to participation in the act of genocide committed in their names at Srebrenica.

Despite the best efforts of the prosecution team, the Rwanda tribunal will probably not be able to break the cycle of impunity that has marred Rwanda's history and brought its people untold suffering. The primary cause of this was the decision making of the United Nations Security Council, and especially the United States and Great Britain. Where is the investigation of the alleged killings committed by the Tutsi militia, the Rwandan Patriotic Front, whose members now belong to Rwanda's government and military? What justice have the innocent Hutu victims received? What does this bode for the future of Rwanda and Central Africa?

Despite this failure, the Rwanda tribunal made significant headway in delivering justice for victims of the genocide. By the time the Rwanda tribunal closes, it will have tried more than sixty high-level *génocidaires*. It pursued its cases against defendants ranging from Théoneste Bagosora, the alleged mastermind of the genocide, to Simon Bikindi, the popular musician whose songs allegedly incited *génocidaires* to kill. The tribunal will have obtained convictions against a former prime minister, military and political leaders, business leaders, and members of the press and clergy.

The Rwanda tribunal considered the Hutus' rape crimes so heinous that it established a worldwide legal precedent recognizing the use of rape as a weapon of war, a form of torture, a crime against humanity, a means of persecution, and an instrument of genocide.

The Yugoslavia tribunal and the Rwanda tribunal had to fulfill their missions in a finite period for a relatively nominal cost that was, nevertheless, an object of ceaseless complaining by United Nations member states as well as United Nations administrators. Compared with the astronomical expense of the developed world's habitual responses to large-scale security crises—humanitarian aid, military intervention, peacekeeping missions, territorial partition, and reconstruction and development efforts—the tribunals did valuable work for a minimal outlay. They also yielded many valuable lessons learned, of which the following are only a few:

- Prosecutors must remain objective in the face of horrendous crimes that tear at the emotions and generate tremendous pressure to hold someone, anyone accountable. Despite the cries of the victims and international appeals for justice, prosecutors must ensure that the rights of the accused are respected. Proper structures and mechanisms within a tribunal's prosecution office must be in place in advance to ensure the ability to disclose exculpatory material to an accused and his or her counsel. Tribunals, from their inception, must have a fully functioning and operational defense counsel unit; sufficient funding, if necessary, for timely translation of relevant documents into the language of the accused; and a proper assessment made of the competency of defense counsel and assessment of whether defense counsel are actually representing their client and not just defending the interests of the entity, state, or ethnic group of the accused.

- Resolutions and other instruments establishing future tribunals must explicitly mandate the prosecution to target the highest-ranking and the most notorious mid-ranking perpetrators. Tribunals must move at speed to direct investigative and prosecutorial efforts against high-ranking accused, and the prosecutorial machinery must be staffed and organized to produce indictments against leadership targets and proceed against lower-ranking individuals only when there is a reasonable likelihood that their prosecution will yield evidence leading to the indictment and conviction of the highest-ranking suspects or when the acts of the lower-ranking individuals are alleged to have been so notorious that their prosecution will have an impact on reconciliation and stability in a given locality or region.

The prosecution of other mid- and lower-ranking accused should be left to domestic, community, or tribal courts. It is not always the highest-ranking perpetrators who carry the most meaning for the victims; one of our witnesses told investigators she was most interested in seeing justice meted out to a neighbor she saw each week at the town market, a man who, she alleged, had killed members of her family.

• Significant differences between the civil law and common law approaches to criminal prosecution must be reconciled, particularly when it comes to procedure.

• Gender-related crimes must be investigated rigorously and professionally, and appropriately indicted and tried.

• Leadership indictments, almost without exception, will be complex instruments. But they must, within the bounds of the law, be kept as simple as possible even as the charges reflect the most serious crimes alleged; "Al Capone–style" tax-evasion indictments are ineffective in breaking the culture of impunity.

• In future tribunals, the trial chamber, and not just the prosecutor, must take firmer and more vocal stands to compel uncooperative governments to hand over all evidence necessary to make informed findings of fact and judgments. If a tribunal does not possess the authority to make arrests, transfer the accused, and enforce subpoenas, then the tribunal must have effective means to compel reluctant national governments to perform these functions. When it came to the Yugoslavia and Rwanda tribunals, the United Nations Security Council failed utterly to take effective action to give teeth to the tribunals' demands for cooperation by uncooperative states, and it would be folly to believe it ever will for future tribunals. Perhaps, in drafting resolutions creating future tribunals, the Security Council should include a basket of preapproved adjustable, Chapter 7–supported sanctions mechanisms for the trial chamber to apply, at its discretion, subsequent to a judicial finding that an individual state is not fully cooperating with the tribunal in good faith.

• Early in their mandates, prosecutors must establish tracking units, with arrest powers, to locate fugitive accused and bring them into custody.

• The United Nations, its member states, and international organizations that invest significant funds and other resources in international tribunals must also assist in the location and apprehension of fugitive accused. A tribunal cannot be left in the dark during efforts by friendly intelligence agencies involved in the process of tracking and arresting fugitive accused, because, otherwise, there is no guarantee that these efforts will be coordinated or produce concrete results.

• Insider witnesses often change their stories when they take the stand and face their old political taskmasters; when dealing with insider witnesses, the tribunal's rules should not bar the prosecution from cross-examining its own insider witnesses and treating them, if necessary, as hostile witnesses.

• The experience of Kosovo has demonstrated that a United Nations tribunal's authority should take precedence over that of United Nations political, peacekeeping, humanitarian, and development efforts.

• In conflict situations where a war crimes tribunal is being created, the body establishing a relevant tribunal should let a period of significant duration immediately after the conflict's end fall within the tribunal's temporal jurisdiction, because, during the immediate aftermath of conflict, reprisal killings and abductions are common and may involve high-ranking individuals who believe they are acting with impunity.

• War crimes trials of high-level leadership figures are complex and time-consuming; if the international community is serious about supporting international justice, it should be prepared to exercise patience and to provide adequate funding. By imposing unrealistic time constraints on the lifetime of the tribunals, the United Nations Security Council effectively interfered by default in how the tribunals meted out justice.

• Cases should not be rushed to trial. Judges should resist public pressure to bring high-profile cases to trial before the cases are fully trial-ready and take steps to explain to the public the ultimate benefits and the necessity of not prematurely commencing a trial. Much time and effort would have been saved had the three indictments against Slobodan Milošević really been consolidated.

• The Trial Chamber of the Yugoslavia tribunal wasted an inordinate amount of time by requiring that the prosecution prove time and again that an armed conflict had occurred in Bosnia and Herzegovina. A period of pretrial management would allow courts to eliminate issues that are not contentious and to further narrow the issues for which direct oral testimony is required.

• Like many people who have attempted to limit the tribunals' lifetime and reduce costs, tribunal judges have placed time constraints upon the prosecution, and too often they have done this in an seemingly whimsical manner with no apparent appreciation for the time, money, and labor expended before the cases have appeared for trial. A tribunal's trial chamber should refrain from unilaterally shrinking complex leadership cases; judicial decisions to remove one or several counts artificially may seriously undermine cases against high-ranking individuals. Certain charges, such as persecution, can be used, however, to capture a vast array of criminal activity within one count, reducing the need for an excessive number of charges.

• A properly functioning scheduling committee, which sets, well in advance, hearing dates for trials that judges cannot change without consulting the parties, enhances the efficiency of any court. Tribunals should have properly functioning scheduling committees.

• Independence of the prosecutor entails independence of purse strings; no registrar should have control over the funding of an office of the prosecutor. A full public auditing of accounts should be a fundamental element of the basic documents under which a tribunal functions.

• Far greater effort should be made to give victims more ownership over the process and to give their needs and wishes greater consideration. In my opinion, victims should even be represented in the courtroom. Tribunals should recognize the importance of making their proceedings meaningful to the communities most affected by the war crimes. The public should be forewarned not to develop unrealistic expectations. Participating in the judicial process does not always lead to "healing" or "closure," and for these effects there might be more thought given to complementary reparation and truth-and-reconciliation measures and other means to help victims get on with their lives. An effective outreach program is crucial to a tribunal's success, and outreach programs must take into account the culture, language, and expectations of the people whom the tribunal affects, on all sides of a conflict. A tribunal should hold trials as close to the conflict area as possible.

• Tribunals must pay particular attention to protecting witnesses, and especially insider witnesses. United Nations tribunals should be able to draw upon the resources of other United Nations entities active in post-conflict areas.

• Efforts must be made to ensure the recruitment of more competent and more experienced judges. The quality of judges might be improved if state governments nominating persons to act as tribunal judges were required to secure recommendations or approval of candidates from local judicial or lawyers' associations. With all due respect to many international justice advocates, tribunals need more experienced criminal judges and fewer legal scholars. Training and legal-education programs for all judges and staff must take place at all stages of the process.

• Tribunals should consider hiring more attorneys who have experience organizing and managing large, complex cases, and even class-action civil suits, and pairing them with attorneys who have experience in criminal prosecutions and expertise in interviewing victims.

• As cherished as the principle of mounting one's own defense may be in common law jurisdictions, allowing a leadership figure to mount his or her own defense in a war crimes tribunal allows such a defendant too broad an opportunity to turn the dock into a bully pulpit and the trial into a political circus. The trial chamber must appoint counsel for defendants who do not retain their own. If the defendant thinks his or her rights are being violated, let the trial chamber involved allow the defendant to submit written comments and questions on a witness-by-witness, argument-by-argument, exhibit-by-exhibit basis, to the trial chamber and appeals chamber. After witnessing how Milošević mounted his own "defense," and after suffering through the antics of Vojislav Šešelj, we know better than ever that an effective defense is crucial for fairness, for a tribunal's credibility, for the credibility of the record the tribunal creates, and, most importantly, for the victims.

• A tribunal's judges should establish sentencing guidelines and, in articulating these guidelines, keep in mind the gravity of the crimes. Wrist-slaps in cases involving mass killing and even genocide do nothing to defeat the culture of impunity, do nothing to create any deterrent effect, and certainly do little to satisfy the victims, many of whom risk their lives to testify against powerful and often ruthless individuals who are subsequently released.

• In instances where accused persons admit their responsibility for crimes and where the judges are satisfied that the evidence supports their responsibility, the resulting guilty pleas can, as the plea of Momir Nikolić demonstrated, have important conciliatory and historical functions.

I am, to this day, more snake hunter than legal scholar. After a quarter century in prosecution, my eyes see more black and white than shades of gray, and I consider this an asset. I make no apologies for being assertive or for speaking my mind.

I certainly could have done my job better, and, looking back, I would have done some things differently. I should have acted more quickly to reassign or dismiss some incompetent attorneys. I should have found the time to become more of a presence on the hallways of the Office of the Prosecutor; I underestimated the value this would have had for morale. I resented the time pressure the completion strategy placed upon the prosecution teams to produce now-or-never indictments where the alternative was to allow impunity to reign. I sometimes lamented not being able to run the Office of the Prosecutor like a real law office, and not under the United Nations personnel rules, which apply so many restrictions and procedures that they detract from performance. Tribunal prosecutors in the future should have a freer rein on recruiting and hiring the best talent. And those persons who choose tribunal prosecutors in the future should understand that longevity in office is crucial, because the job of prosecutor involves so many dimensions and it requires significant time to master them all.

What I have learned, what I have tried to illustrate in this memoir's depictions of successes and failures of my team and me, is that defeating the culture that allows powerful persons, from the *capo dei capi* of the Mafia to military and political leaders, to commit any outrage and not be held accountable is a matter of will that often demands impatience more than patience, a matter of enlisting support, a matter of applying leverage, a matter of taking risks, correcting mistakes, breaking through the *muro di gomma*, ignoring criticism and threats, and, sometimes, suffering the loss of friends and collaborators. Prosecuting war crimes is not some risk-free intellectual game. The past two centuries have demonstrated that human beings are capable of asserting their will to pack millions of children, along with their parents and grandparents and siblings, into gas chambers and ovens, to machete hundreds of thousands of people, to torture and execute prisoners, to surround and bombard entire cities while television cameras broadcast the act itself, to use mass rape and sexual slavery as weapons of war and terror, to expel entire populations from their ancestral homelands. These bloody centuries have shown that victims are extraordinarily courageous, strong, and resilient and that they deserve justice for the crimes so needlessly and ruthlessly committed against them. These centuries have also shown that in too many instances diplomats, world leaders, military officers, intelligence chiefs, bankers and businessmen, and even United Nations officials are willing to regard such criminals as legitimate interlocutors and partners. If the victims of crimes this massive are ever to see justice done and if human society is ever to reduce the instances of criminal violence this massive, the risks to be assumed, the countervailing will to be asserted, and the work to be done must outstrip the risks assumed, the willpower asserted, and efforts made by the worst among us, by those who would have us believe they are above the law.

ACKNOWLEDGMENTS

Any prosecutorial effort requires a team, and my personal efforts would have yielded little had it not been for my advisers and the Office of the Prosecutor's staff of attorneys, analysts, investigators, language assistants, clerical and evidence specialists, and computer technicians, whose names are too numerous to list. I am thankful to all of them. For their assistance on this memoir I am especially indebted to Norman Farrell, whose patience, legal expertise, sound judgment, and editorial suggestions lifted significant portions of the manuscript onto a much higher plane than I ever would have attained alone, and to my editors Raffaele Scelsi and Carlo Feltrinelli. I am also indebted to Jean-Jacques Joris, Jean-Daniel Ruch, Laurent Walpen, and Dominique Reymond of Switzerland; Diana Dicklich, Yves Roy, and Alexandra Milenov of Canada; Anton Nikiforov of Russia; Milbert Shin, Dermot Groome, Mark Harmon, Ken Scott, Clint Williamson, Moya Magilligan, Peter McCloskey, Stephen Rapp, and Bill Tomljanovich of the United States; Andrew Cayley of the United Kingdom; Florence Hartmann, Patrick Lopez-Terres, Cécile Aptel, and, my personal assistant, Christine Bosman of France; Ljiljana Pitesa and Sanja Bokulić of Croatia; Olga Kavran, Julija Bogoeva, and Ljiljana Todorović-Sudetic of Serbia; Michael Hehn of Germany; and for the original *muro di gomma*, Matteo Costi of Italy. Several persons and organizations provided comments, translation assistance, and factual input, including Sabina Zanetta, Laura Silber, Barbara Šurk, Michael Kaufman, Sara and Azra Sudetic, and Jacques Rossier; Nataša Kandić of the Humanitarian Law Fund; Alison Des Forges of Human Rights Watch; the Institute for War and Peace Reporting and James Lyons and the International Crisis Group for their reporting on the political situation in Serbia; Mirko Klarin of Sense; Nina Bang-Jensen and, title-master, Edgar Chen of the Coalition for International Justice; Hirondelle for the news of the Rwanda Tribunal; and Anton, Maartje, and the kind staff of Cafe Room, Den Haag, for maintaining the constant stream of cappuccinos that helped bring the manuscript in on deadline. Finally, special thanks must go to those persons who shared ideas and commentary on the lessons learned: Judith Armatta of the Coalition for International Justice, who generously shared ideas from her own book on the Milošević trial; Gary Bass of Princeton University; Peggy Kuo, whose departure for Wall Street was a loss for the Yugoslavia tribunal; Diane Orentlicher and Kelly Askin of the Open Society Justice Initiative; and, again, Norman Farrell and Ken Scott of the tribunal's staff. While I am grateful to all of the above for providing me advice and suggestions, the views and opinions expressed in this book are solely my own.

APPENDIX A · MAPS

The former Yugoslavia
Bosnia and Herzegovina
Kosovo Region
Rwanda

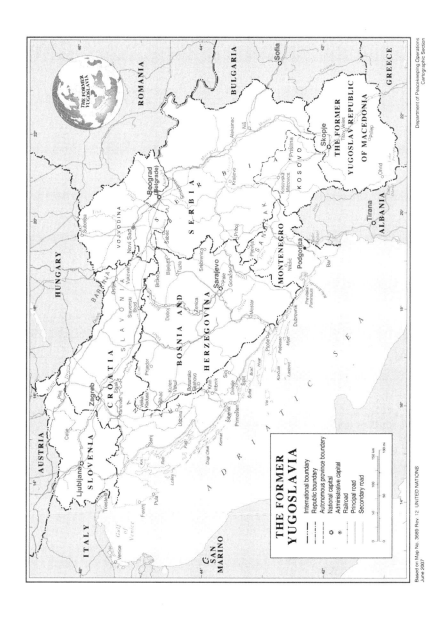

THE FORMER YUGOSLAVIA

International boundary
Republic boundary
Autonomous province boundary
National capital
Administrative capital
Railroad
Principal road
Secondary road

Department of Peacekeeping Operations Cartographic Section

Based on Map No. 3689 Rev. 12 UNITED NATIONS
June 2007

KOSOVO REGION

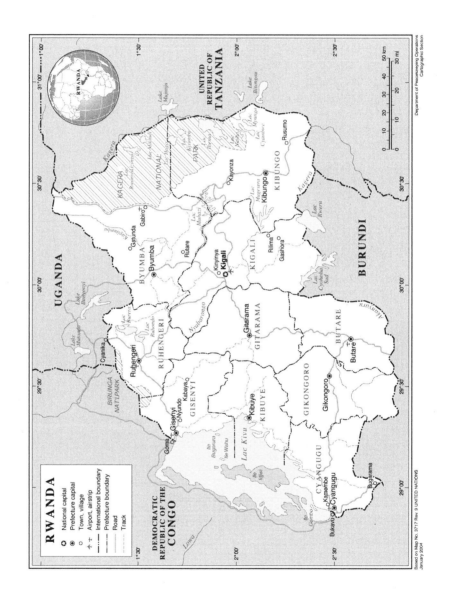

TABLE OF INDICTEES, RWANDA

RELIGIOUS FIGURES	Emmanuel Rukundo Samuel Musabyimana Athanase Seromba Julienne Kisito Gertrude Mukangango
MEDIA FIGURES	Ferdinand Nahimana Hassan Ngeze Georges Ruggio
POLITICIANS	Emmanuel Ndindabahizi Eliezer Niyitegeka
BUSINESSMEN	Félicien Kabuga
INTELLECTUALS	Jean-Bosco Barayagwiza
CULTURAL LEADERS	Simon Bikindi (musician)
MILITARY LEADERS	Théoneste Bagosora

TABLE OF INDICTEES, FORMER YUGOSLAVIA

	SERBS	CROATS	OTHERS
CROATIA (GENERAL)	Slobodan Milošević, Vojislav Šešelj, Frenki Simatović, Jovica Stanišić	Janko Bobetko	
CROATIA (WESTERN)	Milan Martić, Milan Babić, Vladimir Kovačević	Ante Gotovina, Mladen Markač, Ivan Čermak	
CROATIA (EASTERN)	Goran Hadžić, Željko Ražnatović Arkan		
VUKOVAR	Mile Mrkšić, Miroslav Radić, Veselin Šljivančanin		
BOSNIA (GENERAL)	Slobodan Milošević, Ratko Mladić, Radovan Karadžić, Momčilo Krajišnik, Biljana Plavšić, Momčilo Perišić, Vojislav Šešelj, Frenki Simatović, Jovica Stanišić, Mičo Stanišić, Savo Todović		Rasim Delić
BOSNIA (NORTHERN)	Dušan Knezević, Željko Mejakić, Blagoje Simić, Duško Tadić, Stojan Župljanin, Dragan Zelenović		
BOSNIA (CENTRAL)		Tihomir Blaškić, Dario Kordić, Ivica Rajić	
BOSNIA (EASTERN)	Gojko Janković, Milan Lukić, Sredoje Lukić, Željko Ražnatović Arkan		
SREBRENICA	Ljubiša Beara, Ljubomir Borovčanin, Radoslav Krstić, Radivoje Miletić, Drago Nikolić, Vinko Pandurović, Vujadin Popović, Zdravko Tolimir		
SARAJEVO	Dragomir Milošević		
HERZEGOVINA (AND CENTRAL BOSNIA)		Jadranko Prlić, Slobodan Praljak, Milivoj Petković, Berislav Pušić, Bruno Stojić, Valentin Ćorić	Ramush Haradinaj
KOSOVO	Slobodan Milošević, Vlastimir Djordjević, Sreten Lukić, Dragoljub Ojdanić, Nebojša Pavković, Vlajko Stojiljković		

This table includes indictees discussed in this book, and it provides a basic guide to the areas in which they operated during the various military conflicts that ended the existence of Yugoslavia. It is not comprehensive.

KEY POLITICAL AND MILITARY LEADERS AND REGIONS OF INFLUENCE

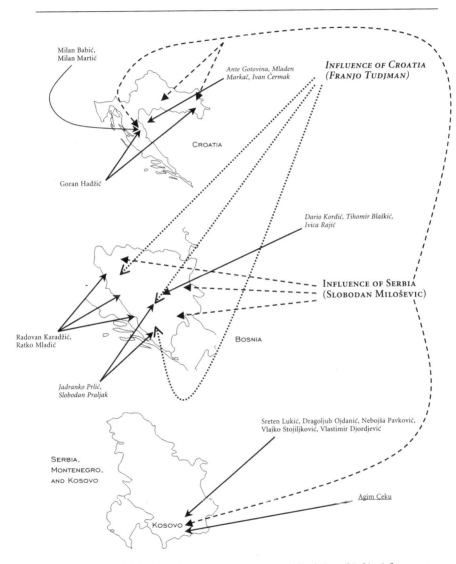

Serbian names are not italicized, *Croatian* names are. Others are <u>underlined</u>. General Serbian influences are indicated in dashed (– – –) lines; general Croatian influence is indicated in dotted (····) lines. Where individuals had a direct influence on events, a single dark line is drawn. This diagram is not comprehensive.

ADEDE, ANDRONICO · former registrar of the United Nations tribunal for Rwanda

AHTISAARI, MARTTI · former president of Finland, special representative of the United Nations secretary-general, responsible for devising a settlement plan for Kosovo's future status

ALBRIGHT, MADELEINE · former secretary of state and former United States ambassador to the United Nations during the Clinton administration

D'ALEMA, MASSIMO · foreign minister of Italy

ANNAN, KOFI · former secretary-general of the United Nations

ANTONETTI, JEAN CLAUDE · judge of the United Nations tribunal for Yugoslavia

APTEL, CÉCILE · political adviser, Office of the Prosecutor, United Nations tribunal for Rwanda

ARAP MOI, DANIEL · president of Kenya

ARBOUR, LOUISE · former chief prosecutor of the United Nations tribunals for Yugoslavia and Rwanda

BABIĆ, MILAN · former president of the self-declared Serb republic in Croatia, committed suicide at Scheveningen prison

BAGOSORA, THÉONESTE · colonel of the Rwandan army, alleged to have planned and executed the genocide of the Hutus against the Tutsis

BAJIĆ, MLADEN · chief state prosecutor of Croatia

BARAYAGWIZA, JEAN-BOSCO · former Hutu media owner, indicted in connection with inciting violence through the mass media during the massacres of Tutsis in 1994

BATIĆ, VLADAN · minister of justice of Serbia

BEARA, LJUBIŠA · officer of the Bosnian Serb Army, indicted on charges of genocide, murder, and other crimes in connection with the massacre at Srebrenica

BERLUSCONI, SILVIO · former prime minister of Italy, returned to office in 2008

BHUTTO BENAZIR · former prime minister of Pakistan

BIKINDI, SIMON · popular singer in pre-genocide Rwanda, arrested in the Netherlands on charges of participating in the slaughter of Tutsis

BISERKO, SONJA · head of the Helsinki Committee for Human Rights in Serbia

BIYA, PAUL · president of Cameroon

BLAŠKIĆ, TIHOMIR · former Bosnian Croat military leader in Central Bosnia

BLEWITT, GRAHAM · former deputy prosecutor of the United Nations tribunal for Yugoslavia

BOBAN, MATE · president of the Croat republic established during the war in Bosnia and Herzegovina

BOBETKO, JANKO · commander of the Army of the Republic of Croatia, indicted on charges linked to an attack on the Serbs in September 1993

BOCCASSINI, ILDA · examining magistrate, Milan, Italy

BONOMY, LORD IAIN · judge of the United Nations tribunal for Yugoslavia

BOROVČANIN, LJUBOMIR · officer of the Bosnian Serb Army, indicted in connection with the Srebrenica massacre

BORSELLINO, PAOLO · examining magistrate, Palermo, Sicily, assassinated by the mafia

BOT, BEN · foreign minister of the Netherlands

BRUGUIÈRE, JEAN-LOUIS · examining magistrate, Paris, France

BUDD, COLIN · United Kingdom's ambassador to the Netherlands

BULATOVIĆ, RADE · head of Serbia's government intelligence agency, the BIA

CALVI, ROBERTO · former Chairman of Italy's second-largest bank, Banco Ambrosiano, found dead under London's Blackfriars Bridge

CANCEMI, SALVATORE · Member of the Corleone crime family who became an informant

DE CAPRIO, SERGIO (*Capitano Ultimo*) · Officer of the Italian special police, the *carabinieri*, arrested the *capo* of the Corleone crime family in a Palermo traffic jam

CARBONI, FLAVIO · Italian, tried and acquitted on charges of murdering Roberto Calvi

CARLOS THE JACKAL (nom de guerre of Ilich Ramirez Sánchez) · Venezuelan, member of the Popular Front for the Liberation of Palestine, carried out hostage-taking at the Vienna headquarters of OPEC

CASSESE, ANTONIO · former president of the United Nations tribunal for Yugoslavia

CAYLEY, ANDREW · former senior trial attorney, United Nations tribunal for Yugoslavia

ÇEKU, AGIM · former chief of staff of the Kosovo Liberation Army

CERIĆ, REIS-UL-ULEMA MUSTAFA · the leader of the Islamic community of Bosnia and Herzegovina

ČERMAK, IVAN · retired general of the Army of the Republic of Croatia, tried on charges linked with Operation Storm in 1995

CHIRAC, JACQUES · former President of France

CISSÉ, CATHERINE · Rwanda tribunal's French–Senegalese legal adviser

CLARK, WESLEY · general, United States Army, former Supreme Allied Commander Europe

CORELL, HANS · undersecretary for legal affairs, United Nations

ĆORIĆ, VALENTIN · former head of the military police of the Croatian republic in wartime Bosnia and Herzegovina

ČOVIĆ, NEBOJŠA · former deputy prime minister of Serbia

DELIĆ, RASIM · former commander, Army of the Republic of Bosnia and Herzegovina

DES FORGES, ALISON · human rights investigator, Human Rights Watch

DJERIĆ, VLADIMIR · legal adviser to the foreign minister of Serbia

DJINDJIĆ, ZORAN · former prime minister of Serbia, assassinated by members of the Red Berets, an elite unit of the Serbian police

DJOGO, JOVAN · former officer in Bosnian Serb Army, reportedly assisted Ratko Mladić while a fugitive

DJORDJEVIĆ, VLASTIMIR · former general of the Serbian police and chief of public safety, indicted in connection with the ethnic cleansing of Kosovo

DJUKANOVIĆ, MILO · former prime minister of Montenegro

DJURO,VLADIMIR · former investigator, United Nations tribunal for Yugoslavia

DODIK, MILORAD · prime minister, Republika Srpska

DRAŠKOVIĆ, VUK · foreign minister of Serbia, one-time anticommunist firebrand

DREYFUS RUTH · former president of Switzerand

DYACHENKO, TATYANA · personal adviser, and daughter, of Russia's former president, Boris Yeltsin

FALCONE, GIOVANNI · examining magistrate, Palermo, Sicily, assassinated along with his wife, Francesca Morvillo, on May 23, 1992

FARRELL, NORMAN · legal adviser and former head of the Appeals Section, Office of the Prosecutor, United Nations tribunal for Yugoslavia, former counsel for the International Committee of the Red Cross

FENRICK, WILLIAM · staff attorney, United Nations tribunal for Yugoslavia

FILARET · bishop of the Serbian Orthodox monastery at Mileševa

GAHIMA, GERARD · prosecutor general of Rwanda

GEORGIJEVSKI, LJUPČO · former prime minister of Macedonia

GOJOVIĆ, RADOMIR · retired general, prosecutor of the Yugoslav Army's military court

GOLDSTONE, RICHARD · former chief prosecutor, United Nations tribunals for Rwanda and Yugoslavia

GOTOVINA, ANTE · former general, Army of the Republic of Croatia, indicted on charges in connection with the military operation that drove the Serb population out of swaths of Croatia in August 1995

GROOME, DERMOT · former senior trial attorney, United Nations tribunal for Yugoslavia

GRUBAČ, MOMČILO · former minister of justice, Federal Republic of Yugoslavia

DE GUCHT, KAREL · foreign minister of Belgium

GVERO, MILAN · general, Bosnian Serb Army, indicted in connection with the Srebrenica massacre

HABYARIMANA, JUVÉNAL · former president of Rwanda, assassinated April 6, 1994, when his plane was shot down

HADŽIĆ, GORAN · former leader of the Serbs in Croatia

HARADINAJ, RAMUSH · former commander of the Kosovo Liberation Army, indicted on charges connected with killings of Serbs in western Kosovo

HARMON, MARK · Senior trial attorney, United Nations tribunal for Yugoslavia

HARTMANN, FLORENCE · spokesperson for the Office of the Prosecutor, United Nations tribunal for Yugoslavia

HIGGINS, GILLIAN · one of the *amici curiae* in the Milošević trial

HIGGINS, ROSALYN · president of the International Court of Justice

HOLBROOKE, RICHARD · former United States ambassador to the United Nations, architect of the Dayton Peace Agreement

HOLLIS, BRENDA · senior trial attorney, United Nations tribunal for Yugoslavia

HOON, GEOFFREY · United Kingdom minister for European Union affairs

IZETBEGOVIĆ, ALIJA · former president of the Republic of Bosnia and Herzegovina and wartime leader of Bosnia's Muslims

JALLOW, HASSAN BUBACAR · Carla Del Ponte's successor as chief prosecutor of the United Nations tribunal for Rwanda

JANKOVIĆ, GOJKO · former leader of Serb paramilitary group, indicted for involvement in the sexual abuse and rape of women detainees in Foča

JASHARI, ADEM · leader of the Kosovo Liberation Army

JELAVIĆ, ANTE · former Croat member of the presidency of Bosnia and Herzegovina

JOJIĆ, PETAR · former minister of justice, Federal Republic of Yugoslavia

JORDA, CLAUDE · former president of the United Nations tribunal for Yugoslavia

JORIS, JEAN-JACQUES · Carla Del Ponte's former diplomatic adviser

JOVANOVIĆ, ČEDO · vice prime minister of Serbia

KABUGA, FÉLICIEN · the Hutu financier, indicted on charges connected with the 1994 genocide

KAGAME, PAUL · president of Rwanda

KAMBANDA, JEAN · former prime minister of the Hutu government of Rwanda, pleaded guilty to genocide

KANDIĆ, NATAŠA · head, Humanitarian Law Center, Belgrade

KARADŽIĆ, RADOVAN · former leader of Bosnian Serbs, indicted in connection with, among other things, the Srebrenica massacre

KAY, STEVEN · one of the *amici curiae* in the Milošević trial

KAYONGA, CHARLES · general of the Rwandan Army, indicted in connection with assassination of President Juvénal Habyarimana

AL-KHASAWNEH, AWN SHAWKAT · vice president of the International Court of Justice

KIRK MCDONALD, GABRIELLE · president of the appeals chamber of the United Nations tribunal for Rwanda

KNEZEVIĆ, DUŠAN · Bosnian Serb Army, indicted in connection with the ethnic cleansing of western Bosnia

KORDIĆ, DARIO · wartime political leader of Croats in Central Bosnia, found guilty on charges related to the massacre of Muslims at Ahmići

KOŠTUNICA, VOJISLAV · former president of the Federal Republic of Yugoslavia, prime minister of Serbia

KOUCHNER, BERNARD · foreign minister of France, former head of the United Nations Mission in Kosovo (UNMIK)

KOVAČEVIĆ, VLADIMIR · officer of Yugoslav National Army, indicted in connection with attack on Dubrovnik

KRAJIŠNIK, MOMČILO · former president of the Bosnian Serb Parliament, found guilty of persecution, extermination, murder, deportation, and other charges

KRGA, BRANKO · chief of staff of the Yugoslav Army

KRSTIĆ, RADOSLOV · a top general to Ratko Mladić

KWON, O-GON · judge, United Nations tribunal for Yugoslavia

LAJOLO, MONSIGNOR GIOVANNI · foreign minister of the Vatican

LAZAREVIĆ, VLADIMIR · general, Serbian Police, indicted for complicity in the ethnic cleansing of Kosovo in 1999

LILIĆ, ZORAN · former president of Yugoslavia

LJAJIĆ, RASIM · coordinator of Serbia's relations with the United Nations tribunal for Yugoslavia

LOPEZ-TERRES, PATRICK · the chief of investigations, United Nations tribunal for Yugoslavia

LUKIĆ, MILAN · Bosnian Serb paramilitary leader, indicted on multiple counts of murder in connection with ethnic cleansing of Višegrad

LUKIĆ, SREDOJE · relative of Milan Lukić, indicted in connection with ethnic cleansing of Višegrad

LUKIĆ, SRETEN · Serbian police general, indicted in connection with the ethnic cleansing of Kosovo

LUKOVIĆ, MILORAD ULEMEK · commander of the Red Berets, the elite Serbian police paramilitary unit

MAHIOU, AHMED · judge, International Court of Justice, from Algeria

MANOLIĆ, JOSIP · former head of Croatia's secret police

MARKAČ, MLADEN · former general, Army of the Republic of Croatia, indicted on charges linked with Operation Storm in 1995

MARKOVIĆ, RADE · chief of state security, Serbia

MAROVIĆ, SVETOZAR · former president of the State Union of Serbia and Montenegro,

MARTIĆ, MILAN · police and military leader of the Serbs in Croatia, indicted in connection with a rocket attack on Croatia's capital, Zagreb

MAY, RICHARD · presiding judge of the Milošević trial at the United Nations tribunal for Yugoslavia

MCCLOSKEY, PETER · senior trial attorney, United Nations tribunal for Yugoslavia

MEJAKIĆ, ŽELJKO · former commander of Omarska concentration camp, indicted in connection with Serb ethnic cleansing of Muslims from Western Bosnia

MERKEL, ANGELA · chancellor of the Federal Republic of Germany

MERON, THEODOR · former president, United Nations tribunal for Yugoslavia

MESIĆ, STIPE · president of Croatia

MIHAJLOVIĆ, DUŠAN · former minister of interior of Serbia

MILETIĆ, RADIVOJE · former chief of operations, Bosnian Serb Army, indicted in connection with the Srebrenica massacre

MILOŠEVIĆ, DRAGOMIR · former commander of the Bosnian Serb Army's forces besieging Sarajevo, indicted for using artillery and snipers to terrorize Sarajevo's populace from 1994 to the end of the siege in 1995

MILOŠEVIĆ, SLOBODAN · former president of Serbia, former president of Yugoslavia

MILUTINOVIĆ, MILAN · former president of Serbia

MLADIĆ, DARKO · son of Ratko Mladić

MLADIĆ, RATKO · former commander, Bosnian Serb Army, indicted in connection with, among other things, the Srebrenica massacre

MONTGOMERY, WILLIAM · former United States ambassador to Croatia and to the Federal Republic of Yugoslavia

MORATINOS, MIGUEL ÁNGEL · foreign minister of Spain

MRKŠIĆ, MILE · former Yugoslav Army colonel indicted on charges connected with the executions of prisoners seized at Vukovar executions in 1991

MUNA, BERNARD · former deputy prosecutor, United Nations tribunal for Rwanda

MURIGANDE, CHARLES · secretary-general, Rwandan Patriotic Front

MUSABYIMANA, SAMUEL · bishop in the Anglican Church, indicted on charges of genocide, conspiracy to commit genocide, and extermination

NAHIMANA, FERDINAND · former director of Radio Télévision Libre des Mille Collines, indicted in connection with the Rwanda genocide

NDADAYE, MELCHIOR · former Hutu president of Burundi, assassinated in October 1993

NDINDABAHIZI, EMMANUEL · former minister of finance of Rwanda, indicted on charges of genocide, inciting genocide, crimes against humanity, and murder

NEGROPONTE, JOHN · former United States ambassador to the United Nations

NGEZE, HASSAN · former editor of an extremist newspaper in Rwanda, indicted in connection with incitement to violence through the mass media

NGOGA, MARTIN · Rwandan diplomat in charge of monitoring the United Nations tribunal for Rwanda

NICE, GEOFFREY · former senior trial attorney, United Nations tribunal for Yugoslavia

NIKIFOROV, ANTON · former assistant to the chief prosecutor of the United Nations tribunal for Yugoslavia

NIKOLIĆ, DRAGO · former officer of Bosnian Serb Army, indicted in connection with the Srebrenica massacre

NIYITEGEKA, ELIEZER · former minister for information of Rwanda, faced charges before United Nations tribunal for Rwanda

NKURUNZIZA, JACKSON · general, Rwandan Army, indicted in France in connection with the assassination of Rwanda's Hutu president, Juvénal Habyarimana

NOBILO, ANTE · defense attorney for Tihomir Blaškić

NTARYAMIRA, CYPRIEN · former president of Burundi, killed with Juvénal Habyarimana, former president of Rwanda, on April 6, 1994, when his plane was shot down

OJDANIĆ, DRAGOLJUB · former chief of staff, Yugoslav Army, indicted in connection with the Kosovo ethnic cleansing of 1999

PANDUREVIĆ, VINKO · former brigade commander, Bosnian Serb Army, indicted on charges connected with the Srebrenica massacre

PATTERSON, NANCY · former senior trial attorney, United Nations tribunal for Yugoslavia

PAVKOVIĆ, NEBOJŠA · former chief of staff, Yugoslav Army, indicted in connection with the ethnic cleansing of Kosovo in 1999

PERIŠIĆ, MOMČILO · former chief of staff, Yugoslav Army, indicted on charges connected with war crimes committed in Bosnia and Herzegovina

PETKOVIĆ, MILIVOJ · the former chief of main staff, Bosnian Croat militia, indicted for grave breaches of the Geneva conventions, unlawful deportation of a civilian, and other charges

DI PIETRO, ANTONIO · examining magistrate, Milan, Italy

PILLAY, NAVANETHEM · former president, United Nations tribunal for Rwanda

PLAVŠIĆ, BILJANA · former Serb member of the collective presidency of Bosnia and Herzegovina, pleaded guilty to war crimes charges

POCAR, FAUSTO · president of the United Nations tribunal for Yugoslavia

POLT, MICHAEL · former United States ambassador to Serbia and Montenegro

POPOVIĆ, VLADIMIR "BEBA" · former chief adviser to Prime Minister Zoran Djindjić

POPOVIĆ, VUJADIN · assistant commander for security, Bosnian Serb Army, Drina Corps, indicted in connection with the Srebrenica massacre

POWELL, COLIN · former United States secretary of state

PRALJAK, SLOBODAN · former commander of the Bosnian Croat militia, indicted for grave breaches of the Geneva convention, violations of the laws or customs of war, and crimes against humanity

PRLIĆ, JADRANKO · the former prime minister of the "republic" the Bosnian Croats had proclaimed on Bosnian territory, indicted for grave breaches of the Geneva convention, violations of the laws or customs of war, and crimes against humanity

PROSPER, PIERRE · former United States ambassador-at-large for war crimes

PUŠIĆ, BERISLAV · former official of Bosnian Croats indicted on charges connected with removal of Muslims from Bosnia and Herzegovina

RAČAN, IVICA · former prime minister, Republic of Croatia

RADIĆ, MIROSLAV · former Yugoslav Army captain indicted on charges connected with the execution of prisoners captured at Vukovar

RADIŠIĆ, ŽIVKO · Serb member of postwar collective presidency of Bosnia and Herzegovina

RAJIĆ, IVICA · confessed commander of Bosnian Croat militia units that killed dozens of Muslims, including women and children, at a village named Stupni Do

RALSTON, JOHN · former chief of investigations, United Nations tribunal for Yugoslavia

RAŽNATOVIĆ, ŽELJKO ARKAN · former Belgrade underworld figure, commander of a Serb paramilitary force, indicted on charges connected with the imprisonment, beating, rape, and execution of prisoners

REHN, OLLI · European commissioner for enlargement

REINHARDT, KLAUS · general, former commander of KFOR

REKUNDO, EMMANUEL · former Rwandan army chaplain and Catholic priest alleged to have taken part in the killings of Tutsis in Kabgayi; captured by the authorities in Switzerland

RICE, CONDALEEZA · United States secretary of state, former United States national security adviser

RICHARD, ALAIN · former minister of defense of France

RIINA, SALVATORE · reputed to have been the boss of bosses, or *capo dei capi*, of the Sicilian Mafia

RISTIĆ, STANKO · former Bosnian Serb military officer, allegedly helped hide Ratko Mladić

ROBINSON, JOHN LORD · former secretary-general of NATO

ROBINSON, PATRICK · judge of the United Nations tribunal for Yugoslavia

RORSCHACHER, VALENTIN · head of Switzerland's Central Office for Drug Trafficking

ROTH, KEN · executive director, Human Rights Watch

RUCH, JEAN-DANIEL · former political adviser to the United Nations tribunal for Yugoslavia

RUGGIO, GEORGES · the so-called white Hutu, Belgian-Italian former journalist with Radio Télévision Libre des Milles Collines, who pleaded guilty to incitement to genocide

RWIGAMBA, ANDREW · lieutenant colonel, Rwandan Army; Rwanda's military prosecutor

ŠAINOVIĆ, NIKOLA · former deputy prime minister of the Federal Republic of Yugoslavia

SALINAS, RAÚL · brother of Carlos Salinas, former president of Mexico

SANADER, IVO · prime minister, Republic of Croatia

SAWERS, JOHN · political director, United Kingdom Foreign Office

SCHEFFER, DAVID · former U.S. ambassador-at-large for war crimes issues, indicted on charges linked with the crimes committed in Croatia and Bosnia and Herzegovina

SCHNEIDER, CYNTHIA · United States ambassador to the Netherlands

SCHROEDER, GERHARD · chancellor, Federal Republic of Germany

SCHULTE, GREG · former senior director for Southeast Europe of the National Security Council

SCOTT, KEN · senior trial attorney, United Nations tribunal for Yugoslavia

SEROMBA, ATHANASE · Roman Catholic priest indicted on charges stemming from the genocide in Rwanda

ŠEŠELJ, VOJISLAV · founder and head of the ultranationalist Serbian Radical Party, indicted on charges connected with activities of the party's militia in Croatia and Bosnia and Herzegovina

SEZIBERA, RICHARD · ambassador of Rwanda to the United States

SIMATOVIĆ, FRENKI · former commander, Special Operations Unit, State Security Service of Serbia, indicted on charges linked with the crimes committed in Croatia and Bosnia and Herzegovina

SIMIĆ, BLAGOJE · Bosnian Serb indicted in connection with the ethnic cleansing of the northern Bosnian municipality of Bosanski Šamac

SKURATOV, YURI · former prosecutor general, Russia

ŠLJIVANČANIN, VESELIN · former Yugoslav Army officer, indicted on charges connected to the execution of wounded men and other prisoners taken from Vukovar hospital

SOBEL, CLIFFORD M. · United States ambassador to the Netherlands

SOLANA, JAVIER · foreign minister of the European Commission

STAKIĆ, MILOMIR · former mayor of the Bosnian town of Prijedor, found guilty of murder and persecution

STANIŠIĆ, JOVICA · former chief of Serbia's State Security Service, indicted on charges linked with the crimes committed in Croatia and Bosnia and Herzegovina

STANIŠIĆ, MIČO · former minister of internal affairs, Republika Srpska, indicted on charges of, among other things, torture, cruel treatment, and deportation of Bosnian Muslims and Bosnian Croats

STEVANOVIĆ, OBRAD · former assistant interior minister of Serbia

STOJIĆ, BRUNO · former defense minister of the wartime Croat republic in Bosnia and Herzegovina

STOJILJKOVIĆ, VLAJKO · former minister of internal affairs of Serbia, indicted on charges connected with the ethnic cleansing of Kosovo in 1999, committed suicide

STRAW, JACK · former head of the United Kingdom Foreign Office

ŠUBAŠIĆ, MUNIRA · chairperson of Mothers of Srebrenica, an organization of the widows and mothers of the men massacred at Srebrenica

ŠUŠAK, GOJKO · former minister of defense of the Republic of Croatia, closest adviser to Croatia's president, Franjo Tudjman

SVILANOVIĆ, GORAN · former foreign minister of Serbia

TADIĆ, BORIS · president of Serbia, former minister of defense of Serbia,

TADIĆ, DUŠKO · former guard in Bosnian Serb concentration camp at Omarska, arrested in Germany and tried by the United Nations tribunal for Yugoslavia

TAFT, WILLIAM · legal adviser to United States Secretary of State Colin Powell

TENET, GEORGE · director, United States Central Intelligence Agency

TERZIĆ, ZLATOJE · general, Yugoslav Army, head commission for cooperation with the United Nations tribunal for Yugoslavia

THAÇI, HASHIM · political director of the Kosovo Liberation Army

TIEGER, ALAN · senior trial attorney, United Nations tribunal for Yugoslavia

TODOVIĆ, SAVO · Commander of Bosnian Serb prison, indicted for persecuting, enslaving, torturing, beating, and killing Muslim prisoners

TOGNOLI, OLIVIERO · convicted former financial manager for the Sicilian Mafia

TOLBERT, DAVID · deputy prosecutor, United Nations tribunal for Yugoslavia

TOLIMIR, ZDRAVKO · former general, Bosnian Serb army, indicted on charges connected with, among other things, the Srebrenica massacre

TOMIĆ, ACO · former general, Yugoslav Army, headed the general staff's security department

TRAJANOV, PAVLE · former interior minister, Republic of Macedonia

TUDJMAN, FRANJO · former president of Republic of Croatia

UERTZ-RETZLAFF, HILDEGARD · senior trial attorney, United Nations tribunal for Yugoslavia

UWILINGIYIMANA, AGATHE · former moderate Hutu prime minister of Rwanda, murdered, with her chidren, by extremist Hutu troops

VASILJEVIĆ, ALEKSANDAR · former general, Yugoslav Army and former head of the Yugoslav Army's counterintelligence service

VÉDRINE, HUBERT · former minister of foreign affairs of France

VUJANOVIĆ, FILIP · president of Montenegro

VUJOVIĆ, NEBOJŠA · special envoy to United Nations tribunal for Yugoslavia

VUKČEVIĆ, VLADIMIR · Serbia's chief war crimes prosecutor, coordinator of Serbia's relations with the United Nations tribunal for Yugoslavia

WALPEN, LAURENT · former chief of investigations, United Nations tribunal for Rwanda

WEINBERG DE ROCA, INÉS · former judge, United Nations tribunal for Yugoslavia

WILLIAMSON, CLINT · former trial attorney, United Nations tribunal for Yugoslavia, United States ambassador-at-large for war crimes

WINKLER, HANS · deputy minister of foreign affairs of Austria

YELTSIN, BORIS · former president of Russia

ZACKLIN, RALPH · assistant secretary-general for legal affaris, United Nations

ZELENOVIĆ, DRAGAN · former Bosnian Serb prison guard, pleaded guilty to charges of torture and rape in connection with assaults on Muslim women

ŽIVKOVIĆ, ZORAN · former prime minister of Serbia, assassinated March 12, 2003

ŽUPLJANIN, STOJAN · Bosnian Serb security commander in western Bosnia, indicted on charges of genocide and persecution connected with the ethnic cleansing of Muslims

PROLOGUE

1 Schopenhauer, "On Women," *The Project Gutenberg EBook of Essays of Schopenhauer*, translated by Rudolf Dircks, 2004, http://www.gutenberg.org/files/11945/11945-8.txt.

2 *Testimony of Witness O, The Prosecutor v. Radislav Krstić*, April 13, 2000, trial transcript, app. 2818–2939, http://www.un.org/icty/transe33/000413ed.htm, translation edited by Chuck Sudetic.

CHAPTER 2

1 *The Prosecutor v. Slobodan Milošević*, Trial Transcript, February 12, 2002, p. 8.

2 Presidential Transcript, December 27, 1991.

3 Ewa Tabeau and Jakub Bijak, "War-Related Deaths in the 1992–1995 Armed Conflicts in Bosnia and Herzegovina: A Critique of Previous Estimates and Recent Results," *European Journal of Population* (2005), Volume 21, Numbers 2–3, June 2005, pp. 187–215.

4 Ball, Patrick, et al., "Killings and Refugee Flow in Kosovo, March–June 1999," an expert report prepared for the International Criminal Tribunal for Yugoslavia (ICTY), January 3, 2002.

5 United Nations, Report of the International Tribunal for the Prosecution of Persons Responsible for Serious Violations of International Humanitarian Law Committed in the Territory of the former Yugoslavia since 1991, August 25, 1999, A/54/187-S/1999/846, http://www.un.org/icty/rappannue/1999/index.htm.

6 *The Observer*, December 26, 1999.

7 "Final Report to the Prosecutor by the Committee Established to Review the NATO Bombing Campaign Against the Federal Republic of Yugoslavia," Office of the Prosecutor, International Criminal Tribunal for the

former Yugoslavia, http://www.un.org/icty/pressreal/nato061300.htm, The Hague, June 13, 2000.

CHAPTER 3

1 Hatzfeld, Jean. *Une Saison de Machettes.* Paris: Éditions du Seuil, 2003.

CHAPTER 4

1 Letter from Kofi Annan, secretary-general, United Nations, to Carla Del Ponte, chief prosecutor, International Criminal Tribunal for the former Yugoslavia, March 6, 2001.

2 The "Vukovar Three" were Veselin Šljivančanin, Mile Mrkšić, and Miroslav Radić, all officers of the Yugoslav National Army.

CHAPTER 6

1 *The Prosecutor v. Slobodan Milošević,* Trial Transcript, February 12, 2002, pp. 1–11, http://www.un.org/icty/transe54/020212IT.htm.

2 *The Prosecutor v. Slobodan Milošević,* Trial Transcript, Testimony of Paddy Ashdown, March 15, 2002, pp. 2355, 2380.

3 Veselin Šljivančanin, Mile Mrkšić, and Miroslav Radić.

4 Report of Carla Del Ponte, Chief Prosecutor, International Criminal Tribunal for the former Yugoslavia, to the United Nations Security Council, October 30, 2002.

CHAPTER 7

1 www.afriquespoir.com/cibles/page20.html, www.chez.com/cprgla/temoinages/Linguyeneza.htm.

2 Human Rights Watch, *Leave None to Tell the Story: Genocide in Rwanda,* www.hrw.org/reports/1999/rwanda/Geno1-3-03.htm#P86_35545.

CHAPTER 8

1 Letter from Chief Prosecutor Carla Del Ponte to the minister of foreign affairs of the State Union of Serbia and Montenegro, Svilanović, May 24, 2003.

2 *The Prosecutor v. Slobodan Milošević,* Trial Transcript, Cross-Examination of Zoran Lilić, July 9, 2003, and Exhibit D 160.

3 "Alors, Général, il est encore en fuite, Mladić, c'est inacceptable, il faut l'arrêter immediatement."

4 International Crisis Group, "Serbian Reform Stalls Again," *Europe Report* No. 145, by James Lyons, July 17, 2003, citing Hugh Griffiths, "Humanitarian or War Criminal," *Transitions Online*, and The International Criminal Tribunal for the Former Yugoslavia, *The Prosecutor vs. Slobodan Milošević*, Written Statement, Exhibit 143, OTP Reference K1136, May 9, 2002.

5 Report of Chief Prosecutor, International Criminal Tribunal for the former Yugoslavia, to United Nations Security Council, October 9, 2003.

6 *The Prosecutor v. Slobodan Milošević*, Trial Transcript, February 10, 2004, p. 31709.

7 International Criminal Tribunal for the former Yugoslavia (ICTY), Press Release 824e, "Statement of Judge Theodor Meron, President of the ICTY, upon the Resignation of Judge Richard George May," February 22, 2004.

8 *The Prosecutor v. Slobodan Milošević*, Trial Chamber, Decision on Motion for Acquittal, June 16, 2004, http://www.un.org/icty/milosevic/trialc/judgement/index.htm.

CHAPTER 9

1 S/RES/United Nations Security Council Resolution 1503 (2003).

CHAPTER 10

1 Report to President Franjo Tudjman by Markica Rebić, June 4, 1998, Annex 4 attached to the Prosecution Response to Appellant's Motion to Admit Additional Evidence, *The Prosecutor v. Tihomir Blaškić*, September 13, 2001.

2 Report to President Franjo Tudjman by Markica Rebić, June 4, 1998, p. 20, Annex 4 attached to the Prosecution Response to Appellant's Motion to Admit Additional Evidence, *The Prosecutor v. Tihomir Blaškić*, September 13, 2001.

3 Stewart, Lieutenant-Colonel Bob, *Broken Lives* (London: HarperCollins, 1993), 295–298.

4 http://www.un.org/icty/blaskic/appeal/judgement/index.htm, footnote 705.

5 Cited in *The Prosecutor v. Tihomir Blaškić*, Prosecution Request for Review or Reconsideration (Public Redacted Version), July 10, 2006, p. 19,

CHAPTER 11

1 Humanitarian Law Center, *Abductions and Disappearances of non-Albanians in Kosovo*, Belgrade, 2001.

2 "Protests in Priština," Beta, January 7, 2003.

3 United States State Department, Human Rights Report for 2003.

4 OSCE Mission in Kosovo, "Kosovo, Review of the Criminal Justice System, March 2002–April 2003, pp. 11, 18.

5 Jeta Xharra, Muhamet Hajrullahu, and Arben Salihu, "Investigation: Kosovo's Wild West," BIRN Kosovo, February 18, 2005, http://kosovo.birn.eu.com/en/1/51/1770/.

6 *The Prosecutor v. Beqa Beqaj*, Trial Chamber Judgment, May 27, 2005, p. 13. www.un.org/icty/limaj/beqa/beq-tj050527f.htm.

7 Place names appear first in Serbo-Croatian and then in Albanian.

8 www.unmikonline.org/press/2005/pr1325.pdf

9 *Koha Ditore*, September 2, 2006, p. 10.

10 *Lajm*, August 31, 2006, pp. 1, 3.

CARLA DEL PONTE was chief prosecutor of the United Nations War Crimes Tribunal for the former Yugoslavia from 1999 to 2007 and chief prosecutor of the United Nations War Crimes Tribunal for Rwanda from 1999 to 2003. Born in Lugano, Switzerland, she studied law at the universities in Berne and Geneva and entered private practice in 1972. Del Ponte began to acquire an international acclaim in 1981, when, as an examining magistrate and a public prosecutor, she collaborated with the late Giovanni Falcone and other Italian prosecutors on financial investigations into drug-trafficking and other criminal activities of the Sicilian Mafia. Ms. Del Ponte was appointed Switzerland's federal attorney general in 1994; during her tenure, she supported lawmakers in Switzerland in their efforts to outlaw money laundering and curtail bank secrecy; Del Ponte also investigated financial improprieties involving Boris Yeltsin, the late president of Russia, Raúl Salinas of Mexico, the Bhutto family of Pakistan, and persons with links to Middle East terrorist networks. Her work at the United Nations tribunals contributed to the indictment, arrest, or prosecution of dozens of persons accused of genocide and other war crimes, including Slobodan Milošević, the former president of Serbia; Théoneste Bagosora, the former Hutu military leader charged with having masterminded the genocide in Rwanda; and two of the world's most wanted men, Radovan Karadžić and General Ratko Mladić, who faced charges stemming from the massacre of Bosnian Muslim prisoners at Srebrenica in 1995. Del Ponte has received numerous awards and honors. She is currently Switzerland's ambassador to Argentina.

CHUCK SUDETIC reported for the *New York Times* from 1990 to 1995 on the breakup of Yugoslavia and the transition from communism in other Balkan countries. His first book, *Blood and Vengeance* (1998), a chronicle of the experiences of two Bosnian families during the century of turmoil ending with the Srebrenica massacre, became a *New York Times* Notable Book and was named a "Book of the Year" by *The Economist*, the *Washington Post*, and *Publishers Weekly*. His articles have appeared in *The Economist*, *Atlantic Monthly*, *Rolling Stone*, *Mother Jones*, *Das Magazin* (Zurich), and other periodicals. Sudetic studied English, journalism, and Slavic languages at The Ohio State University,

Indiana University, and Davidson College and was a Fulbright Scholar in Yugoslavia. From 2001 to 2005, he worked as an analyst for the Yugoslavia tribunal. He is now a senior writer for the Open Society Institute (Soros Foundation) and is completing a book about the Adriatic town of Dubrovnik. He resides in France.

in Kigali, 74–75
life in the Hague, 33–34
management of Office of the Prosecutor, 131–132
mandate nearing end, 366–368
marriages of, 15, 18
moves to unseat from war crimes tribunals, 236–237
reappointment as Special Prosecutor, 233–234
reception in Belgrade, 93–94, 151
reception in Yugoslavia, 93–94, 98
Rwanda not granting visa, 74, 83
as Swiss attorney general, 4–5, 24, 29–30
wanting position in International Criminal Court, 230
Del Ponte, F. (brother), 11–12, 15, 30, 221
Del Ponte, father, 14–15, 18
Del Ponte, M. (son), 16, 18, 20, 222
Delić, R., 365
deportations/expulsions
from Kosovo, 37, 46, 58, 273, 292
from Krajina, 244
Des Forges, A., 65, 76
detention centers. *See* concentration camps
Di Pietro, A., 22
Djerić, V., 169–170, 202, 206–208
Djindjić, R. (wife), 101–102, 193, 332
Djindjić, Z., 172
    assassination of, 176, 194, 196, 219, 305
    cooperating with tribunal, 98–99, 102–104, 106, 148, 153–154, 159, 173–175
    Del Ponte and, 106, 154, 193
    injury to, 173–174
    on limited possibilities for tribunal's prosecution, 159–160
    Milošević and, 102–104, 110, 115–116, 119, 219, 332
    on Milošević's possible trial in Serbia, 112, 115–116
    Mladić and, 152, 174
    planning reforms of army, 175–176
    state funeral of, 193–194
Djinović, R., 277
Djogo, J., 336, 339, 367
Djordjević, V., 196
    as fugitive, 326, 329, 362–363
    indictment of, 195, 197, 209–210, 213–214, 216
    Serbian government and, 197, 215, 307
Djukanović, M., 171–172, 175–176
Djuro, V., 254
Dodik, M., 50–51, 335

donors conference, Yugoslavia waiting for aid from, 109, 115–120
Drašković, V., 104
Dreyfus, R., 30
Drina River valley, deportations and killings in, 58
drug trafficking, 44, 346
    capture of money from, 22–24
    by Italian mafia, 4–5, 19
    money laundering through Swiss banks, 4–5, 24–26
Dubrovnik, bombing of, 37, 53, 58, 250
Dukagjin Operational Zone, 292, 301–302
Dyachenko, T., 27

economy
    Croatian, 253
    Serbian, 316
Egypt, 26
environment, damage from NATO bombing, 61–62
Erdut, Serb crimes against Croats in, 254
ethnic cleansing, 314. *See also* genocide
    in Bosnia and Herzegovina, 27, 160–161, 247–250
    in Kosovo, 44, 58, 89, 143–144, 175, 273, 275, 319
    trials in Serbia for, 307
ethnicity, in identity of Yugoslavians, 35–36
EUFOR (European military force in Bosnia), 334
Europe
    pressure on Serbia by, 116–118, 316, 354
    Rwandan fugitives arrested in, 188–189
    support for International Criminal Court in, 116
    support for tribunal waning in, 352–354
European Commission, 258
European Council, report on Croatia's cooperation to, 267, 270–271
European Union, 271, 341
    aid for Yugoslavia, 109
    capture of fugitives and, 319, 326, 347
    conditions for Serbia's entry into, 170, 348
    Croatia's entry into, 246–247, 250, 253, 258
    Croatia's entry stalled by lack of arrest of Gotovina, 256–257, 266–267, 318
    Europe softening on conditions for Serbia's entry into, 342, 344–347, 349–353, 354
    military force in Bosnia and Herzegovina, 329–330